Official Hayes Modem Communications Companion

AT Command Quick Reference Card

Note: This tear-out card lists some commonly used AT commands. All modems do not use the same commands. See Appendix A for a more complete listing and details on using the commands.

AT Command Descriptions

Command	Description
ATA	Enter answer mode, go off hook, attempt to answer incoming call, and go online with another modem.
ATD	Enter originate mode, go off-hook, and attempt to go online with another modem. The dial modifiers tell the modem what, when, and how to dial.
ATDT	Dial by using tone method.
ATDP	Dial by using pulse method.
ATDT,	Dial by using tone method and wait two seconds.
ATH0	Hang up and place modem in command state.
ATL0, LI	Set low speaker volume.
ATL2	Set medium speaker volume.
ATL3	Set high speaker volume.
ATM0	Turn speaker off.
ATMI	Turn speaker on until carrier detected.
ATM2	Turn speaker on.
ATM3	Turn speaker on until carrier detected, except while dialing.
ATQ0	Return result codes.
ATQI	Do not return result codes.
ATSn?	Read and respond with current value of register n (n is the register number; ? requests the value assigned to that register).
ATSn=value	Set the value of register n to value.
ATV0	Display result codes as numbers.
ATVI	Display result codes as words.
AT&F	Recall factory configuration as active configuration.
AT&Q5	Communicate in error-control mode.
AT&V	View active configuration, user profiles, and stored telephone numbers.
AT&W0	Write storable parameters of current configuration in memory as profile 0.
AT&WI	Write storable parameters of current configuration in memory as profile I.
AT&Y0	Specify stored user profile 0 as power-up configuration.
AT&YI	Specify stored user profile I as power-up configuration.

Result Code Descriptions

Number	Word	Description
0	OK	Command executed.
1	CONNECT	A connection has been established.
2	RING	Ring signal indicated
3	NO CARRIER	Carrier signal not detected, or lost, or inactivity for period of time set in the automatic timeout register (set with **S30**) caused the modem to hang up.
4	ERROR	Invalid command, checksum, error in command line, or command line exceeds 255 characters.
5	CONNECT 1200	Connection at 1200 bps (disabled by **X0**).
6	NO DIALTONE	No dial tone detected. Enabled by **X2** or **X4**, or **W** dial modifier.
7	BUSY	Engaged (busy) signal or number unobtainable signal detected. Enabled by **X3** or **X4**.
8	NO ANSWER	No silence detected when dialing a system not providing a dial tone. Enabled by @ dial modifier.
10	CONNECT 2400	Connection at 2400 bps (disabled by **X0**).
11	CONNECT 4800	Connection at 4800 bps (disabled by **X0**).
12	CONNECT 9600	Connection at 9600 bps (disabled by **X0**).

S-Register Descriptions

Register	Description	Range/Units	Default Setting
S0	Select ring to answer on.	0-255 rings	0
S1	Ring count (incremented with each ring).	0-255 rings	0
S2	Escape sequence character.	0-127 ASCII	43
S3	Carriage return character.	0-127 ASCII	13
S4	Line feed character.	0-127 ASCII	10
S5	Back space character.	0-32,127 ASCII	8
S6	Wait before blind dialing.	2-255 sec	2
S7	Wait time for carrier/silence.	1-255 sec	50
S8	Duration of delay for comma.	0-255 sec	2
S9	Carrier detect response time.	1-255 1/10 sec	5
S10	Delay carrier loss to hang up.	1-255 1/10 sec	14
S11	Duration/spacing of DTMF tones.	50-255 msec	95
S12	Escape sequence guard time.	0-255 1/50 sec	50

⊞ Official Hayes Modem Communications Companion

Official Hayes Modem Communications Companion

by Caroline M. Halliday

Foreword and Introduction by
Dennis Hayes
President and Founder
Hayes Microcomputer Products, Inc.

IDG BOOKS

IDG Books Worldwide, Inc.
An International Data Group Company

San Mateo, California ✦ Indianapolis, Indiana ✦ Boston, Massachusetts

Official Hayes Modem Communications Companion

Published by
IDG Books Worldwide, Inc.
An International Data Group Company
155 Bovet Road, Suite 310
San Mateo, CA 94402

Library of Congress Catalog Card No.: 9475047

ISBN: 1-56884-072-1

Printed in the United States of America

10 9 8 7 6 5 4 3 2 1

1C/QU/RZ/ZU

Distributed in the United States by IDG Books Worldwide, Inc.

Distributed in Canada by Macmillan of Canada, a Division of Canada Publishing Corporation; by Computer and Technical Books in Miami, Florida, for South America and the Caribbean; by Longman Singapore in Singapore, Malaysia, Thailand, and Korea; by Toppan Co. Ltd. in Japan; by Asia Computerworld in Hong Kong; by Woodslane Pty. Ltd. in Australia and New Zealand; and by Transword Publishers Ltd. in the U.K. and Europe.

For general information on IDG Books in the U.S., including information on discounts and premiums, contact IDG Books at 800-762-2974 or 415-312-0650.

For information on where to purchase IDG Books outside the U.S., contact Christina Turner at 415-312-0633.

For information on translations, contact Marc Jeffrey Mikulich, Foreign Rights Manager, at IDG Books Worldwide; FAX NUMBER 415-358-1260.

For sales inquiries and special prices for bulk quantities, write to the address above or call IDG Books Worldwide at 415-312-0650.

 is a registered trademark of IDG BooksWorldwide, Inc.

 The text in this book is printed on recycled paper.

About the Author

Caroline M. Halliday

Caroline M. Halliday shares her passion for PCs and telecommunications with her husband. They like to explore new BBSs and online services and keep abreast of current trends in the industry. Unfortunately, Caroline keeps stumbling across new computer games that divert her attention. Her husband can pick up the slack, however, and keep their phone companies profitable.

To pay for these exploits, Caroline uses her electrical engineering degree to write books and magazine articles for the PC industry. She focuses particularly on making the technology understandable to the home user and small-business owner. Caroline is on the *InfoWorld* review board, and her other best-selling book is *PC SECRETS*, also published by IDG Books Worldwide.

About IDG Books Worldwide

Welcome to the world of IDG Books Worldwide.

IDG Books Worldwide, Inc., is a subsidiary of International Data Group, the world's largest publisher of computer-related information and the leading global provider of information services on information technology. International Data Group publishes over 195 computer publications in 62 countries. Forty million people read one or more International Data Group publications each month

If you use personal computers, IDG Books is committed to publishing quality books that meet your needs. We rely on our extensive network of publications, including such leading periodicals as *Macworld*, *InfoWorld*, *PC World*, *Computerworld*, *Publish*, *Network World*, and *SunWorld*, to help us make informed and timely decisions in creating useful computer books that meet your needs.

Every IDG book strives to bring extra value and skill-building instructions to the reader. Our books are written by experts, with the backing of IDG periodicals, and with careful thought devoted to issues such as audience, interior design, use of icons, and illustrations. Our editorial staff is a careful mix of high-tech journalists and experienced book people. Our close contact with the makers of computer products helps ensure accuracy and thorough coverage. Our heavy use of personal computers at every step in production means we can deliver books in the most timely manner.

We are delivering books of high quality at competitive prices on topics customers want. At IDG, we believe in quality, and we have been delivering quality for over 25 years. You'll find no better book on a subject than an IDG book.

John Kilcullen
President and CEO
IDG Books Worldwide, Inc.

IDG Books Worldwide, Inc. is a subsidiary of International Data Group. The officers are Patrick J. McGovern, Founder and Board Chairman; Walter Boyd, President. International Data Group's publications include: **ARGENTINA'S** Computerworld Argentina, Infoworld Argentina; **ASIA'S** Computerworld Hong Kong, PC World Hong Kong, Computerworld Southeast Asia, PC World Singapore, Computerworld Malaysia, PC World Malaysia; **AUSTRALIA'S** Computerworld Australia, Australian PC World, Australian Macworld, Network World, Mobile Business Australia, Reseller, IDG Sources; **AUSTRIA'S** Computerwelt Oesterreich, PC Test; **BRAZIL'S** Computerworld, Gamepro, Game Power, Mundo IBM, Mundo Unix, PC World, Super Game; **BELGIUM'S** Data News (CW) **BULGARIA'S** Computerworld Bulgaria, Ediworld, PC & Mac World Bulgaria, Network World Bulgaria; **CANADA'S** CIO Canada, Computerworld Canada, Graduate Computerworld, InfoCanada, Network World Canada; **CHILE'S** Computerworld Chile, Informatica; **COLOMBIA'S** Computerworld Colombia; **CZECH REPUBLIC'S** Computerworld, Elektronika, PC World; **DENMARK'S** CAD/CAM WORLD, Communications World, Computerworld Danmark, LOTUS World, Macintosh Produktkatalog, Macworld Danmark, PC World Danmark, PC World Produktguide, Windows World; **ECUADOR'S** PC World Ecuador; **EGYPT'S** Computerworld (CW) Middle East, PC World Middle East; **FINLAND'S** MikroPC, Tietoviikko, Tietoverkko; **FRANCE'S** Distributique, GOLDEN MAC, InfoPC, Languages & Systems, Le Guide du Monde Informatique, Le Monde Informatique, Telecoms & Reseaux; **GERMANY'S** Computerwoche, Computerwoche Focus, Computerwoche Extra, Computerwoche Karriere, Information Management, Macwelt, Netzwelt, PC Welt, PC Woche, Publish, Unit; **GREECE'S** Infoworld, PC Games; **HUNGARY'S** Computerworld SZT, PC World; **INDIA'S** Computers & Communications; **IRELAND'S** Computerscope; **ISRAEL'S** Computerworld Israel, PC World Israel; **ITALY'S** Computerworld Italia, Lotus Magazine, Macworld Italia, Networking Italia, PC Shopping Italy, PC World Italia; **JAPAN'S** Computerworld Today, Information Systems World, Macworld Japan, Nikkei Personal Computing, SunWorld Japan, Windows World; **KENYA'S** East African Computer News; **KOREA'S** Computerworld Korea, Macworld Korea, PC World Korea; **MEXICO'S** Compu Edicion, Compu Manufactura, Computacion/Punto de Venta, Computerworld Mexico, MacWorld, Mundo Unix, PC World, Windows; **THE NETHERLANDS'** Computer! Totaal, Computable (CW), LAN Magazine, MacWorld, Totaal "Windows"; **NEW ZEALAND'S** Computer Listings, Computerworld New Zealand, New Zealand PC World; **NIGERIA'S** PC World Africa; **NORWAY'S** Computerworld Norge, C/World, Lotusworld Norge, Macworld Norge, Networld, PC World Ekspress, PC World Norge, PC World's Produktguide, Publish& Multimedia World, Student Data, Unix World, Windowsworld; IDG Direct Response; **PANAMA'S** PC World Panama; **PERU'S** Computerworld Peru, PC World; **PEOPLE'S REPUBLIC OF CHINA'S** China Computerworld, China Infoworld, PC World China, Electronics International, Electronic Product World, China Network World; IDG HIGH TECH BEIJING'S New Product World; IDG SHENZHEN'S Computer News Digest; **PHILIPPINES'** Computerworld Philippines, PC Digest (PCW); **POLAND'S** Computerworld Poland, PC World/Komputer; **PORTUGAL'S** Cerebro/PC World, Correio Informatico/Computerworld, MacIn; **ROMANIA'S** Computerworld, PC World; **RUSSIA'S** Computerworld-Moscow, Mir - PC, Sety; **SLOVENIA'S** Monitor Magazine; **SOUTH AFRICA'S** Computer Mail (CIO), Computing S.A., Network World S.A.; **SPAIN'S** Amiga World, Computerworld Espana, Communicaciones World, Macworld Espana, NeXTWORLD, Super Juegos Magazine (GamePro), PC World Espana, Publish, Sunworld; **SWEDEN'S** Attack, ComputerSweden, Corporate Computing, Lokala Natverk/LAN, Lotus World, MAC&PC, Macworld, Mikrodatorn, PC World, Publishing & Design (CAP), DataIngenjoren, Maxi Data, Windows World; **SWITZERLAND'S** Computerworld Schweiz, Macworld Schweiz, PC Katalog, PC & Workstation; **TAIWAN'S** Computerworld Taiwan, Global Computer Express, PC World Taiwan; **THAILAND'S** Thai Computerworld; **TURKEY'S** Computerworld Monitor, Macworld Turkiye, PC World Turkiye; **UNITED KINGDOM'S** Computing /Computerworld, Connexion/Network World, Lotus Magazine, Macworld, Open Computing/Sunworld; **UNITED STATES'** AmigaWorld, Cable in the Classroom, CD Review, CIO, Computerworld, Desktop Video World, DOS Resource Guide, Electronic Entertainment Magazine, Federal Computer Week, Federal Integrator, GamePro, IDG Books, Infoworld, Infoworld Direct, Laser Event, Macworld, Multimedia World, Network World, NeXTWORLD, PC Letter, PC World, PlayRight, Power PC World, Publish, SunWorld, SWATPro, Video Event; **VENEZUELA'S** Computerworld Venezuela, MicroComputerworld Venezuela; **VIETNAM'S** PC World Vietnam

Dedication

For all who "push the envelope of technology," particularly in the fields of medicine and computers.

Acknowledgments

I want to acknowledge *all* the talented staff at Hayes Microcomputer Products, Inc., for their help, particularly the founder and president, Dennis Hayes.

Special thanks to Peggy Ballard, who focused much of her time and energy on this product.

Thanks to Dwayne Arnold and Ricky Lacy for enriching my list of frequently asked questions.

Thanks to Paul Curtis, partner at The Coastal Group, for sharing his information for the "First BBS Teleconference to the USSR" sidebar.

Thanks to Alan Fuerbringer at Mustang Software, Inc., for his useful solution.

Thanks to Bruce Ansley for reviewing the chapter on the Internet.

Thanks to Tim Stanley for modifying the AT Command Quick Reference Card.

Thanks to H. Leigh Davis and Sandy Reed for excellent editing and support.

Thanks to Dow Jones News Retrieval, Dialog, and America Online.

Thanks to Hayes for supplying various supporting materials.

Software Creations BBS screens are used with permission of Dan Litton.

Credits

VP & Publisher
David Solomon

Managing Editor
Mary Bednarek

Acquisitions Editor
Janna Custer

Production Director
Beth Jenkins

Senior Editors
Tracy L. Barr
Sandra Blackthorn
Diane Graves Steele

Production Coordinator
Cindy L. Phipps

Associate Acquisitions Editor
Megg Bonar

Editorial Assistant
Darlene Cunningham

Project Editor
H. Leigh Davis

Copy Editor
Sandy Reed

Technical Review
Hayes Microcomputer Products, Inc.

Production Staff
Tony Augsburger
Valery Bourke
Mary Breidenbach
Chris Collins
Sherry Gomoll
Drew R. Moore
Kathie Schnorr
Gina Scott

Proofreader
Henry Lazarek

Indexer
Steve Rath

Book Design/Jigsaw Puzzle Illustrations
Jo Payton

Contents at a Glance

Table of Contents

Part II: Communications Basics 54

Table of Contents

Foreword and Introduction to the Book

At Hayes, we built the on-ramp to the information highway. Over the last decade, computers revolutionized the way we work and play. Computer communications made it possible for online information services to grow in popularity and to increase in number and type of services available. With the widespread use of modems over the global telephone network, it's now possible for computers at virtually any location to connect. As the speed of communications technology increases, new applications are opening that will allow the novice as well as the experienced computer user to conduct business or enjoy entertainment interactively at any time with information systems or people who may be located anywhere. All this — and at prices that almost everyone can afford.

For the last 15 years, we at Hayes Microcomputer Products, Inc. have worked very hard to take the mystery out of modems and computer communications. In fact, I felt so strongly about providing a resource to eliminate the discomfort you may feel about computer communications that we did something at Hayes that we've never done before. We provided Caroline Halliday and IDG Books with an inside look at Hayes that no one else has ever seen. She interviewed our research and development engineers, talked at length with our technical service and support team, toured our labs, and spent a lot of time getting to know Hayes from the inside. That insight, coupled with her vast knowledge of the computer industry and her successful track record as a writer, provides you with the most thorough and detailed computer communications guidebook ever written.

This authoritative reference taps into the Hayes knowledge base unlike any other book ever written. We have a unique perspective concerning what people want to know about using modems and computer communications. Our customer and technical support team members speak with more than one million modem users every year. I know firsthand that this type of interaction can build a huge information and knowledge base among Hayes employees. I say that because I answered the phones myself during our early years, and today I spend much of my time talking with customers and use what I learn from them to improve our products and our company. Now, you can benefit from our years of experience and enjoy the exciting world of computer communications like never before.

When my partner, Dale Heatherington, and I began our company some 15 years ago, our goal was to make our company a global leader in computer communications. We wanted to do that by making products that took computer communications out of a technical environment and let them migrate to the real world where almost anyone could use them productively. Our first goal was to take the mystery out of modems. It is now my desire that the *Official Hayes Modem Communications Companion* become an extension of that vision, which can take the mystery out of modem communications for you.

When the first Hayes Smartmodem shipped on June 16, 1981, a new era in computer communications began. We introduced the Hayes Standard AT Command Set to allow software to use a command language for controlling modem features, such as Auto Dial and Auto Answer. Up to that time, most early modems were not intelligent devices but simply translators that required complicated technical setup for a specific use. Now, thanks to the original Hayes Smartmodem, a modem is a system element that is easier to integrate into the computer environment. Its ease of use was coupled with a powerful capability that had been unavailable prior to 1981. That capability was a standard set of commands we designed to make it easy for software to tell the modem what to do — the Hayes Standard AT Command Set. It has been adopted worldwide for modem communications and continues to be copied "more or less" by most modem manufacturers and supported by communications software developers. Its use is so widespread that it gave birth to the term *Hayes-compatible* or *AT-compatible* products, a whole new category of modems known as PC modems.

In hindsight, I think you can look at that first Hayes Smartmodem as being the foundation for the on-ramp to the information highway and, when coupled with communications software and the telephone network, a whole new world of information at a user's desktop. In the 1980s, we weren't contemplating the superhighway that is receiving so much attention today. But in the beginning stages, the information highway needed explorers to open new territories for dial-up communications. I'm very proud that our company was there as a pioneer.

Speed has also played a great role in our ability to use the information highway and is increasingly more important to what we can reasonably do with the infrastructure. That first Hayes Smartmodem was a 300 baud modem. Since then, modem speeds have doubled about every 18 months. With today's files and programs being measured in megabytes and telephone charges being measured in dollars per minute, we need faster modems. With a 300-baud modem, transferring a megabyte of data would take more than 9 hours! Today, our OPTIMA 288 V.FC + FAX supports data-throughput speeds of up to 230,400 bps, hundreds of times faster than our first modem! That's a megabyte of data transferred in less than a minute, an increasingly valuable capability when you consider the vast number of huge data, graphics, and program files being transferred today. These increases in speed translate into shorter transfer times, lower operating costs and phone charges, and more convenience. That's good news for every user. Advances in speed have also led to exciting, powerful communications applications for remote control, remote LAN access, and multimedia applications that are ready to burst onto the scene with information services and bulletin boards supporting pictures, video, and desktop conferencing.

Our design philosophy today is a direct reflection of our vision from the early 1980s — design a product that is technologically complex and powerful on the inside, yet simple to use from the outside. Furthermore, we want to bring the product to the market at a price that makes the technology more available to growing and varied segments of the marketplace. So, whether it's Hayes LANstep, our network operating system, or Smartcom for Windows communications software, our design philosophy is the same as it was in the beginning. Time has shown that our philosophy is sound and that it has provided a solid foundation for future computer communications technology.

One of the most gratifying aspects of the success of our design philosophy is knowing that because modems no longer require a technical expert, we have freed users to go on a nearly limitless journey beyond their desktops. The telephone network has become the largest computer peripheral in the world, with the modem providing the electronic link to a wide array of communications applications and information available from such industries as the medical, legal, and entertainment fields, as well as the government. You may have already experienced the communications excitement of calling an online service, like CompuServe, America Online, or Prodigy, or explored the variety of topics and people who communicate regularly on one of the more than 200,000 bulletin board systems around the world that represent special interest groups as diverse as home improvement, botany, computer clubs, or business communications systems for customer service.

Whether you need to maintain a worldwide, intercompany e-mail system, use your modem as a fax machine, oversee a network for placing orders with suppliers, or play a game, modems provide the critical link. From the very practical to the ridiculous, computer communications has something for everyone.

I'm excited about the possibilities for you when you combine the capabilities of your modem and communications software with the wealth of information in this book. So, no matter what your communications application might be, go ahead and start your own computer communications revolution and jump on the information highway. The on-ramp is only an AT command away.

Dennis Hayes
President and Founder
Hayes Microcomputer Products, Inc.

An Armchair Tour

Part I of the *Official Hayes Modem Communications Companion* introduces this book, the communications world, and the technology. You learn about the necessary elements to make efficient and productive use of the remaining parts of the book.

Chapter 1 introduces the important elements in the book. It gives an overview of telecommunications, how the material is presented in the book, and what to look for when using the book as reference material.

Chapter 2 introduces the communications world and defines communications, what you can communicate with, and what you need to communicate. It also includes information on interesting and unusual applications for telecommunicating. You don't need any technical knowledge to understand this chapter.

Chapter 3 introduces the technology. You learn about data modems, fax modems, and their associated software. This chapter focuses on a general understanding and serves as a springboard for the more technical details introduces in later parts.

A Guide to Using This Book

Welcome to the *Official Hayes Modem Communications Companion*! This authoritative guide to PC communication will make you comfortable with the technology, improve your productivity, and widen your horizons. Above all, it is a benefits-oriented practical tool that addresses the most frequently asked questions about communication.

This chapter is the guide to the rest of the book and introduces the following topics:

- ❖ Electronic communication
- ❖ What is and is not in this book
- ❖ Keys to finding information
- ❖ Where to go from here

Changing World

Electronic communication is one of the most rapidly changing and exciting technologies of this century. It has radically altered our view of the world. No longer do we hear about revolutions or natural disasters in distant places months or years after they occur. Now, we see and hear events as they happen and can even communicate directly with people involved.

Not only has our perspective of the world changed, but our everyday lives are also different. It is inconceivable to run any business without a telephone, and even the smallest business typically has a fax machine, voice mail, or an answering machine.

Modems and all the associated technology are now available to anyone with a computer at an affordable price and in an understandable presentation. In the same way that millions who use PCs now would never have imagined using a computer 10 to 15 years ago, millions now use modems, faxes, and other telecommunication tools as easily as an ordinary telephone or television. Telecommunication has become a major application for computers, now ranking in importance with word processors, spreadsheets, and databases.

It was natural for personal computers to evolve to include communication facilities. After all, mainframes have used modem technology since the 1960s. Telephones had become commonplace, inexpensive, and a primary means of communication. In fact, modems have been available for personal use since before the IBM PC and date back to the first microcomputers, which came in kits, such as the Altair.

Modems used with mainframes required dedicated phone lines. To link with another modem, you specified the phone number so mechanical switches could be set internally. If you needed to access a different phone number, the modem's switches had to be adjusted — usually by a qualified technician.

Dennis Hayes, founder of Hayes Microcomputer Products, learned about telephone networks while at Georgia Tech as a co-op student with AT&T Long Lines. After leaving Georgia Tech, he joined National Data Corporation. NDC ran a service bureau that handled electric membership cooperatives, which provide power and telephone service to rural communities. Part of Hayes job was to help the local independent telephone companies install modems.

Realizing how cumbersome the modem installation and configuration process was, Dennis Hayes and Dale Heatherington pioneered the concept of a microprocessor-controlled modem rather than having to call a technician every time a parameter needed changing.

In 1977 — four years before the introduction of the IBM PC — Hayes and his partner, Dale Heatherington, built a microprocessor-controlled modem that could be directly controlled by computer software. The first models were aimed at the hobbyists who were building microcomputers from kits, particularly the S100, and soon after that Apple II computers.

Although the first models were for hobbyists, the potential for personal and small-business use was obvious. Additionally, Hayes realized that the early computer companies did not have experience in data communication and that the large established companies, such as AT&T and IBM, would not immediately recognize the potential of the small-user market.

What became Hayes Microcomputer Products was incorporated by Hayes and Heatherington, an engineer, as D.C. Hayes Associates in January 1978. The voracious appetite of typical early microcomputer users for things to do with their computers spurred modem sales. For example, Hayes sold more than 1,000 modems for the Apple II before Apple introduced a hard disk drive.

Early modems worked only with specific computer models. Customer requests for modems to connect to computer A or computer B quickly drove Hayes to look for device independence in the modems. This would enable the company to build a single model modem that would connect to any computer, whether it was a minicomputer or a microcomputer or mainframe.

Linking modems to each other was not a problem, because all modems had to meet a specific standard. The problem was getting the electronic signals from the modem to a computer. The computers all had their own method of connection and used different standards.

This device independence was a driving force in the Hayes modem design. Each had to be able to be connected to a terminal, a microcomputer, or a printer. Additional features could not compromise this criterion. As a result, intelligent modems (with microprocessors that can accept commands from external software) became the standard means for linking computers, terminals, and printers.

By 1982, only a year after the IBM PC's introduction, Hayes annual sales hit $12 million, and in 1983 the company added Smartcom II software for the IBM PC to its product line. Since then, modems have become a standard part of many PC setups and are increasingly important for both business and home use.

Nowadays, modems are used most frequently to link two computers, but they continue to be able to link other devices, such as a terminal or printer, to a computer as well. Throughout this book, I assume you will be using a PC and a modem as one end of the connection. You may, however, be linked to another computer or a printer. Using a modem with a dedicated terminal rather than a PC, although feasible with modems, is not covered in this book.

What Is in This Book

Although communication is no longer limited to a technical audience, the perception lingers that modems are complicated "black boxes." This book, for introductory and intermediate users, focuses on the essential tools needed to take advantage of your modem, PC fax, and the telecommunication world. It is a practical reference that introduces the necessary concepts and terms and shows how to apply them.

The decision of what material to include in this book and what to omit was based in part on using the concept of providing answers to commonly asked communication questions. I gathered these questions from a variety of sources including the Hayes customer support staff, electronic bulletin boards, user groups, magazines, and, of course, my own experience.

This book explains PC communication, modems, faxes, and how to link to and exchange data with other computers. You learn what modems and faxes are, how to choose them, when to use them, and how to use them most effectively.

The early chapters lay the groundwork for the intermediate and more-advanced chapters. Armed with the concepts, you can move on to selection, installation, and configuration. After "getting it to work," you can discover how to streamline your communication and optimize your configuration to minimize online costs.

The gigantic array of online information is another main focus. Just as a library is a much wider resource than is your personal book collection, online information can expand your personal program library into a huge collection and give you limitless information on any topic.

However, just as a specialized library may be better in some instances, information may exist in various forms in different places online. To avoid frustrations, online services should be considered carefully and used appropriately.

Online information is not just reference material. A worldwide community of people use PC communication to share and exchange messages and information. They are not elite or (typically) eccentric, but they do have a desire to communicate.

Telecommunicating makes this possible 24 hours a day, seven days a week. Not only is the world becoming a smaller place, but time-zone differences, national borders, and even continental boundaries are irrelevant. Access to all this information can be as close as a local phone call.

The different types of online services are introduced in this book, and a sample session of each type illustrates applicable techniques that you can use to tap into this incredibly rich resource.

What Is Not in This Book

This book is not an encyclopedic tome that incorporates every tiny detail relating to communication. Because it is a practical tool, unnecessary engineering detail is not included. I do not, for example, describe the intimate details of how a modem or fax is designed so that you can design one for yourself. However, I provide sufficient conceptual information so you are able to appreciate what a modem or fax does, why it does it, and how to optimize its performance.

This book does not cover the details of linking a terminal to a modem. However, it does explain how to use your PC as a terminal to link to other computers. The information relating to terminals linking to remote computers tends to be very vendor specific.

This is not a speculative book. If the technology is not widely available and actually being used in practical situations, it is not covered in detail. Wireless communication, for example, is not included.

Although an important focus for this book is the available online services, both commercial and free, my intent is to give you a solid understanding of the possibilities and typical flavor of these services — not to provide an exhaustive guide. Once you have chosen an online service that suits your needs, you can probably find other books that focus on that particular service.

How the Parts Fit Together

The *Official Hayes Modem Communications Companion* is divided into four main parts: "An Armchair Tour," "Communications Basics," "Survival and Efficiency Tools," and "The Online World Tour." The book introduces terms and techniques so beginners will understand the necessary concepts and can apply their knowledge. It also includes, as sidebars, in-depth explanations for readers interested in more details or background.

Part I, "An Armchair Tour," introduces the concept of the whole communication picture being composed of a variety of connected but separate elements. It serves as a guide to the rest of the book. It introduces the technology, explains what is included in the book and what is excluded. It shows what is possible with communication, what you need to achieve your goals, and how the parts of the book fit together.

Part II, "Communications Basics," introduces the fundamentals necessary to use modems and PC faxes effectively. It covers the important terms and elements needed to communicate. By the end of this section, you know when to use a fax and when to use a modem, as well as how to select, install, and make a connection with another computer. You understand the essentials of serial ports, telephones, modems, communication software, connecting, terminal emulation, file transfer, and disconnecting.

Part III, "Survival and Efficiency Tools," moves you from the elementary connection to making the most of the modem, fax, and communication software. By the end of this section, you understand modem features and know what to look for in communication software, such as dialing directories, scripts, and file-transfer protocols. You understand your fax software and OCR software. Additional chapters cover other automation techniques, such as off-line readers, methods for reducing costs, and remote control software.

Armed with the techniques from earlier sections, Part IV, "The Online World Tour," introduces the wide scope of available online services. The perspective is practical, emphasizing what each type of service should be used for, and includes a brief tour. This makes you aware of the potential for online communication rather than providing a reference guide to any particular service. With the fear of the unknown removed, you gain the confidence to use a particular service without mentally counting the costs. As general topics, the covered services include BBSs, the Internet, message-based services such as MCI Mail, information-exchange services such as CompuServe and Prodigy, and information-searching services such as Dialog and Dow Jones News Retrieval.

Part V includes four appendixes to serve as references: "AT Command Set," "Resource Guide to Popular Online Services," "Guide to Smartcom for Windows LE," and "100 Most Frequently Asked Questions."

Keys to Finding Information

Three design elements used throughout the book help guide you when using the book as a reference, provide more technical detail for the interested reader, and emphasize the authoritative practical tools included.

The sidebars

Each chapter in Parts II through IV also includes sidebars. These are usually one page in length and allow the inquisitive reader to gain an in-depth understanding of a specific topic. You often see sidebars in magazines. They are separate boxed areas of text, often with a shaded background, that stand separately from the main text but are related to the subject.

How to Identify a Sidebar

Boxed sidebars introduce additional details, historical or more advanced information on a particular topic. They are set apart from the main text by being boxed and have a shaded background.

For example, Chapter 4, "Selecting Your Equipment," includes a sidebar on understanding a UART

(Universal Asynchronous Receiver/Transmitter). Although this is an important topic that will be of interest to most readers, it is not essential reading for understanding the concepts introduced in the chapter.

The questions

Throughout the book, you will see commonly asked questions in large type. These questions are used as a graphical element throughout the book to stand apart from the main text. The questions start in the margin, appear in italics, and are surrounded by quotation marks to indicate that these are questions that many readers have.

"How do I find answers to my communications questions?"

The main text surrounding the question will directly answer the question. This element also helps you focus on a particular problem by posing questions likely to occur.

Appendix D lists these commonly asked questions and provides a page cross-reference to where you can find the answers in the book.

The jigsaw puzzle

At the beginning of each chapter, the jigsaw puzzle shows how the particular chapter relates to the whole book. This will serve as a quick guide for the reader interested in exploring only particular features. (See Figure 1-1.)

Each of the 12 jigsaw puzzle pieces represents a benefit or feature of communications. For example, the picture of winged running shoes represents speeding your communications, and the envelope being mailed represents sending mail electronically. The puzzle pieces in the chapter opener show the major topics covered in that particular chapter. For example, the chapters that have the winged running shoes as one of the chapter opener puzzle pieces include sections that help speed your communications.

The 12 puzzle pieces represent the following concept:

1	Time savers
2	Speeding communications
3	Automating communications
4	Transferring files
5	Chatting online
6	E-mail and messaging
7	Broadcasting your messages
8	Reading online
9	Researching online
10	Entertainment and games online
11	World exploration
12	Reaching an audience around the world

Figure 1-1: The 12 jigsaw puzzle pieces used in this book.

Where to Go from Here

Typical readers of the *Official Hayes Modem Communications Companion* include:

1. Non-computer people, probably professionals and business owners, who recognize the need to expand their understanding and use of communication to compete in the market.

2. Home users who dabble in communication and want their children to have access to online information and games.

3. Network administrators, again possibly non-computer professionals, who are expected to expand a company's information base or implement electronic mail services both internally and externally.

4. Modem owners who want to better understand the technology. They are likely to be user-group members and extensive magazine readers.

These readers need to know how to select, install, configure, and use the equipment and software they have or need to buy. They are looking for a fundamental understanding of what they are doing, where to go for data sources, and how to collect the data, but they do not want a lecture in electronics or speculative information on future technologies.

When the basics are understood, these readers want real solutions and practical methods to reduce expenses by getting the required data as fast and as inexpensively as possible. Even without understanding the technology, many readers are aware that ongoing costs are necessary for phone service but want to feel in control of their expenses.

If you are a newcomer to communications, although you may be a PC expert, Chapter 2, "Understanding the Communications World," and Chapter 3, "Understanding the Technology," are essential reading. These chapters show the full scope of communication and serve as a launching point for exploring the remainder of the book.

Even if you already own and use a modem, these chapters may let you discover new opportunities. Skim through them quickly to get an idea of all the concepts before moving on.

Part II, "Communications Basics," is the next stopping place for all readers. The essential concepts and practical methods introduced in this section are built on in later chapters. If you know what you want to do but do not know quite how to do it, this is the place to start. Along with Part III, "Survival and Efficiency Tools," it is also the section to read if you are considering purchasing equipment or software.

Intermediate users can go directly to Part III to learn how to make the most of the equipment they already have up and running. If terms that you do not understand are used, they will have been explained in Part II, so you may need to refer back for areas where you are less knowledgeable. Part III can also help in purchasing decisions.

As Part II introduces the essentials to make a connection, communicate with another computer, and transfer files between computers, Part III shows the myriad of tools that make this connection more efficient, streamlined, and cost-effective. If you are upgrading equipment, Part III shows what might be missing from your current configuration. Chapter 12, "Special Purpose Communications," focuses on less-common connections, such as remote control software, communicating on the road, and international communication. These are becoming increasingly important but need special consideration to be feasible.

Part IV, "The Online World Tour," is beneficial for all readers. It shows what you can connect to. This is the section for finding where to look for computer games, doing patent searches, getting a pen pal in Siberia, or finding technical support for your favorite word processor. It is also the place to find where to market and distribute the programs you have written, advertise your better mousetrap, or tout your solution to world poverty.

Summary

This chapter described the general scope of the book and explained the design elements that will help you find the specific techniques you are looking for.

If you're new to telecommunications, thoroughly read Chapters 2 and 3. If you already know some basics about your modem, skim Chapters 2 and 3, and move on to Part II.

2

CHAPTER

Understanding the Communications World

This chapter introduces the concept of human communications and telecommunications. You will learn about the following topics:

- ❖ Understanding human communications
- ❖ Understanding telecommunications
- ❖ Appreciating the many reasons for communicating
- ❖ Knowing what you need to communicate

Defining Communications

As humans, we no longer depend on our ability to hunt, kill, and keep away animal predators but instead have established an elaborate set of social skills and methods of interacting for survival. In many ways, we still use our hunting and survival skills, but we depend heavily on communications rather than actually killing our prey. We typically define successful people as those who have made better business decisions, can manage more people, and have accumulated more money. The respected "tribal" leader is no longer the man who has killed the most animals, but now is the person who has the most control of money, people, and data.

We also continue to be social animals and communicate in many different ways. The most obvious is speech, but mime, body language, and the written word are also important elements, as well as the more recent radio, television, and computer communication.

Data communications, or *telecommunications*, where information is transferred between two computers, is a logical extension of human communications skills. We are by nature inquisitive and have extended our skills, moving from semaphore to telegraph, telephone, and the current computer electronics era. There is little doubt that this evolution will continue, and the next generation will have even more data at its fingertips.

Communications on a computer can seem like a daunting field that you will never understand. Even a PC expert may find all the new terminology intimidating. However, once you have learned a couple of basic items, PC communications is easier to understand than many other PC concepts.

Before discussing computer communications, let's briefly consider human communication in general. These analogies illustrate successful and unsuccessful communication. As I introduce you to the various telecommunications techniques throughout the rest of the book, I will restate the "human" equivalent so that you have a quickly understandable comparison.

Let's first consider communication between two people. One person signals in a way that must be understood by the receiving person. Despite the apparent simplicity of this scenario, many different parameters need to be satisfied for successful communication. For example, the two people need to be within earshot, speak the same language, and be ready to listen and talk to each other.

In conversation, the sending and receiving often occurs at the same time in both directions. One person smiles as the other says something funny, or one person's blood pressure rises as another person shouts abuse. You have direct feedback as to whether your message is being received as you desire and, if necessary, can alter your response until the desired effect is found.

As humans, our speech involves a lot of body language, voice intonation, and other signals that impart more than the words themselves. Some forms of communication remove some of the human senses and reduce the ease of communication. For example, the telephone removes sight from the interchange. Unless the receiving person provides verbal feedback, you cannot tell whether your message is being understood or misinterpreted. Some people, including myself, continue to use hand signals while on the telephone even though they cannot be heard or seen by the receiver.

Other forms of communication can still involve two people but are less direct, such as letter writing. One person writes a letter and mails it; at a later time, the recipient reads the letter. Parameters similar to those for direct communication must be satisfied, such as language barriers and correct routing of information (equivalent to being within earshot). This indirect approach can also have problems if that information is lost along the way or misinterpreted or if the situation changed between its being sent and received.

Mail, like the telephone, removes senses from the communication, both sound and vision. However, its indirectness—the information is not read as soon as it is written— is a tremendous advantage. You can read what you have written before sending it and reconsider your phrasing. Ultimately, however, the indirectness means you are unable to see the recipient's immediate reaction.

Strictly speaking, books are also a form of communication that involves two people. The author has written material that is mass produced and read at a later time. As before, the communication requires correct routing of information and no language barrier, but you can also look at this form of communication in a different way.

The author has gathered and arranged related material that is intended to be seen as a single entity by the reader. A major application for telecommunications involves the electronic equivalent of a library. You browse through "book" titles and select topics of interest so that you can withdraw books or abstracts from books for later reading. In this communications example, the emotional response of the reader is less important than the usefulness of the material itself. The best communication is achieved by the "library" that has the most accurate and accessible indexing system.

Most types of communication are variations on the three basic forms: conversation, mail, and books. These have direct equivalents in telecommunications: chatting, messaging, and databases.

The Potential for Communications

Webster's Ninth New Collegiate Dictionary defines *telecommunication* as "communication at a distance (as by telephone or television)" and *teleconference* as "a conference among people remote from one another who are linked by telecommunication devices (as telephones, televisions, or computer terminals)."

Although accurate, this definition only hints at the reality and potential for telecommunications with your PC. Even if you know little about computers, you can appreciate the potential by considering what you can do with television and existing technology. The telecommunication problems you will run into have parallels with typical telephone, television, and VCR use.

You can use an antenna and pick up local television stations, or you can connect to a cable television company and pick up more stations. If you use a satellite dish, however, you have many more television stations from all around the world available at the click of a button (or two).

Not only can you get access to more television stations, but with newer televisions, you can also watch more than one channel at once, get better quality sound, bigger (and smaller) pictures, and automate your watching by having the television turn off after a predefined time or blocking out specific channels.

If you add a VCR, your resources multiply. You can watch prerecorded tapes, record your own tapes, watch the television while recording another channel, get higher resolution pictures on your television, and program the VCR to turn on and off automatically. Now add a video camera, and you can videotape your family and friends, record events that are remote from your VCR, and bring them into your home.

Each of these devices has more options and gizmos each model year, and whatever you buy now will be outdated in a couple of years. If you wait a while before purchasing, you will be able to do more things than present equipment will permit. However, while you wait, you are missing out on many possibilities.

Telecommunications on your PC is comparable. Armed with a modem, communications software, and a phone line, you have access to limitless resources bounded only by your imagination. The field is so wide that generalizations are essential.

As discussed previously, communications can be divided into three main topics: speech, mail, and books. Telecommunications has equivalents: chatting, messaging, and databases.

You can use your modem, communications software, and phone line to communicate with another modem that is attached to another computer. You can, for example, call a friend or business colleague. Depending on your communications software, you can "chat" with your friend by typing on your keyboard and waiting for him to type a response, send a message to the other computer so that your business colleague will read it when she returns to her computer, transfer files between the two computers, or look something up on your friend's computer.

However, except in special circumstances, you are unlikely to want to communicate only with a particular friend. All around the world, in rapidly increasing numbers, online services supply the same features as the simple scenario of communicating with a friend but on a much grander scale.

Online services, covered in detail in Part IV, are computers with modems and specialized communications software that act as repositories for the database information and messages that are exchanged between modem owners. Most have multiple phone lines, and several, if not thousands, of people can be calling the same computer at the same time. Some systems even include features that allow you to "chat" or play games with other people who are currently calling the same computer.

As with many new technologies, a large variety of terms are used for similar items. *Online services* is a general term that encompasses such well-known commercial services as CompuServe as well as the estimated 200,000-plus *bulletin board systems* (BBSs) available in the U.S. Although many of these BBSs are run as hobbies from basements, do not assume that they are amateurish. Each online service is unique and offers different features and contents.

Databases

The most popular application for online services is the collection of software. People want to extend their personal software libraries, and literally millions of computer files are available online. You simply call up the online service and transfer the file to your computer.

The types of files available online are even more varied than the people who run the services. Many programs, utilities, and data are free for the taking. For example, one file may be a template to create newsletters in Microsoft Publisher, another may contain a spreadsheet model template for calculating your mortgage payments in Lotus 1-2-3, and another may be clip art. Each file was created by someone and transferred to the online service for anyone to access and use.

The First BBS

Across the nation, thousands of people sign on to bulletin board systems everyday to perform a wide range of tasks, from downloading important business information to ordering groceries. The inventors of the first BBS didn't have such commercial uses in mind on a snowy Chicago day in 1978. Ward Christensen and Randy Suess were simply two snowbound computer hobbyists who needed an easier way to transfer data to one another than sending cassette tapes in the mail.

The preceding summer, Dennis Hayes shipped the first hobbyist modem, the 300-baud internal modem. Hayes built the first Smartmodems on his kitchen table in small production runs of five. The Smartmodem was the missing component needed to make the connection between computers and telephone lines easily. In the setup manual, Hayes wrote that modems could be used for a number of applications, including establishing a bulletin board.

Christensen and Hayes knew each other from industry meetings. So, when Christensen called Hayes on that snowy Saturday, Hayes agreed to donate a modem for use in their history-making project.

Christensen and Suess then developed software and hardware for the first BBS in a short two weeks. Two years earlier, Christensen had written software to allow him to "beep" the contents of a floppy disk to a cassette tape by using an acoustic coupler. Although Christensen didn't know it at the time, he had just invented the 128-byte Xmodem standard, which is still used today.

While Suess worked on the hardware side, Christensen wrote a bulletin board program patterned after corkboard bulletin boards used to post information for a computer club. With that program finished, all the components — computer, phone line, modem, and software — came together to produce the first, and to this day, the oldest BBS in the world.

The most important file type found in online services is called *shareware*. These commercial products, often of a very high quality, are distributed by using the shareware principle, which means you can obtain and copy these programs for no charge. You can use them for a limited period to see whether they fit your needs. If they do, you pay the registration fee to the original author. If you do not find the program useful, you simply delete it from your computer and owe nothing.

Shareware programs, like programs found in retail and mail-order outlets, vary in quality. However, you have to pay only if you actually like the product. Even if you do not like the product, you are more knowledgeable about what to look for in another company's product.

I find that about half of the programs I use on a regular basis are shareware and are much better than typical commercial equivalents because they fit my needs more closely. This is due in part to the fact that I can actually try them out before purchase.

In particular, I find that shareware products, such as communications programs, bookkeeping programs, electronic databases, and virus detectors, often incorporate valuable additions much more quickly than do their commercial counterparts. For example, if I am concerned that my antivirus program is out of date, I can get the latest update within minutes by using telecommunications.

Programs found online really do include the full gamut. Games are extremely popular, as are utility programs, but you can find almost anything you need. If you cannot find it, ask by leaving a message and you are very likely to be directed to several files fitting your needs.

Do not overlook telecommunications as an economical means of file distribution as well as file collection. For private use, you can rapidly distribute updated sales reports, new form layouts, and other data by using your modem instead of an overnight courier service or mail. The data arrives almost instantaneously for the cost of a phone call.

For more public consumption, you can rapidly get your program seen by more people than is possible through traditional selling channels. Do not assume that if you use the shareware approach you will not get registrations. If your product is any good, people will register. Recent reports estimate that the top shareware antivirus program manufacturer made $2 million in profits in a single quarter. Although multimillion-dollar enterprises are in the minority, many shareware authors make a reasonable living by supporting and updating their programs. Shareware is also distributed by other methods, but the primary sources are online services and disk vendors that charge a small disk-copying fee.

The other more specialized application for online databases is research. Some online services are organized as huge reference libraries. You pick a topic and gradually focus in on the data you are looking for. For example, you may need to know how and why the economy of China has changed over the last 100 years, or you may need to know current financial information for your stock portfolio.

By accessing the most appropriate online service, you can sift through enormous databases and rapidly focus on the information you need. When you find the data, you will be able to extract only the information you need and ignore the rest.

Some companies offer a service in which their staff will do the searching for you. You might use this, for example, as a newspaper clipping service, where you hire a company to read particular newspapers and magazines and provide copies of articles mentioning your company's or your competitors' name. Because the search is done electronically (most newspapers and magazines are now available in electronic form), searching can be much more accurate and inclusive than depending on a human to spot the names.

Messages

Apart from files, most online services include a messaging system. *Messages* are usually divided into *topics*, often known as *conferences*. You look at the conferences or topics, choose the ones of interest to you, and read the messages being sent. You can also type in your own message in response to someone, or you can start a new series of messages. Topics or conferences are very diverse and are not necessarily computer related. A few examples are politics, cooking, word processing, science fiction, and geology.

Messaging is typically designed for public discussion. Although messages can be marked as private, they are not private in the sense that they cannot be read by anyone. They can be read by the computer operators who run the computer system. You might use a private message to invite a fellow computer user to a movie, but you would not disclose confidential information that you didn't want anyone other than the recipient to read.

Messages are a mainstay on online services. They come in various guises but can provide more diverse and rapid information than other means. Many PC vendors, such as Hayes, Borland, Microsoft, and WordPerfect, have their own conferences on at least one popular online service. You can read information about upcoming products, get detailed qualified technical support, and find out what other people are complaining about or praising in a new product.

You can also contact many vendors by using their bulletin boards. When you purchase a computer product, the documentation often includes the phone number for a BBS. A vendor's BBS may include tips on configuration, updated documentation, or even full technical support resources. Companies with BBSs include Hayes, Microsoft, and Symantec. Online With Hayes, for example, enables users to read information about new products, obtain technical support, and download files (800-874-2937).

Some online services offer variations on the messaging system. You can do online shopping, make airline reservations, find the weather, or obtain stock market information, for example. This is an area where there is a blurring between using the online service as a database and using it as a messaging system.

Online services also provide interest at a variety of levels. You can find local, regional, national, and international information if you look in the right places. In many cases, all of these services are only a local phone call away.

Messages are intended to be an open forum type of mail. However, private mail, known as *electronic mail* or *e-mail*, is also available on some online services. These services, or this aspect of a service, are equivalent to the U.S. Postal Service or a courier service providing a mechanism for private delivery of your mail. In these cases, neither the online service operators nor other subscribers to the online service can read the information.

You can send your message to anyone who subscribes to the same service as you do or who subscribes to a service that can exchange data with your service. This interchange of data between services is an evolving feature that is gradually becoming less of an issue as more services can interconnect.

With e-mail, you write a message to be sent to a particular person or group of people, and the service distributes the information. Depending on the service, the message can be text only, or you may be able to attach a binary file, such as a program, to the message so that the file and message are sent together.

Some e-mail services offer more than mail service to their subscribers. MCI Mail, for example, will send a message to the addressed person. However, if the person is not an MCI Mail subscriber, the message will be printed and mailed via U.S. mail from the closest service location to the recipient. In many cases, this is faster than using U.S. mail directly and, for short messages, costs less than an overnight courier service. It is also more convenient.

Before using one of these services, be sure to understand whether anyone else, such as the system operator, is able to read your mail. Although you probably do not care if someone reads that you are holding a meeting in Chicago on Tuesday, you may care if others learn that you are about to make a hostile takeover of a competitor. This can be important when you are sending mail from one service to another because the receiving service may not offer the same privacy as the sending service.

Another major application for telecommunications and mail is PC faxes. You can use a PC fax modem, which is now often incorporated into the modem board in your computer, in the same way you would use a stand-alone fax machine. You choose what you want to send from your computer and send it via the fax software. In this case, the receiving computer is a fax machine and may or may not be a PC fax modem. Chapter 3, "Understanding the Technology," details the differences between a data modem and a fax modem. However, for this chapter, you need to understand that a PC fax modem provides a method of sending data to a potentially non-PC end user and that the fax received is a graphical representation of the text or material sent. You would not use a fax modem to communicate with an online service.

You need to understand that the data you send is not limited to being read the instant it is sent. The computer or remote fax is a storage medium, equivalent to a mail box. The information is read or retransmitted only when the receiver is ready.

Chatting

The database and messaging information found on online services share both a big advantage and a big disadvantage. You can access any of the information at any time of the day or night, but you are not directly interacting with the sending person.

However, direct interaction, known as *chatting*, is available in various forms on many online services. Some online services offer conferences where you can "chat" with other people online. Suppose, for example, that when you are online, you choose to look at a chat conference. You would type the command to join the conference and a message would appear on everyone's screen in this conference saying that you joined. You would then watch for a few moments while you read what everyone is discussing. Suppose the topic is local restaurants. A typical message may ask "Where do I go for good seafood?" When you want to add your input, you type your comment at the keyboard, and your comment is shown to everyone in the chat conference.

While discussing local restaurants may seem trivial, another section of the same conference might include a guest "speaker," such as a famous author, politician, or industry leader, giving you the opportunity to ask questions of people you would not normally be able to meet. This type of chatting is often advertised by the service. When you connect with the service, a list of upcoming "events" shows you who will be chatting when.

Interactive games are an increasingly popular application for online chatting. Unlike ordinary computer games in which you pit yourself against a computer opponent, with *interactive games,* you call an online service with your modem and participate in computer games where the other players are also "humans" calling in from their respective computers. This is like a computerized version of the very popular Dungeons and Dragons role-playing games. The games offered, however, are not all mystical characters. There are also plenty of opportunities to drive a tank and shoot your opponents, for example.

Another minor application for chatting online may occur when you call a BBS, especially if it is a small local BBS. The system operator, the person who runs the BBS, may see that you are having difficulty doing something or may want to respond to a message you are leaving immediately, and will chat with you by interrupting the bulletin board software and typing a message to you on the screen.

I regularly call a couple of local bulletin boards very early on Saturday mornings. The system operator of one of them (run from the local vet's office!) does system maintenance at about the same time as I call. He often breaks in to have a quick chat. We discuss, for example, what we have read in the trade journals or what new software or hardware we have seen or bought. This is unlikely, if not impossible, on many of the large online services.

Technology potential

Technology is changing so rapidly that even the most detailed description of online applications barely scratches the surface of the potential.

In the same way that PCs have completely changed the way we do business and how we need to present ourselves to look "professional," telecommunications has and will continue to change the way we use our computers.

Consider, for example, how word processors changed mass mailing. You now regularly receive mail with your name seamlessly included in the address and main text of a letter, as if it had been written specially for you. You can do similar things with telecommunications. With a single phone call, you can communicate with hundreds of thousands of people. It's up to you what you want to say to them or hear from them.

First BBS Teleconference to the USSR

"Greetings from the United States of America. This moment shall go down in history because it marks the beginning of the Global User Group, a momentous occasion." With these words, the first International BBS Teleconference involving uncensored access to the then-USSR was conducted on June 15, 1990.

It all started when Paul Curtis, systems operator for GLOBALNET, the worldwide electronic bulletin board system of the Association of PC User Groups (APCUG), wrote a White Paper in April 1989 describing the possibilities and opportunities for reducing tensions among nations of differing political and economic systems. With the help of GLOBALNET sponsor Borland International and equipment donations from other U.S. software and hardware manufacturers, Curtis' possibility became a reality.

The first BBS teleconference to Russia used Hayes modems and was held at the First International Computer Forum in Moscow. At the Moscow site, the entire teleconference was projected on a large screen so that the audience could observe the proceedings and ask questions. "There was such disbelief that such a thing could even take place or that the technology could make it possible," Curtis remembers.

Through this historic event, channels of communication were opened between the East and the West that had never been opened before. "The combination of communicating and computing is an empowering technology," emphasized Curtis.

Using Modems in One of the First Closed Loop Traffic Systems

If you've ever been stuck in traffic because of a malfunctioning traffic light, you can appreciate the role Hayes modems played in helping to revolutionize traffic control systems.

Until the early 1980s, traffic control was monitored by urban traffic-control systems that only connected traffic-control boxes at intersections to a mainframe computer. These systems were expensive and often inefficient. Complaints about traffic light malfunctions had to be checked through the mainframe or in person.

Cities needed a decentralized system that would allow traffic-control monitoring at the desktop. In the early 1980s, Transyt Corporation in Tallahassee, Florida, developed such a system. Using Hayes

Smartmodems, Transyt's Closed Loop System connected intersections on the airport loop road in Atlanta to PCs operated by the city's traffic-monitoring team. Hayes modems, installed in traffic-control boxes near the intersections, allowed the traffic team to monitor traffic lights, change traffic patterns, and watch intersections on the airport loop without leaving their desks or logging on to a mainframe.

The Transyt Closed Loop System was a huge success, and the Transyt Corporation currently has approximately 2,000 systems installed internationally. More than 11 years after the first installation, the primary communications link from the office to the field continues to be the Hayes modem.

What You Need to Communicate

To communicate, you ultimately need at least two people: one to send information and one to receive it. Telecommunications is similar in that you need to send information and have it received.

As a general rule, a telecommunications link has five elements: the sending computer, sending modem, telephone link, receiving modem, and receiving computer. The electronic devices that you use to connect your computer with another computer are called *modems* (short for *mo*dulator/*dem*odulator). The transmitting modem accepts signals from the sending computer and translates (*modulates*) data into a form that can be sent on a telephone line. The receiving modem, attached to the other end of the phone line, translates (*demodulates*) the received data and passes the signals to the receiving computer. The receiving modem may be attached to a printer rather than to a computer.

A modem can be an external device, the proverbial "black box," or a device installed inside your computer. Chapter 3, "Understanding the Technology," introduces modems and their purpose in more detail. For this chapter, you need to understand that you link two modems together and control them from computers to make a telecommunications link.

As a modem owner, you will need communications software. This software does two things: it controls the connection and is responsible for sending or receiving the desired data. This connection control involves controlling the link between the modem and the computer as well as the link between the modems. Chapter 1 explains how Dennis Hayes realized the value of being able to control a modem by sending it commands from software, cofounded Hayes Microcomputer Products, and created the PC modem industry. This allows you, the computer operator, the ability to control the modem via software commands.

Most modems come with communications software. Some of these programs are very elementary and provide only the minimum required to make a connection, and others are flexible and versatile enough to fit all of your communications needs. If you prefer, you can purchase communications software from a third-party company or another modem manufacturer.

The typical stumbling block for most new modem users is establishing the first connection and transferring the first file. The ease of doing this is directly related to the communications software. Before you give up telecommunications as a very technical and overwhelming topic, try and judge whether your frustration is due to communications software that is unnecessarily difficult to use.

Communications software has two primary purposes. First, it controls the modem. Second, it sends and receives your data to and from another modem. The modem must be controlled to make it operate with appropriate parameters (equivalent to talking the same language in human communication) as well as to establish and maintain the link between the two modems (equivalent to dialing the correct phone number and keeping the phone off the hook).

The receiving computer must also use communications software to control its modem and open the way to allow the data to be received. The receiving computer does not have to be the same type of computer as the sending computer, nor does it have to be running the same communications software. But the two modems must be able to communicate with each other for the communications link to work. The receiving device can be a printer, and the printer can accept the control codes and data sent from the originating computer to print a document. In this case, the printer sends data back to the originating computer and signals its status.

With the two modems, and consequently the two computers, linked, you use the communications software to send data to and receive data from the other computer. Regardless of whether you are chatting, messaging, or using a database, the communications link involves sending and receiving data between two modems that are controlled by computers with communications software.

The automation possible with computers can remove the need for a second person to be active in a telecommunications link. However, it does not usually remove the need for a second computer. In many cases, such as when you call an online service, you are able to control the communications software attached to the remote modem (the modem at the other end of the phone line). You instruct the online service to accept your message or file without direct interaction with anyone at the service.

Using a PC fax modem instead of a data modem is a similar conceptual connection. The fax software on your computer controls the PC fax modem. It sends signals to the fax modem that make the fax modem adjust its parameters or establish a connection with another fax modem and send or receive data. Although you may have a PC fax modem and a data modem as a single expansion board or device, you actually have two separate devices: a data modem and a fax modem. A telecommunications link can either link two faxes together or can link two modems together. You use communications software to link two data modems together and fax software to link two faxes together.

Strictly speaking, the term modem means modulator/demodulator. Types of modems include data modems, fax modems, and voice modems. As is typical with PC terminology, the terminology has become abbreviated, and *data modems,* which are used to transmit data from one place to another, are known simply as modems. Now that fax modems are also available for the PC, the terminology is more confusing. A *fax modem* can send data that conforms with the fax standards from one place to another.

If you think about it, the term fax is meaningless. Does it refer to the hardware, the paper, the action of transmitting, or the printed document? A stand-alone fax machine is actually a fax terminal, because it is a terminal device capable of sending and receiving faxes. When installed in a PC, the equivalent device lacks the terminal capabilities but includes the modem features for sending and receiving documents to fax communication standards.

In this book, the term *modem* is used to mean *data modem,* and the term *fax modem* relates to the electronic device installed or attached to a PC that can receive and send facsimiles of documents.

Summary

This chapter introduced the concept of telecommunications. Telecommunications between computers is an extension of human communications. By considering the three main means of human communication—conversation, mail, and books—you can understand the three main types of telecommunications—chatting, messaging, and databases.

You use telecommunications to transfer data between two computers. The other computer can be the same as or completely different from yours. You make your computer communicate with your modem. Your modem communicates with another modem, which in turn communicates with its computer. For the connection to be successful, the two modems must be able to communicate with each other.

Chatting is equivalent to holding a conversation with another person. When connected to another computer, you type on your keyboard, and someone else types on his/her keyboard in response. *Messaging* is when you type a series of sentences, a "message," that is stored on another computer and can be read by the recipient. Messaging lacks the direct interaction available with chatting but is the most typical way of interacting when online.

Much data stored online is in databases and can be divided into two general types. One database type is a collection of files and programs that you can gather by using your modem. The other is more of a research resource that you search for pertinent information on a particular topic. This type is roughly equivalent to a sophisticated encyclopedia.

Online services include large-scale commercial services, such as GEnie, as well as bulletin board systems. A typical commercial service can handle thousands of users calling at once; a BBS typically handles only tens of concurrent users. However, each online service has an individual character and offers unique features. A data modem is typically referred to as a modem, and a fax modem is a modem that can transmit and receive facsimiles of documents.

Chapter 3 builds on the knowledge gained from this chapter to introduce the specifics of telecommunications as it applies to PCs.

3
CHAPTER

Understanding the Technology

This chapter introduces telecommunications technology. You learn about the following topics:

- ❖ Understanding data modem and fax modem communication
- ❖ Understanding data modem and fax modem hardware
- ❖ Knowing your data modem and fax modem software
- ❖ Understanding remote control software

This information provides the basic knowledge to enable you to take advantage of the *Official Hayes Modem Communications Companion.* Subsequent chapters are more specialized and will focus on one or more of the topics covered in this chapter. The terminology introduced in this chapter will be assumed in later chapters.

Introducing Modem Communications

As explained in Chapter 2, a telecommunications link involves five main elements. A computer with communications software is linked to a modem. The modem is linked to a phone line and subsequently to another modem. This remote modem is in turn linked to another computer with communications software or to a printer.

The two computers, two communications software programs, and the two modems do not need to be the same. In fact, you do not actually have to use a phone line to link the two modems; a cable will serve but obviously has distance limitations.

The key to a communications link is making the two modems communicate with each other. This involves making the communications software at each end of the connection control the modems appropriately so the modems will interact.

Introducing a modem

To understand modem communication, you need to understand the basics. A *modem* (*mo*dulator/*dem*odulator) is a piece of electronic hardware that you attach to your computer. As shown in Figure 3-1, it can be an external box that is connected to your computer by a cable, or as shown in Figure 3-2 and Figure 3-3, it can be an internal device that is plugged into your computer directly.

Note: Many newer modem models include a PC fax modem as standard. If you purchase a data and fax modem, you have essentially bought two different devices in a single unit. You have the ability to connect by using the modem portion or the fax modem portion of the data and fax modem. This section of the chapter refers only to the data modem. Fax modems and their software, because they are used for different purposes than data modems, are detailed in subsequent sections.

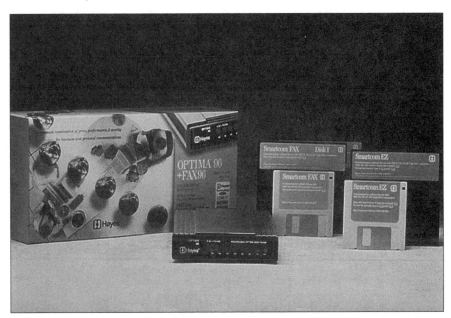

Figure 3-1: An external modem, the Hayes OPTIMA 96 + FAX96 is a data and fax modem combined in a single unit.

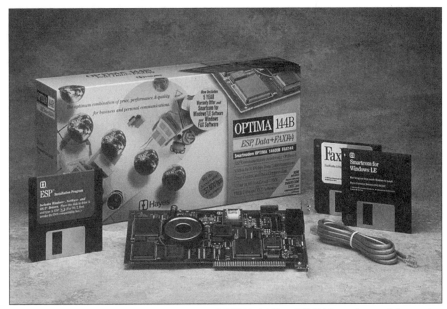

Figure 3-2: An internal modem, the Hayes OPTIMA 144B + FAX144 is a data and fax modem with a communications accelerator combined in a single expansion board.

Figure 3-3: A PCMCIA modem, the Hayes OPTIMA 144 + FAX144 is a data and fax modem combined on a PCMCIA expansion board used in some laptop and notebook computers.

As an external unit, a modem is typically a small rectangular box with a series of LEDs (light-emitting diodes) along the front and a series of connectors and an on/off switch on the back. Most modems also include a separate power supply, a small black cube with an incorporated electrical plug, that you plug into the electrical outlet and the rear of the modem.

An external modem typically has two or three other connectors. The larger connector, known as a *DB25 connector*, is the data connector that accepts the cable linking your computer and the modem. You will need a cable that can join this connector to a serial port on your computer.

Serial ports are covered in detail in Chapter 4, "Selecting Your Equipment." For this chapter, you need to understand that your modem is controlled by your computer via this cable.

The other one, or two, connectors are *RJ-11 phone jacks*. These are the same as the connectors typically found on telephones and telephone outlets. They are used to connect your modem to the phone line and possibly to another telephone extension.

Do not be embarrassed if you did not realize that you need to connect the modem to the phone line. It may be very obvious once you know, but an acquaintance of mine spent more than an hour trying to help someone call a BBS with a new modem and software without thinking to ask whether the modem was connected to a phone line.

A modem's electronic circuitry includes a microprocessor. You control the modem from your computer by using communications software, which sends two types of information to the modem: data and modem commands.

A special sequence of characters, known as the *escape sequence*, switches the modem into command mode so that it is ready to accept instructions. These instructions tell the modem to perform such tasks as the equivalent of picking up the phone receiver, dialing a phone number, and making a connection with another modem.

A modem can accept many more commands than those necessary to simply dial the telephone. Successful telecommunication involves many more parameters and coordination between the two modems. Commands can set the desired speed of data transfer between the modems, the number of times the phone should ring before the modem answers, and the form of modem status information that is sent back from the modem to the computer.

Chapter 5, "Understanding Your Modem," explains the essentials of these commands; but for this chapter, you need to understand that the modem is a microprocessor-controlled box that interfaces between your computer and your phone line. You control it from communications software on your computer. The modem can accept commands when in command mode and can send and receive data to the other computer when not in command mode.

Linking the computer to the modem

Your PC is a digital computer. A bit of data has one of two discrete levels, on or off, also known as high or low, or one or zero. The patterns generated by your PC, the sequences of ones and zeros, make up the data that you see as characters on the video screen, numbers in a spreadsheet, or keystrokes on the keyboard, for example.

In a telecommunications link, you are sending digital data from one computer to another. However, the telephone system is an analog system designed to accept the human voice. Although parts of it take advantage of digital electronics technology to move the speech more efficiently, the telephone system in its current form is intended for speech and not a series of ones and zeros. Analog signals do not have discrete levels like the zeros and ones in digital signals, but can have any value between the minimum and maximum.

An ordinary light switch provides an approximate analogy. The on/off switch is considered digital because the light bulb is either on or off. If you replace the light switch with a dimmer switch, the light bulb's glow is considered analog because its brightness can have a variety of levels between on and off.

You can think of your PC as a microprocessor with memory and a series of devices attached to it. The devices include the keyboard and display. However, the PC system architecture allows you to add other devices, such as a printer or mouse, via standard connections, known as serial and parallel ports. Most printers, for example, are connected to your computer via the parallel port.

A modem is a serial device and is attached to the PC's microprocessor via serial port. Unfortunately, despite the simplicity of the concept, attaching a modem to an available serial port in a way that everything continues to work in your PC is not necessarily simple. Chapter 4 shows logical approaches to making your modem installation easy.

If you have an internal modem, the modem is plugged into the computer and the modem acts as a serial port. If you have an external modem, the electronics that make up the serial port are located in your PC and you connect a cable from a serial port to the modem.

Your communications software sends the digital data to be transmitted to the other computer to the modem via the serial port, and the modem translates this data into an analog form that can be transmitted efficiently along the phone line to the receiving modem. The receiving modem translates the analog data back into digital data and passes this digital data on to the receiving computer via the serial port.

Your communications software also sends digital data to the modem to control the modem. The modem is able to determine when the data is to be used for control and when it is to be transmitted.

Introducing the link between two modems

So far, you have learned that the PC sends digital data to the modem via the serial port and the modem can translate this into an analog form that can be sent down the telephone line for the receiving modem to translate back again. The translation from digital data to the analog form is known as *modulation*, and the translation from the analog form to digital data is known as *demodulation*.

You no doubt have encountered the term modulation in radio and television transmission. Consider the AM and FM bands on your radio. AM is the abbreviation of *amplitude modulation,* and FM is the abbreviation of *frequency modulation.* Television is also transmitted by using modulation techniques. You listen to a particular radio station by setting your radio's tuning circuits to a particular frequency where the radio station transmits its signal, for example, 98.1 MHz FM.

You can think of the modulation process as the radio station transmitting a steady signal, known as the carrier signal (98.1 MHz in the example) and then superimposing the music and speech on top of this carrier. The way the music and speech are superimposed is the modulation technique. In the same way, the sending modem modifies (modulates) a tone or tones by the digital data. The receiving modem recovers the digital data from the modulated tone or tones.

Your radio picks up the signal transmitted by the radio station (the carrier and music or speech combined). The radio can strip away (demodulate) the carrier signal from this combined signal and leave the music and speech. The music and speech are then sent to the radio's speaker for your listening pleasure.

The modulation techniques used by modems are more complex than the radio example and, depending on the particular communications standard being used, may even involve no carrier signal being sent. However, you can think of the procedure as the sending modem modulating (encoding) the data in some known way and sending the digital data in a form suitable for analog phone lines. The receiving modem, because it knows how the data was modulated, can perform the reverse and demodulate the data to change it into digital form for transmission to the receiving computer.

For a successful communications link, the two modems must be able to communicate with each other. The receiving modem must know, for example, what modulation method or methods are being used, what the carrier signal frequency or frequencies are, how fast the data is being sent, and the form of the data.

In the same way that there are a variety of PCs manufactured by different manufacturers and with different microprocessors and performances, there are different modems that conform with different standards and operate at different speeds. To someone who has been involved only with PCs, telecommunications standards can seem unnecessarily complicated. The PC industry has become so large that it has been able to create its own unique standards, or variations on more universal standards, that are commonly accepted. It is easy to assume that there are no other computer standards. However, telecommunications is not isolationistic and, unlike computers, can be used to link.

PC owners, for example, have a tendency to dismiss mainframe computers and Amiga personal computers, for example, as remote and irrelevant. Standards that apply to mainframes or Amigas may not seem to have any significance to a PC owner. Owners of IBM PC-compatible systems and Apple Macintosh computers often have similar views about the importance of each other's standards.

However, it is vital to realize that telecommunicating has been around longer than PCs, is not a PC standard, and is independent of the computers attached to the modems. Early telecommunication standards, still in use today, were different in the U.S. from the rest of the world. However, the more-recent communications standards, now the most common primary standards, are truly international.

The communications standards dictate details such as the carrier signal frequencies, how the data is modulated, and how fast data is transmitted. Your modem will conform with at least one of these standards, and you can communicate with another modem that conforms with the same standard. Chapter 5, "Understanding Your Modem," explains the relevant specifics of some of the communications standards.

To create a communications link, both modems must be working to the same standard or they will not be "speaking the same language." The modem and communications software can automate the creation of a successful link. The bleeps, clicks, and hisses you hear when your modem makes a connection are part of the automated linking procedure. Chapter 5 explains the important aspects of this automation.

Introducing Communications Software

You need communications software to make your modem operate. This software may have been supplied with the modem, or you may have purchased it elsewhere. The software must serve two basic purposes but will probably include many additional features.

When you run the communications software, you issue commands that control your modem. These set such items as the speed you want the modem to try and connect at and whether to answer the telephone line when it rings. Other commands make the modem do the equivalent of picking up the phone, listening for a dial tone, and dialing a phone number.

When another modem answers the phone, the two modems establish a communications link. This connection is a negotiation procedure trying to find the highest common standard at which both modems can communicate. Once found, the two modems use this standard, and you can start to communicate with the other computer.

You also use communications software to send data from one computer to the other via the established communications link. You can type on your keyboard and have the characters control the other computer, or you can transfer a file between the computers. When you have finished communicating, you tell the communications software to instruct the modem to hang up the phone, and the modem terminates the phone connection.

Communications software comes in many forms, ranging from the most elementary to the most sophisticated. You can compare the range with the range of word processors available. A word processor at its most simple is a text editor.

At its simplest, when in a text editor, you type characters on the keyboard; they appear on-screen and can be stored in a file. Different fonts and special formatting, such as centering or automatic word wrapping at the end of a text line, may not be available. Even inserting, moving, or copying text may require knowledge of some esoteric command names and methods. These programs are usable but are not particularly user-friendly.

At its most sophisticated, a word processor can do advanced desktop publishing. You can use lots of fonts, reformat whole manuscripts with a single command, insert and manipulate graphics with ease, and produce masterpieces with every bell and whistle possible. These programs are undoubtedly the best if you need most of their features.

Hundreds of word processors fall between the extremes. The most suitable one is the one that includes at least all the features you need or will want in the near future but is easy to use with logical commands.

Communications software is comparable. You will be more successful rapidly with communications software that is beyond the most basic, because you will find it much easier to use. On the other hand, you do not need to rush out and buy the most sophisticated program unless you need a particular feature.

Chapter 8, "Beyond the Basics," and Chapter 9, "Making the Most of Your Modem and Software," introduce all the features a communications program needs to be reasonably easy to use and perform all the communications tasks. When you understand these features, Chapter 10, "Streamlining Your Communications," shows the extra features you can look for in a communications program that make telecommunicating easier, faster, and more streamlined.

Introducing Fax Machine Communication

The popularity of fax machines has expanded dramatically in the last few years. Faxing is an economical way to transfer printed material almost instantly from one location to another.

Like a modem, a fax machine is a microprocessor-controlled device that links with another fax machine via a telephone line. The telecommunications link is similar to that shown in Chapter 2. A computer is linked to the fax modem, which is in turn linked to the phone line, another fax modem, and another computer.

Unlike modems, which are available only as computer peripheral devices, many fax machines are stand-alone units and do not attach to a computer. Most of these incorporate a telephone and may include an answering machine as well. These fax units combine the computer and modem portions of the connection.

A modem is designed to link you with another computer and communicate directly with that computer. A *fax machine*, as its full name *facsimile machine* suggests, produces a replica of a document found on the sending fax machine on the receiving fax machine's paper. The methods used to generate the data for sending and printing at the receiving end are totally different than for modem communication.

When the fax machine sends a fax document, you can think of it as a scanner and modem. The scanner portion reads the page for transmittal as a series of dots, one line at a time. This data is sent from the scanner portion to the modem portion as a series of ones and zeros representing the presence or absence of a dot on the original document.

The modem portion modulates this data into a form suitable for transmission on the phone line. This modulated data conforms with a telecommunications standard. However, the standards used for fax transmittal are different from the standards used for data modem transmittal.

The receiving fax machine can be thought of as a modem and printer. The modem demodulates the transmitted data and passes the series of ones and zeros to the printer portion. The printer portion of the receiving fax machine takes the data and either prints or does not print a dot in the corresponding place on the page to replicate the original document.

PC fax modems are a further development from stand-alone fax machines. Rather than needing to print a document or graphic before it can be transmitted to another fax machine, PC fax modem boards send the document directly from the PC without the need for printing first and then passing it through a fax machine. Similarly, when receiving a fax document on your PC fax modem, rather than it being printed, the image of the page is stored in a file on your computer.

As shown in Figure 3-4, you can purchase PC fax modems as expansion boards that fit into your PC and provide fax machine services.

Figure 3-4: The Hayes JT FAX 144B Dual, a PC fax modem that provides similar services to a stand-alone fax machine but is controlled from the PC to support high-density enhanced fax servers as well as LAN fax servers on gateway applications.

However, many new modems also include fax modem features so you can purchase a combined unit on a single expansion board, or as an external unit.

To avoid confusion between when to use a modem and when to use a fax modem, consider the two features — the data modem and the fax modem — as two separate items, even though they are located on a single expansion board or external case and use the same cables. You cannot, for example, use communications software to send a fax document and you cannot use a fax machine to send a computer file.

Fax machines (whether stand-alone or PC fax modems) are preferable in some situations, and modems are preferable in others. Knowing when to use which device is important.

Think of a fax machine as a device that can replicate a document or graphic by scanning the document and sending the scanned image to the other fax machine for printing. The receiving fax modem may be located in another computer, or it may be a stand-alone fax machine. A modem can send electronic files and characters to another computer.

When you receive a fax document, even if you receive it via your PC fax modem and it is stored on your computer, you have a series of dots that make up a scanned image. You do not have text; you have a picture of text.

Chapter 7, "Understanding Your Fax Modem," introduces how to use your fax modem and Chapter 11, "Making the Most of Your Fax Modem," shows how to make the most of your fax modem and its software.

Introducing Fax Modem Software

If you have a stand-alone fax machine, the buttons and displays serve as the controls for it. A PC fax modem, even though it includes a microprocessor, is controlled by fax modem software installed on your computer.

The fax modem software has two main purposes: preparing your document for transmittal or display and controlling the fax modem board for transmittal or receipt.

First consider sending a document. The fax modem software is responsible for converting your document or graphic image into a series of scanned lines made up of dots and spaces. In a stand-alone fax, a scanning head actually views the page and detects dark and light areas on a scanned line. In a PC fax modem, the software performs an equivalent function.

Note: This is not the same as reading your text. The PC fax modem software takes your document regardless of its type and reads it as a series of a narrow lines, called *scan lines.*

The fax modem board's control for transmittal or receipt of documents is equivalent to that of a data modem, except that different communications standards are used.

The fax modem software tells the fax modem board to perform such functions as the equivalent of taking the phone off the hook, dialing the phone number, and establishing a mutually compatible communications standard with the receiving fax machine.

When connected, the document is transmitted between the two fax machines. If the receiving fax machine is a stand-alone unit, the document is reproduced one scan line at a time as the data is transmitted. If the receiving fax modem is a PC fax modem, the document is reconstructed electronically and is stored as a single graphic file on the computer.

Fax modem software, like communications software, is available in a variety of different flavors, but you are most likely to use the software supplied with your fax modem board. The commonality between modems doesn't exist between fax modem boards, so you need fax modem software that supports your particular fax modem board.

Some PC fax modems come with very basic fax modem software, and others are supplied with more-advanced software. Some PC fax modems also come with extra utilities that can help with file conversion so that your fax document can be loaded in other PC programs.

The basic fax modem software can send a graphic file to the specified phone number and receive faxes when the phone rings and a fax transmission is detected. More-advanced fax modem software may allow you to send the same document to multiple people by one selection or to group your commonly used lists of recipients. The utility software may include programs to convert from one graphic format to another or may include an OCR (optical character recognition) program that can convert your graphic file into text.

The typical home user can make do with less-advanced fax modem software and supplement the functionality by using other PC software such as graphic conversion programs or OCR programs available from other vendors. Unlike communications software, where there are literally hundreds of extra things beyond the basics that can be added to the software, far fewer bells and whistles can be added to fax modem software.

However, the business user can purchase more-specialized software for specific applications needs, such as using a fax modem as a fax-back server, which gives an automated fax response to a phone call. For example, some companies have automated telephone numbers you can call, and they automatically fax you sales literature.

The appeal of fax machines is their ubiquitous presence in so many locations, including rest stops on interstate highways, hotels, and businesses of all sizes. You do not need a computer to send a fax. In many situations, a fax document is considered written confirmation; consequently it is used for quotations, purchase orders, and many other business applications. It has become the equivalent of permanent voice mail. Rather than leaving a telephone message, people send confirming faxes.

Introducing Remote Control Software

Another interesting application for modems is remote control software. This is an extension of more-typical modem communication. You link the two computers as you would for a normal telecommunication connection and can operate the remote computer (the one at the far end of the telephone connection) as if it were in front of you.

For example, remote control software enables you to call your office computer from home and use all of the usual application programs, such as word processors and spreadsheets, that are located on the office computer. You see on your home monitor the same thing as on your office computer, and when you press a key on your home keyboard, your office computer behaves as if you had pressed a key on its keyboard.

Being able to use your main computer remotely allows you, for example, to take advantage of all the applications software on the remote computer. You do not have to have that software on the computer in front of you. You can use the large hard disk on the remote computer and do not have to have such resources on your connecting computer.

Remote control software also may enable you to perform maintenance and configuration changes remotely. Because you have control of the remote computer, your keyboard causes actions on the remote computer, and your monitor displays the correct screen, you can rearrange the hard disk contents and alter configurations at will.

It also can provide remote technical support and training in a way not possible unless you are physically in the same room as the remote computer. As discussed in Chapter 2, "Understanding the Communications World," the telephone removes the sense of sight from a communication. In a way, remote control brings sight back into the situation.

Suppose that you install a spreadsheet on a customer's computer. When that customer needs to know how to enter a formula into a cell, he or she may call you for technical support. With remote control software, you can see the same screen that your customer sees and press keys for him or watch him press keys. If you have ever done technical support via telephone, you will appreciate how remote control software can be a boon to productivity.

One problem with remote control software is that both computers must have the software installed and ready to use, so it typically is employed in situations where you know you are going to need it rather than being a coincidental part of most PC users' software set.

Other problems relate to compatibility and system resources. You need to run applications programs that will allow the remote control software to operate correctly, but not all application programs will support the software, and not all computers have adequate resources to allow both the application and the remote control software to run at once.

However, the advantages of remote control software for technical support and home/office use can be tremendous. Chapter 12, "Special Purpose Communications," explains remote control software in more detail. It also includes information on using your communication software's host mode, which makes your remote computer behave like a bulletin board, allowing you to exchange files or find files on a remote computer without needing to be at that location.

Where to Go from Here

To choose and install your modem and communications software, you need to read Chapter 4, "Selecting Your Equipment," next. Chapter 5, "Understanding Your Modem," which deals with actually making the connection, communicating, and disconnecting, assumes your modem and software are installed correctly.

To choose and install your PC fax modem and its software, you also need to read Chapter 4 next. Chapter 7, "Understanding Your Fax Modem," covers actually sending and receiving your fax document, but it assumes you have a PC fax modem already installed.

Other variations on telecommunications, such as remote control software, international communications, and using modems on the road, are also covered in Chapter 12. This chapter assumes you understand how and when to use your data modem and fax modem in more common situations. This information is found in Chapters 4 through 11.

Summary

Part I introduced the world of telecommunications. It showed what communication is, what you can communicate with, and what you need to communicate.

It introduced the major items involved in telecommunications: modems and their software, fax modems and their software, and online services.

Although it avoided detail, Part I also showed the basics of a modem connection and fax modem connection, knowledge that is assumed in subsequent chapters.

Part II, "Communications Basics," details how to choose the equipment, install it, and get it up and running. You can begin to focus more on a particular chapter to identify the specific items you need to make a successful communications link.

When you have your modem or fax modem up and running, you can examine Part III, "Survival and Efficiency Tools," to learn more about making the most of what you have, and Part IV, "The Online World Tour," to discover the limitless opportunities for online data resources.

II

PART

Communications Basics

Part II introduces the concepts and practical tools you need to make your data modem or fax modem work. By the end of this part, you will have your equipment up and running and will know enough to make a connection, communicate with another computer, and transfer files and fax documents between the computers. However, you will not necessarily know the most efficient or fastest way to make the transfer or know streamlining and automation techniques. These techniques are covered in Part III.

Chapter 4 introduces selecting your equipment and installing it. By the end of this chapter, you know whether you want to use a modem or fax modem and will be ready to make your first connection.

Chapter 5 explains how to make a telephone connection with your modem and how to communicate with another computer via modem. You learn such terms as terminal emulation as well as how and when to use AT commands.

Chapter 6 extends your modem use to include file transfer. You learn how to transfer a file to and from another computer and when to use which file-transfer protocol.

Chapter 7 explains how to make a connection with your fax modem. You learn the pros and cons of PC fax modems as well as fax machines and how to send and receive fax documents.

4

CHAPTER

Selecting Your Equipment

This chapter covers the essentials for selecting and installing your data modem or fax modem. Even if you already own a data modem or fax modem, this chapter shows the important features you should understand to make the first connection. Most new modems include a plethora of features, and you only need the essentials to start with. In particular you will learn about the following concepts:

- ✦ Understanding telephone essentials and serial ports
- ✦ When to choose a data modem and what to look for
- ✦ When to choose a fax modem and what to look for
- ✦ Installing your data modem or fax modem and making it work

Serial Ports, RS232, and Telephone Essentials

Installing and operating your data modem or fax modem is the most important part of telecommunications. When you have the data modem working, you can start choosing from all its options. You can think of this process like installing a VCR: Until you can make a tape play on your television, learning about setting the clock and automatic programming isn't worth too much.

Before you learn when to use a fax modem and when to use a data modem, you need to understand a little about the telephone connection and serial ports in your computer. You make a connection between two computers and two modems by connecting the first computer to a modem and the modem to a telephone line; the second computer is connected to its modem, which is in turn connected to the phone line.

Telephone line essentials

Using a phone line is a convenient way of linking the two modems. The whole country, and most of the world, has telephone lines linking businesses and residences. In concept, these telephone lines are cables that connect one place with another. In reality, there are a wide variety of methods for actually making the connection, but you can think of it as a long cable.

The telephone exchanges include switching equipment that route the telephone call in different directions, and the actual route may not include a physical cable. For example, most international and some long-distance calls are transmitted to a satellite in space and sent back down to earth in or near the receiving area. In most connections, different types of cables are used. The phone cable that is actually attached to your phone outlet is probably a four-wire cable; when that cable reaches a junction box, the connection is continued via cables with many more wires or wires that use more advanced technology, such as fiber optics and packet-switch networks, so that many phone calls can be routed along the same cable.

As a modem user, you should understand that the phone companies involved make the connection in many different ways. This variation, as well as other factors, including the weather, can affect the quality of your connection. For example, you may get a very clear connection one time you call your mother but a noisy line the next, even if you hang up the phone and redial immediately. When you use a modem, you do not actually hear the clarity of the connection, although its effect is noticeable when you try to communicate or transfer files.

If your connection and transfer run smoothly, you do not need to think about the telephone connection. However, when you experience intermittent problems, such as losing data or getting random or unexpected characters appearing on-screen, remember that your equipment and settings may be perfect, but the phone line connection may be noisy.

The telephone is designed to transmit the human voice from one location to another via cable. As explained in Chapter 3, the human voice is *analog*, rather than *digital*, and consists of a variety of signal levels. Digital data has only two states, on or off, which are often referred to as zeros and ones.

To transfer information between two computers, the digital data must be converted into a form suitable for transmission along telephone lines that are designed for analog data transmission. The modem *modulates* the data into a form for transmission and also *demodulates* the data for the receiving computer or device. The modem does not change the data — only the form of the data.

Modem technology is reaching the point where increasing the speed of data transmission (shoving more data down the line at once) will require better connection equipment. The fastest modems currently available, when used with all the special data-compression features, are stretching the limits of analog phone connections. To move beyond this speed, replacement connections will be necessary. Although the majority of users do not need to transmit faster, the new technology is available in some geographical areas, and some people have started to use it. However, not every phone connection will ever exceed the current analog telephone standards.

Three types of telephone lines are typically available: voice grade, conditional voice grade, and leased lines. The vast majority of phone lines are voice grade; they are designed to be of a sufficiently high quality for transmitting the human voice well. However, if you have special needs, such as transmitting a lot of data, you can get higher-grade lines. You will pay more for these lines and may need to pay for their installation at your location and at any receiving locations.

The conditional voice grade line provides a better-quality phone line by using more-modern technology, such as packet-switched networks. A leased line, as its name implies, is a phone line that you lease. It is "permanently" connected to a particular phone and is used most frequently for connecting terminals, which may be PCs, to a minicomputer or mainframe. This permanent attachment means that you do not have a dial tone and you do not have the ability to dial a phone number.

Why Not More Data, Faster?

You may wonder why the modem manufacturers do not make faster and faster modems. The problem is not with the modems but with the relatively antiquated analog phone system. Because the phone system is designed for the human voice and consequently analog data, the digital data from your computer is modulated into analog form for transmission down the phone line.

The current modems, such as V.FC and V.FAST, are transmitting data at just below the theoretical limit of the phone lines. They probably could send data just a little bit faster, but not reliably, with every phone connection in the world.

There are two ways of increasing data rate. You either send the data faster or send more data at once. However, it requires power to send the data along the telephone line, there is inherent noise on the telephone line, and there is a limited amount of bandwidth on the telephone line. You are limited by the physical limitations.

This limitation, known as Shannon's Law — after Claude Shannon who proved the limits for an ideal situation — shows it is related to the power of the signal, the power of the noise, and the bandwidth of the channel. In reality, this limit cannot be reached because of other problems found in a practical situation. (For example, Shannon's Law assumes only random noise.)

The amount of power available is limited by the design of the telephone system. The bandwidth of the telephone system, which can be thought of as the amount of room available to send multiple bits of data at once, is limited. You reach a point where you cannot distinguish the difference between two bits of data being sent at the same time, you cannot distinguish between two bits of data being sent one after the other, and the signal is so weak that you cannot distinguish the bits of data from the noise on the phone line.

"Do I need a special telephone line for my modem?"

All home users and most small- to medium-sized businesses will need only a voice-grade phone line. Specialized needs, such as typesetting or printing services that transmit data more or less continually to the printers, are possible exceptions. If you have applications that need these capabilities, you will probably be told by your software or hardware supplier as well as the phone company.

Most telephone companies offer a variety of extra services on the standard voice-grade line. Some of these are beneficial to modem users. Others are hazardous.

One option is pulse or tone dialing. A pulse dial phone sends a series of pulses that sound like clicks when you dial the phone. When you press 6, for example, you hear six clicks on the line. A tone dial phone sends a different tone for each digit on the keypad. (When I lived in Florida, I regularly called a local engineering company regularly whose number sounded like "Mary had a little lamb!")

Tone dialing is an extra cost item in most areas; in others, it is a standard part of the service. Tone dialing is much faster, and when using a modem, which sends tones or pulses down the phone line faster than you can dial manually, the extra cost is well justified. If you have tone dialing, you can use pulse dialing, but in some cases, if you only have pulse dialing, the telephone exchange equipment that routes your call will not be able to recognize the tones as digits in the dialed number.

Another option increasingly being offered by telephone companies is call waiting. Call waiting adds a signal to the phone line — in some areas, it sounds like a beep, in others a clicking noise — to indicate that someone else is trying to call your phone number.

Although you may not consider it rude or inconvenient to have someone interrupt your phone call, because you can keep talking without interruption, the modem cannot ignore the signal. You may lose some data, or you may lose the connection completely because the two modems lose track of each other.

"How do I disable call waiting?"

You have two alternatives for call waiting besides not subscribing to the service in the first place. You can disable call waiting before making a phone call. This typically involves dialing *70 from a tone phone or 1170 from a rotary phone. You can program your modem to send this dialing sequence before dialing the desired phone number. Chapter 9 explains how to do this with communications software, and Chapter 11 explains how to do this with fax software.

However, there are several problems. Your phone company service may use a different number sequence or may not allow you to disable call waiting. Additionally, if you are receiving the phone call rather than dialing out, call waiting is not disabled.

Another technique, which requires some experience to set up properly, involves setting a parameter in your modem so that the modem ignores interruptions that are only as long as the call-waiting beep. However, this technique requires a balancing act of making the modem ignore the call-waiting signal while recognizing interruptions that prevent corrupted data. If at all possible, disable call waiting before making a phone call.

If you have a single phone line into your home, you should be able to use this to connect a modem. All PC modems that connect directly to the phone line use a modular connector known as an *RJ-11* jack. You plug a phone cable into the modem in the same way that you plug a phone cable into an extension phone.

Most homes now use these modular connections rather than the previous four-terminal system. If not, you can inexpensively purchase adapter kits that convert to the modular jack system, or you can get a telephone installer, such as the phone company, to make the conversion for you.

To give your modem the best line possible, remove as many other phone extensions as possible. The more telephone extensions you have attached to the phone line, the more potential for problems. In particular, be wary of very cheap phones, especially old ones, because they can cause many problems related to noisy phone lines and poor data connection. Cordless telephones are another potential problem.

"Can I use my telephone at the same time as the modem?"

In the same way that call waiting adds beeps to the phone line that interfere with the data connection made between the modems, picking up a telephone receiver while a modem is using the phone line introduces extraneous noise (even if you only listen and do not talk). This noise may cause your computer to receive or send corrupt data or lose the telephone connection between the two modems.

If you use a modem in a house with many phone extensions, create a system so that people do not inadvertently use the phone when the modem is connected. For example, you may decide that a second phone line is justified specifically for the modem.

Although a typical phone wire to your house includes four wires, only two are used to make a connection to a typical phone. The phone cables you attach have a similar modular RJ-11 jack that can accommodate the four wires, but only two of the wires may be connected. These two wires are named *tip* and *ring* and harken back to the early days of telephones when a telephone operator at the local telephone exchange made the connection for you.

"How do I attach a modem to my second phone line?"

In many cases, your home may be already wired for two telephone lines. The second two wires in the four-wire cable, also named *tip* and *ring* but for a second phone number, allow you to have a second phone number. To use this second line with a telephone, you purchase a two-line phone or you buy an adapter.

A two-line phone uses an *RJ-12* jack instead of an RJ-11. These are physically the same size, but all four wires are connected and used with the RJ-12. The phone has a button of some sort that connects with the first or second phone line.

Depending on your modem, you may be able to use the second phone line in an RJ-12 jack (or even other less common phone jack types that are most typically found in businesses). However, this feature, which you may need to enable using software, is not available on all modems.

A more common alternative is purchasing an adapter that makes the second phone line appear like the first phone line to the modem. To connect a modem or single-line phone to the second phone line, you can purchase an adapter that is sold at most electronic stores or your local telephone store. This adapter is a small plug that plugs into your phone outlet and has three sockets in it. One socket is labeled *L1+L2*, another *L1*, and the third *L2*. To plug a modem or phone into line 1, you can use the L1+L2 or L1 socket. To plug a modem or phone into line 2, you use the L2 socket. The L2 socket makes the third and fourth wires in your phone outlet appear in the locations normally used for the first and second wires. (To plug a two-line phone into this adapter, use the L1+L2 connector.)

In a business situation, or in homes with more than one phone line, you may have different types of telephones. If your company uses a private branch exchange (PBX), you may or may not be able to attach a modem so that it goes through the exchange. You may need a separate phone line that bypasses the PBX to connect your modem to the phone line. In particular, if you have a digital PBX, you cannot connect a typical modem. However, you can purchase modems designed to work on digital PBXs.

In some business environments, you can't know whether someone is already using the phone line that is attached to a modem because each extension attached to the same line may be in a physically different location. Additionally, you may not want to supply all users with their own modems but may want them to share a modem or a few modems. In this situation, consider a more advanced connection arrangement, known as *modem pool*. If your users are connected via a *local area network* (LAN), you can probably add a modem so that multiple people can share a single-user modem. This is comparable to sharing a printer on a LAN. Only one person can use each modem at a time, but the arrangement can be economical if implemented sensibly.

Other more-specialized telephone situations include using a modem in situations where modular telephone jacks are not feasible, such as in a hotel room or at a public telephone. A device known as an *acoustic coupler* may help in these cases. This kludgy-looking device connects a typical phone handset and a modem's RJ-11 jack. Chapter 12 includes examples of unusual situations, especially when using a modem on the road, and explains acoustic couplers in more detail.

Serial port essentials

A modem is the interface between the computer and telephone line. After deciding that you can plug the modem into a telephone line, you need to determine how to plug the modem into the computer. Unfortunately, this is not always as easy as plugging into the phone line.

As explained in Chapter 3, you can consider your PC as a microprocessor with a series of devices attached to it. These devices are attached via a connection known as a *port*. Typical devices are the keyboard and monitor. The PC also includes support for two additional, industry-standard ports, known as a *serial port* and a *parallel port*.

You can attach serial devices to serial ports and parallel devices to parallel ports. Because the PC's ports conform to an industry standard, rather than a PC-specific standard, you can choose from a wide variety of serial and parallel devices rather than having to buy a PC-specific device.

Most PC users know the general definitions of bits and bytes and serial and parallel. However, these bear repeating. Digital data consists of ones and zeros, known as *bits* of data. In a PC, these bits are typically moved around in groups of eight. These groups are known as *bytes* of data.

A typical printer is a *parallel* device that can accept data one byte at a time. A typical mouse, digitizer, or external modem is a *serial* device and can accept data one bit at a time. A typical internal modem is a *serial port* and modem combined into a single expansion board that you plug into your PC.

The parallel port in a PC can take the data given to it and arrange it in a form so that one byte of data is sent out of the port at a time. The parallel port communicates with the device, such as a printer, to coordinate the sending of data at a rate that the device can accept.

The serial port is similar, but its job is more involved. A serial port takes the data presented to it as a byte of data and arranges it so that the data is sent from the port one bit at a time. Similarly, the serial port accepts data one bit at a time and rearranges the data into bytes so that the PC's microprocessor can manipulate the data. This conversion is done by an *integrated circuit* (a chip), known as a *universal asynchronous receiver/transmitter* (UART), and its supporting circuitry.

The following sidebar gives you more detail on this process. For the purposes of making your modem work, you probably do not need to understand more than the preceding paragraph. However, to take full advantage of the faster transmission speeds, you need more-detailed knowledge to understand terms like overrun and to know what type of UART is in your serial port and understand its speed limitations.

"What do RS-232 and RS-232C mean?"

The serial port on a PC is said to conform with the Electronic Industries Association's (EIA) standard number RS-232. (The RS stands for *recommended standard.*) The C is added after the name to refer to the revision level of the standard. Formally, the RS-232 standard specifies the interface between data terminal equipment (DTE) and data communication equipment (DCE) using serial binary data interchange. In other words, the standard gives details on sending serial data from one piece of equipment to another.

The RS-232 standard is a written document that actually specifies only a limited portion of what has come to be known in the PC world as the RS-232 standard. For example, revision C does not specify the shape of the connector. However, it does specify the connector's gender—whether it has pins or holes. IBM, and as a result almost all PC-compatibles, use the wrong gender connector for their serial ports according to the specification.

Revision D of the standard is now released and actually makes some PC-compatibles even less in compliance because it specifies a 25-pin D-type connector. Many PCs, most notably AT-compatibles, use 9-pin connectors for their serial ports.

Understanding a UART

In most situations, such as using a serial mouse, the speed at which data is sent from or received by the serial port is relatively slow, and no problems occur. However, problems can occur when using high-speed modems because the UART and the way in which it interacts with the PC may not be fast enough to avoid data loss.

For example, the UART may signal to the microprocessor that it has data to be transferred, but the microprocessor may be busy doing something else and take too long to respond. If the UART receives more data than it has room to store, data will be lost. This is known as *dropping characters* or *overrun*. In modem communications, this phenomenon manifests itself as lost data or data that appears to be corrupted. Your file transfer may abort because too many errors in the data were detected.

The early PCs used a UART chip from National Semiconductor called an 8250B. Faster PCs, such as AT- and 386-based computers, used a functionally comparable chip called the 16450. The 16450 is typically placed in a socket in your computer, rather than being soldered directly into the circuit board.

These UART chips include a serial port and baud rate generator. In simplistic terms, the *baud rate generator* is the mechanism that controls when, what, and how fast data is sent from the serial port.

The 16550AFN UART is used in IBM PS/2 computers and some newer PCs. This UART is a direct pin-for-pin replacement for the 16450. It includes a serial port and baud rate generator but has the advantage of also including a 16-character FIFO buffer on both the receiver and transmitter portions. A FIFO buffer is a *first-in first-out* storage area. The first character to be placed in this buffer is the first character read from the buffer.

This UART is less likely to experience overrun because a temporary storage area exists for the characters that are waiting for processing. As a minimal cost upgrade, many communications experts recommend replacing the 16450 with the 16550AFN.

If you are not using high-speed communications (say 9600 bps or higher), this upgrade is unnecessary. If you are using high-speed communications, it is an inexpensive alternative where physically possible, but it is not a panacea. Be sure to examine other potential causes of data loss, such as unshielded long wires or noisy phone connections.

Some manufacturers offer alternative solutions, such as replacement serial ports, sometimes known as communications accelerators. These are introduced in Chapter 9.

Now that I've stated that PCs do not conform with the RS-232 standard and have probably confused you, you should realize that the PC conforms with the RS-232 standard well enough so that if you can make your PC talk to the serial port and connect the modem to that port, you probably can make the modem talk to the computer and make the appropriate connections.

Port addresses, interrupts, and names

For most PC operations, you do not need to know the technical details of how the application program uses the operating system and how the operating system controls the microprocessor and hardware. However, this detail becomes important when installing or configuring software that needs to use extra hardware, such as mice and modems. It's a pity that you can't learn about the detailed stuff after you have the program working, but unfortunately, you need the knowledge to make it all work together.

Because you are adding a serial device to your computer when you add a data modem or fax modem—regardless of whether the modem is internal or external—you need to know what serial ports you have, what they are named, and part of how they are configured. The PC can only control one thing at a time, so your addition must appear to the software as a distinct and separate item. If, for example, you have a mouse and a modem both responding to the microprocessor's instructions at once, neither device will work correctly.

This basic understanding is the most confusing part of installing a modem. When it is installed and configured appropriately, you can forget most of the detail until you install new software or replace or rearrange your hardware.

First, the information you probably know. Your application programs, such as word processors or communications software, interface with the operating system, which in turn manipulates the computer hardware. The most prevalent operating system on the PC is DOS.

DOS Version 3.3 or later supports up to four serial ports. Earlier DOS versions support up to two serial ports. These ports are named by DOS as COM1, COM2, COM3, and COM4. In your communications software, you probably need to specify which serial port your modem is attached to.

The microprocessor communicates with the devices by using I/O (input/output) addresses commonly referred to as *port addresses*. The port addresses can be thought of as the "positions" of the devices. Each serial port is assigned a group of eight port addresses. (You specify the first address, and the subsequent seven addresses are assigned as the rest of the group.)

Additionally, each serial port is assigned an *interrupt* number. An interrupt number is often referred to as an interrupt level or interrupt request level. Interrupt level 3, for example, is abbreviated to IRQ3, and interrupt level 5 is abbreviated to IRQ5. An interrupt is a signal line that the serial port uses to indicate to the microprocessor that it needs attention. For example, the serial port may signal that it has some data ready for the microprocessor to collect.

"What are the typical address and interrupt assignments for serial ports, such as COM1?"

You can (theoretically) assign an address and interrupt to a particular serial port, such as COM1 or COM2. In fact, the flexibility of this assigning depends on the sophistication of your software. The typical assignments are shown in Table 4-1.

Table 4-1	Typical Serial Port Assignments	
Port name	**Address**	**Interrupt**
COM1	3F8	IRQ4
COM2	2F8	IRQ3
COM3	3E8	IRQ4
COM4	2E8	IRQ3
COM3 (PS/2)	3220	IRQ3
COM4 (PS/2)	3228	IRQ3

Notice that COM1 uses the same interrupt as COM3, and COM2 uses the same interrupt as COM4. This is because the PC was actually designed to support only two serial ports, and the addition of COM3 and COM4 are workarounds.

IBM PS/2 computers have a different I/O address map, and you can assign different addresses to your additional serial ports.

You need a unique name, interrupt, and address for each serial port in your computer. For example, if you have a mouse, you place it on one serial port and your modem on another.

The usual approach is to attach your first serial device to COM1 and the next to COM2. Wherever possible, avoid reconfiguring the devices you already have installed. If you change them, you will probably need to change the configuration of each of the software programs that use that particular device.

For example, if you have a mouse on COM1, avoid moving it to COM2 if at all possible. If you move it, you may need to change the configuration of each of your application programs that use a mouse.

To attach a serial device to your computer, you need a serial port. DOS can access them only if they are physically present on your computer. As explained earlier, a serial port comprises electronic circuitry that contains a UART or equivalent chip that performs the necessary data manipulation for serial data to be sent from the port.

Most PCs, made after about 1985, include two serial ports as standard. These may be built into the computer's main system board or may be in an expansion board. Earlier PCs typically had only one serial port. However, you can purchase inexpensive expansion boards that contain a serial port (or two), or you can purchase an internal modem that incorporates a serial port.

All serial ports that you can plug serial devices into are revealed by a connector in the computer's case. This connector will be either a 25-pin D-type connector (so called because it is D-shaped) or a 9-pin D-type connector. The typical PC standard is for this connector to be male (have pins rather than holes), but some early PCs had female connectors. (The serial port on an internal modem cannot be used to plug in a different serial device.)

If your display adapter is an EGA or earlier, it may also have a 9-pin D-type connector. This must be used to attach your monitor and is not a serial port.

To communicate by conforming with the RS-232 standard, you do not actually need to use all the wires in the 25-pin connector. In fact, all the required connections can be made with the 9-pin connector. IBM used the 9-pin connector in the IBM AT for space considerations (a 9-pin connector is much smaller than a 25-pin connector). Consequently, many PC compatibles also use the 9-pin connector.

Note: The serial ports with a 9-pin connector cannot be used for synchronous communication because this requires more than 9 wires for the signals. Unless you are using a leased line (covered earlier in this chapter), you will be using asynchronous communication and can use the 9-pin connectors without a problem.

You typically assign a serial port's name, address, and interrupt number by altering switches or changing jumpers on the circuit board. Some serial ports can be adjusted by using configuration software instead of physically changing switches.

If you are adding an internal modem, the serial port is incorporated into the expansion board, and you need to assign an available port name, address, and interrupt number.

As with the serial ports, this may be achieved by physically altering switches on the board or by running software. The manufacturer's documentation is essential reading.

An external modem can be plugged into an available serial port in your computer. Whether you add an internal or external modem, you need to write down the serial port name, address, and interrupt number. You need this information for your communications software. If any of your hardware or software does not work after installing a modem, the first question asked by technical support will be "Do you know your serial port name, address, and interrupt number?"

As more and more PCs include extra devices, such as sound boards and network adapters, the port address and interrupts become an important issue. There are a limited number of addresses and an even more limited number of interrupts. Because you only want one device to respond at a time, the assignments can become tricky.

For example, most network adapters are configured to use interrupt 3 when supplied. If you then try to add a second serial device, you may experience conflicts because the second serial device may be configured to also use interrupt 3. These conflicts may not occur when you are not actually using the second serial port but *do* occur when you try to add a modem. In this case, you may need to change the interrupt number assigned to your network adapter or to your second serial port.

Several programs — commercial, shareware, and free — are available that will interrogate your computer hardware and tell you what devices are assigned to which ports. Microsoft Diagnostics (MSD), shipped as part of DOS 6 and later, is particularly convenient, but your computer or modem may be supplied with a utility program. Many Gateway 2000 computers, for example, are supplied with QA Plus, and Qualitas' 386MAX memory management program is supplied with ASQ, a system analysis program.

You can use a serial device on COM1 and another on COM3, and similarly a serial device on COM2 and another on COM4, if you usually only use one serial device at a time.

For example, you may have a mouse on COM1 and a plotter or serial printer on COM3. Because you use the printer only when printing and the mouse to move the cursor around the screen, you can probably make both devices work successfully.

Problems arise when you try to use both devices at once. For example, if your program moves the mouse around while printing to a serial device, you can end up sending incorrect information to the mouse and the serial printer, and neither will work correctly. (This does not occur with parallel printers and mice, because the mouse and printer are configured as different devices with different port addresses.)

This conflict is particularly important for modems and mice. As a general rule, if you are using a mouse on COM1, avoid COM3 for your modem; and if you are using a mouse on COM2, avoid COM4 for your modem. Read the documentation that comes with your modem to help avoid problems.

Choosing a Modem

Like PCs, modems are advertised with lots of buzzwords, and different manufacturers emphasize different features to make a particular modem stand out from the crowd.

Also like PCs, your particular needs will be different from other people's requirements, and selection really is a matter of personal preference. You can buy very inexpensive modems that will probably operate under most conditions but may lack the extra features, technical support, warranty, or company reputation, and not be tolerant of slightly noisy phone lines or work with all other modems.

In contrast, you also can buy expensive top-of-the-line modems from well-known companies with every conceivable feature, excellent technical support, and good warranties. However, you may not need all these features and may be wasting your money.

One important difference between modems and PCs is that you need two modems to communicate, but many PCs never have their compatibility with other PCs tested. Any modem you buy, including fax modems, must be able to establish, maintain, and disconnect with another modem, which may or may not be of the same brand or standard.

Choosing a data modem, fax modem, or combined unit

Your first choice is relatively easy. Decide whether you need or will need a data modem, a fax modem, or a modem that combines data and fax capabilities. (Many new model modems automatically include a fax modem.)

If you know you want to transfer files between computers, call such online services as CompuServe or BBSs, or link your computer to another computer through telephone lines, you need a data modem.

If you want a substitute for a stand-alone fax machine and want to send documents (equivalents of pieces of paper), consider a fax modem. As the concept of the electronic desktop becomes more of a reality, where nothing is handed around on pieces of paper, the desirability of PC fax modems increases. As discussed in a later section, choosing a fax modem requires careful consideration.

Choosing the modem's form factor

After deciding whether you need a data modem or combined data modem and fax modem, you need to assess your current computer system, because this may limit your options. If you are going to use the modem with a desktop or tower computer, you have two main choices: internal or external.

An *internal modem* fits into an expansion slot inside your computer and incorporates a serial port. You need an available slot in which to place it, and you need to assign it an unused serial port name. If you already have four serial ports on your computer, you need to remove one to use an internal modem.

If you have a PS/2 computer and want to use an internal modem, you may need to select one that uses the Micro Channel Architecture (MCA) bus connection rather than the more common Industry Standard Architecture (ISA) or PC bus connector. (Not all PS/2 computers have the MCA bus; some low-end computers, such as the Model 25, use the ISA bus.)

If you want an external modem, you have two general choices. The typical box style is about 6 inches wide, 1½ inches high, and 10 or 11 inches deep, although some companies offer futuristic shapes rather than the boring box. Alternatively, you can choose a small modem, often known as a *pocket modem,* that can be used with a desktop or tower computer or (because of its small shape) taken on the road with a laptop.

If you want to use a modem with a laptop or notebook, you can use an external modem and attach it to a serial port. Some laptops come with built-in modems or modems that are available from the computer manufacturer as upgrade options. Alternatively, if your computer has a PCMCIA type 2 slot, you can purchase a PCMCIA modem that plugs into the expansion slot in your notebook. (These may be products offered by the computer manufacturer or a third-party company.) These modems are also small and lightweight for relatively easy travel.

If you are not limited in your choice, consider the following advantages of external modems:

- Most external modems have LEDs (light-emiting diodes) on the front that give an indication of the current modem status.

- You can use the serial port for other purposes, such as attaching a plotter.

- You can move the modem from one computer to another. This is good if you own multiple computers or decide to upgrade your computer.

- External modems have a separate power supply and do not use PC power. (This is only a factor with older PCs that don't have a power supply sufficient to power the modem along with everything else.)

Consider the following advantages of internal modems:

- Internal modems do not need a data cable connecting the serial port to the modem.

- Internal modems come with a built-in serial port.

- You don't need extra room for the modem on the desk.

- You don't need an extra electrical outlet for the modem's power supply.

Apart from the physical shape of your modem, you need to consider its features. Some modems can transfer data faster than others. The majority of buzzwords, in particular the ones that are not acronyms or abbreviations, used by communications people are related to the communications standards. These standards dictate the speed at which data can be transferred from one computer to another. In some standards, more data is sent at once. In others, the data is compressed before transmission and uncompressed by the receiving modem, which results in more data being sent in a certain amount of time.

Selecting compatibility

For PCs, the first consideration is to buy only a Hayes-compatible or AT-compatible modem. (As explained in Chapter 5, the AT is not the same as IBM's AT but refers to the two characters that are used as the start of modem commands.)

The analogy with PCs is worth reiterating here. The term PC-compatible has come to mean PCs that run and support all software and hardware designed for the IBM PC. In some cases, the PC-compatible standard has been expanded and enhanced by other manufacturers, and these extras may be desirable features. In other cases, increasingly less significant nowadays, PC compatibility may mean supporting almost all software and hardware designed for the IBM PC. This is where name brand — not necessarily IBM, but a major computer manufacturer — plays an important part in the support you will get from the computer manufacturer and software vendors when you find an incompatibility. They are more willing to support a computer that has brand recognition, because there are more likely to be many customers with the same computer.

The term AT-compatible is comparable. Buying a modem that claims to be AT-compatible is essential for you to use PC-communications software easily and consequently make a connection with another modem easily. However, it does not guarantee full compatibility and/or it may buy you extra features that are not available on all other AT-compatible modems.

For most PC users, there is only one type of telecommunication, and you use an AT-compatible modem to link with other modems. This type of communication is called more formally *asynchronous communication.* Asynchronous (as opposed to synchronous) communication is communication that occurs between two computers without regard to the precise clock timing sequences of the connected computers.

Synchronous communication is used between two computers when the events at each end of the phone line must occur in sync with (or in step with) the devices and computers attached to each other. People who need synchronous communication are usually aware of it, because they either have specialized computer knowledge or are supported by people who do. The most common implementation is linking a terminal to a mainframe computer. You can purchase specialized adapter boards for your PC that perform this type of communication.

However, if you need synchronous communications, you can purchase modems that will do both asynchronous and synchronous communication. You can do synchronous communication on dial-up phone lines and don't need a specialized synchronous communication adapter.

Note: The Hayes AutoSync protocol handles the situation this way. The synchronous application talks to the AutoSync driver, and the AutoSync driver sends special formatting signals to the modem so that the modem can convert the data. The modem has firmware in it that converts the asynchronous data into synchronous and puts it out on the phone line. Between the computer and the modem, the connection is asynchronous, but to the software, it appears to be a synchronous channel, and the data going over the phone line is properly formatted synchronous data. It's a clever way of tricking the hardware to do what the software needs to do.

Modem communications standards

Modems can operate at a variety of speeds and with different options that affect the effective data rate and insensitivity to data errors. A modem's data transfer rate is specified in bits per second (bps). However, this is not the only number you need to consider. When choosing a modem, you want to pick the most advanced standard you can afford.

Remember, however, that you must communicate with a second modem. The fastest and the highest standard that you will be able to communicate to second modem is the *highest common denominator*. For example, if you are only going to communicate with a 1200 bps modem, you do not need the fastest modem on the market.

The history of the modem provides insight into the apparently random numbering of communications standards and the apparent duplication of standards for certain data rates. You simply need to understand that from the time of the very first modem in the 1920s, people have wanted to send more data faster.

As a consequence, when a national or international standard for faster transmission had not been defined but public demand existed, manufacturers created proprietary standards to accommodate their customers. However, in most cases, the manufacturers also supported existing standards as fallback positions. If a modem was not connected to a modem that could support the faster standard, a fallback, and probably slower, standard was agreed on by the modems and used instead.

You don't have to worry about whether the modem you are calling has a particular standard. You set your modem to communicate with all its features, and it negotiates with the other modem automatically to find the best common denominator. However, when you buy a modem, you need to know which features you want, because its top feature will be the best at which you can communicate.

In the U.S., early microcomputer modems conformed with the Bell 103 standard. This transmits data at 300 bps. Although now rarely used, it is still supported by most high-speed modems as the final fallback standard. The next standard in the U.S. that is still used is Bell 212A. This transmits data at 1200 bps.

However, in Europe and the rest of the world, the two equivalent standards that were adopted were specified by the United Nations agency Consultative Committee on International Telephony and Telegraphy (CCITT) and were V.21 for 300 bps transmissions and V.22 for 1200 bps. CCITT is now renamed ITU-T (International Telecommunication Union).

Unless you purchase a very old modem, most modems support both Bell 212A, Bell 103, as well as V.21 and V.22. Bell 212A or V.22 are likely to be the lowest standards your modems will ever use.

For speeds above 1200 bps, U.S. manufacturers tend to adopt the international standards as they become available. However, there are some modems that also incorporate proprietary standards that you can use only when calling a modem of the same brand.

The 2400 bps standard is V.22bis (pronounced *bizz* or *biss* depending on who you talk to), and the 4800 bps and 9600 bps standard is V.32. The 14,400 bps standard is V.32bis.

So far, apart from slightly strange numbers, the bigger the standard number, the faster the modem, and the addition of *bis* to the standard number means a faster modem. As an additional help, most manufacturers use the data speed as part of the product's name to indicate its maximum speed.

Two more important standards are commonly available on newer modems: V.42 and V.42bis. Both of these standards may be available on any 1200 bps or faster modem.

A modem that supports V.42 can do error-checking on your data to help ensure that the data received is the same as the data sent. (Error-checking is explained in more detail in Chapter 6.)

A modem that supports V.42bis can compress and uncompress the data you are transmitting. As a consequence, you send more data between the modems in a given amount of time. Although manufacturers clearly tout the V.42 and V.42bis support, they do not usually make the potentially faster data-throughput speed with data compression part of the product name. The amount of data compression you actually get depends on the data that you are sending.

The ITU-T will agree on a further communications standard called V.FAST in 1994 and will probably name it V.34. This was intended to be the fastest possible standard possible on typical analog phone lines. In fact V.34bis is already being discussed. However, eventually further speed advancements beyond a standard will require specialized telephone lines and other techniques as yet not considered.

However, V.FAST has been very slow in being defined and agreed upon, and many people are clamoring for faster modems now. As a result, several U.S. manufacturers, headed by Multi-Tech Systems Inc., AT&T Paradyne, and AT&T Microelectronics, created a standard known as V.32terbo as an interim solution. This standard has a maximum speed of 19,200 bps. (As with memory capacities, 19,200 bps is usually represented as 19.2 kbps and is often spoken of as nineteen dot two.)

Understanding Modulation

Although you don't need to know the intimate details of the communications standards, a conceptual understanding of *modulation* is valuable. It will help you understand commonly confused terms, such as *speed* and *baud*, and understand why the current analog phone line cannot transmit data infinitely faster. These topics are covered in Chapter 5.

A covered in Chapter 3, the modem is a modulator/demodulator. When sending data, the modem modulates digital data into an analog form, and when receiving data, it recovers the data and changes it into a digital form again.

There are many different ways of modulating data, and each communications standard uses one or several different methods. To understand the basics, consider that steady alternating signal, known as a *carrier signal,* is transmitted at a particular frequency with a particular amplitude. The data signals are detected as changes in the carrier signal. The carrier signal is a *sine wave*, which you may remember from high school mathematics. All modulation schemes use amplitude, frequency, or phase modulation, or a combination of them.

Consider first *amplitude modulation*, which is similar to AM radio. The amplitude, or signal level, of the carrier is changed to indicate the data. A carrier signal with a normal signal level may represent a zero, and a carrier signal with a slightly lower signal level may represent a one. The carrier's signal level goes up and down to represent the data bits. Amplitude modulation on its own is not used in data modems.

In *frequency modulation*, which is like FM radio, the carrier signal's frequency is altered to indicate the data bits. Low-speed modems use frequency modulation.

The third type of modulation is called *phase modulation*. This requires two sine waves with the same frequency to be sent. A sine wave is an oscillating wave; at one point in time, its signal level is a minimum; at another, it is at a maximum. The number of times per second the signal is at a maximum (or at a minimum) is the signal's frequency. Phase modulation delays or advances the second sine wave relative to the first sine wave.

Depending on the communications standards, the modems use one or more of the modulation methods to transmit data. The details of what represents a one and what a zero are part of the communications standard. However, in many of the standards, you are sending more than one bit of data at a time.

Using amplitude modulation again as the example, because it is the easiest to visualize, a normal carrier signal amplitude may represent two zeros in a row. A slightly lower signal may represent a zero followed by a one. A slightly lower signal may represent a one followed by a zero, and a slightly lower signal still may represent two ones in a row. Consequently, each change in the carrier signal represents more than one bit of data. Sending two data bits at a time rather than one means that twice as much data can be sent in a given time.

In a separate effort, a different group of manufacturers, including Rockwell International Corp. and Hayes Microcomputer Products, has created another standard called V.Fast Class or V.FC. Rockwell has developed a modem chip that is available to all modem manufacturers as well as computer manufacturers. Computer manufacturers may include this chip on a system board so that the modem is an integral part of the computer. This standard has a maximum speed of 28,800 bps.

Many manufacturers have announced support for this V.FC standard, but it should be considered an interim standard. If you need to communicate at 28,800 bps now, rather than waiting for V.FAST standard to be finalized, V.FC is of interest. If not, it is worth waiting for the new standard modems.

Table 4-2 summarizes the specification numbers in increasing speed order. Remember that any modem 1200 bps or faster may include V.42 and V.42bis features. Both of these standards are desirable features for your modem to support.

Table 4-2   Summary of Modem Specification Numbers

Speed	Standard
300	103 or V.21
1200	212A or V.22
2400	V.22bis
4800	V.32
9600	V.32
14,400	V.32bis
19,200	V.32terbo
28,800	V.FC or V.FAST (V.34)

Note: V.42 and V.42bis are available on modems 1200 bps or faster. V.42 adds error-detection and V.42bis adds data-compression.

Selecting extras

Besides communications standards and physical shape, you should consider the extras that come with your modem when considering price. The warranty, technical support, or any money-back guarantee offered may be important to you.

If you buy a modem that supports a new or less commonly used standard, examine the upgrade path being offered. The biggest complaints I hear on bulletin boards are from modem buyers who thought they would be able to upgrade their modems inexpensively, but when the time came, the upgrade cost a couple of hundred dollars.

The analogy with PCs applies here again. In most cases, PC upgrades are not as smooth or inexpensive as you may think. A modem is not the same as software, and upgrading costs the modem manufacturer more than the shipping costs.

If you are purchasing a data modem and fax modem combination, take special care to read the product's specifications. Fax modems follow different communications standards than data modems. As a result, you may think that you are purchasing a modem with a particular speed when you are actually reading the fax modem's specification. Consider your data modem needs and your fax modem needs separately, and then look at products that can fill both needs. The following section on choosing a fax modem gives details on what to look for in fax modems.

The other extras that come with modems are the cables and communications software. The cables, typically a data cable for external modems and a phone cable for all modems, are fairly inexpensive to buy for yourself, but you do need to remember to purchase them. Check with the supplier regarding the length of the phone cable in case you need a longer one to reach the phone outlet.

For external modems, check whether a data cable is supplied and the type of connector on the end. You may need to buy a different cable to fit your serial port. Remember that serial ports on the PC may have a 9-pin or 25-pin connector. You can purchase a 25-pin to 9-pin adapter cable or complete replacement cables if necessary. These cables are called a variety of names, including serial cables, RS-232 cables, and DTE to DCE cables.

"Do I need a null modem cable?"

You sometimes hear about a null modem cable, and people get confused about whether this is the cable they need to connect their modem. A *null modem cable* is a cable that allows you to link two pieces of equipment together without using modems. It is also known as a crossover cable, a modem eliminator cable, or a DCE-to-DCE cable, or DTE-to-DTE cable. You don't need one for connecting your modem to a PC.

You also do not want to purchase a specialized plotter cable to use with a modem because, like the DCE-to-DCE cable, the connectors on the ends may be right, but it may not have the correct wires going to the correct pins. This specialized plotter cable may be a DCE-to-DCE cable, which will not work correctly connecting a modem to a PC, or it may be a completely custom cable for a specific plotter configuration.

Understanding Flow Control or Handshaking

The concept of flow control is fairly simple. The flow control settings establish "who talks, when". A ham radio operator, for example, uses the term "over" to signal when it is time for the listener to speak. A committee discussion may use rules so that the person speaking stands up; when the speaker sits down, another person can stand up and speak. This controls the flow of information and prevents two people speaking at once.

The RS-232 specification, used by the serial ports in your computer, supports two forms of flow control, known as *hardware handshaking* and *software handshaking*. As the names vaguely suggest, controlling data flow with software handshaking involves sending a signal within the data stream (comparable with saying "over" in the ham radio example). Controlling data flow with hardware handshaking involves using extra signals separate from the data stream (comparable with the committee discussion example).

In a typical communications connection, you have two areas of flow control. The *local flow control* dictates the type of handshaking used between the serial port and the modem. The *end-to-end flow control* dictates the type of handshaking used between the two modems.

The end-to-end flow control is determined automatically by the error-control features in your modem or by the file-transfer protocol from the communications software you are using. (File transfer is covered in Chapter 6.)

You can alter the local flow control method and choose between hardware and software handshaking. Lower-speed modems may only support software handshaking, in which case you have no choice. However, most higher-speed modems, which include error-correction features, support both hardware and software handshaking. When transmitting data at higher speeds, hardware handshaking is preferable.

Hardware handshaking involves two signal lines called clear to send (CTS) and request to send (RTS). When a serial device (modem or computer, for example) is ready to receive data, it raises the CTS line. When the serial device is ready to send data, it raises the RTS line. When both the CTS and RTS lines are raised, the data is sent. When the CTS or RTS line is lowered, the data transmission between the two serial devices is stopped.

Software handshaking involves characters added to the data stream that signal the beginning and end of the transmission. The XON character (pronounced ex-on) starts the transmission, and the XOFF character stops the transmission. The XON character is the character sent when you press Ctrl+S and XOFF character is the character sent when you press Ctrl+Q.

Occasionally, the XON or XOFF character appears in the middle of a file transmission, due to the particular combination of bits, and the receiving computer gets confused. It sends a message, or your communications program issues a message, depending on which program detected the XON or XOFF in an unexpected location, that indicates an XON or XOFF character was found.

For example, if the data stream starts with an XON character, the receiving program is expecting to see an XOFF to indicate the end of the transmission. If a file contains an XON character, the receiving program may send a message. You can manually send an XON or XOFF character as required, by pressing the relevant keystrokes.

Because it is likely that XON or XOFF may appear occasionally in a file, hardware handshaking is preferable to software handshaking. However, apart from the local control, the handshaking type is determined by the communications protocols and not by the user.

Table 4-3 lists the pin assignments needed to connect a 9-pin serial port connector to a modem. (The names of the signals are also included for reference.) A 25-pin serial port connector needs a straight-through cable where pin 1 at one end of the cable is connected to pin 1 at the other end, and pin 2 is connected to pin 2. You actually need only nine wires connected, but some serial cables have all 25 wires connected at each end of the cable.

Table 4-3	Serial Port Pin Assignments
9-pin Serial Port	**25-pin modem connector**
1 (CD)	8
2 (RD)	3
3 (SD)	2
4 (DTR)	20
5 (SG)	7
6 (DSR)	6
7 (DTR)	4
8 (CTS)	5
9 (RI)	22

The RS-232 standard works well only with short cables. It is not intended for use with cables much longer than a yard. If you use a longer cable, you are more likely to pick up extraneous noise and consequently data errors. You are better off with a longer phone cable and short serial port cable, although longer phone cables are also susceptible to noise. The serial cable should also be shielded. Many users make an inexpensive cable by using *ribbon cable* (a flat strip of wires frequently used to connect different internal parts within PCs). These will work under ideal conditions, but if you experience data loss, your serial cable may be at fault. Consider investing in a shielded serial cable before blaming noisy phone lines. (You can buy shielded ribbon cable.)

Besides cables, you need communications software to operate your modem. Almost all modems come with some sort of communications software, but the available features in this software vary dramatically, depending on the modem. Choosing communications software is covered later in this chapter.

If you want a data modem and fax modem, you need communications software to operate the data and fax communications software to operate the fax modem. These are two separate communications programs, although a future trend will be to make a single program perform both tasks. As with the data and fax modem combination, you should still consider your needs for transferring data and faxing separately and then compare them with the software's features.

Choosing a Fax Modem

Fax modems are, on the one hand, obvious add-on products for PCs, but on the other hand, they are not totally suited for the job of faxing and receiving documents. The suitability of fax modems depends on what you want to send out, what you want to receive, and what you want to do with the received fax documents.

Note: Fax is short for *facsimile.*

Data modems are well suited to PCs because they transfer data that is stored on a computer to another computer or peripheral device. Fax documents can be documents or drawings that are stored on a computer, but they are just as likely to be handwritten material, including signed documents or drawings, sales brochures or other informational material.

A brief summary of the advantages of fax machines over fax modems and fax modems over fax machines is worth considering.

The advantages of fax machines over fax modems include the following:

- You can use any fax machine from more or less anywhere. You do not have to carry a computer and fax modem around with you.

- You can send information that is not stored on the computer, such as handwritten notes, sketches, and printed brochures.

- The recipient does not need to own a computer. You can arrange for fax documents to be received at local service centers, hotels, or your customer's site.

- In theory, a fax document is easier to send than a file.

- You can use the fax machine (but not a fax modem) as a low-volume copy machine.

The advantages of fax modems over fax machines include the following:

* You can transfer large files, such as text, programs, or graphic files, complete and without degradation. A fax document is always received as a relatively low-resolution *graphical* representation of the original.

* You can typically transfer the file faster than a document.

* You can do far more with a fax modem than a fax machine. For example, you can do online research. You can send electronic mail intended for many possibly unnamed people to read.

Choosing a fax modem first involves deciding whether you need a fax modem or a stand-alone fax machine. There is no slot for you to insert your paper on a PC fax modem. This may seem obvious to many people, but it is asked about more often than you would think.

Considering sending documents

First consider the material you want to send. If you send only information you have previously printed from your PC, you may make good use of a fax modem. However, if you send handwritten information or signed documents, the fax modem is less applicable because you must find some way of getting the written material into your computer.

The signed-document issue is worth emphasizing. It is actually relatively easy to add a graphic image of your signature onto a fax document in your PC. However, you need to be very comfortable with your PC security before you would want to use that type of mechanism due to the legal implications of anyone having access to your signature.

Sending handwritten or preprinted documents with a fax modem and performing the equivalent of stuffing the document in the fax machine's slot are time-consuming and require extra software and hardware. You need a scanner and scanning software. The scanner translates your paper document into an electronic form and stores it as a file on your computer. You can then use the fax modem and its software to send the document as if you had created it on your computer. The scanning process often takes as long as, if not longer than, sending the document.

Considering receiving documents

To receive a fax document on a fax modem, your computer must be turned on and the fax communications software loaded. (There are ways to install the software so that you can work on your computer while waiting for a fax.)

However, you cannot use the fax modem and the data modem at the same time. Nor can you use a telephone attached to the same phone line. They can share the telephone line, but only one device can use the line at a time.

The fax modem behaves like a fax machine. It can answer the phone, establish a communications link with the sending fax machine, and collect the sent document.

Received fax documents are always graphical representations of the original material. Graphic files are large compared to typical text files.

A single-page document that is 4 KB when stored as ASCII text, might be 1 MB — about 250 times larger — when stored as a graphic file. If you expect to receive 10 to 20 pages of fax documents a week and have a need to keep them all, you can rapidly fill your hard disk.

You can print the graphic file and then delete it from your hard disk if you do not actually need to store the received fax on your PC. Many stand-alone fax machines, particularly the less expensive ones, use photosensitive paper that curls and fades with time. Most PC printers use ordinary paper, so the output from the printer may be better than from the stand-alone fax machine.

However, you need a printer that can print graphic files, and you need to consider the time needed to print. A laser printer, for example, can take several minutes to print a page with a graphic image.

If you need to use the received fax on your computer to make modifications, for example, you probably need to convert the received graphics file into text. This can be done by using an optical character recognition (OCR) program. A few fax communication programs include OCR programs, and many other OCR programs are available. Chapter 11 details the advantages and disadvantages of these programs.

An OCR program looks at the graphic file and tries to interpret the shapes into text characters. Depending on the OCR program, this method is very successful for clear typewritten and printed documents and is useless for handwritten, dirty, or complex documents including a mixture of fonts. For example, it is quicker to retype a document with handwritten marked-up notes and pictures than to try to make the OCR program convert it accurately.

Another potential problem with handling documents received by a PC fax modem is your filing system and organization. The documents are saved with a DOS filename, and you need suitable software that can identify the document easily, or you may spend hours trying to find the fax again.

With printed documents, even if you don't have a filing system, you can skim and dismiss a document within a couple of seconds. On the computer, you will be loading and unloading large graphic files unless you have a good filing system that can identify the document without reading it.

Text documents that you are going to alter rather than just read and throw away are much more appropriate for sending with a data modem than a fax modem. However, fax modems are relatively inexpensive ways of providing yourself with faxing capabilities, especially if you purchase a data modem and fax modem combination. The ability to give people a fax number is becoming an essential part of business today.

If you are buying a data modem anyway, consider getting a combined data modem and fax modem to supplement a stand-alone fax machine. You can use the PC fax modem for outgoing faxes that are documents you created on your PC and the stand-alone fax machine to send pre-printed or handwritten material.

Choosing a fax modem's form factor

As with data modems, you need to consider the physical attributes of the PC fax modem as well as the communications standards. The previous section on choosing a data modem's form factor applies equally to your fax modem.

A PC fax modem will probably be an internal device. However, the data modem and fax modem combinations are commonly available as external units. You need to select an internal fax modem that conforms with the expansion bus of your computer. For example, if you have a PS/2 computer, you may need a fax modem with a Micro Channel Architecture connector, or you may want a PCMCIA fax modem for your laptop.

The fax modem is similar to the data modem in that it uses the serial port to connect to your PC. If you already have four serial ports in your computer, you will have to remove one to make a serial port available for an internal fax modem. An external fax modem needs one of the serial port connectors.

Choosing fax modem compatibility and communications standards

Fax machines (stand-alone and PC fax modems) send documents between each other by using established communication standards. These standards predate PCs and are different from all the standards covered earlier in this chapter for data modems.

However, these standards were established by the same United Nations group, ITU-T (previously CCITT), as for data modems. Fax machine communication standards are known as Groups, and there are standards for Group 1, Group 2, Group 3, and Group 4. Almost all fax machines produced today are Group 3 compliant.

Group 1 and Group 2 fax machines are analog devices and do not include modems. Group 3 faxes are digital devices and scan the document, convert the digital data, and then modulate it for transmission. Upon receipt, they demodulate the data back into digital data for printing. Group 4 fax machines can transmit the fax data over digital telephone lines, such as leased lines or ISDN lines. They are not covered in this book.

"What are fax modem communications standards?"

The group number may be abbreviated in the manufacturer's specification. For example, Group 3 may be referred to as G3. Choose a fax machine or fax modem that is Group 3 compliant. Group 3 modems use ITU-T communications standards that specify how the data is modulated for transmission. Like data modems, the different modulation schemes result in different speeds of data transmission.

The V.21 Channel 2 standard is used for 300 bps fax transmission. V.27ter is used for 4800 bps transmission with 2400 bps transmission as a fallback speed. V.29 is used for 9600 bps transmission with 7200 bps fallback speed. V.17 is used for 14,400 bps fax transmission with 12,000 fallback speed. Table 4-4 lists the standards.

Table 4-4	Fax Modem Standards
Maximum Speed	**Standard**
300	V.21 Channel 2
4800	V.27ter
9600	V.29
14,400	V.17

As with PC data modems, you should buy the fastest fax modem you can afford. When buying a data modem and fax modem combination, be sure to read carefully and determine which is the data modem's speed and which is the fax modem's. You can, for example, buy a 9600 bps data modem that has a fax modem capable of 14.4 kbps transmission. This will not give you a 14.4 kbps data modem.

PC fax modems, rather than fax machines, also conform with other standards. These standards are the equivalent of AT-compatibility and dictate how the PC will communicate with the fax modem. The standards do not affect how the fax data is transmitted so are not relevant to stand-alone fax machines.

The command set used by the PC to communicate with the fax modem is determined by the fax modem's Class. The Telecommunications Industry Association (TIA, also referred to as EIA/TIA) has established the Class standard for fax modems. However, some PC fax boards, including the most popular, use a proprietary standard.

Class 1 fax modems conform with EIA/TIA-578 and are the most commonly found PC fax modems. Class 2 is a fairly recent new standard that is likely to be more popular than Class 1 because of performance improvements.

The selection of a Class 1, Class 2, or a proprietary fax modem depends on the software you are using. The Class standard for the fax modem affects how the PC talks to the fax modem, not how the data is sent over the phone line. The issue for fax modems is a matter of fax communications software support. A Class 1 or Class 2 fax modem will be supported by almost all fax communications software. If you pick a popular proprietary fax modem, such as Hayes JT Fax or Intel SatisFaxtion, any supplied fax communications software will support it. Do not consider proprietary fax modems that are not specifically supported by the fax communications software you are considering.

A fax modem using proprietary techniques for communicating between the data and fax modem may outperform or be more flexible than Class 1 or Class 2 fax modems. For example, you may be able to send a fax document in the background more efficiently while working on another program. Now that Class 2 fax modems have become available, this is a preferable choice to Class 1 fax modems. (The Class 3 standard is also being discussed.)

Fax modem extras

As with the data modem, you need to consider the extras that may or may not be supplied with your fax modem. This includes such physical items as the phone cable as well as the warranty, technical support, and money-back guarantee. The previous section on modem extras applies to fax modems as well, except that you are less likely to have an external fax modem and consequently will not be concerned about data cables.

The fax communications software is typically a weak point with PC fax modems. The programs work satisfactorily, but you may need other programs to provide file management or conversion utilities. The following section on choosing communications software and Chapters 7 and 11 provide more detail.

Choosing Communications Software

Most modems come with communications software, and most fax modems come with fax communications software. You should consider only modems with associated software. This helps with installation and fault-finding, because the supplier will be unable to argue that they have not tried that particular communications program.

The software supplied with data modems and fax modems varies in quality and features. However, most will probably get you up and running even if they do not include all the extra features you may want when you can do the basics.

You have a wide choice of communications programs to choose from. The most appropriate choice depends on what you want to do. For example, if you want to call BBSs, you will want a different program than if you want to call Prodigy, an online service that requires its own communication software. You probably want a general-purpose communications program and should be prepared to get add-on programs or specially written programs as you communicate with different online services.

For example, a general-purpose communications program will allow you to connect with a friend or business colleague as well as get access to most online services. However, you will dramatically reduce your online charges, which in some cases include a charge for the time you are connected to the service in addition to the telephone connection charges, by using a product that streamlines your actions while connected. If you need a special program to connect with a particular online service, you purchase this program as part of the start-up kit when you first subscribe to the service.

The best communications program to use is the one that includes the features you need and you can get the most help with. It's rather like word processors — you get the best help with your word processor if you talk to other people with the same program.

As a starting point, use the communications software supplied with your modem. If you are unable to make it work and cannot get adequate help from the modem manufacturer, choose a well-known third-party program that supports your modem. For example, QModemPro from Mustang Software and Procomm Plus from Datastorm Technologies are two of the most popular programs used on BBSs. If you are using Microsoft Windows, choose a communications program designed to work with Windows, such as Hayes Smartcom for Windows or DCA's Crosstalk for Windows.

As mentioned in Chapter 3, do not give up on telecommunicating because you cannot understand the communications software supplied with your modem. Chapter 5 introduces the basics of making a connection, and Chapter 6 covers how to transfer files between computers. Your communications software should be able to perform both of these tasks.

Part III explains specific features supplied in communications programs and shows how to consider whether you need a better program than that supplied with your modem. In most cases, if you do more than the very occasional connection, you will want to take advantage of software with more features. If you catch the telecommunications bug, you will have very specific requirements.

Fax communications software is slightly different in scope. Most fax modems are supplied with software. Do not consider a fax modem unless it comes with software. Unlike data modems, where you have a lot of control over the communications parameters, you cannot do many different things with a fax modem. You simply send a document or receive a document.

The fax modem communications software must be able to the basics, such as sending and receiving documents, but needing extra features, such as viewing the received document or converting the file into another form, depends on your application. Rather than expecting your fax communications software to do much more than communicate, you may consider third-party utility programs.

For example, fax software can save your graphic file. To work with the received file, you want a graphic viewing or editing program. You may need to convert the graphic file into another file format before you can edit it in your editing program. You may choose a third-party (or is it sixth-party?) program that can do the file conversion. If you want to convert the file to text, you need an OCR program. OCR programs are sophisticated and will probably not be included in your fax modem.

Chapter 7 shows how to send and receive a fax. The supplied fax communications software should be able to perform this task. Part III explains the extra desirable features, such as file management, that you may want for use with your fax modem. When considering the cost of modems and in particular fax modems, assess the associated software carefully.

Installing Your Equipment and Software

As an external unit, a modem is typically a small rectangular box with a series of LEDs (*light-emitting diodes*) along the front and a series of connectors and an on/off switch on the back. Most modems also include a separate power supply, a small black cube with an incorporated electrical plug, that you plug into the electrical outlet and the rear of the modem. (See Figure 4-1.)

There are typically two or three other connectors on an external modem. The larger connector, known as a DB 25 connector, is the data connector and accepts the cable linking your computer and the modem. You need a cable that can join this connector to a serial port on your computer. Serial ports are covered in detail earlier in this chapter.

The other one, or two, connectors are RJ-11 phone jack connectors. These are the same as the connectors typically found on telephones and telephone outlets. They connect your modem to the phone line and possibly to another telephone extension.

You link one connector, probably labeled *Line* or *Telco*, to your phone line via a normal phone cable. This links your modem to the phone line in the same way that a phone is linked to the phone line. When you issue the appropriate instructions in the communications software, the modem can perform the equivalent of taking the phone off the hook and dialing a phone number.

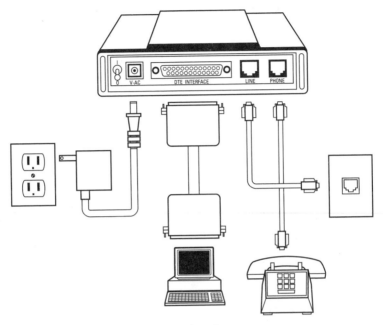

Figure 4-1: The setup of a typical external modem.

The other RJ-11 phone jack, when present, will probably be labeled *Phone* or *Ext.* You can connect a phone via a phone cable to this connector. If there is only one connector on the rear of your modem and it is labeled *Phone*, you should use a phone cable and this connector, the telephone line, and not an extension phone.

Don't be embarrassed if you didn't realize that you need to connect the modem to the phone line. It is very obvious once you know, but an acquaintance of mine spent more than an hour trying to help someone call a BBS with a new modem and software and did not think to ask whether the modem was connected to a phone line.

On some modems, the RJ-11 connectors are not labeled. In this case, they often are linked internally; it doesn't matter which one you use to connect to the phone line and which to an extension phone. However, check your modem documentation to be sure. If the documentation tells you to use a specific one for the phone line and the other for the extension phone, take the time to label the connectors so you avoid confusion later.

If the space around your computer is limited, you should label the cables themselves as you install them. It is surprising how often you have to unplug your external modem to move telephones or computers around.

An internal modem, as its name suggests, is plugged into your PC, laptop, or notebook. It draws its power from the computer and does not include a separate power supply. You can put the modem into any available slot that it will fit into. (See Figure 4-2.)

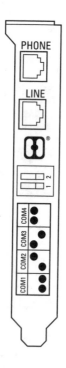

Figure 4-2: A typical internal modem.

Modems have moderate power supply needs, and if you are using a laptop or notebook, you will quickly run down your battery. Wherever possible, plug your laptop or notebook into the main power when using your modem. Because you must be near a telephone anyway to transmit, the addition of external power to the computer is not normally a big problem.

An internal modem has fewer visible connectors than an external modem. The data connector is not required because the computer is linked to the modem via the expansion board or PCMCIA connector.

Like the external modem, the internal modem has one or two, RJ-11 telephone connectors on the rear panel. (The PCMCIA modem also has an RJ-11 connector.) If there is only one connector, you plug a phone cable into the rear panel of the modem and into the telephone outlet in the wall.

If there are two connectors, one probably will be labeled *Line* and the other *Phone* or *Ext*. Use a phone cable to join the connector labeled *Line* to the telephone outlet in the wall, and use a phone cable to join the other connector to a telephone if you prefer.

Tip: Even if you do not want to leave a telephone attached permanently, it is worth adding a telephone while you install your modem and make it work. You can then check that you are actually getting a dial tone and can dial numbers manually from the modem's location.

If there are two connectors and they are not labeled, check the modem documentation for details. As with the external modem, if you must use one for the phone line and one for the extension phone, take the time to make a sticky label and label the connectors so that you avoid confusing the connections.

Take the time when installing your modem to label your phone cables as well as the connectors. This is especially important with internal modems. You will probably need to unplug your modem from the phone line every time you move your computer. Reconnection is much quicker with labeled connectors.

With the hardware installed, you need to install the communications software supplied with your modem. This usually involves running an installation program that copies and uncompresses the files onto your computer. Refer to your modem or communication software documentation for specific details.

After copying the files to your hard disk, you need to configure the software to fit your computer hardware configuration and the modem. This can involve such items as specifying the serial port, its address, and interrupt level, as well as choosing niceties such as screen color.

The actual process depends on the specific modem as well as the specific software. Some communications programs can examine your hardware and determine the modem's location automatically. Others will supply lists for you to choose from, and still others will require to do all the specifying explicitly.

Note: Hayes modems support a feature called AutoStart that enables software to automatically determine the modem capabilities and feature set and configure the software to support them. This feature is supported through the I4 command. With Smartcom for Windows, for example, the software automatically interrogates the modem to find the speed and feature set and can set up the software to support those feautures.

Make sure that your modem is turned on before starting your communications program. (An internal modem gets its power from the PC and is "turned on" whenever your PC is turned on.) In this way, any initializing or interrogation done by the communications program will occur automatically.

"Why doesn't my communication software start when I type AT and press Enter?"

Although this chapter introduces the concept of modems being Hayes-compatible or AT-compatible and mentioned the term AT commands, this is not the name of your communications software program. AT commands are used within your communications software program to communicate with your modem. In most cases, the software program sends the commands and you do not type them separately.

To start your communications program, you need to type its DOS filename at the DOS command prompt and press Enter. (Although this may seem obvious to experienced DOS users, it can be confusing because an operating mode found within communications programs, known as *terminal mode*, can look deceptively like a DOS command mode.)

The communications program's name will probably be the product name or an abbreviation of the name. For example, you run QModemPro by typing **qmpro** and Smartcom Exec by typing **exec** and pressing Enter.

Your fax software is comparable with the data communications software. Installing involves copying and uncompressing files onto your hard disk or creating working copies. This process is usually automated and may or may not include configuring your fax modem. Be sure to turn your fax modem on before doing the configuration. (As with data modems, if the fax modem is internal, the fax modem is powered on whenever your computer is turned on.)

Your data modem or fax modem requires a communications program to be running as well as the modem being powered on to communicate.

Chapter 5 shows how to communicate with your modem, make your modem communicate with another modem, and create a communications link. Chapter 6 explains file transfer, which you can do after you understand how to make the two modems talk to each other. Chapter 7 shows how to establish a connection and send or receive fax documents at your fax modem.

Summary

This chapter introduced the telephone and RS-232 port essentials. You learned the type of phone line you need and techniques for getting the best service from that line. You also learned the basics on serial ports, their DOS names, port addresses, and interrupt levels.

You determined whether you need a data modem, fax modem, or a combination data and fax modem. The selection depends on many factors, including the specific types of information you want to exchange, the computer's form factor, and other criteria such as warranty or technical support.

You were introduced to the ITU communications standards used in data modems. Some of these specify the speed at which your modem can communicate, and others add data-compression or error-detection into the process.

You also were introduced to the ITU communications standards for fax modems. These are not the same as the standards used for data modems.

This chapter covered installing your modem and communications software in preparation for the subsequent chapters. Chapter 5 introduces data modem communication, and Chapter 7 introduces fax modem communication.

5

CHAPTER

Understanding Your Data Modem

This chapter explains how to communicate by using your data modem. You learn the following important steps:

- Preparing to communicate
- Issuing commands to a modem
- Establishing a connection
- Communicating with another computer
- Breaking the connection

This chapter does not explain how to send a fax but focuses on data modems. Chapter 7 is the equivalent chapter for fax modems. Your modem and communications software should be installed before using the techniques in this chapter. Chapter 4 explains modem selection and installation.

Preparing to Communicate

Unless you have used your modem recently and made successful connections, it is well worth checking that you have the following connected:

❖ A phone line plugged into the rear of the modem and the telephone outlet in the wall

❖ The data cable for an external modem plugged into the rear of the modem and into the serial port on your computer

❖ The power supply for an external modem plugged into the rear of the modem and into an electrical outlet

If you find a missing cable or loose connection, be sure to turn off the computer and modem before correcting the problem. When you plug in a connector, you actually make and break the connection multiple times. This can damage the electrical equipment it is attached to. For example, plugging in the power supply to the modem when it is already plugged into the electrical outlet can break your modem. It rarely happens, but there is a chance.

After checking the cables, turn on your modem and start your communications program. An external modem may have an LED to indicate that the power is on and will probably light at least one of the LEDs on its front panel.

An internal modem lacks these LEDs, but you may use a terminate-and-stay-resident (TSR) program on your computer to display the equivalent of the LEDs on your computer screen. A TSR is a program you load into your computer, typically from AUTOEXEC.BAT. It remains in memory and you can run your normal programs with the TSR still resident.

Your internal modem may be supplied with a program of this type or you can obtain one from a computer user group or BBS. These programs remove the disadvantage of not having visible LEDs on an internal modem but may not allow all your other application programs to run successfully. This program is worth considering when you are experiencing problems rather than being a requirement for all situations.

Table 5-1 lists the most common LEDs found on external modem front panels and gives a brief description of their purpose. You will not need to look at these LEDs other than to check that power is on, but they are a valuable tool in troubleshooting. For example, if you do not hear a dial tone when you ask the communications software to dial a number, you can look at the OH LED and see whether the modem performed the equivalent of lifting the phone receiver.

Table 5-1		Modem LEDs
LED	**Name**	**Description when lit**
HS	High Speed	Modem is operating at what it considers to be a "high speed."
AA	Auto Answer	Modem answers when phone rings.
CD	Carrier Detect	Modem detects a carrier signal from other modem.
OH	Off Hook	Modem has done equivalent of lifting phone receiver.
RD or RX	Receive Data	Data is being sent from modem to computer.
SD or SX	Send Data	Data is being sent from computer to modem.
TR	Terminal Ready	Computer and modem are linked via serial port.
MR	Modem Ready	Modem is turned on.
DC	Data Compression	Modem is able to compress data.
EC	Error Control	Modem is able to detect errors.

You need to know five items in order to connect with another modem:

1. The phone number
2. Whether you are calling the other modem or the other modem is calling you
3. The *character format*
4. If you are doing the calling, the fastest desired transmission speed
5. The *terminal emulation* both computers will use

Each of these items is detailed in the following sections. Most communications programs include all of these settings within their menus. However, you also can control your modem by sending commands directly. Issuing commands to your modem is covered later in this chapter.

Knowing where you are calling and how

To make a communications link, two modems are connected via a telephone line.

If you are calling another modem, you need to know its phone number. You also want to choose whether you use tone or pulse dialing. As covered in Chapter 4, tone dialing is faster, but you need a phone line that can accept it.

When dialing another modem, you are originating the call. You may need to select this option, called *modem originate,* in your communications program. In most programs, this is the default setting, and if you select a phone number to dial from your program's *dialing directory* (list of phone numbers), this setting is assumed.

If another modem is calling your modem, you need to know the phone number that your modem is attached to. Remember that you cannot use the phone for a voice call at the same time as the modem.

When a modem calls your modem, your modem answers the phone. You need to select the *auto-answer* option or the *modem answer* option in your communications software. This instructs the modem to listen for the phone ringing and then pick up the phone call.

Choosing character format

As explained in Chapter 4, your computer sends serial data to the modem, which is modulated and sent to the other modem for translation back into digital data, where it is accepted by the receiving computer's serial port.

Although the data is sent from the serial port one bit at a time, it is arranged in groups known as *characters.* The character format is comprised of three parts: start bits, data bits, and stop bits. Both computers need to be set to send and receive characters with the same character format.

You define the character format for your connection by choosing the number of *data bits* (7 or 8), the number of *stop bits* (1 or 2), and the *parity* (None, Even, Odd, Mark, or Space).

"What do 7E1 and 8N1 mean?"

The sidebar, "Understanding Character Format," explains parity and gives more detail on how the character is actually formatted when you change these parameters.

In general, if you are calling another PC, such as a BBS or your office personal computer, you will want to choose eight data bits, no parity, and one stop bit. If you are calling a mainframe computer — many commercial online services are run on mainframes — you will probably need to choose seven data bits, even parity, and one stop bit. These are commonly abbreviated to 8N1 and 7E1 respectively.

These values can be changed in most communications programs in a variety of places. The menus are typically named *port settings, device settings,* or format settings. In many programs, you can choose a setting that will be the default if you do not specify a different one, and you can specify a different setting for a particular telephone number. (Choosing default settings and customizing settings for particular places you call are covered in Chapter 8.)

For example, you may set 8N1 as the default because you will usually be calling bulletin boards. However, your settings for when you call the online service Genie may be 7E1.

Understanding transmission speed

In addition to specifying the format of the character, the serial port must be set to transmit data to the modem at a particular speed. Surprisingly, the maximum possible speed is not always the most desirable.

With a few exceptions, which are noted in the following sidebar, choose a transmission speed that matches your modem's maximum speed or choose the *automatic* or *maximum* speed option. For example, if you have a 2400 bps modem, choose 2400. If you have a 9600 bps modem, choose 9600.

Many users, experts included, use the term *baud,* or *baud rate,* instead of or as well as *speed* or *bits per second* (bps). You can provoke many arguments trying to understand the correct definition. The technical sidebar "Understanding Baud and Data Rates" addresses these debates.

Understanding Character Format

Your computer sends data to the serial port one byte at a time. The UART and other circuitry rearrange this data into serial data form for transmission from the serial port. The receiving serial port accepts the data one bit at time.

So that the receiving port understands where one byte begins and ends, the bits of data are arranged into characters. The data bits have extra bits known as *framing bits* added on either end of the byte of data. You can control the format of the character by altering the number of data bits, the number of stop bits, and the parity.

The sending and receiving serial ports must be set to use the same character formats to translate the data correctly. Some computers, typically mainframes, can use only seven data bits in a byte, and consequently, the PC, which can use eight data bits in a byte, must alter its serial port settings to conform with the more limiting standard.

Similarly, some serial ports expect one bit to indicate the end of a character being sent on the serial port, and others expect to see two bits to indicate the end of a character.

Using human communication as a comparison, think of needing the same character format at both ends as the difference between local accents. I was in a car accident once in Texas, and the other driver came from New York. I could not understand the slow-talking Texas policeman who left gaps in the middle of words as well as between them. I spoke very precisely with my British accent, pronouncing every syllable, and the policeman had problems understanding me. The New Yorker, who talked extremely fast with no gaps between sentences, let alone words, ended up repeating what the policeman and I said so we could all communicate with each other. You would not have believed that we were all talking English.

The parity bit is an error-checking mechanism that can be added to the data. The parity bit is added so that the receiving serial port has a check that the character sent is the same as the character received. The receiving serial port compares the *parity bit* in the character with the *parity* of the received character. If the two are the same, there is a reasonable assurance that the character actually received is the same as what was sent.

To understand a character's parity, consider a character containing eight data bits, which is a row of eight ones and zeros. The character is considered to have even parity if there is an even number of ones in the row and is considered to have odd parity if there is an odd number of ones in the row.

If you set even parity on your serial port, the serial port will make the parity bit a one or a zero to make the character along with its parity bit have an even number of ones in the row of data. For example, if the eight data bits were 10011001, the parity bit would be a zero to maintain an even number of ones.

You may have odd, even, mark, space, or none parity. Odd parity is similar to even parity, except that the parity bit is made a one to make an odd number of ones in the character. No parity, usually designated as a setting of none, does not add a parity bit.

Mark and space are also no parity, in that they do not represent the parity of the character, but they do add a bit in the parity bit location. Mark adds a one in the parity bit location, and space adds a zero in the parity bit location. They are used most frequently in serial device applications, such as plotting, other than modems.

If you want to avoid the detail, understand that baud (pronounced *bod*) and baud rate are most frequently used incorrectly. As a modem user, talk about your modem's speed in bits per second or bps and you will be correct. I think the confusion has arisen because baud is easier to pronounce than bps.

Your communications software, and other documentation, such as guides to online services, may use the term baud or baud rate to mean transmission speed or data rate. This is where you set the transmission speed. (The modem's actual baud is defined by the communications standard being used and is not directly controlled by the user.)

The speed of the modem you are connecting to is usually not important to the data speed setting. Your modem will try to connect at the fastest speed you specify, and if this is not possible will automatically negotiate a slower speed with the other modem.

The following three sections address the times when you will not want to set the communication software's transmission speed to the maximum value.

Slow modem, fast software

Your communications software may be able to send data at rates that your modem cannot handle. For example, if you have a 2400 bps modem, you don't want to set the port speed to 115200 bps. If you do not pick an appropriate speed, you may experience overrun or dropped characters. (Chapter 4 explains overrun.)

Connect charges

Many online services charge you a connect time charge. You pay an hourly rate for the length of time you are connected to the service. Because you can get more data in a given amount of time if you connect at a faster speed, these services often charge more per hour if you use a faster speed.

For example, you may pay $1 per hour if you connect at 2400 bps or $5 per hour if you connect at 9600 bps. As a beginner, do the basic mathematics to choose the best connection speed. In this example, 2400 bps seems a better choice. You will need to set your communications program to the slower speed, or your modem will try to connect at the faster speed, and you will connect at the higher hourly rate.

As you become more familiar with communications, this is an area well worth revisiting, because understanding the true cost of a connection can save you a lot of money. Even in the preceding example, you may want to use the faster speed for certain operations and the slower speed for others. For your first few connections, the difference of a few cents an hour is probably less important than actually making the connection and doing the communicating. However, when you are spending ten hours a week online, the few cents add up. Part IV explains how to find out your true online costs and what choices are available.

By the way, if spending ten hours a week online seems a lot to you, consider this. A popular online service changed its rate schedule from a fixed monthly charge to an hourly rate. Many people (home computer users) complained that this would be cost prohibitive for them because they spent in excess of 200 hours a month online to this particular service!

Understanding Baud and Data Rates

When a modem manufacturer called me in 1986 to tout a brand new product that was a 9600 bps proprietary modem with 7.5 baud, I realized I needed to brush up on my engineering degree. I didn't know how to repsond. I knew the terms but bandied them around haphazardly. Baud and data rates are the most abused and confusing terms in modem technology.

First the definitions. *Data rate* is the amount of data that is transmitted in a given amount of time. For example, a data rate of 2400 bits per second means that 2,400 bits of data are sent every second. *Baud* is the signaling rate. For example, 2400 baud means that data is sent 2,400 times per second. (Notice that this definition does not say how much data is sent, only how often data is sent.) Strictly speaking, there is no such thing as *baud rate*. It is like saying "frequency rate" rather than frequency.

Any modem that conforms with the commonly accepted standards, such as V.22bis or V.32, and operates faster than 1200 bps has a baud rate lower than the data rate. To conform with the standards and make best use of the telephone system, more than one bit of data is transferred between the modems at a time.

For example, a 2400 bps modem operates at 1200 baud. Two bits of data are being sent every 1/1200 of a second. The faster modems, such as the 9600

bps modems, have even lower baud rates because even more data is being sent at one time. In my earlier example of 9600 bps at 7.5 baud, 1,280 bits of data were being sent at a time, and they were sent 7.5 times per second.

Many communications programs include a baud setting rather than a bps setting, and many people, including modem manufacturers, refer to their modems as being, for example, 9600 baud modems. In fact, the communications programs are correct and the modem manufacturers are wrong!

Your communications program communicates with your modem through the serial port. The baud setting you choose in the communications program dictates the data speed between the serial port and the modem. Because the data is only sent out of the serial port one bit at a time, the signaling rate is the same as the data rate.

However, the data being sent between the two modems may or may not be sent one bit at a time. The baud is decided by the modems and not the user. In some cases it is chosen based only on the communications standards being used, in others it depends on the standard as well as on the amount of noise on the phone line. When you refer to a modem, you should talk about the data rate and ignore its baud.

Data-compression included

You want to pick a sufficiently fast speed for your communication, which may not be the specified speed of your modem. As explained in Chapter 4, the V.42bis communication standard adds data compression features to your modem. V.42bis is a feature that may be available on all 2400 bps or faster modems.

Other modems may use different data compression methods. These may be proprietary to the particular brand and model of modem or may conform with another fairly common standard called MNP Level 5.

When your modem uses a compression standard, such as V.42bis or MNP Level 5, it compresses the data supplied from the computer and transmits it to the other modem. The receiving modem uncompresses the data and passes it on to the receiving computer. This compression results in more data being passed between the modems in a particular length of time than if the data is sent uncompressed.

In this case, if you set the serial port to the maximum speed of the modem, such as 9600 bps, the modem will not be sending data the whole time because it will compress the data and wait for more data. In effect, the compression will not increase the overall throughput.

However, if you set the serial port speed on both the receiving and the transmitting computer to faster than the modem's speed, the overall throughput can exceed the modem's maximum transmission speed. The sending modem collects a chunk of data and compresses it, then it sends the smaller-sized data to the other end for uncompression or extraction. The data transmission speed (the number of bits per second) remains the same, but the amount of data contained in those bits is more due to the compression.

The amount of compression, which may be none, depends on the type of data being sent. If you have used file compression programs, such as PKZIP, you may be familiar with the concept that certain file types compress more than others. A typical text file, for example, can be compressed by a substantial amount, but a typical program file can be compressed only a small amount.

This compression is possible because of the actual patterns in the data bits and the type of compression techniques used. Text files, for example, include a lot of repetitive characters; words such as "the" or "and" or lots of space characters in a row may occur frequently. A compression technique may take advantage of this to reduce the amount of data sent. Consider the difference in voice communication between ordering "Same again" in a restaurant as opposed to "I'll have a gin and tonic with lots of ice and a lime twist, please."

As a beginner, you don't need to worry about the degree of data compression possible on the material you are sending or receiving. Because the maximum data-throughput with data compression can be eight times your modem speed, you should set your serial port speed higher than your modem speed. (If you do not know about the receiving computer, set the speed higher and be prepared to lower it at a future time if you experience data loss.)

Choosing between compressing data before transmission or using a modem's compression techniques is an intermediate topic that is addressed in Part III. Chapter 9 expands on the possible approaches. Like using the most economical speed if you are being charged based on the time you are on-line, you also want to reduce the time you are on line by using the best compression method.

Understanding terminal emulation

In addition to setting the speed and format of the transmitted information, you need both computers to operate with the same or compatible *terminal emulations*. The parameters discussed previously allow the data to be sent and received at their respective serial ports. The terminal emulation is what the two computers mean by the data that is being sent.

You must remember that you are actually linking two modems together with a communications link. Although each modem may be attached to a computer, the computer types do not have to be the same. Additionally, a second computer does not have to be involved. One modem may be attached to a printer or a device called a terminal.

Terminals consist of a video screen, keyboard, and some control electronics and are typically used to attach to minicomputers or mainframes. They do not contain the processing power of a PC, nor do they usually contain disk drives, but they use the communications link to connect the keyboard to the programs and data on the minicomputer or mainframe. The remote computer in turn controls the terminal. It may send particular data or controlling codes to alter the terminal's operation.

There are a variety of terminal types. Logically, each type is used to connect to each type of computer. Some are very simple, and others are more sophisticated with many more functions available. You can make your PC appear to the other computer as a terminal, hence the name *terminal emulation*. The two computers are able to "talk" to each other because they are using the same terminal emulation.

Using voice communication as a comparison, the terminal emulation is equivalent to establishing the language you are going use, such as French or Spanish. If the two people talking to each other do not use the same language, some information may be heard correctly, but other information may be misinterpreted.

The voice communication analogy can be extended beyond language to gestures and expressions. This is equivalent to the computer sending controlling data and expecting a certain result. In America, looking at the person you are speaking to shows a degree of interest and respect. But in another culture, say Japan, you show respect by keeping your eyes and head lowered. Hand gestures in particular have very different meanings around the world. Even within Europe, a relatively small geographical area, a polite gesture in one country may be lewd in another.

The terminal emulation you choose dictates the effect of your pressing a key on the keyboard and what the receiving computer thinks that key means. For example, when you press an A on your keyboard, the receiving computer considers it as an A. However, if you press F1 on your PC, this may have no meaning to the computer at the other end. Additionally, the remote computer will send data to your computer, and you need to choose the terminal emulation mode that will respond in the expected way to the data or control information sent.

The most basic terminal emulation is known as TTY. This is supported by most computers but has the disadvantage of providing only basic functionality. (TTY was used for teletype machines, an early form of fax machines still in use in many places around the world.) If you do not know what sort of computer you are connecting to, you are unlikely to fail with TTY. Even if the other computer is actually using another terminal emulation, you may still be able to understand most of the characters because TTY is a subset of many more-advanced terminals.

"How do I make BBS menus appear in color?"

If you are connecting with another PC — and most BBSs are run on PCs — you should choose ANSI as the terminal emulation being used by your communications program *and* the BBS. This allows you to see characters in color, bold, or flashing where applicable. Additionally, you will be able to see line characters. These are the characters that make your menus have lines around them instead of funny looking characters.

"When I log on to a BBS, I see funny characters around the menus. Why?"

If there is a mismatch between your terminal emulation selections, your screen will not appear as intended. The BBS probably offers a menu option, and you can adjust the setting in your communications program.

You may have seen similar funny characters by pressing Print Screen and printing a screen with menus on to a laser printer or dot matrix printer.

A recent addition to many BBSs is a graphical user interface called RIP (Remote Image Protocol). This allows you to see graphical menus and to use your mouse on-line. To take advantage of RIP, you need to use RIP Script or RIP emulation as your terminal emulation. As graphical user interfaces on BBSs become more popular, this will become a preferable alternative to ANSI.

The other terminal emulation types found in many communications programs are very important if you need to connect to other types of computers and are features worth looking out for in your communications software. As a PC user, you will probably be told whether you need to use one of these other emulations. Common terminal emulations include VT 52, VT 100, VT 102, VT 220, and VT 230. These are Digital Equipment Corporation (DEC) terminal emulations. Other popular ones are Wyse 50, IBM 3101, and Heath 19; Prestel and Teletel are widely used in Europe.

When you connect with a system for the first time, you will often be given a choice of terminal emulations. You will probably want to choose the most advanced one your computer can support. If you do not know which to choose, make a note of all of them and try them in turn. For example, choose RIP over ANSI, and choose ANSI over TTY.

The more-advanced terminal emulation may make the system less responsive. For example, the time it takes to redraw the screen with RIP may be much longer than with TTY. If you have a fast modem and fast computer, you may not see any significant difference between the speeds and can enjoy the "pretty screens". However, on slow computers with relatively slow modems, the redrawing can be annoying.

Issuing Commands to a Modem

Almost all communications software includes a menu system that allows you to choose the phone number, character format, transmission speed, terminal emulation, and if necessary an auto-answer feature. You pick the relevant menu and select from a list of options. You are then ready to make a connection.

However, the ease with which you can select these items varies dramatically with the software program. This may be the point where you decide that the communications program provided with your modem is unusable.

As explained in Chapter 3, AT-compatible modems can be controlled from software. (You, or more likely a telephone technician, made adjustments in early modems by opening it up and altering switches inside the cover.) When you make a selection from a menu, the communication software sends commands to the serial port and modem to make the appropriate adjustments.

You can also make these and many other adjustments directly rather than using the communications software. As you become more experienced with communications, you are more likely to need to make the adjustments directly, because your software may not include all the particular modem-controlling commands you need.

For example, you are likely to want to configure your modem in a particular way every time you start your communications software. One method of doing this is to make your software issue a series of commands to the modem, known as an *initialization string*, when you start the communications program. Initialization strings are covered in Chapter 10, because they are an intermediate-level topic. However, controlling the modem directly is an introductory topic.

When you turn on your modem, it powers up in *command mode* and is ready to accept commands that are sent from the computer's serial port. The modem commands (with two exceptions) all begin with the prefix **AT,** and sending commands directly to the modem is commonly referred to as issuing *AT commands.* For example, the command to dial the phone number 555-1111 is ATD555-1111.

"*What does AT stand for?*"

AT is not an abbreviation but is used by the modem to determine the character format and transmission speed being used by the serial port. The AT allows the modem to self-calibrate. It is expecting to see the two characters AT and can adjust its internal settings so that it will understand the subsequent characters sent as commands from the serial port.

This AT character sequence is not the same as IBM's PC AT computer designation. The AT in an IBM AT computer is an abbreviation for Advanced Technology, because it is a more advanced computer than the IBM PC.

To issue AT commands, you need a method of sending characters from the serial port. For modems, this is done from within your communications program. Your communications program will have a mode where, when you type characters on-screen, they are sent to the serial port. This is most frequently known as *terminal mode* or the *terminal screen* (because you are using the PC as a terminal).

This is the area on your screen where you see data from the computer you are connected to. In a DOS-based communications program, the terminal screen is typically a blank screen with a line of status information at the top or bottom of the screen. In a Windows-based communications program, it is usually a blank window.

"When I type AT at the DOS command prompt, nothing happens. Why?"

Because the terminal screen is mostly blank or has a series of commands with the cursor at the bottom, it can be confused with the DOS prompt screen that may be displayed when you turn on your computer. The two screens may appear similar, but they serve different functions.

The DOS prompt screen, which usually has a drive letter and path, such as C:\>, followed by the cursor, is used to issue commands to DOS. The terminal screen is within your communications software program.

To reach a terminal screen, you need to type the name of your communications software program, such as **qmodem** or **exec**, and load your communications software then access the terminal screen. The method for accessing this screen varies, but you may automatically be in this screen when you load the program or may need to press Esc to remove a dialing directory (list of places you can call). Alternatively, your communications program may use the term direct connection to give you access to the terminal screen. Some communications programs do not include a method for you to enter AT commands directly.

When at the terminal screen, the keys you press on your keyboard are sent to the modem. If your modem is in command mode, the keys you press are considered modem commands and the modem tries to respond to them. If your modem is not in command mode (it is in *online mode*) and is connected to another modem, the keys you press are sent to the modem, passed to the other modem, and in turn passed onto the other computer.

You will need to issue AT commands in two typical situations: configuring and trouble-shooting. You may want to change some modem settings, such as how long the modem is to wait after dialing before giving up on making a connection or how many times the phone must ring before your modem should answer it. You may also need to use AT commands to find problems, such as verifying that your modem actually can communicate with the computer or hang up the phone when the remote computer appears to be unresponsive.

There are literally hundreds of AT commands, and no single modem supports them all. Some of these commands are found on all modems, some are found on specific modems, and some are applicable only to fax modems. In most cases, a particular AT command is used in the same way on each modem that supports that command. However, there is no clear-cut definition that says "buy a modem that supports the following AT commands and you won't go wrong." In general, an AT-compatible modem will include support for sufficient AT commands to make communications successful.

Unfortunately, there is no definitive core AT command set. The TIA/EIA 602 standard for data modems, TIA/EIA 578 for Class 1 fax modems, and TIA/EIA 592 standard for Class 2 fax modems are minimum lists of AT commands that a modem or fax modem will include. However, these lists are not enough for most modem use.

This book presents the AT commands in various forms. This chapter includes seven AT commands that all users should memorize. Even if you know about AT commands, you should read the following section because it defines terms like result codes that are used throughout the book.

Appendix A includes a list of the AT commands. Your modem will include many of these commands, but it may include additional ones as well.

Verifying that your modem is there (AT)

The first command all users should know is AT. From the terminal screen, type **AT** and press Enter. As you press each character, it is sent to the modem. However, the modem will not respond until you press Enter to indicate that the command is completed.

Most modems are not case-sensitive, so you can type **AT** or **at**. However, some modems are case-sensitive and only respond **to AT**.

"Can I type **at** or must AT commands be capital letters?"

Your modem should respond, by displaying on your terminal screen, with OK or less commonly 0. If you do not see the OK or 0, you typed the command incorrectly or your modem is not responding. Check that your modem is turned on and verify that your cables are plugged in. (You may need to exit your communications program and restart it if your modem was not turned on.)

The OK and 0 are called *result codes* and are the modem's method of signalling its status as a result of the commands you have sent. Modems support two types of result codes: verbose and short form. As the name suggests, one is brief and the other is more descriptive. See the ATV and ATQ commands later in this section.

If you make an error when typing a command, you cannot use the backspace key to erase it because the modem has already received it. Press Enter and retype the command; remember to press Enter at the end.

You may not see the letters AT on-screen as you type them. You can make them appear by using another AT command (**ATE1**) to make the modem echo the commands back to the screen. However, some communications programs do not operate correctly when you do this, so if you do it for testing, use the **ATE0** command to turn the echo off before resuming normal communication. See the later section on "Communicating" for more information on the local echo command.

Making your modem go off hook (ATH1)

Use **ATH1** to make your modem do the equivalent of picking up the phone receiver. You can use this to make sure that the modem is plugged into a phone line. Type **ATH1** and press Enter. The modem performs the equivalent of taking the phone off the hook. It will return the result code OK or 0, and you should hear a dial tone through your speaker and the OH LED on your modem should light. Type **ATH** or **ATH0** to hang up the phone.

If you type the **AT** correctly, but the modem is unable to understand the rest of the command, your modem will respond with ERROR or 4. You can reissue the command.

If you do not hear a dial tone, your modem may have its speaker volume turned down or off. (Some modems do not include a speaker.) Early-model modems have a knob on the back that you turn to alter the speaker volume. Newer modems use two AT commands to alter the sound from the speaker. **ATM1** turns the speaker on, **ATM0** turns the speaker off. **ATL0** provides the lowest volume and **ATL2** a medium volume.

Making your modem dial (ATD)

The ATD command is used to make the modem dial a phone number. On its own (without the accompanying number), you can use it like ATH1 to make sure the modem is plugged into a phone line. Type **ATD** and press Enter.

To make the modem dial a phone number, you add the phone number to the ATD command. For example, to make it dial directory inquiries, you type **ATD555-1212** and press Enter.

There are many modifiers to this command so that you can make the modem dial in different ways and with different delays. For example, you can add a T to the command to make it dial in tones or add a P to the command to make the modem dial in pulses. You can add a W to make the modem wait until it hears a dial tone before dialing or add a comma (,) to make it pause while dialing.

For example, the command **ATDTW9,555-1212** dials the same number as before but will use tone dialing, will wait to hear a dial tone before dialing the 9, and will pause before dialing the rest of the number. As you may have guessed by now, there are additional AT commands to alter the length of time the modem will pause when you include a comma in the dialing command and additional modifiers that affect the dialing.

You may need any or all of the modifiers depending on how you are configured. For example, many company phone systems require you to dial a 9 to get an outside line, and you may have to pause for a couple of seconds before you get the line.

As a beginner, you do not need to learn all the modifiers, but you should understand that your communications program is issuing these instructions to your modem. It will probably require you to add such items as commas to indicate delays and add the number you would dial to get an outside line.

Getting result codes (ATQ and ATV)

It is much easier to fault find if your modem is supplying result codes. If you are having trouble connecting with a new online service, any one of many things may be going wrong. You may not be dialing the right number, the phone line may not be working, your modem may not be working, the phone number may be busy or ringing with no answer, et cetera, et cetera.

The ATQ command enables and disables the result codes. If you type **ATQ0** and press Enter, result codes are enabled; if you type **ATQ1** and press Enter, result codes are turned off.

The ATV command enables and disables the verbose result codes. If you type **ATV1** and press Enter, you will get verbose result codes that are much more meaningful than the short form. Typical examples include OK, RING, BUSY, CONNECT 2400, CONNECT 9600, and COMPRESSION: V.42BIS.

The short form codes, enabled by typing **ATV** or **ATV0**, return a one- or two-digit number. Most PC users will not use these codes, although obscure communications programs may require their use. These codes are used most frequently when the modem is attached to specialized equipment, such as control circuitry. Rather than the circuitry needing to translate long words, it can translate the number.

Making your modem hang up (ATH)

After the AT command, the most important command you can learn is how to hang up the phone. The AT command to make your modem hang up the phone is ATH or ATH0. Type **ATH** and press Enter or type **ATH0** and press Enter. Your modem should hang up the phone.

This is not as easy as it sounds and is explained in more detail in the section on disconnecting later in this chapter.

Resetting your modem (ATZ)

To reset the modem to a predefined state, use the ATZ command. Type **ATZ** and press Enter.

If no one has reconfigured your modem, this returns you to the factory default settings. However, you should be aware that you can store your own selection of settings in many modems. These settings are known as a *profile*. Profiles are an intermediate topic and are covered in Chapter 9. When you use the ATZ command, the *preferred* profile that you have previously chosen is restored.

Connecting

To make a connection with another modem, you need to set the phone number, character format, transmission speed, and terminal emulation for your connection. This can be done via menus in your communications software or, if necessary, by issuing AT commands directly to your modem.

When each item is chosen, you select the dial command in your communications software to start the connection process. The communications software sends the commands to the modem, which in turn alters its settings where necessary, takes the phone off the hook, and dials the specified number.

The terms *local* and *remote* are frequently used in communications. As with Einstein's theory of relativity, the terms you use depend on your frame of reference. The local computer and the remote computer may vary, depending at which end of the phone connection you are standing. For the following explanation, assume that the local computer is the one you are dialing from (the *originating* modem) and the remote modem and computer (the *answering* modem) are the ones at the other end of the phone line receiving the phone call.

At the other end, the remote, or answering, modem is set to auto-answer and performs the equivalent of picking up the telephone receiver when the phone rings.

(If the phone number is busy, your modem may signal to your communications software that it is busy or it may continue to wait for an answer.) You can make adjustments to many modems (by using AT commands) that alter how long the modem should wait for a connection.

The tones, bleeps, buzzes, and squeals you hear while your modem is making the connection indicate the negotiation process. When the remote modem answers the phone, it sends a tone or series of tones to the local modem that originated the phone call. The particular tone or series of tones specify the particular speed and particular modulation scheme that it is able to connect at.

The local modem either responds or fails to respond to the tones sent from the remote modem. The two modems negotiate the highest possible connection speed that both modems can achieve (or have been set to achieve). Depending on the particular speed and modulation protocol established, the two modems may exchange further information. This information is used, in part, to further tailor the connection by altering the modems' electronics. In this way, the best possible connection, with the least noise and potentially the most error-free transmission characteristics, for the particular phone line connection is made.

On modems that do not support data compression or error detection, when the highest mutually acceptable speed and modulation standard has been agreed to by the modems, the connection is complete, and the modem sends the result code indicating connection at a particular speed to the communications program (unless the result code feature has been disabled).

However, on modems that support data-compression or error-detection, such as V.42, V.42bis, or MNP 5, the connection is not yet complete. The modems do further negotiation to agree on the data compression or error-detection standards. When complete, the modem sends the result code to indicate the connection speed and the compression or error detection to the communications program.

When you are connecting with another modem, look out for this result code. You will not see codes that your modem is not capable of achieving, but you may see standards that are lower than you are expecting.

For example, if you have a 9600 bps modem and connect with a BBS, you may see a result code such as `CONNECT 2400`. This means you are connected at 2400 bps, not 9600 bps. Read the BBS's menus carefully because you may find that if you call an alternate number, you can connect to the BBS at a faster speed, such as 9600 bps. Typically, the commonly advertised phone number for online services is a 2400 bps number.

As another example, you may see a connect result code that says, `CONNECT 2400, COMPRESSION: V.42bis, PROTOCOL: V.42/LAPM` indicating that you have connected at 2400 bps, but the modems are able to use V.42bis compression and V.42 error detection.

After the negotiation, the two modems "keep in touch" with each other by establishing a signal between them, known as a carrier signal. This is the signal that is modulated to transmit the digital data between the modems. Chapter 4 introduces modulation and carrier signals. When a modem stops detecting a carrier signal, the connection is lost. You will have to reestablish the connection by redialing the phone number.

Communicating

After the modems finish negotiating and establish the carrier signal, the two computers, or the computer and the remote serial device, can communicate with each other by using the chosen terminal emulation.

When you press a key on your keyboard, it is received by the remote computer, and if the remote computer sends characters to your computer, you see them on-screen. The computer you call, such as an online service, usually displays a prompt, such as `Last`

`Name`, or will display a screen of information and a menu. If you call a friend, rather than an online service, you see the modem result codes, and when you press keys on your computer, they will display on your friend's computer screen. When your friend presses keys on the keyboard, you will see them on your screen.

Part IV explains in more detail the type of information you see when you access an online service. For this chapter, you need to understand that the remote computer is running a program that you control when you call it. This program will probably ask for your name and password before providing access to its resources. If you follow the prompts and type carefully, you will quickly reach the menus for the system. If this is the first time you access the system, you may need to register with the system or fill out a questionnaire, but the remote computer sends characters (or graphical images depending on the terminal emulation) that are displayed on your screen.

You respond to the prompts sent from the other computer, and the remote computer follows your instructions. For example, you may ask to read mail or send a message. Depending on what computer you are connected to and what program is running on that computer, you may have to alter a further communications setting. If you do need to alter this setting, make a note of it and set it before the next time you connect with this system.

As explained in the section on issuing AT commands to your modem, when you power up your modem, it is in command mode and your modem tries to interpret any keys you press on the keyboard as commands. When you make the modem dial a phone number, the modem switches from command mode to online mode, and any key you press on the keyboard is passed to the remote modem and onto the remote computer.

"Why do I see repeated characters when I connect to a particular computer?"

In most cases, the remote computer echoes (repeats) the character in the data it sends back to the local computer, so when you press a key, it appears on your screen. However, some computers, depending on how they are configured, do not do this echoing. The remote computer will still accept and process the key press correctly, but you will not see it on the screen. You can correct this by turning on *local echo* and making the local modem echo the characters you press back to your screen.

In the opposite case, where you have local echo turned on and the remote computer also sends back the characters you press, you will see double characters. For example, if you type **hello** you would see HHEELLOO. In this case, turn local echo off.

Local echo is turned on and off either directly from a command in your communications program or by issuing an AT command to your modem. In many communications programs, it is a single key combination to toggle the setting. For example, QModem uses Alt+E and calls it *Duplex toggle;* Smartcom Exec uses the term *Echo typed characters* and you choose yes or no. The AT command to turn echo on is ATE1 and to turn echo off is ATE0.

Unfortunately, this is another area like baud and data speed where terms are misunderstood. Local echo on is sometimes called full duplex, and local echo off is sometimes called half duplex.

Strictly speaking, the terms full duplex and half duplex refer to how the data is transmitted between two serial devices. In half duplex, data is sent in only one direction at a time; in full duplex, data is sent in both directions at once.

As covered in Chapter 6, some file transfer protocols are full duplex and others are half duplex. This is different from local echo being on and off. Local echo on makes the connection between your computer and modem a duplex connection and has nothing to do with the connection between the two modems.

In most cases when you are calling an online service, you want local echo set to off, and the remote system will echo the characters you press. You are most likely to need to turn local echo on when you call a friend's computer and not a BBS. In the calling-a-friend situation, the symptoms of not having local echo on will show as you seeing what your friend types but not what you are typing. Similarly, if your friend can see what you type but not what he is typing, he needs to turn local echo on his computer.

Apart from local echo, communication between the two computers involves you sending characters, which are created by pressing keys on your keyboard, and the remote computer sending characters back to you. Even the graphical interfaces are doing a similar thing — when you pick a menu item this is translated into a series of characters that are accepted by the remote computer. This *character transfer* will allow you to read the information and send information between the two computers.

However, on many occasions, you will send more information than you can type easily at your keyboard, and you will want to send or receive files of information that may or may not consist of characters. *File transfer* is an important part of modem communications and is introduced in detail in Chapter 6.

As a beginner, you should differentiate between *character* and *file transfer* so that you know when you are doing one and when the other. When you press a key, you are doing character transfer, and when you activate a command (run a program) comparable with the DOS copy command, you are doing a file transfer between the two computers.

ASCII, which is an abbreviation for American Standard Code for Information Interchange, is a national and international standard for representing characters that are used on most computers. The internationally approved ASCII character set includes representations for all the alphanumeric keys and punctuation keys and many symbols. There are 128 characters in the set, although not all of the characters are printable. For example, one character represents a carriage return. You can represent 128 characters with seven bits of binary data.

The IBM PC popularized a variation of the standard character set, called the extended character set. This included an additional 128 characters and requires eight bits of binary data for the full set.

"Why do I see gibberish when I connect?"

Sometimes when you are online, you see characters that look peculiar, including for example, smiley faces, squiggles, and other strange shapes. This is a mismatch between your communications program's terminal emulation and the terminal emulation being used on the remote computer.

Your terminal emulation is taking the number of the ASCII character and displaying the character from the extended character set instead of from the basic character set. For example, instead of displaying 2, which is ASCII character number 50, the screen will actually display the extended ASCII character number 178 (128 + 50), which is a shaded rectangle.

Most communications programs have a command that switches the representation so that you see the correct character. This is often called 8-bit toggle or 8-bit on and off, and in QModemPro is toggled by pressing Alt+8. Note that changing this option does not affect characters that are already displayed, but will affect any new characters sent from the remote computer to your screen.

Disconnecting

In theory, disconnecting from the remote modem and computer appears easy. Unfortunately, it is not always simple to make the modem perform the equivalent of hanging up the phone.

When you have made a connection, the modems are transparent to the connection, and you are linked to the remote computer. You expect any data that you send from your computer to the other computer or that you receive from the remote computer to be passed on by the modems and not be changed en route.

However, when you want to hang up the phone, you need to make your modem hang up the phone or the remote computer needs to make the remote modem hang up the phone. You need the modem to stop passing the data it receives onto the other modem and accept an AT command to hang up the phone. When one modem hangs up the phone, the carrier signal is lost and the other modem is aware the connection has been broken.

Unless configured differently by the use of AT commands, Hayes-compatible modems monitor the connection by two methods. They look in the stream of data being sent for a special sequence of characters, referred to as an escape sequence to instruct the modem to switch from on-line mode to command mode. Additionally, they look for the presence of a carrier signal.

When you want to make the modem pay attention to you, rather than pass data onto the other modem, you issue this escape sequence and the modem switches to command mode and awaits AT commands. When you have made any adjustments you need, you can issue a final instruction to make the modem return to online mode if applicable.

"How do I hang up?"

Because the modem uses three different ways to determine whether it can send data, you can use two different ways to break the connection yourself, or you can get the remote computer to break the connection.

If you are connected to an online service, you can use the remote computer program's commands to break the connection. A typical menu will include a command option such as goodbye or logoff. When you enter this command, you will be disconnected from the service. Wherever possible, particularly if you are paying a connect time charge for the service, use the facilities offered by the remote computer to disconnect. In this way, you can be certain that the remote computer considers you disconnected immediately and does not wait until nothing happens for a certain length of time before considering you disconnected.

If you need to hang up at a time when you do not have a menu option, use your modem to break the connection. For example, if the remote computer locks up or you are unable break out of a file transfer, you can try to make your modem hang up.

The easiest method, and the one you should always use first if you are breaking the connection, is the hang up command. The hang up command in your communications program issues the escape sequence followed by the hang up command. Your modem detects the escape sequence, switches to command modem, then accepts and acts on the hang up command.

Alternatively, you can issue the hang up command directly. You first need to switch the modem to command mode using the escape sequence and then issue the ATH command as described earlier.

The term *escape sequence* does not mean the Esc key on your keyboard. It is a series of keystrokes that you designate as "the keys I want the modem to pay attention to." By default, it is assigned to the plus key, but, surprise, surprise, you can use AT commands to alter the assignment.

To explain the escape sequence, assume the default setting of the plus key. For a true AT-compatible modem, the escape sequence is a period of no data of at least one second (where nothing is typed on the keyboard or is being sent to the modem) +++ followed by another period of no data of at least one second. These no-data periods are known as Guard Time. Hayes Microcomputer Products has a patent on this escape sequence, and other modem manufacturers have been issued a license by Hayes to use it in their modems. This escape sequence is formally called Hayes Improved Escape Sequence with Guard Time.

When the modem sees this escape sequence, it switches to command mode and accepts AT commands. (The escape sequence is one of the two commands that does not use the prefix AT.)

Some modems do not require the Guard Time and will respond to an escape sequence of +++AT followed by a carriage return in most cases without needing a no-data period before or after it. This escape sequence is formally called Time Independent Escape Sequence (TIES).

Understanding an Escape Sequence

Dale Heatherington, inventor of the Hayes Smartmodem along with Dennis Hayes, very carefully chose the escape sequence needed to switch the modem from online mode to command mode. The idea was to create a sequence of characters that would not appear in any data being sent from one modem to the other.

Suppose that the escape sequence had been "cat." The internal electronics in the modem would have been programmed so that when it saw the sequence of characters "c a t," it would switch from online mode to command mode. This would mean if any file transferred with the word "cat" in it — or whenever you typed the word cat when connected — the modem would stop passing data to the other modem and wait for AT commands. The likelihood of the word "cat" occurring in files is high, especially if you consider it as part of other words, such as catalog, advocate, or scathing, and the escape sequence would interrupt far too many transmissions.

On the other hand, you cannot pick an obscure sequence of bits because the user must be able to type it at the keyboard. Remember that the modems were designed to work with any computer, so unusual keys, such as the function keys on a PC or special keys found on terminals, were not suitable.

The addition of Guard Time before and after the escape sequence reduces the chance that a file will switch the modem to command mode. Using the "cat" example again, the need for you to leave a one second no-data period before and after typing the word "cat" probably makes it unlikely that the word catalog or advocate will make the modem switch to command mode. File transfer, which is a continual stream of data, is very unlikely to trigger the modem.

The default escape sequence chosen was a one second no-data period +++ followed by a one second period of no data. On most modems, you can reprogram this sequence to be another character, such as !!!, if you prefer.

The sidebar uses a specific example to explain the escape sequence. However, for a beginner, you need to understand that the modem is designed to respond and switch to command mode when it sees the escape sequence. If you transfer files or data that contain the escape sequence, the modem will assume that the sequence of data bits was intended for it and will interrupt the data transmission by switching to command mode.

The issue is how often the escape sequence actually occurs during data transmission. If you never send a file that has the particular sequence of bits that make up the escape sequence, you will detect no difference between the two types of modems (the one that uses Guard Time and the one that is time-independent).

However, you will not be able to send a file or sequence of characters that make up the escape sequence without the modem switching to command mode and disrupting the transmission. By employing Guard Time, where nothing is transmitted for a second before and after the escape sequence, it is far less likely, as in almost improbable, for the escape sequence to be detected in a normal data stream.

On the other hand, the Guard Time requirement can make it harder to attract the modem's attention. If, for example, you want to sever a connection while a file is being transmitted or streams of characters are scrolling across your screen, the one-second delay without transmission can seem impossible. In this case, you must resort to one of the other methods for breaking the connection.

However, Guard Time may be preferable to you because the transmission will not be broken unintentionally by the data that is being transmitted. Although it is harder to interrupt and get the modem's attention, it is not due to strange — and probably unrecognizable to the user — data content.

The other method for hanging up the phone is to remove power from the modem. Use this as a last resort. An external modem is relatively easy to turn off at its power switch. Exit your communications software, turn your modem back on, and restart your communications software before making another connection.

With an internal modem, you can only remove power by turning off the computer or by pressing the reset button. (This is not the same as pressing Ctrl+Alt+Del.) Wherever possible, exit your communications program before turning off. If you turn your computer off, rather than pressing the reset button, wait until the hard disk drive and cooling fans have stopped before turning it back on again.

Summary

This chapter introduced the basics of making a connection with your modem. You learned the five items needed before making a connection: phone number, call originator, character format, data speed, and terminal emulation. You also learned that you may need to adjust local echo to be able to see the characters you type.

In most cases, the communications program can issue the commands to the modem, but as you become more experienced, you will need to be able to issue AT commands to your modem directly. This chapter explained that modems can accept commands when in command mode and pass on the data you send from your computer to the other modem when in online mode. You can issue AT commands from the terminal screen, and you were introduced to seven of the most frequently used AT commands in this chapter.

Before reading the next chapter on file transfer, you should understand the three stages of a connection: dialing, connecting, and disconnecting. You should also understand the difference between character transfer, which uses terminal emulation and transfers one character at a time, and file transfer, which uses the equivalent of a DOS copy command to transfer groups of data.

6

CHAPTER

Understanding File Transfer

After users learn to make their modems call other modems and they have access to all these online services, file transfer becomes the primary application. You can copy files from your computer to another, or you can copy files from the other computer to your computer.

This chapter introduces file-transfer protocols. Specifically, you will learn the following techniques:

- ❖ Extending your communication to include file transfer
- ❖ Understanding the importance of the appropriate file-transfer protocol
- ❖ Defining the types of available file-transfer protocols
- ❖ Choosing a file-transfer protocol

Extending Your Communication to Include File Transfer

Chapter 5 introduces how to establish a connection with another modem. When you are linked to another computer via two modems, you can type characters on your keyboard and control a program running on the remote computer.

In many cases, in addition to typing messages, you need to transfer files between the two computers. File transfer is comparable to using the DOS copy command: You want to move a file from one computer to another.

However, because different computers are involved, and you probably won't have the same communication software running on both computers, and you may not even have the same operating system running on both computers, you need to use commands that will operate on both computers.

These commands are actually small programs that you run on both computers. You have a choice of programs that you can run. These programs support a particular standard, and the standards are known as *file-transfer protocols*.

In human communication, the analogy for file-transfer protocols is mailing a letter. In most countries, the general principle is to write the address on an envelope, put a stamp on it, and mail the letter in a mailbox. The postal service handles the routing and delivery.

In reality, the precise rules vary from country to country. In the U.S., for example, mail boxes are blue; in England, post boxes are red. In Germany, you typically place the town below the name and the street below that. In the U.S., the street address comes below the name and the town on the subsequent line. However, you can still send mail from one country to another without worrying about the details related to the receiving countries.

"What are uploading and downloading?"

In modem communication, the terms *uploading* and *downloading* refer to sending and receiving a file respectively. Like the remote and local computers, if you are standing at the other end of the connection, the uploading and downloading terminology is reversed.

The general procedure is to prepare the communication program at one end of the connection to send or receive the desired file and then start the program at the opposite end. For example, if you are calling an online service and want to download a file to your computer, you issue the command on the remote computer to start the download. Then you issue the command to your communication software to accept the downloaded file.

In most cases, when you control the program at both ends of the connection, you start the process at the remote end and then instruct your program to receive or send the file. If you are calling a friend, one of you should prepare to accept the file, and the other can instruct the communication program to send it. The typical procedure is to start the download command (the Page Down key in many communications software programs), and then start the upload command (the Page Up key in many communications software programs).

Remember that you are uploading the file from the sending computer. The receiving computer, which is accepting the file, needs to use the download command to receive the file. In the case of an online service, both ends use the terms downloading or uploading, because the program is only being controlled from one end. In the case of you and a friend, you are both controlling your own ends of the connection.

Although you probably will not use exactly the same file-transfer *program* at both ends of the connection, both computers must agree on the file-transfer *protocol*. There are a variety of protocols in use; some are variations on each other; others have specialized applications.

Although the technical detail may seem cumbersome to understand, you should realize that the faster the protocol you use, the faster the file is transferred. Different file-transfer protocols operate at different speeds and have different levels of error-checking.

On the other hand, it does not matter how fast the file is transferred if it is received inaccurately. Inaccuracies occur during file transfer because of noise on the telephone lines. You do not get 10, 20, or 30 minutes of completely noise-free phone lines. When you are talking, you can easily repeat a sentence or stop talking when the noise occurs; but in telecommunications, you need a mechanism to verify that what was sent is what is received.

Understanding Error-Correction

Apart from ASCII, the file-transfer protocols, such as XMODEM and ZMODEM, are *error-detecting* protocols, although they are often referred to as *error-correction* protocols. As a modem user, you should understand the difference between error-detection and error-correction, because you may need to be the judge of how long you are prepared to let a poor transfer last.

An error-detection protocol can identify when an error has occurred during transmission. It then signals the equivalent of "That can't be right" and resends a portion of the file.

An error-correction protocol, which is not employed by the file-transfer protocols, is actually able to *correct* an error rather than *detect* it. This is much more difficult than simply detecting the error.

Suppose that I send you an equation, and I tell you that it will be three numbers added together, such as 8 + 6 + 3 = 17. If you actually receive 8 - 6 + 3 = 17, you know there is an error and can correct the minus sign to a plus sign. On the other hand, if you actually receive 7 + 6 + 3 = 17, you know there is an error, but you cannot tell which number is incorrect.

The different error-detection methods, such as checksum, 16-bit CRC, and 32-bit CRC, offer different levels of error-detection. You can think of them as providing different levels of detail about the transmitted block. The additional detail gives the receiving computer more of a chance of detecting an error.

File Compression (Zipped Files)

File transfer takes time. Anything you can do to reduce this time saves you in telephone and connect-time charges. Most files stored by online services ready for you to download are stored in compressed form. This makes the file much smaller and consequently reduces the file transfer time.

The most commonly used file compression program is PKZIP, a shareware program from PKWare. This program can compress a file or many files into a single file. The compressed file is typically referred to as being *zipped* and has a file extension of .ZIP. Other file compression programs include ARC, from SEA, and LHA, a public domain program created by Haruyasu Yoshizaki (familiarly known as Yoshi).

However, you cannot run these files in their compressed form. After you download them, you need to uncompress them before use. Consequently, one of the first files you should obtain is the set of zipping and unzipping programs. This file, which has a name that includes its version number, such as PKZ204G.EXE, which means Version 2.04 of PKZIP, is available on most online services as well as from most user groups. It is a special type of zipped file, known as a *self-extracting* file, which can uncompress itself to give you the various utility programs and documentation.

If you find an online service using a different file compression program, you need to obtain the equivalent program. In general, you can find the appropriate file compression program for a particular online service in the files listing for that service.

"What do I do with this zipped file?"

PKZIP, which zips the files, and its partner, PKUNZIP, which unzips the files, are a vital part of your PC utility programs. If you intend to do any telecommunicating, you will use PKZIP on a regular basis and should register your shareware copy.

The PKZIP utility is used to group files together and enables you to download a single file to obtain all the elements you need. Suppose that you download a popular game with the filename MICEMN.ZIP. This single zipped file contains all the files you need to play, configure, and register the game, including the documentation.

You look for the game in a files list on the online service and download it to your computer. You then exit your communications program and issue the command **PKUNZIP MICEMN.ZIP**, at the DOS prompt. PKZIP uncompresses and separates all the files, and you have the game file, MICEMEN.EXE, the documentation, MICEMEN.DOC, and other supporting files.

Many online services accept files that you upload. However, many require you to zip the files before you upload them to save disk space and online time. Zipping files involves compressing them, which is the reverse of unzipping them. This process is easy when compressing only one file but requires a little care when compressing multiple files into a single zipped file. However, the documentation supplied with PKZIP provides good instructions.

Determining when to use PKZIP and when to take advantage of your modem's compression is an intermediate topic covered in Chapter 9.

File-Transfer Protocols

The following sections introduce the popular file-transfer protocols. Although you do not need to remember the technical details, you should understand the basics and make sensible selections. Additionally, this section can be used as a reference when you have trouble matching a file-transfer protocol available in your communications program with a file-transfer protocol available on an online service.

ASCII

The most basic file-transfer protocol is *ASCII,* which is used to transfer *text* files between computers. As Chapter 5 explains, ASCII is used on most computers throughout the world, and IBM PCs and compatibles have popularized the extended character set, which provides even more characters. The ASCII file-transfer protocol is *not* used to transfer programs. (Hayes communication software, including Smartcom for Windows LE, uses the term *autotype.*)

The ASCII file-transfer protocol sends each character in the file in turn as if you had typed it on the keyboard. It does not include error-checking features nor any compression features.

Understanding File Compression

File compression is extremely important when doing file transfer because it can dramatically reduce the size of your files and consequently reduce the file-transfer time. For example, I regularly capture screen shots for inclusion in magazine articles, and a file-compression program can compress the file to about 4 percent of its original size.

There are many ways to compress files, and a good file-compression program will use the best method for each particular file. Some compression algorithms are quite complex, but an understanding of simple algorithms can help you understand why some files cannot be compressed and others can be compressed substantially.

If a file contains truly random data, it cannot be compressed. However, most files, including program files, contain repetitive patterns. A file-compression program looks for these repetitions and, instead of sending the full pattern each time, sends an abbreviated version.

One approach is to eliminate the repetition in a series of bits. For example, a typical bit-mapped screen (without color) is a series of black dots and a series of white dots. Instead of sending the code for "white, white, white, white, black, black, black," the compression program may say "four whites, three blacks."

Another, much more involved approach is to use substitution and send the decoding instructions for the substitution. For example, if the text of this chapter was considered, the words *communications* and *file-transfer protocol* would occur very frequently. If I said "substitute Fred for communications and Jane for file-transfer protocol," I could save a lot of space.

This substitution approach is complicated because the substitutions are not the same for each file. For example, if the file was a bird-watching guidebook, the expression *file-transfer protocol* would not occur. However, *Fred* could be used as a substitute for *binoculars* or *winter habitat.*

XMODEM

XMODEM is the next most common file-transfer protocol found on PCs after ASCII. XMODEM was invented by Ward Christensen, the designer and programmer of the first BBS (see sidebar in Chapter 2). It is known as a half-duplex, error-correcting protocol. In fact, it is an error-detecting protocol and not an error-correcting protocol. *Half-duplex* means that data flows in only one direction at a time.

The file is divided into blocks that are 128 bytes in length, and a checksum is added to each block. The *checksum*, which is, as its name suggests, a number that verifies the data within a block, serves a similar purpose to a parity bit. See the sidebar "Understanding Error-Correction" for more detail.

The transmitting computer sends the first block of data along with its checksum. The receiving computer calculates the checksum for the block and compares its compared value with the checksum value sent with the block.

If the two checksums are the same, the receiving computer sends a character, called an *ACK* (for acknowledge), to the originating computer. The originating computer then sends the next block of data and its checksum.

If the checksums do not correspond, the receiving computer sends a *NACK* character (for no acknowledge) to the originating computer. The originating computer resends the block of data and its checksum.

"Why is the file bigger after I download it?"

The process of sending a block, verifying the checksums, and sending the next block continues. The last block of data in the file contains a special code called an *EOT* (end of text) code that logically indicates the end of the file. When the receiving computer gets the EOT code, it combines all the blocks received into a single file and completes the file transfer.

XMODEM blocks are all 128 bytes in length. If your file is not an even multiple of 128 bytes, XMODEM adds bits to the last block to make it a complete block. These are not removed by the receiving computer. Consequently, you may see a slightly larger number of bytes in the file on the receiving computer than on the sending computer. This does not affect the file because the end-of-file indicator within the last block is unchanged, but the padding on the end is stored on the disk.

XMODEM variations

Several variations on the basic XMODEM protocol are used in the PC environment. *XMODEM/CRC* uses a *cyclic redundancy check* (CRC) instead of a simple checksum. The CRC is a two-byte code that provides better error control than the one-byte checksum. Its value is derived from a more complex algorithm, and as a result, any transmission errors are more likely to be detected.

In many cases, XMODEM/CRC has replaced the original XMODEM. Consequently, you may run into poor nomenclature and find an online service referring to XMODEM/CRC as XMODEM. If you choose XMODEM in your communications program and XMODEM on the online service, but have trouble with a file transfer and none of the blocks are accepted, the nomenclature may be the problem. Try setting XMODEM/CRC in your communications program, keep XMODEM on the online service, and try again.

Although XMODEM, with its 128-byte blocks, is reliable, it is not particularly fast. Additionally, the transfer protocol does not provide a method of keeping the time and date stamp for the file. For example, if you download a new version of your favorite game by using XMODEM, the date and time that appears with the filename is the date and time of your downloading and not the file-creation date.

XMODEM-1K is another variation of XMODEM. It is similar, except that the block size is 1,024 bytes (1 KB) instead of 128 bytes. The larger block size gives a faster transfer rate because the receiving computer sends fewer ACK or NACK signals. Terminology is mixed with XMODEM-1K, too. Some online services use XMODEM-1K but call it *YMODEM.* YMODEM is explained in the following section. You may need to choose XMODEM-1K in your communications software to use the YMODEM protocol on the online service.

YMODEM

YMODEM is an extension of XMODEM-1K but includes two important but optional extra features: time and date stamp transfer and batch file transfer. YMODEM uses a 1 KB block size but also transfers such file information as the file date and time stamp.

You can also specify more than one file at a time to be transferred. This is known as a *batch-file-transfer protocol*. YMODEM is used on many online services but is often not implemented with the batch-file-transfer protocol feature and is sometimes not implemented with the time and date stamp transfer.

ZMODEM

ZMODEM has become the most popular file-transfer protocol in recent years. It is faster than the XMODEM variations and is usually implemented with the batch-file-transfer protocol and is more tolerant of errors.

In a ZMODEM transfer, the blocks are sent continuously to the receiving computer. Each block includes a 16-bit or a 32-bit CRC. The 32-bit CRC picks up more errors than the 16-bit CRC, in the same way that the 16-bit CRC detects more errors than a checksum. Consequently, you can be more confident that your data-transmission errors (due typically to noise on the telephone line) will be detected.

The sending computer does not expect to receive an ACK signal until the file is completely sent. If the receiving computer detects an error, however, it sends a NACK signal immediately and specifies which block contained an error. On receipt of the NACK signal, the sending computer aborts and restarts the file transmission, beginning with the incorrectly received block. ZMODEM also supports batch-file transfer; you specify a series of files and start uploading or downloading. ZMODEM automatically handles each file in turn.

ZMODEM is faster than the other file-transfer protocols because even less response is necessary from the receiving computer. If there are no detected errors, the receiving computer acknowledges at the end of a file transfer. However, its recovery from errors is particularly desirable. If you are downloading (or uploading) a file and start to see a lot of errors, you can assume that the telephone line has become noisy. You can hang up the phone, redial, and restart the file transmission. ZMODEM will not retransmit the whole file but will start from where it left off.

Suppose that you are downloading a 1 MB file and have received half of it when lots of errors start appearing. With the other file-transfer protocols, such as XMODEM, it's a toss-up whether it's quicker to let the file transfer continue with the error detection and retransmission or hang up and start all over again. With ZMODEM, when you try to download the file again, only the unreceived part is sent.

Other protocols

Several other file-transfer protocols are used in PC communications, and new ones are developed as new technology is available or programmers become more creative. Some are used for specialized purposes, and others are enhancements that can squeeze that extra ounce of performance for you.

When selecting communications software, look for a program that supports all the file-transfer protocols you need and that has the capability to add additional file protocols through add-on programs. In this way, you can expand your communication program's features without buying a whole new program.

For example, HSLINK is a relatively new file-transfer protocol that is not yet supported in every communications program but may be very popular in the online services you choose to frequent. You can buy an add-on program that allows you to use HSLINK with a communications program that supports external file transfer protocols. DSZ and GSZ, enhanced implementations of ZMODEM, are other examples of external protocols you may need.

The communications programs that support external file-transfer protocols allow you to select them from the upload or download menu as if they were part of the main program. In fact, the communications program passes control to the external file-transfer program and waits until the file-transfer program passes control back again to continue.

The following sections introduce two specialized but important file-transfer protocols: CompuServe B and Kermit. You may never run into these, but if you need them, nothing else will suffice.

CompuServe B

As its name suggests CompuServe B, along with its close relatives CompuServe B+ and Quick B, are proprietary file-transfer protocols used by the popular online service CompuServe. They are optimized for use with the particular software used by CompuServe. If you do not subscribe to CompuServe, you won't need it. On the other hand, if you do subscribe to CompuServe, it's the file-transfer protocol of choice.

Kermit

Kermit is another specialized file-transfer protocol. It is actually very flexible but has not become popular in the PC-to-PC communications world. It's the only commonly available file-transfer protocol for transferring 7-bit files.

As described in earlier chapters, you are not necessarily connected to another PC when you use your modem. The remote computer may be a minicomputer or mainframe. Most mainframes use 7-bit characters and not the more familiar (to PC users) 8-bit characters. You need to use Kermit to transfer files to a system that uses 7-bit files.

Kermit transfers can include blocks with varying sizes. This feature is useful if the receiving computer can accept only particular block sizes, but it is also particularly useful on noisy line conditions. When a line is clear, the blocks can be larger and received accurately, but when the line is noisy, smaller blocks are sent, which reduces the number of retransmissions of data necessary to receive the file accurately.

Kermit also allows you to specify wild-card transfers, (similar to the DOS wild-card feature) and employs some file-compression techniques. However, all this flexibility can make successful Kermit transfers difficult because of the number of options that must match, and consequently, it has not gained extensive popularity in the PC communications world, although it is used extensively in academic circles.

HSLINK

HSLINK is a bidirectional file-transfer protocol that is used with full-duplex modems, and both computers can send data at the same time. For example, you can use HSLINK with 9600 bps modems that support V.32, V.32bis, and V.FC communications standards. (As other communications standards bocome able to connect at full-duplex, they will also be able to use HSLINK.) HSLINK takes advantage of this feature and allows you to upload and download files at the same time.

This bidirectional protocol has tremendous performance advantages because you can transfer your files more rapidly. However, because it only works on high-speed modems that are operating in full-duplex, it is not very popular yet.

GSZ and DSZ

The ZMODEM file-transfer protocol was developed and put into the public domain by Chuck Fosberg. He also created two popular ZMODEM implementations called DSZ and GSZ. These shareware products are examples of add-on products that can supplement your communication software. Other add-ons for different purposes are covered in Chapter 10.

GSZ (an implementation of ZMODEM that uses graphical characters) and DSZ (an earlier implementation) include ZMODEM compression and MobyTurbo (TM) accelerator features. You may see 2-5 percent improvements in the time required to download a file when you use this program. Although this may seem small, every minute you save online is saved connect time and, where applicable, phone call expenses; these minutes leave you with more time for other online activities when you call a time-limited system that may, for example, allow only 90 minutes connect time each day.

Selecting a File-Transfer Protocol

With the exception of ASCII transfer, which is used for a particular purpose, you can choose any file-transfer protocol that your communications software and the remote computer's software support. However, there is a significant difference in performance between the protocols, and faster is probably better.

When to use ASCII

You are most likely to use the ASCII file protocol for uploading messages you have previously typed. For example, if you are looking for information on a new type of motor car oil you heard about, you may want to leave the same message on several online services. Typing the message before going online will save typing the same thing several times. Alternatively, you may want to ask detailed questions about a problem you are having with configuring your word processor, and writing the message before going online will ensure accurate typing.

Which protocol to choose

If you are transferring a file of data, rather than a text file, you cannot use ASCII and must choose another protocol. As a general rule, choose ZMODEM. Remember that the chosen protocol must be supported by the receiving *and* sending computers. If ZMODEM is not supported by your computer or the receiving computer, choose XMODEM. Although it's not a particularly faster protocol, it is widely supported.

The following are exceptions to this rule:

- When transferring 7-bit files, choose Kermit.

- When transferring from CompuServe, choose CompuServe B or one of its variants.

- If you have a modem that supports V.32 and are connected to a modem that supports V.32 and HSLINK is supported, HSLINK is preferable.

- If you have a modem operating in full-duplex mode at 9600 bps or higher and HSLINK is supported, HSLINK is preferable.

Summary

This chapter introduced file transfer, the other application for communication by modem besides sending and receiving messages. In particular, you learned that most files are stored in compressed form. You need a file compression and uncompression utility, such as PKZIP, to use the compressed files that you obtain.

You also learned that you upload a file from your computer to another computer and download a file from a remote computer to your computer. You must choose the same file-transfer protocol at both ends for the transfer to occur. In general, you should choose ZMODEM or XMODEM, except in specialized situations. You choose ASCII to upload or download text.

Chapter 7 introduces fax modem use. Part III extends your modem knowledge so that you can streamline your modem use and make the best use of your communications software.

7

CHAPTER

Understanding Your Fax Modem

This chapter shows how to use your fax modem to send and receive documents. There are distinct differences between sending and receiving fax documents on your PC fax modem. Consequently, this chapter separates these two major functions. The following specific items are covered in this chapter:

- ❖ Preparing your fax document
- ❖ Sending your fax document
- ❖ Receiving fax documents
- ❖ Handling a received fax document

Preparing to Communicate

On the one hand, your fax modem is similar to a stand-alone fax machine; on the other hand, it is similar to a data modem. A stand-alone fax machine is like a long-distance copy machine. Your job is to prepare the document and dial the phone number. You feed a document into the fax machine, and it produces a copy at a remote location. When receiving, you simply verify that the fax machine is on and pick up the pages as they are received.

A fax modem needs preparatory work similar to a data modem as well as document preparation. (The preparatory work for a data modem is presented in Chapter 5.) However, after you dial the phone number, the fax modem behaves like a stand-alone fax machine, and you don't need to be actively involved in the process; the document sending is automated. In fact it's easier, because you don't have paper jams and misfeeds, unless the receiving modem runs out of disk space, which is equivalent to running out of paper.

With a data modem, you typically perform tasks, such as reading messages or performing file transfer, while online. The connection, when you are actually linked to another modem via the telephone line, is an interactive one. Although you can automate various parts of the process, your actions generally are a necessary part of the connection.

Receiving a fax document with a fax modem can be as easy as receiving with a stand-alone fax machine, if your computer is configured to accept a fax document. However, unlike a fax machine, which only serves one purpose, you can use your computer for other purposes, and you might change the computer's configuration and leave your fax modem inoperative and not prepared to receive documents at any time.

Chapter 4 explores the differences between using a stand-alone fax machine and using a fax modem. A PC fax modem can only *send* documents that it has in electronic form. *There is no paper slot in a fax modem.* You must prepare the document on your computer or use a scanner to convert a paper document to electronic format for transmittal.

Similarly, a PC fax modem *receives* documents in electronic form as graphic images. You can print the document as a graphic image, or you can use another program, usually not supplied with the fax modem, to convert the file into a text form so that you can edit it in your word processor. Keep in mind that graphic images are large, and storing many fax documents in graphic form on your computer can rapidly fill hard disk space.

Before considering the necessary preparation of your fax document, you need to install your fax modem and its software. This process is explained in Chapter 4. Like a data modem, unless you have used your fax modem recently and successfully sent or received a fax document, you should check the following connections:

❖ A phone line plugged into the rear of the fax modem and the telephone outlet in the wall

❖ The data cable for an external fax modem plugged into the rear of the modem and into the serial port on your computer

❖ The power supply for an external fax modem plugged into the rear of the modem and into an electrical outlet

If you find a missing cable or a loose connection, be sure to turn off the computer and fax modem before correcting the problem. After checking the cables, turn on your fax modem and start your communications program. An external modem may have an LED indicating that power is on, and at least one of the LEDs will light on its front panel. An internal modem is powered on whenever your computer is turned on.

Fax Limitations

Consider the following topics before using a fax modem extensively:

If you are dealing with computers, transferring files by a data modem is preferable in most cases to using a fax modem or stand-alone fax machines. If you have only a computer at one end of the connection, fax modems are a good alternative.

A fax machine sends a graphic representation of a document between two modems. If you need to send text, it is converted to a graphic image (a series of dots) before transmission.

The received image is in black and white — not color. If the sent image was stored electronically in color, the color is lost during conversion.

File conversion from one format to another is rarely perfect. The reason that different formats exist is that different application programs offer different features. Every time a file is converted into another format, you will probably lose detail. Wherever possible, minimize the number of file-format conversions to get the best possible translation.

Fax resolution is relatively low. The typical resolution is 300 dots per inch in a horizontal direction and 150 dots per inch in a vertical direction. This is lower than most laser printers and newspapers. You will see little detail on a fax document.

Sending a Fax Document

Sending a fax document by using a fax modem requires the document preparation, cover sheet preparation, and fax modem preparation. You can then actually send the document to another fax machine. The following sections detail these steps.

Preparing your fax modem to send a fax document

When the fax software is installed and loaded into memory (by typing the program's name at the DOS prompt or choosing the program from Windows), your fax modem is comparable to a stand-alone fax machine. The software incorporates the features you get on most fax machines — such as adding a line to each page of the document with your fax phone number and company name, or programming frequently dialed numbers to dial automatically.

You need to consider two sets of parameters: those that will apply to every fax you send and those that apply only to the particular document you are sending. The general parameters that apply to every document can be configured once and remain unchanged, but other parameters are part of the document preparation. Document preparation is covered in a later section.

The available general parameters vary, depending on the particular fax software you are running. However, they usually include communication configuration information, such as the fax modem's serial port assignment, dial type (tone or pulse), and the number of times you want a busy phone number to be redialed. Additional information that you can set is the filename for your fax cover page, word processor types, and a DOS directory name as a location for your dialing directory of commonly called numbers.

As a beginner, you should choose only the parameters you need, such as the port assignment. Chapter 4 gives the information you need about your serial ports and installation. Chapter 11 explains methods for streamlining your fax transmission and receipt, which include setting up directories to store your received fax documents and dialing directories.

Unlike a data modem, you don't have to be concerned about data-connection speeds and standards with a fax modem. These settings are important when you purchase the modem but are used automatically when you send or receive a fax document.

If the software is installed and loaded, you need to decide on three items before sending a fax: the document you want to send, the phone number of the fax machine you are sending it to, and whether you want to add a cover sheet.

Knowing whom to call

The fax software can perform the equivalent of dialing the phone number of the receiving fax machine for you. As explained in Chapter 5, the modem accepts commands from the software and can do the equivalent of taking the phone off the hook, dialing the number, and making the connection.

You need the phone number of the receiving fax machine and need to enter it into the fax software. Depending on the software, you may simply need to add the phone number to the cover page, or you may need to type it when you make the actual call.

Dialing directories, where frequently called numbers are stored for easy retrieval, and other automating techniques are covered in Chapter 11. This chapter covers the essentials of sending a fax that are applicable to all fax modems and software. Chapter 11 includes desirable rather than essential features that you can use with your fax software and hardware.

Knowing what to send

The concept of sending a fax document seems obvious: You find the document and press the equivalent of a start button. However, in practice, a fax modem requires different considerations than a stand-alone fax machine.

The document you want to send must be stored in electronic form; it can be a text file or a graphic image. Although you don't need a hard copy of the document, you must have a file that you can print or an image you can display on-screen. For example, you can print a word processing document or a spreadsheet. Although you may not have a color printer, a color graphic image is printable and can consequently be sent by fax.

You cannot send handwritten notes or drawings, marked up documents, or preprinted forms or brochures unless you can convert them to electronic form. (You can make this conversion by using a scanner and scanning software.)

"How do I load my document into the fax software?"

Your document files are stored on your computer in a variety of formats. Files are usually in the format appropriate for the particular application program software that you use to generate them. For example, a document created in WordPerfect is in a different electronic format than a spreadsheet created in Excel.

Depending on the sophistication of your fax software, you may be able to use some document files directly, and you will need to convert others into a form that can be used as input for the fax software. This is explained in more detail in the following section.

Another alternative, suitable for such short fax documents as a brief memo, is to use the text editor supplied with your fax software program to type your fax directly into the fax software.

Preparing the fax document

A typical fax document includes a cover sheet that specifies the number of pages in the accompanying document, who the fax document is for, and who sent the document. Most fax communication software includes a sample that you can use. (Some feature many samples—serious and frivolous.)

Your fax document is a file stored on your computer. The cover sheet is a separate file, rather than part of your document, that is sent before your fax document file. Some software programs give you the option to send a document without this cover sheet if you prefer.

Consider the form of your electronic document. Your application program, such as the word processor or spreadsheet, probably allows you to add such items as different fonts, centering, and other formatting features that make your document look professionally produced. You want your fax software to preserve these elements wherever possible.

Read your fax software documentation carefully, and consider these features prior to purchasing it. The manual should include a list of application programs and file format types that can be entered into the fax software without conversion by you. (The fax software converts the file into a graphic image for transmission.)

For example, typical fax software may support: ASCII text, WordPerfect, Microsoft Word, and WordStar word processors as well as PCX, TIFF Class F, or TIFF uncompressed graphic files. Any file that you can create in one of these listed formats probably won't need modification before sending. However, before sending a critical document to an important customer, experiment with samples and, when available, use the preview image to verify that what you are sending is what you expect. Remember that when you upgrade an application program, such as a word processor, the fax software may not be able to accept this new version directly.

If you use a word processor or other application program that does not create a supported file format, you need to convert your file into a format that *is* supported. For example, you can save your document as an ASCII text file from most word processors. If you change a document's file format—save it as a text file, for example—you may lose formatting and other items that make the document look professionally prepared.

Similarly, although many graphics programs use proprietary file formats, you can usually save the image as a PCX or TIFF format file. If you use this approach, you should check the fax image you are sending so that there are no surprises. TIFF files, for example, can be one of five or six different formats, and your fax software may only support one variation.

You can take another approach if the fax software accepts print files. This approach is useful because it can be applied in unusual situations. Most applications support a wide variety of printer types. In your application program, choose a printer type that is acceptable as an input file type for your fax software. For example, you may be able to choose a Hewlett-Packard LaserJet or an IBM Proprinter.

You create a document in your application program and issue the Print to File command. This creates a file that contains all the necessary codes to print the document on the specified printer type. You then use this print file as the input to your fax software. Keep in mind that the output quality of your document is only as good as the printer type you select.

Your fax software may include other utilities that can help automate more unusual situations, including print-capture and screen-capture utilities. Again, your results may vary, depending on the specific software (the application program and the fax software).

A print-capture program is a *terminate-and-stay-resident* (TSR) program that you load before starting your application program. You create the document in your application program as normal. To create a file suitable for your fax software, you activate the print-capture TSR and print your document. The TSR takes the output intended for the printer and saves it in a form suitable as input for the fax software.

A screen-capture program is similar. It also is a TSR that you load into memory before starting your application program. You create the document page or display the image on-screen. You then activate the TSR to capture the displayed image. The TSR saves the image in a format suitable as input for the fax software.

As explained in the "Preparing to receive a fax document" section, TSRs are a mixed blessing. They may be too large so that you do not have sufficient room in memory to run your application program. TSRs may or may not operate correctly with a particular application program, and they may or may not capture the correct image. Even if your fax software does not include conversion utilities or features, you can purchase third-party conversion utilities that produce excellent results and may enable you to send documents not possible otherwise.

I frequently capture program screens for inclusion in magazine articles and books. I also frequently need to convert files between different formats. Sometimes, my editors do not have the same word processor; sometimes, they use different graphic formats. I have a large collection of screen-capture programs and a couple of file-conversion programs. Although I have my favorites, I cannot use a single product for every occasion, and in some situations, I am unable to capture or convert an image.

In addition to using the fax preview mode of your fax software, it is worth noting that fax documents are in black and white, not color, although standards for color fax documents are being discussed. If you send a color picture, it appears in shades of gray. In some cases, this is difficult to view or read. If you use the fax preview mode, you will be able to see which shades of gray were used when the fax software changed your color image into black and white. It gives you the opportunity to alter the colors in the original and make a better selection for transmission in shades of gray.

Tip: If you find yourself somewhere without a printer but with a fax machine, you can always fax your document to the fax machine and get a hard-copy printout. This is especially useful when staying in hotels. Send yourself a fax to the hotel's fax machine. (Some hotels charge for incoming faxes.)

Connecting to send

After you prepare the document for sending and arrange the cover sheet, the hard work is over. You instruct your fax software to send the fax document to the desired number. The fax software issues the appropriate instructions to the fax modem. (These instructions are AT commands, comparable to those being used by data modems.) The modem dials the telephone and waits for the receiving fax machine to answer.

"Why do I hear a beep after dialing with my fax modem?"

When the receiving fax machine answers the phone, the two modems must establish a mutually acceptable communication standard. Like data modems, they negotiate this standard by exchanging signals that you hear as bleeps and whistles.

Unlike data modems, you don't have to worry about the standard that is actually chosen. The selected speed will be the fastest possible. Although you may have some documents transfer more slowly because they are connected to a slower fax machine, you cannot improve the situation by altering settings or precompressing files as you can with data modems.

After connection, your modem sends the document to the remote fax machine. It takes the document one page at a time and converts it into a series of horizontal lines that are sent between the modems. The receiving fax machine either prints the document one line at a time or, if it is a fax modem, saves the image in a file for later viewing or printing.

Receiving a Fax Document

When a fax machine calls your fax machine's phone number, your fax machine answers, negotiates a communication standard with the sending fax machine, and then the sending fax machine sends the document to your machine. On a stand-alone fax machine, the fax document is printed onto paper; on a fax modem, the document is stored as a file on your computer's hard disk. To read your fax, you must use the fax communications software supplied with your fax modem to display it on-screen, print it, or convert it into another file format to view in another application program.

Preparing to receive a fax document

Using a stand-alone fax machine to receive documents is easy. When it is plugged in and turned on, you only need to check the paper supply periodically. A power break may disrupt your settings, but you can check it when you reset the clocks or the answering machine.

A fax modem requires similar preparation but different knowledge. The power to an internal fax modem is available whenever the computer is turned on, and the MR LED on an external fax modem is lit when power is applied. However, this isn't enough to receive fax documents.

You need a program loaded into your computer's memory that can detect the telephone line ringing and activate the fax modem. Your fax software will probably include a utility for this purpose, usually a terminate-and-stay-resident (TSR) program you load whenever you expect a fax. You can load it from your AUTOEXEC.BAT file so that it is loaded into memory automatically when you turn on your computer.

A TSR will, as its name suggests, sit in memory until the ringing telephone line activates it. The fax software then leaps into action and performs the necessary tasks, such as answering the phone, sending the appropriate connection signals, and receiving the fax document.

TSRs are good and bad. They are good because you can run other software while they are waiting for the correct moment to activate. They are bad because you cannot always run other software while they are loaded into memory. A TSR may occupy too much memory so that you don't have sufficient memory remaining to load your other program, such as a word processor or spreadsheet. (This is true even if you have several megabytes of total memory in your computer.)

Alternatively, a TSR may not be completely compatible with your other software. This may be due to poor TSR program, but you can't do two things with the same serial port. For example, if you want to use an external fax modem to receive fax documents, you cannot use that serial port for any other purpose, such as attaching a mouse or plotter.

If you can make your application programs operate with the fax software's TSR program, you can load it each time you start your computer and be ready to receive a fax whenever the phone rings. If you load and unload the fax software TSR into memory, you must be aware of when you can receive a fax. Think of it as having a telephone answering machine that you must remember to turn on. If you want to receive a fax, the computer must be turned on. This means you will probably want the computer turned on all the time — at night and on weekends.

I do not use a fax modem for receiving fax documents unless I am expecting to receive a document within the next few minutes. I use my stand-alone fax machine and have it turned on permanently so that I do not miss a fax document. I change my computer configuration too often to be certain that the fax software will always be loaded.

Depending on your fax software program, the installation and removal of the TSR may be automated. Read the supplied documentation carefully to understand how you verify that you are prepared to receive fax documents.

Besides needing the software loaded in memory, you need the equivalent of having enough paper available. As explained in Chapter 4, fax documents are received as graphic images, and graphic images can be very large. You must always have plenty of room on your hard disk to accept the documents. Avoid using floppy disks for receiving many or long documents because their capacity is so limited.

This disk space requirement is another reason that I don't use a fax modem to receive documents. The usual document that I need to edit is written electronically, and I can use the data modem to transfer it as a text file, probably in my word processor's format, including all the style and page formatting. The usual fax document I receive is intended for reading and then discarding. It may be page proofs of an article, sales literature, or a confirmation of a fact.

Note: You cannot use the serial port or the phone line that is waiting for a fax document for another purpose at the same time. For example, you cannot use your data modem and receive a fax at the same time. Although this is obvious when sending a fax, it is not so obvious when you are using the computer for other purposes and expect the fax modem to automatically answer the phone.

Connecting to receive

If you have the fax software's TSR program for receiving a fax loaded into memory, you can use your computer as normal while waiting for a fax. When the phone rings, your fax modem will answer it. It then exchanges signals with the sending fax machine to establish a mutually compatible communications standard.

Unlike a data modem, where you can select a different transmission speed than the maximum, you want the fax modem to connect at the highest possible speed so that you receive the document as fast as possible. The fax machines will agree on a mutually compatible communications standard, and the document transfer will begin.

The sending fax transmits the document one line at a time. The receiving fax takes the data and stores it on the disk as a graphic image. When all the pages of the document have been received, or the transmission is stopped for some reason, the fax modem saves the document in a file on your hard disk. It is then available for viewing.

Knowing what you have received

It is vital that you understand that your fax modem saves a graphic image of a document. You have not received a document that can be directly edited in a word processor. The graphic image is stored as a series of bits of data, representing black dots on a white page of paper. The fax software probably includes a viewing utility so that you can see this image on-screen. If you have a printer that can print graphic images, you can print your document to your printer. This is equivalent to printing the document on a plain-paper stand-alone fax machine.

"How do I read my fax document?"

The viewing features in your fax software, if available, provide a way of reading your document. For single-page fax documents, such as a memo or short note, these features are adequate because you can read the information and then delete the file.

Pictures, sketches, and handwritten notes also can be read efficiently with your fax software's viewing features. Some viewers are quite sophisticated and include extra features. For example, some allow you to rotate the image, if the sender put a sheet of the document in upside down. Others allow you to adjust the contrast so that the document becomes more legible.

Multi-page documents can also be read in this way. However, as with all long documents on a computer, reading them from a video screen is not very efficient. You cannot see much at once, and you cannot refer to several places in the same document at once.

Avoid sending fax documents, particularly text, by inserting a page into a fax machine sideways, because the human eye can read text more easily with the lines of text running horizontally across the page. The problem is compounded with smaller text. The *vertical resolution* (the number of dots per inch) on a received fax document and its *precision* (its alignment with the previous row of dots) are much lower than the horizontal resolution and precision. On a fax modem, the precision is unaffected by the rotation, because the document is not physically moved through the fax machine, but the resolutions are still different. (If you don't believe me, try it and see.)

You have two alternatives to using your fax software's viewing features. You can print your document so that you have a hard copy to work from, or you can convert your fax file into another format so that it can be edited with your other application program. In some cases, conversion utilities are supplied with the fax software, and in most cases, so is a printing utility.

Printing your fax document

The print utility in your fax software will print your document on a printer that can print graphic images. These include Hewlett-Packard LaserJet, Epson graphic printers, and many other printers. The image stored as a series of dots is copied to your printer.

Printing fax documents can be extremely slow because the information is usually sent to the printer one line at a time. A single page may take several minutes to print. Again, the important thing to remember is that the fax document file is a graphic image and not text.

The fax modem has a tremendous advantage over many stand-alone fax machines because most printers use ordinary paper but most stand-alone fax machines use light-sensitive paper. The light-sensitive paper, as its name suggests, is affected by light. Fax documents, even when stored in file folders, tend to fade with time and should not be considered permanent. You must photocopy fax documents from most stand-alone fax machines to preserve the image. You only need to print fax documents from a fax modem to get a permanent image. (You can purchase stand-alone fax machines that use ordinary paper, but they tend to be more expensive.)

Converting your fax document

If you want to edit the fax document, you need to convert the received fax document into another form so that you can use it in other application programs. This file conversion falls into two main categories: graphic-image conversion and graphic-image-to-text conversion.

Some fax software includes graphic-file conversion utilities. You may have used the utility to change the graphic image form so that you could send a document. However, the reciprocal utility that can convert the received fax document format into another graphic-image format may not be available.

For example, the fax software may be able to convert from PCX and several different TIFF formats but only able to convert back to PCX format. Read the supported file format documentation very carefully. A third-party file-conversion program, such as HiJaak from Inset Systems, may be a valuable addition to your software library if you intend to handle graphic images in many forms.

Note: Even if the fax document sent was in color, the fax document is received in black and white. A conversion program is not going to restore the color for you.

"How do I get a text file from my fax document?"

Conversion of graphic images into text files, known as *optical character recognition* (OCR), is the only alternative for converting your fax documents into a form that can be read by a text editor or word processor. OCR software is not usually supplied with the fax software that is bundled with your modem.

Some scanners are supplied with OCR software, and many OCR programs are available from third parties. Some of these programs are excellent, fast, and accurate, and others are more or less useless. Because of its importance, OCR is covered in more detail in Chapter 11.

Beginners need to understand that OCR software takes the image of the page with text on it and examines what it considers to be a single letter. This small image is compared with the OCR software's library of letters, and a letter is chosen. The software then takes the next area and runs a similar comparison to determine the next letter.

In some cases, using OCR software is the only method of getting a document into electronic form. However, if you find you are making this conversion frequently with fax documents, evaluate whether you are making more work than is necessary. If the original document was in electronic form, you can probably use a data modem to transfer the file in electronic form. Even if you need to add formatting, such as fonts and centering, this approach probably will be more accurate and faster than using OCR software.

Summary

This chapter introduced sending and receiving fax documents with your fax modem. Although fax modems are an inexpensive form of fax machine, they require different preparation and document handling than stand-alone fax machines.

When sending fax documents, the document must be prepared in electronic form, converted into a form that the fax software can accept, and then sent, with or without a cover sheet. If you convert the file before sending, verify that the converted document looks as you expect.

When receiving fax documents, a TSR program must be loaded so that the fax modem is prepared to answer the phone. The received document can be viewed, printed, or converted into another file format. If you find that you are converting received documents frequently, consider using a data modem instead.

Part III takes you beyond the basics so that you can choose the best communications and fax software, streamline your communications, and perform special purpose communications.

PART

III

Survival and Efficiency Tools

Part III extends your communications knowledge beyond the basics of getting up and running. By the end of this part, you will know how to make the best use of your data modem, fax modem, communications software, and fax software.

Chapter 8 provides the launching point for this part. It introduces the types of opportunities for possible improvement. It explains whether the additional feature is software or hardware related or elementary or more advanced, so that you can read the details in the subsequent chapters.

Chapter 9 explains how to make the most of your data modem and its software. The chapter presents optimization guidelines that help you choose the most appropriate modem and software options.

Chapter 10 shows how you can streamline your communications. You learn when and how to use your communications software programming features and how to remove the drudgery and repetition. By employing these techniques, you can minimize your online expenses.

Chapter 11 explains how to make the most your fax modem and its software. It covers automation techniques and methods of reducing your expenses. It also provides guidelines on how to improve fax document quality and translation from graphics to text.

Chapter 12 covers special purpose communications. This includes using modems on the road, international communication, and communicating with a Macintosh. It also covers methods of controlling a remote computer, such as using remote control software or host mode in your communications software.

8

CHAPTER

Beyond the Basics

This chapter suggests many ways to make your modem communication easy, faster, and more efficient. Subsequent chapters provide more detail on the methods, but this chapter divides the possibilities into categories so that you can rapidly explore the opportunities. This chapter covers the following topics:

- ❖ Making the most of your equipment
- ❖ Potential software and modem improvements
- ❖ Potential fax software and fax modem improvements
- ❖ Alternative uses for modems or fax modems.

Making the Most of Your Equipment

Although electronic communication can be intimidating until you make a few connections and transfer a few files, the procedure soon becomes more routine. The general method of deciding who and what you are calling, dialing the phone number and making the connection, controlling the remote software and exchanging files, and then terminating the connection is the same for all the connections you are likely to make. These procedures apply regardless of whether you are using a data modem or a fax modem.

However, there are many ways you can improve your modem use beyond the basics. These techniques are similar to the difference between making yourself understood in a foreign language and holding an interesting conversation in that language.

As discussed in earlier chapters, telecommunicating involves making two modems communicate with each other over a telephone line. Each modem is attached to another device, such as a computer or printer, and you can control the remote device from your PC. Your task as a computer user is to choose options and settings that enable the modems and devices to establish and maintain a connection. The process is a logical series of events, and each stage has a variety of options.

Part II removes as many of the choices as possible so that you can make your first connection. As you may have noticed, however, there are many opportunities for improvements. These make establishing the connection more automated, make your actual communications faster, reduce your online time, or, in the case of fax documents, make the results higher quality.

Part III divides the improvements in each chapter. Chapter 8 sets the stage for the remaining chapters in this part. This chapter divides the potential improvements by separating the fax modem changes from the data modem and making two classes for data modems.

The first set of improvements (see Chapter 9) for the data modem connections is possible with most modems and communications software. The second set of improvements (see Chapter 10) applies mostly to communications software and gives you some indication of the power of the more advanced communications software. Fax modem techniques are discussed in Chapter 11. Chapter 12 discusses techniques possible in only the most advanced communications software.

Understanding Modem Features

Your modem is the serial device that takes the serial data supplied from your PC's serial port and modulates it into a form suitable for transmission along the telephone line. Similarly, the modem can take data sent from a remote modem and demodulate it into a form suitable for transmission from your modem to the serial port.

The modem is also programmable and can respond to commands sent from your PC. When you first power up, the modem is in *command mode* and ready to accept instructions. When switched to *data mode*, any data sent is passed to the remote modem. You can switch the modem from data mode to command mode by sending an escape sequence. You can then issue AT commands to instruct the modem.

"What other types of AT commands exist?"

The basic instructions, discussed in Chapter 5, include dialing a phone number or hanging up the phone. Most modems actually include many more commands; some support more than 100.

Although some commands are unique and you are unlikely to use them except in special circumstances, many are more general. For example, some modems (especially newer ones) have a speaker that can be controlled by AT commands. If your modem is buried in modular furniture, you may need to turn up the volume to hear it dial the phone. Conversely, if you use your modem late at night and do not want to wake other family members, you may want to turn down the speaker volume. (See Chapter 9, the section "Adjusting your speaker volume.") Obviously this is not an essential command, but it is valuable.

Your modem determines how it responds to commands and the other modem by examining internal storage areas. The modem's storage areas include integrated circuits or chips known as *read-only memory* (ROM) as well as memory areas known as *S-registers*. These areas are explained in more detail in Chapter 9, but the ROM contains unchangeable information placed by the modem manufacturer. Some S-registers contain information that remains stored in the modem even when the power is turned off; others give ongoing information about the modem's current status, but much of the information can be changed by using the appropriate AT commands. The S-registers contain information that determines such items as result codes (explained in Chapter 4) or how fast to dial a phone number.

"What's an S-register?"

Although you may need to alter a few S-registers, you won't need to change them all. Most people have only one or two preferred configurations. Your modem comes preprogrammed with the factory default settings. Some modems allow you to store other configurations as an alternative. This configuration, which allows you to store a collection of all your preferred S-register settings and other settings, is known as a *profile*.

"What is a profile?"

Additionally, you may wish to issue the same series of instructions to your modem every time you start your communications program. In this way, you can be certain that the modem is configured in the way you expect. You can configure your communications program so that it sends an *initialization string* of commands to your modem as soon as you start it.

"Why do I need an initialization string?"

Profiles and initialization strings are very important, especially if you will be calling different locations. If you only call your office PC, you will always use the same parameters. If you call, for example, several different BBSs or online services, the profiles and initialization strings become much more important.

Additionally, if you use more than one communications program, profiles and initialization strings are valuable. They enable you to use each program in the best possible way. Many modem owners may use multiple communications software programs without even realizing it. For example, you may use fax software and data communications software, or you may use a front-end program, such as that supplied when you register with Prodigy or another online service, and data communications software, such as QModem, Smartcom Exec, or Smartcom for Windows.

The optimum settings for your modem when you send a fax document may be completely different from the setting you use when you call a particular online service, which may in turn be completely different from the best settings for calling your office computer.

You can often adjust your modem settings from menu options within your communications programs. The more sophisticated the program, the more adjustments you can make without specifically issuing AT commands. For example, you may be able to choose the number of times the phone rings before the modem answers from a menu selection, such as Modem Configuration, or you may need to issue the AT command itself.

Altering the speaker volume or number of rings are commands that can be considered useful but not essential in particular user situations. Chapter 9 explores many available commands. However, no modem has all possible commands. Older modems in particular will have fewer available commands.

Other AT commands are more technical and control whether the modem uses error correction or compression when available or modem control when operating in synchronous mode. For most users, these settings should not be changed.

Besides the modem settings, your modem use will improve if you clearly understand how your modem is operating. As mentioned in Chapter 5, when your modem makes a connection, it sends result codes to your communications software that you may be able to see on-screen. For example, your screen may say `CONNECT 2400`.

To reduce online time, you should usually make the fastest connection possible and take advantage of error correction and compression. Although you may set these options, however, your modem can apply them only if the other modem can conform with these standards.

Chapter 9 discusses looking for information on how your modem has actually connected and how this knowledge affects your other selections, such as file-transfer protocol.

More on AT Commands

Chapter 5 introduces seven of the most important AT commands found in all AT-compatible modems. All modems include more commands than these seven, and some include more than 100 commands. Although there is an approved standard for AT commands, these represent only a small number of those actually found in modems.

Over the years, as communications standards have evolved, many manufacturers have produced modems that conform with the generally accepted previous AT commands and add new AT commands. Some of these additions may add proprietary communications standards, and others add user configuration convenience.

For example, when 9600 bps modems first became available, there were several different proprietary standards. If you had a 9600 bps modem, you could only communicate at 9600 bps with another modem of the same type. You could, however, communicate with other modems at 2400 bps by using the existing standards. These modems used (and still use) new AT commands to select the faster speed or otherwise change the modem configuration.

Other additions to the AT commands came from manufacturers trying to gain a market edge and have something different in their modems. Commands to store profiles, for example, are an enhancement to the standard AT command set.

The result is that there is no such thing as the complete AT command set, and even the most advanced modems do not include all the AT commands. In some cases, particular AT commands are implemented in different ways by different modems. These differences may be subtle or significant.

It doesn't matter that your modem does not include every single AT command. However, it is important that you know what AT commands your modem can support and use your communications software to take the best advantage of the commands that you do have. If you are purchasing a new modem or are using more than one modem type, you should compare the commands available in the two modems and see whether you need to reconfigure or even replace your communications software to get the best use out of your new modem.

For example, I own a very inexpensive but fast modem that does not perform as well as its more expensive competitors on noisy phone lines. A local BBS is a particular problem. As a result, I use a particular configuration with my inexpensive modem to help it connect with this BBS. It is not an ideal configuration, because the settings increase the chances of my getting communications errors. However, it makes the difference between being able to connect or not. When I use a different modem, I change its configuration to give me the best performance.

Understanding Communications Software Features

Your modem is controlled by software on your PC. Your communications software does not need to include many features. It must be able to send data to and receive data from the serial port and support a terminal emulation.

Even the most basic communications programs usually include the capability to send some AT commands to the modem by selecting options from the program's menus. However, these commands may be limited to resetting the modem, dialing a phone number, and hanging up the phone. You should be able to issue other AT commands directly from the terminal emulation screen.

To use this primitive type of communications program, you must be a sophisticated user or have very simple needs. As discussed in Chapter 4, if you find you have a primitive communications program and need more support, consider another program before giving up on telecommunicating.

"What extras are in my communications software?"

Most communications programs offer many more features than the absolute minimum. Your modem will work more or less with any of these programs, but you will get the best from your modem by using a good-quality communications program suitable for your task. This may involve using more than one communications program.

For example, the CompuServe Information Manager program supplied when you subscribe to CompuServe is not the most sophisticated communications program available, but it is one of the best for finding your way around CompuServe. It is written specifically to navigate CompuServe and help you read mail and find user forums, technical support areas, games areas, and other services without effort.

On the other hand, QModem is a more general-purpose communications program with some excellent advanced features. These include its "learn" feature where you can call a particular service or BBS and have the communications program record your keystrokes. With a little work, you can then use this learned sequence, known as a *script*, every time you call the service. The communications program will replay your keystrokes, saving you the repetition.

The most basic options in your communications program will include choosing the character format, speed, and terminal emulation. In almost all cases, your program will include a method of storing telephone numbers for online services that you call regularly.

Most communications programs, such as QModem and ProComm, have a dialing directory, which is equivalent to an electronic list of phone numbers. You can store some settings with each phone number. For example, apart from the phone number and name of the service, you can usually store such settings as the character format and speed. When you run your communications program, you select the service to connect with from this dialing directory.

Other communications programs, such as Smartcom Exec, organize around activities rather than using a dialing directory. Others, such as Smartcom for Windows, use both concepts. This metaphor is used on Apple Macintosh computers where all activities are stored as separate documents. Each online service or place you call with your modem is considered a separate activity. You select the activity by filename rather than from a list within your communications program.

The ease with which you can add more numbers to dial and the required specifications, such as speed and character format, also varies with the communications program. In most cases, you configure your communications program with a default set of information and then only customize the settings for specific connections.

Beyond the more basic options, a good communications program includes extra items that can streamline your modem use. The number and type of file-transfer protocols supported will affect your communications performance. You want a program that supports ASCII, XMODEM, and ZMODEM as a minimum. However, Kermit and YMODEM are desirable extras.

One particularly good alternative is to choose a communications program that allows you to add additional programs that can expand your communications features. Then, when a new file-transfer protocol becomes available, you can find an add-on program that supports the new standard and continue to use your current communications program. For example, the ZMODEM file-transfer protocol is available as an add-on program for many communications programs. You may be able to update your older communications program to include the relatively new standard.

"What is a capture file?"

You probably will want a communications program that supports session capture. The interaction that takes place from when you call the other modem until you hang up the phone is considered a *session*. The *capture file* stores a record of your online proceedings in a file on your disk so that you can read the events again. It's like tape-recording your online connection. You turn on or open the capture file, and everything you type and everything displayed on your computer screen is saved in this file. After you turn off or close the capture file (or exit the communications program), the file can be read by using a text editor, such as the EDIT program in MS DOS 5 or later versions.

You can use the capture file for a variety of purposes, including reading messages at leisure or listing the options available on the service you called. For example, if you call a new BBS, you can open a capture file, have a quick look around the service and list a few menus to see what's available, and then disconnect. By reading your capture file, you can determine whether the BBS includes messages or file areas or chat areas without reading and digesting all your options while online. Consider a capture file as a tape recorder that records everything that happens in session. It does not do anything more than record.

Scripts and *key macros* are another option in better communications programs. Scripts and key macros are similar to playing back portions of a recorded tape. A key macro feature allows you to assign a series of keystrokes to a single key press. For example, you may want to assign your password to a single key, such as F4. (Consider your security before you automate your passwords.) In this example, when an online service prompts you for your password, you can press F4 instead of typing all the characters of your password.

"Are scripts only for programmers?"

A script file is more complicated than a key macro, but all users can benefit from them. As its name suggests, script files play back information like a film script that contains instructions and dialog. For example, you can create a script that responds by typing the letters in your last name when it sees the prompt Last Name: from the online service. More-sophisticated script files can automate most, if not all, of your communications session.

You usually create a key macro for something you use in a variety of sessions. However, a script is tailored to a particular online service. For example, you may have one script file for calling your local BBS and another for calling the electronic mail service MCI Mail.

More-advanced communications software programs include a variety of tools for creating script files. Some have a programming language that you can use. For example, you may be able to include lines in the script that perform the equivalent of waiting for 10 seconds before responding, or pressing Y every time you see the prompt More (Y/N).

Some communications programs make creating script files relatively easy by including a learning feature that records the information sent by the remote computer and your responses and makes the first draft at generating a script.

"Why do I need an offline reader?"

Another feature, particularly useful when calling BBSs for messages, is a communications program that supports an *offline reader.* The offline reader may be incorporated into the communications program or may be available as an add on product.

An offline reader is useful when you call a BBS or other online service that also supports offline readers. You choose a special menu item and the BBS automatically collects all the messages you have requested into a file and downloads that file to your computer. You then log off from the BBS and read the messages with your offline mail reader without being connected to the BBS.

Chapters 9 and 10 discuss making the most of your communications program and consequently making the most of your modem. To make all your options digestible, Chapter 9 focuses on your software configuration, including modem profiles and initialization strings. Chapter 10 partly assumes an understanding of Chapter 9 and covers the options possible with some communications programs to remove the repetitious portions of communicating and speed your communications so that you reduce online time.

Although you may not want to get involved with the details of configuring your modem, Chapter 10 can automate your connection at a simple level. For example, you can use a script (rather like replaying a series of recorded keystrokes) to automate connecting with online services.

More-sophisticated scripts and offline readers can completely automate your connection. For example, I call a national BBS and automatically download messages, find new files, and log off the system. I only select the phone number to dial; the rest is automated. I am only online for 10 to 15 minutes, but I collect messages that take me between 1 and 2 hours to read, which enables me to keep current at minimal expense. (See Chapter 10, the section, "Understanding offline mail readers.")

Tip: When you use a front-end communications program, supplied with your subscription to an online service, such as CompuServe, Prodigy, or America Online, many of the enhancements suggested in this section are not possible. The front-end program does a good job of streamlining your interface with the system, because the communications program is tailor-made for that service. However, you should look at the configuration settings in these programs to see whether you can make some alterations. For example, you may be able to send an initialization string before connecting, but you are unlikely to be able to alter all aspects of your connection.

Understanding Fax Features

As with stand-alone fax machines, you can purchase fax modems with varying degrees of sophistication. At its most basic, the fax modem must be able to take a file containing the image you want to send and deliver it to the remote fax machine as well as receive the image from a remote fax machine and save the image as a file. It must be able to dial the phone number, establish the connection, transfer the file, and break the connection.

Fax modems in PCs are a more recent development than data modems. Additionally, the task involved in transferring the file from one modem to the other involves fewer options and variables than are possible with data modems.

Like data modems, fax modems accept AT commands, and different fax modems support different AT commands. However, like data modems, all fax modems support the minimum necessary AT commands, and many support additional ones.

You can generally buy a data modem and use any communications software with it. The modem is independent of the communications software. Your modem may not support all the features of your communications software, but you can successfully use the software with any modem.

Apart from speed, you have far fewer features to choose from when selecting a fax modem. Most of the variability of features between fax modem features comes from the supplied software rather than the hardware, and fax modems are not as independent as data modems. When choosing a fax modem, choose carefully. Unlike data modems, which will work with your selection of communication programs, your fax modem may not work with alternative fax software.

Understanding Fax Software Features

Because of the typical fax modem's lack of independence, you probably will use the fax software supplied with your fax modem rather than purchasing separate fax modem software. However, you should consider third-party utility software to enhance your fax modem's software.

The fax software must be capable of taking an image stored on disk and getting it to the remote fax machine. Additionally, it must be capable of receiving a fax document.

"What extras do I need in my fax software?"

The desirable extras for fax software fall into two categories: control and flexibility preparing *for* and *during* the communications session and flexibility with document handling *before* transmission and *after* receipt. The control you want for preparing the document is comparable to the control and flexibility you want from a data modem. The document-handling features are unique to fax documents and do not have a data modem equivalent.

Your fax modem can accept AT commands like a data modem. However, it uses fewer AT commands because there are fewer necessary alternatives. For example, your fax modem must be able to dial the telephone and hang up the phone. Your fax communications software will probably hide most of the communications features within menu selections, which usually are named System Configuration.

After you choose the desired configuration, you probably won't change it again. Unlike a data modem, where you need different configurations depending on the service you are calling, almost all of your fax documents will be sent to similar systems, and reconfiguration is not necessary. However, you may be able to improve your configuration after the initial installation. After you have managed to send and receive a couple of fax documents, you should review your configuration to see whether any changes can be made.

The fax modem configuration is the area you need to consider if you find that your fax modem is no longer working. This will probably occur because you changed your computer configuration in some way. For example, if you change CONFIG.SYS or AUTOEXEC.BAT, your fax modem may no longer work. Chapter 11 provides a checklist of techniques for reviewing your fax software configuration.

As explained in Chapter 7, consider your fax modem like a stand-alone fax machine or an answering machine. You can receive faxes only if your computer is turned on and the terminate-and-stay-resident (TSR) program is loaded. Most problems with receiving fax documents relate to this TSR.

Your software may have different options for receiving fax documents. You may, for example, be able to print each document automatically upon receipt or place the documents into a separate area of your hard disk. Other desirable options for sending fax documents relate to ease of use and quality of the document. You can store fax machine phone numbers in a dialing directory, for example. Or, you can optionally enhance the fax document you send by adding a cover sheet to your document or by adding your company logo or signature to the document.

More-advanced fax software may allow you to prepare multiple fax documents and send them all at one time. Alternatively, you can send the same fax document to multiple people. Or, you can schedule the document sending time to take advantage of lower telephone rates. In this case, a feature for turning off the modem's speaker may be very important. You might want to keep a transaction log showing what you sent to whom and when. (See Chapter 11.)

When sending documents, you must import your document in a format that your fax modem software can understand. As explained in Chapter 7, there are several approaches to this, including using screen capture utilities or capturing the output from an application program by using a fax software utility program that can capture the data you would ordinarily send to a printer. Few, if any, fax software programs are exceptional in this area.

However, many third-party programs can perform good file translation when your fax modem software does not match your application software file formats. Remember that your application program, such as a word processor or spreadsheet, may be able to do the translation so that your fax software can accept the document.

When you receive documents, you want to read them and possibly convert them into another format, including text. Again, fax software programs usually are not exceptional in this area. Ideally, your fax software should include the capability to view your received documents and rotate them so they are readable without you standing on your head. Documents can easily be sent sideways or upside-down from a stand-alone fax machine.

Like sending documents, you can use third-party file-conversion programs to change the format of the received document into a format that one of your graphic programs can read. However, you may wish to convert a received fax into text so that it can be edited as text.

Be certain that you are using the correct tool for the job. If you want to edit a text document, consider the possibility of transferring the document as a file by using a data modem rather than a fax modem. This will preserve the accuracy of the file as well as keep all the formatting features of the document.

If the document was not in electronic form, or a data modem is not available, you need to use an optical character recognition (OCR) program to convert the received fax, which is a graphical image of the document, into text. Chapter 11 presents OCR software and techniques you can use to help improve your conversion accuracy. It also includes techniques for improving the document quality of sent and received faxes.

Understanding Remote Control Software

As covered in Chapter 5, you can make your modem communicate with another modem via your communications software. This remote modem is also controlled by communications software. In the case of online services, the remote computer runs special communications software, often BBS software. In the case of your calling a friend or your office, the remote computer is probably running a general-purpose communications program similar to your own.

When you call an online service, you can control your end of the communications link and the remote end. The remote computer displays lists of available commands, and you type your requests. When you call your friend, however, you have two people involved—one at each end of the connection. Each person controls his or her own end of the connection.

To transfer a file from one computer to another, the following is the general procedure:

1. The first person activates the upload command and specifies the filename and file-transfer protocol.

2. The second person activates the download command and specifies the filename and file-transfer protocol.

3. The second computer recognizes the signals to transmit being sent from the first computer, and the file transfer occurs.

Having two people involved in the connection is often not practical. The person calling the remote computer wants control of both computers. This is important in two situations, the previously described case where you want to transfer information from one computer to another and the case where you want to control the remote computer as if you were sitting at the remote computer.

The first case, where you only want to control both ends of the connection to save someone typing commands at the remote computer, is possible with more-advanced communications programs. You don't have to use special BBS software but can activate a feature in your communications software known variously as *host mode* or *remote access*.

"How do I control my office computer from home?"

Again, the performance and flexibility of these features depends on the communications program. However, the general idea is that you can set up your computer so that it is like a mini-BBS. The caller can control both ends of the connection and download or upload files or perhaps read messages as if he or she were calling a BBS. You may want to set up your office computer in this mode so that you can call and collect data when you are at home.

I find this setup particularly useful when someone needs to call me and collect files, but he or she has only one phone line. The host mode provides the caller with menu prompts and options. If I am controlling my end of the connection, I need to talk someone through the process on a second phone line, or I need to switch between chatting and file transfer. This can be especially disconcerting for callers who have not done much telecommunicating.

The other situation where you want control of the remote computer is when you want to use the remote computer as if you were seated at the remote computer's keyboard. For example, you may want to call your office from home and use the word processor and files stored on your office computer as if you were actually in the office. You want to press keys on your home computer and have the appropriate keystrokes activate the commands on the remote computer.

This type of software is called *remote control software*. You run a TSR on your office computer, and when you call from home by using the special communications software, you can control the remote computer. This is like your office computer having two keyboards and two displays — with one keyboard and one display in your home. Host mode and other remote control operations are covered in Chapter 12.

Understanding Special Situations

Most of this book has focused on the most general communications situations where you call another modem from your computer, but your computer is always located in the same place and is attached to the same telephone line.

In some cases, you need to use your modem or fax modem in more unusual situations. You may want to use your modem from a hotel room or send a fax from a public pay phone. Using your modem on the road is becoming easier every day as more hotels, airports, and even road rest areas become aware of communication needs. However, these special situations bring their own unique problems to the table, and Chapter 12 solves the most common.

Other special communication situations may or may not pose a problem. In some cases, the problems are perceived rather than real, such as taking your modem overseas and calling overseas with your modem. Calling overseas is at one level a perceived problem in that you only add more numbers to the dialing string. However, you may be dealing with different standards, and the two modems may not talk to each other because each follows its own standard. Taking your modem overseas and getting it through customs and plugged in and working are very real problems. In some cases, you will have your equipment confiscated at the border. Plugging in is often impossible if not illegal.

You also can use your modem to communicate with another type of computer. The perceived problem is linking with another computer type. Remember that your modem is communicating with another modem. The remote modem can be attached to any sort of computer, including Macintosh or mainframe. Chapter 12 covers the potential problems, typically perceived rather than real, of communicating with another computer type.

Summary

This chapter introduced some of the myriad ways you can enhance your communicating beyond the basics. These improvements include simple tasks, such as reconfiguring your communications software and your modems to use them to their full potential, as well as more-involved options, such as taking advantage of extra features in your communications programs.

Depending on your specific communications needs, you may want to make elementary changes that make the best use of the hardware and software that you own. These enhancements are covered in Chapter 9. Chapter 10 extends these enhancements to cover features possible only with more-sophisticated communications programs or by using add-on programs with your current communications program.

Your fax modem can be a particularly useful tool when used correctly—or a boat anchor when not used appropriately. Chapter 11 shows how to make the best use of your fax modem and its software for sending and receiving fax documents. The value of third-party software is also included in the discussion in that chapter.

9

CHAPTER

Making the Most of Your Modem and Software

This chapter presents techniques for making the most of your modem and communications software. In particular it covers the following topics:

❖ Configuring your modem

❖ Using AT commands to tailor the configuration

❖ Understanding profiles and initialization strings

❖ Understanding connection speed and compression

❖ Choosing serial port options

Reconfiguring Your Modem and Software

After making your first connections and transferring a few files, you should reconsider your modem's configuration and the communications software configuration. As you become more experienced with calling other modems, you move from needing guidance every step of the way to connecting faster, wringing an extra ounce of performance from your modem, and streamlining your communications.

This chapter focuses on choosing the best configuration for your modem in your particular situation and for your communication needs. These techniques take your configuration from a general-purpose modem to an optimized version. Most suggestions in this chapter relate to improving how your modem works, and Chapter 10 focuses on methods for streamlining the communications session itself.

You may find that you cannot achieve all the optimization suggested. You may not have a modem that contains all features, or you may not have a communications program with all the relevant options.

Modem type selection

When you first install your modem and communications software, you make selections relating to the serial port assignment and port addresses. You probably select the modem type from a list within your communications program. (Some communications programs can automatically choose a modem type, and others allow you to choose for yourself.)

Unless you can see the precise modem model on your communications software list of selections, you probably choose the option of Hayes-compatible, AT-compatible, or generic Hayes modem. You may choose based on your modem's speed, such as 2400 bps or V.32.

Consider re-examining your modem type selection to see whether a better match exists for your modem. Although your modem may claim to be "fully Hayes-compatible," there is actually no such thing. Not only do the modem manufacturers have their own interpretation of compatible, but the communications software manufacturers also have their own version.

"What modem type do I choose in my software?"

Additionally, some modems may have different models with the same features, and your communications program may supply the best configuration for one version but you own another.

Selecting the most appropriate modem type in your communications software is like understanding local dialects or even more subtle language differences, such as the difference between the American and English pronunciations of *mall*. Americans make "mall" rhyme with "doll," and the English make it rhyme with "shall." In both cases, the same word is being spoken, but they are not heard as the same word.

You should pay special attention to your modem type selection if you have an unusual modem or one that supports a proprietary standard. Some differences exist because the 9600 bps standard was slowly accepted over a period of years. Users were clamoring for faster speeds before there was a 9600 bps standard that was affordable for PC modems. Several modem manufacturers created a proprietary standard. These modems could communicate at 9600 bps with another modem from the same manufacturer but only at 2400 bps with another manufacturer's modem. Since that time, the V.32 standard has been accepted, and 9600 bps communications between different manufacturers' modems is possible.

However, if you have one of these older USRobotics 9600 bps modems, it may support the HST proprietary standard. This is not compatible with the older equivalent (speedwise) Hayes V-Series 9600 bps modem when the modems try to operate at 9600 bps. If you choose the Hayes V-Series instead of the USRobotics in your communications software, you will not connect at 9600 bps — but only at 2400 bps.

In addition to the modem's communications standards, there are differences between the supported AT commands. For example, one modem may allow you to store two profiles while another allows three. If you choose the modem type that supports only two profiles in your communications software, you won't have access to the third profile. There also may be differences between the way two modems from different manufacturers implement the same AT command.

Even if your communications software lists your modem's product name specifically, you may want to alter or add to its configuration. Most communications software programs allow you to choose and add to the supplied settings. Wherever possible, retain the original configuration, and create a copy of it for experimentation. You can then return to the original if necessary.

Finding what your modem can do

Before exploring details of S-registers and other configuration settings, you need your modem operating manual to determine whether particular AT commands are available. The manual supplies lists and tables showing the available commands and summaries of their purposes.

Some modems, such as the Practical Peripherals 9600 SA modem, include an AT command that supplies information about the modem. From your communications program's terminal screen, type **AT$H** and press Enter. If the command is supported, you see the first of several screens of information about your modem, including the supported command list. Use Print Screen to print this information to your printer for reference. If your modem does not support this command, you will see the message ERROR when you press Return.

Understanding S-Registers

As explained in Chapter 8, your modem contains storage areas where data is stored. Some data is permanent, and some can be adjusted by the user. The permanent data is stored in *read-only memory* (ROM), and the more alterable data is stored in *nonvolatile memory*. Nonvolatile memory is memory for which the current contents are preserved when you remove power. However, you can change the contents by sending appropriate AT commands.

"What is an S-register?"

The memory areas can be compared with the memory areas in a PC. The ROM in a PC contains permanent data that is used, in part, to boot the computer when you first turn it on. The PC (except for early models) also contains nonvolatile memory. This memory contains, in part, the date and time. Although the date and time are preserved when you turn off power to the computer, you can issue a DOS command to alter the date or time.

The ROM in a modem contains a variety of information, including the factory default configuration. Part of the nonvolatile memory area is a series of storage locations called S-registers. The S-registers, which are numbered, contain the settings that your modem uses. For example, one register named S0 contains the setting for the number of rings the modem must receive before answering the phone. The register S1 contains the number of rings the modem has received. (Register S0 is a register you may wish to change, but register S1 is a register you won't want to change.)

For the most part, the S-registers are implemented in the same way regardless of the modem. However, different modems contain different S-registers. For example, a 2400 bps modem may contain 28 S-registers, and a 9600 bps modem may contain 96 S-registers.

Note: Arbitrarily changing the values of S-registers may make your modem stop working or work erratically. Change only the registers you need, and learn the reset command to remove any errors you have made.

Reading S-registers

Before changing any S-registers, you need to know what they currently contain. To view the contents of a particular S-register type **ATS*n*?** (where *n* is the particular S-register number) and press Enter. For example, to view the contents of S1, you type **ATS1?**. To view the contents of S0, you type **ATS0?**.

You can view the contents of several registers at once by stringing your requests together on a single command line. For example, to view the ASCII values for the Escape code character, the carriage return character, the line feed character, and the backspace character, stored in registers S2, S3, S4, and S5 respectively, you type **ATS2?S3?S4?S5?** and press Enter.

Your modem returns with something comparable to the following:

```
OK
ATS2?S3?S4?S5?
043
013
010
008
OK
```

(If you can't see what you're typing on-screen, remember to turn on local echo so that the modem will echo the characters back to the screen.)

Note: Local echo is typically a toggle in your communications program. For example, it is assigned to Alt+E in QModemPro, and is an option called Local character echo in the terminal settings in Smartcom for Windows. (Chapter 5 covers this in more detail.)

The example shows the values you probably will find in your modem. However, as covered in Chapter 5, you can change any of these values.

You probably will view an S-register's contents just before changing it. For example, if you think that your modem is dialing slowly, you will at the relevant S-register (S11) determine the meaning of its value and change to a new value that makes the modem dial more quickly.

If you want to know the values of all your alterable S-registers, you will probably view the profile for your modem — if your modem supports profiles — rather than explicitly calling each S-register's value. Profiles are covered in the later section, "Understanding Profiles."

Changing an S-register

You can change the value stored in an S-register by using the appropriate AT command. You type **ATS***n=value* and press Enter.

For example, to change the value of S0 to four and instruct the modem to answer the phone after four rings, you type **ATS0=4** and press Enter. Your modem responds with OK to indicate that it has accepted and executed a command. In this case, the number you type is an actual number and represents the number of rings the modem should receive before answering the telephone.

However, other S-registers, such as S2, contain a number, but the number represents something other than a number. For example, S2 contains the ASCII code for the Escape-code-sequence character. S12's contents determine the amount of guard time around the Escape-code sequence, expressed in 0.02 seconds (1/50 seconds). If you enter the value 50, the guard time is one second.

You should verify that you changed the register you intended by issuing a read command and checking that the new value is in the register.

You may never need to alter an S-register setting. But, by reading your modem manual carefully, you can get a performance improvement in many cases (by increasing the speed of dialing, for example) or can otherwise tailor the configuration to your particular situation (by instructing the modem to answer the phone only after ringing five times, for example).

However, you need to understand S-registers and know how to change them in two circumstances. If your modem starts behaving strangely, you may need only to change an S-register value. Alternatively, if you find something slightly unusual about your configuration, such as your modem dialing a telephone number before it gets a dial tone, you can change the S-register to make the modem work in your situation.

If you do need to alter an S-register's setting, look carefully to see whether you can make the change once and make the modem and communications software change the setting automatically each time by using profiles and/or initialization strings. These topics are covered later in this chapter in the sections "Understanding Initialization Strings," and "Understanding Profiles."

Valuable Commands

Chapter 5 introduces seven AT commands that all modem users should know. These include dialing a phone number and hanging up the phone. Even when explaining only the basic AT commands, other AT commands crept into the explanation to give you some idea of the flexibility of your modem's configuration.

So that your modem works when you first install it, your modem manufacturer creates a default configuration that works for many installations. However, most modems, especially the newer more advanced ones, have settings that involve personal preferences. As a result, you may prefer to make adjustments away from the factory default.

Before changing any modem settings, verify that your modem and communications software are installed and operating. The time to fine-tune your installation is after you have the basics working. Do not try to change everything at once.

The following sections introduce AT commands that have widespread usefulness. If you have a special situation, you may need other commands that are not included in this chapter. Refer to Appendix A, "AT Command Set," for ideas for further changes you might make.

Modifying your dial command

As presented in Chapter 4, the dial command is ATD followed by the desired phone number. To dial by using tones, you use ATDT, and to dial by using pulses, you use ATDP. So, to call 555-5555, you might issue the command **ATDT 555-5555**.

The sequence of characters the command comprises are known as a *string*. In this case, the characters ATDT 555-5555 are the dialing string. Most modems ignore spaces, hyphens, or parentheses in the dialing string, so you can add them for clarity. However, your modem dials fractionally faster if you leave them out.

If you use your communications software to issue this command, you probably will select tone or pulse dialing during the installation and enter the phone number in the dialing directory.

However, in many cases, you need to use a different arrangement. Keep in mind that the modem does exactly as you instruct and will probably do it faster than you could manually. If you need to pause during dialing, you will need to tell the modem to pause. If you need to dial a 1 in front of the number, you need to tell your modem.

The pause modifier

Including a comma (,) in your dialing string makes the modem pause. For example, if you use **ATDT 9,555-5555,** your modem dials the 9, pauses, and then dials the rest of the phone number.

The modem waits for the number of seconds specified in S-register S8. The factory default is usually two seconds.

The wait modifier

The wait modifier is different from the pause modifier. When you issue the dial command, the modem usually takes the phone off the hook and waits for a specified period of time before dialing. The modem does not attempt to detect a dial tone. The length of time that the modem waits is specified by the contents of S6, which usually is set as a default of 2 seconds, and on most modems, the minimum wait is 2 seconds regardless of the S6 contents.

Note: Whether to look for a dial tone when issuing a dialing command without the wait modifier is enabled and disabled as one of the result code options. If you choose a particular version of extended result code (by issuing the AT command ATX2), you can make the modem always look for a dial tone.

Including a W in your dialing string makes the modem wait for a dial tone before continuing. When the modem processes the W in the dialing string, it waits until it hears a dial tone, in which case it continues to process the rest of the dialing string, or if it does not hear a dial tone within the time specified in S7, it hangs up the phone. Depending on the selected result code format, you may see the NO DIALTONE result code if the dial tone is not detected within the specified time.

S7 is used for two purposes. If you use the W modifier in your dialing string, it controls the time the modem must wait before giving up on finding a dial tone. S7 also controls the amount of time the modem must wait before giving up on getting a carrier signal from a remote modem. The default value in S7 is often 30 seconds or greater. This allows time for the modem to dial the number, the remote telephone to ring, and the remote modem to pick up the phone and send a carrier signal.

You can use the W modifier in front of your phone number or in the middle of the number. In a situation where you get a dial tone when you pick up the phone receiver, you can allow the modem to "dial blind" and not actually listen for a dial tone. You probably need to use W in the middle of a dialing string when you have to dial a number to get an outside line and then have to wait for a telephone exchange to give you a dial tone. The necessary delay may vary, and in some cases, you may not get a dial tone if all the outside lines are busy. In this case, the W modifier can be a better alternative than the pause modifier.

Note: Your modem can detect only a normal dial tone. Other dial tones may not be recognized by the modem, such as separate tones for internal and external phone lines.

To instruct the modem to wait for a dial tone, place the W within the dial string. For example, if you use **ATDT 9W555-5555**, your modem takes the phone off the hook, pauses for the time specified in S6 or 2 seconds (whichever is longer), and then dials 9. It then waits until it hears a dial tone or for the time specified in S7. If it hears a dial tone, it continues dialing 555-5555. If it does not hear a dial tone, it hangs up the phone and sends the result code NO DIALTONE to the serial port.

Dealing with long dialing strings

When you issue a dialing command, the command is accepted by the modem and temporarily stored in a buffer. This buffer is limited in size, and as a consequence, there is a limit to the length of a dialing string. For example, the buffer may be limited to 36 characters.

The length of the dialing string does not include the spaces, hyphens, or parentheses if your modem ignores them, but it does include the ATDT in front. In some cases, especially if you are calling internationally or from a hotel room, this limitation can be a problem.

"*How do I dial a long telephone number?*"

When you issue a dialing command, the modem usually dials the number and then switches out of command mode in preparation for communicating with the remote modem. If you end your dialing string with the semicolon modifier (;), you can make the modem stay in command mode, ready to receive another AT command.

You can use this modifier to divide your dialing string into multiple parts and overcome the buffer size limitation. Suppose that you want to call a modem from your hotel room and want to use a long-distance telephone service credit card. You may need to dial a digit to get an outside line, an 800 number to access the long-distance service, enter your security code, and then dial the actual phone number. The two telephone numbers are 10 or 11 digits each, and the security code may be 14 digits, and that does not include any pauses or waits or the ATDT portion. You can quickly rack up long strings.

Additionally, you may want to keep the dialing string portion related to the long-distance carrier separate from the actual phone number your are dialing in your communications program. Most communications programs allow you to specify a prefix that must be added to all telephone numbers, and some allow you to store multiple prefixes. When you work from your office, you use the simple prefix; when on the road, you use the more extensive one.

The semicolon must appear as the last digit of your dialing string. Your modem responds with OK after each dialing string is sent. Remember not to put a semicolon at the end of the last portion of the dialing string so that the modem will switch out of command mode and prepare for a connection.

For example, you may issue the following command:

```
ATDT 9,1-800-555-1212;
```

The modem responds with OK, and then you can issue the remainder of a dialing string, such as:

```
ATDT ,555-5555
```

The modem treats the two strings as if they were a single one. Remember that you must issue the dialing command itself both times, and you do not place the semicolon after the final dialing string.

Monitor for busy

Another feature that can speed your dialing and redialing is making the modem detect a busy signal. When a busy signal is detected, the modem hangs up the phone and awaits your next command, which probably will be repeat the last command so that you can retry the number as soon as possible (see the section "Repeat the last command").

To monitor for busy, you must know the various result codes options. The AT command that adjusts the result codes is **ATX***n*, where n is 0, 1, 2, 3, or 4.

The command **ATQ** or **ATQ0** enables result codes. To disable result codes, use **ATQ1**. In almost all circumstances, you need result codes enabled. The factory default typically enables result codes.

The command **ATV** or **ATV0** enables the short form of result codes. As explained in Chapter 5, short result codes return a number rather than a word such as CONNECT or BUSY. In most cases, you want to enable the long version of result codes unless you are using specialized computer equipment. Use the command **ATV1** to enable them. The modem's factory default typically enables long result codes.

After you enable result codes and choose the long version of result codes so that words rather than numbers are returned from the modem, you can choose between the various ATXn commands.

ATX0 offers 300 bps compatibility. The modem does not recognize dial tones or busy signals. However it does send the result code CONNECT when a connection is made.

ATX1 is slightly more advanced than ATX0. The modem returns such result codes as CONNECT, CONNECT 1200, or CONNECT 2400 depending on your connection speed (300, 1200, or 2400 bps respectively in this example). As with ATX0, the modem does not recognize dial tones or busy signals.

ATX2 is slightly more advanced than ATX1. The modem looks for a dial tone before dialing and reports NO DIALTONE if one is not found within 5 seconds. It sends the connect result codes found with ATX1.

ATX3 is similar to ATX2 except that it does not recognize a dial tone and does recognize a busy signal.

ATX4 is the most advanced and usually the preferred setting for result codes because it supplies the most information and detects the most things. You see the connect messages that tell you how fast your connection speed is, and the modem can detect a dial tone and busy signal. On most modems, ATX4 is the default setting; however, your communications program may change this value.

By making your modem detect a busy signal, you can learn sooner whether your telephone connection can be made and attempt a redial. These result codes are particularly important when you use a modem without a speaker or with the speaker volume turned down. Some modems may dial the number very loudly, but the busy signal or ringing may be much fainter.

You may need to select a redial-enabled option in your communications program. The communications program probably can look for a BUSY result code from your modem and act on it by automatically redialing the number. However, some communications programs make this an optional part of the configuration.

In QModemPro, for example, you specify the modem result codes that QModemPro should consider as a successful and unsuccessful connection. (The typical values are supplied.)

Repeat the last command

The A/ command allows you to repeat the last command. You use this command when you dial a number and find it is busy. Your communications software may use this command automatically if it has an automatic redialing feature.

Note: This is one of the two commands that do not start with AT. (The other is the escape sequence.)

To repeat the last command, you type **A/**. Unlike the other AT commands, you do not follow it by pressing Enter.

Adjusting speaker volume

Most early model modems that included a speaker had a knob on the back that you could adjust to alter the volume of the speaker. You can change the volume of newer modems that have a speaker by using AT commands.

You should choose a modem that contains a speaker so that troubleshooting is easier. However, you might choose a modem without a speaker in special situations. For example, a portable modem that you want to take on the road may be smaller if it does not include a speaker. The weight and size benefits may outweigh the benefits of having a speaker.

"How do I turn off the speaker?"

The speaker can be enabled or disabled by using the **ATM*n*** command. ATM0 turns the speaker off all the time. ATM1, usually the default setting, leaves the speaker on until the data carrier signal is detected.

ATM2 leaves the speaker on all the time. In this case, you can hear the noise made as data is sent between the two modems. Although this is interesting, when you've heard it once, it's not usually a desirable option.

ATM3 turns the speaker on after dialing and leaves it on until the data carrier signal is detected. This allows you to hear the negotiation for the transmission speed and protocols between the two modems, but you do not have to listen to the phone being dialed.

Most people want the speaker to be set with the ATM1 command. Of more interest is the speaker volume command. The volume is controlled with the **ATL*n*** command where n is 0, 1, 2, or 3. ATL0 and ATL1 make the volume low. ATL2, usually the default, gives a medium volume and ATL3 a loud volume.

Warning: Depending on your modem, the speaker can be extremely loud and even make the unit vibrate. I had a modem that had a volume control knob on the back, and the slightest adjustment changed the volume from a discrete set of bleeps to an alarm clock that could wake the dead. A different modem, controlled by software commands, literally shakes when set to a high speaker volume. (I assume that the speaker is not mounted firmly in the chassis. It is still under warranty, but it seems a petty thing to send it back for repair!)

Understanding Initialization Strings

As explained earlier in this chapter, your modem contains two main areas of memory: ROM and nonvolatile memory. The ROM contains information that cannot be changed; the nonvolatile memory contains information that can be changed. The S-registers are numbered storage areas in the nonvolatile memory. Some S-registers are intended to be changed by the user, while others are changed by the modem during operation.

Your modem contains a set of default settings that are applied each time you turn on your modem. The stored configuration is called the *factory configuration* or *factory profile*.

You may be able to specify an alternative group of settings that are automatically loaded when you turn on the modem. (See the section "Understanding Profiles.")

The default settings applied when you turn on your modem are copied into the from the factory profile into another set of memory. This copy is called the active configuration. This is the copy that you alter when you issue AT commands and alter S-registers.

Certain parameters, although they can be changed by your issuing AT commands, are not saved when you turn off the modem. When you turn the modem back on again, the factory settings are placed in the active configuration.

For example, the ASCII value for the carriage return character, stored in register S3, is restored to the factory default whenever the modem is repowered or reset.

"What is an initialization string?"

Most communications programs include an option in the modem configuration that allows you to change the modem's configuration from the default to your desired setting. This *initialization string* is a sequence of AT commands that is sent to the modem every time you start your communications program.

Note: The initialization string provides a method of sending a predefined set of commands to your modem using your communications program. A profile on the other hand is the modem's method of being able to restore a standard configuration to itself.

Some communications programs, such as Smartcom for Windows, include additional configuration commands that are comparable to an initialization string. For example, in Smartcom for Windows you can save two different modem setups (two initialization strings), a string that is sent prior to dialing, a string that is sent before answering, and a string to send after hanging up.

If you use your modem's profiles, you will be able to select a profile in the initialization string. If you are not using an alternative profile from the manufacturer's default, you can send a series of AT commands that change the desired parameters by saving it as an initialization string.

If you are using profiles, your best initialization string is probably ATZ0 or ATZ1 which reset the modem and restores the profile number 0 or 1 respectively.

The initialization string is particularly important if you use more than one communications program. You will have a preferred set of parameters for each program, and using an initialization string makes it possible to assume that the modem is the same configuration each time you run a program.

As you investigate the online world, you will find that initialization strings are a regular topic in messages. Although there is actually no perfect initialization string, the sequence of commands AT&F&C1&D2 is a good generic command string. However, because it restores the factory defaults, it does not include any personal preferences described in this chapter.

&F restores the factory defaults, &C1 makes the modem track the status of the remote modem's carrier signal, and &D2 makes the modem track the computer's data terminal ready (DTR) signal and hang up the phone and return to command mode when DTR is lowered.

My personal initialization string is only ATZ, but I use profiles to store a long sequence of AT commands that set many options, including the speaker volume, result code format, as well as making the modem track the remote modem's carrier signal and monitoring DTR.

Understanding Profiles

As discussed earlier, your modem may include the ability to store one or more configurations known as profiles. The modem will come with a factory default profile in ROM; however, you may be able to add alternatives.

By using an AT command, you can load a profile from nonvolatile memory into your modem's active configuration. This command overwrites the configuration currently stored in the active configuration with the information stored in the profile.

You can use other AT commands to write the information currently stored in the active configuration into a profile. Other AT commands allow you to select one of the profiles as the one that is loaded into the active configuration when you turn on your modem. You can also restore the factory default profile with another AT command.

Viewing the stored profile

The profile includes AT commands and some S-register settings. You can view the profiles stored in your modem by typing **AT&V** command and pressing Enter. Figure 9-1 shows an example of the response from a modem.

```
OK
at&v
ACTIVE PROFILE:
B1 E0 L2 M1 N1 Q0 T V1 W2 X4 Y0 &C1 &D2 &G0 &J0 &K3 &Q5 &R0 &S0 &T4 &X0 &Y0
S00:000 S01:000 S02:043 S03:013 S04:010 S05:008 S06:002 S07:060 S08:002 S09:006
S10:014 S11:050 S12:050 S18:000 S25:005 S26:001 S36:007 S37:000 S38:020 S44:003
S46:138 S48:007 S49:008 S50:255

STORED PROFILE 0:
B1 E0 L2 M1 N1 Q0 T V1 W2 X4 Y0 &C1 &D2 &G0 &J0 &K3 &Q5 &R0 &S0 &T4 &X0
S00:000 S02:043 S06:002 S07:060 S08:002 S09:006 S10:014 S11:050 S12:050 S18:000
S25:005 S26:001 S36:007 S37:000 S38:020 S44:003 S46:138 S48:007 S49:008 S50:255

STORED PROFILE 1:
B1 E1 L2 M1 N1 Q0 T V1 W2 X4 Y0 &C1 &D2 &G0 &J0 &K3 &Q5 &R0 &S0 &T4 &X0
S00:005 S02:043 S06:002 S07:060 S08:002 S09:006 S10:014 S11:050 S12:050 S18:000
S25:005 S26:001 S36:007 S37:000 S38:020 S44:003 S46:138 S48:007 S49:008 S50:255

TELEPHONE NUMBERS:
0=12125551212                              1=
2=                                         3=

OK

 ANSI    Offline 38400 8N1  [Alt+Z]-Menu  HDX 8 LF X ♪ ♪ CP LG ↑ PR  16:47:09
```

Figure 9-1: Viewing a modem's profiles. The modem has a currently active configuration as well as two user-created-and-saved configurations.

This modem has four stored profiles. One is the *factory default*, which is not displayed when you issue the AT&V command. Another contains the current settings, known as the *active profile.* The other two profiles are named *stored profile 0* and *stored profile 1.*

This modem also can store four telephone numbers. In Figure 9-1, only the first telephone number storage area has a number in it. The display from the profile viewing command shows the contents of each profile. The profiles consist of various AT command selections and a list of the contents for many S-registers.

Note: Not all S-registers are suitable for alteration by the user, and not all S-registers that can be altered by the user are stored within a profile.

The two profiles stored in this modem are very similar and differ only by one command and one S-register. Stored profile number 1 uses the E0 command rather than E1. The E0 and E1 are the second commands in the line below the stored profile's name.

The E0 setting makes the communications software responsible for echoing the characters you type at the keyboard while in command mode. The E1 setting makes the modem echo the characters you type at the keyboard while in command mode.

The other difference between the two profiles is in the contents of S-register S0. The S-register contents are listed on the line below the command settings. They are in the form Sxx:yyy, where xx is the S-register's number and yyy is the S-register's contents. In Figure 9-1, register S0 contains a zero in stored profile 0 and 5 in stored profile 1. The contents of S0 specify the number of rings the modem must hear before answering the phone.

To copy a profile to the active area, you use the **ATZ***n* command, where n is the number of the stored profile. To restore profile number 0, for example, type **ATZ1** and press Enter.

Storing a new profile

If you want to store a profile, use a two-step process. First, make all the changes you want to the modem by using AT commands and adjusting S-register contents. When you have precisely the configuration you want, you can write it to a stored profile.

Note: You should use this command with care because it overwrites the existing profile. You should keep a record of the profiles before you start playing with them. (Press Print Screen with your printer turned on after issuing the AT&V command.)

Use the AT&V command to view the current profiles. Verify that the active profile contains what you expect. Then write the profile to a stored area by typing **AT&W0** to write it to profile 0 or **AT&W1** to write it to profile 1. After writing, use the view command again to make sure you performed the operation correctly.

Selecting the factory default profile

Your modem is supplied with a default profile that is the active profile unless you or your communications program make any changes. A copy of these settings is stored in ROM. This allows you or your modem manufacturer to have a complete configuration that is always the same.

Be prepared to use the factory default profile when troubleshooting. If you have made changes to the profiles, you probably will need to print a copy of their contents before restoring the factory defaults. Although the factory defaults are restored to the active configuration, you also may want to copy them into a profile to remove a problem setting.

This procedure is equivalent to having a floppy disk containing DOS that you can use to boot your computer. (DOS 6 includes features that perform the equivalent procedure without actually needing a disk.) Booting your computer from a floppy disk gives you a "clean" configuration. It allows you to troubleshoot when you have problems making all the parts of your computer work together.

To restore the factory defaults, type **AT&F** and press Enter. This copies all the factory settings from ROM into the active configuration. This is not the same as turning off the modem's power and turning it back on again. Nor is it the same as issuing the reset command.

When you purchase the modem, the profiles probably contain copies of the factory default settings. However, if you have changed profiles, it is the changed profile that is loaded into the active configuration when you turn the modem on — not the factory defaults.

Selecting a stored profile on power up

Your modem may allow you to save more than one profile, and one of these profiles is copied into the active configuration when you apply power to the modem. You can change which profile is loaded by issuing an AT command.

If you type **AT&Y0** and press Enter, profile number 0 is loaded when you apply power. If you type **AT&Y1** and press Enter, profile number 1 is loaded when you apply power.

Resetting your modem

If you want to restore a known configuration to your modem, you may need to issue the reset command. The reset command copies a profile into the active memory area. If the modem is online, the connection will be broken.

If you type **ATZ** or **ATZ0** and press Enter, the modem is reset and profile number 0 is loaded into the active configuration. If you type **ATZ1** and press Enter, the modem is reset and profile number 1 is loaded into the active configuration.

Note: Using the reset command does not have the same effect as turning the modem on and off. When you turn the modem on and off, the setting of AT&Y determines which profile is loaded. When you use the reset command, the form of the reset command determines which profile is loaded.

Connecting at an Optimum Speed

When you make your modem call another modem, you can specify whatever speed and other communications standard you prefer. However, this standard is applied only if the modem that is being called is capable of achieving that standard.

When the second modem answers the phone, the two modems negotiate first for a connection speed and then, if applicable, for other protocols, such as compression and error-correction. The modems select the highest mutually acceptable standard.

The result is that the communications speed and other protocols that you think you have selected may not be what you have actually achieved. However, there are a couple of different ways you can tell what communications standards are being used.

Dialing the correct number

If you set your communications speed and options within your communications program to the fastest your modem can achieve, your modem will connect at that speed wherever possible. For any given connection, your modem will choose the standards that achieve the highest possible data throughput. The compression standard, for example, is not "faster," but you push more data across because it is stored in a smaller space.

Faster Serial Ports

DOS is a *single-tasking* operating system. This means it can only do one thing at a time. Other operating systems, such as OS/2 and UNIX, are *multi-tasking* operating systems and can do multiple tasks at one time. In fact, they also do only one thing at a time, because there is only one microprocessor in the computer, but they are able to divide the available time between several different tasks so that it appears to you that multiple things are happening at the same time.

Microsoft Windows is an operating environment that runs on DOS. (It actually depends on your precise definition of operating system whether you consider Windows as an operating system in its own right.) Windows is a multi-tasking environment and can do multiple things at the same time by allocating small amounts of time to each task.

You can buy a communications program that runs under Windows and can run it at the same time as other application programs. However, you may experience problems when running at high speed due to limitations in the PC.

In a multi-tasking operating system, each task running is given a small amount of time to run before the next task is given some time. For example, the communications program may have time to pick up a few characters from the serial port, and then it is the next task's turn to have control of the microprocessor. The data being sent to the serial port by the other computer, however, continues to arrive, although the communications program cannot look at it.

The PC's serial port contains a *buffer*, a temporary storage area, where received characters are stored until the communications program is able to collect them. However, the storage area is not very big, and at high data speeds, there is a possibility that some characters will be received but lost because there was not enough room in the buffer.

This is not a problem for DOS communications programs, because the communications program

has complete control of the microprocessor and is able to process the data as fast as the modem can send it. However, in a multi-tasking operating system, such as Windows, you can reach situations where the serial port in the PC is inadequate.

As the new V.FAST modems become readily available, the capability of your serial port to handle the faster data speed starts to become an issue regardless of whether you are running DOS or Windows. The problem is more likely in Windows, because there is more chance the communications program will not have uninterrupted control of the serial port.

You can purchase special serial port boards, such as Hayes ESP Communications Accelerator, or internal modems with a faster serial port, that ease the problems. As covered in Chapter 4, the serial port in a PC contains a UART (universal asynchronous receiver/transmitter) chip with other support circuitry. The particular chip used is not the most advanced available, and the faster serial port boards use more-advanced circuitry. For example, the more-advanced circuitry may operate faster and include more buffers. Consequently, you are less likely to get data loss because of overrun.

Note: Because you are using different serial port circuitry, the communications program must recognize the different serial port. This requires your communications program to support it directly, or you must choose a faster serial port that includes the necessary device driver program. For example, if you are running under Windows, you need a special Windows device driver; if you are running under another operating system, such as OS/2 or DOS, you will need different device drivers.

The boards can be configured to behave like typical PC serial ports, but in this mode you will probably lose the advantage of the extra features. However, if you are using high-speed modems (over 9600 bps) with Microsoft Windows, you should consider a faster serial port to make the connection as error free as possible.

However, many online services, particularly BBSs, offer a variety of phone numbers that you can call. The modems attached to these phone numbers will probably vary in type, and you may be able to achieve faster speeds by calling a number other than the one most widely publicized.

For example, my local BBS advertises one phone number. However, if you call on this number, you can connect at only 2400 bps. On the opening screen, this BBS shows its other numbers and encourages 9600 bps modem owners to call an alternate number so that they can connect at 9600 bps.

The slower number is advertised because it is a single number that will allow anyone to connect. The sysop is trying to discourage people with only 2400 bps modems from calling the 9600 bps lines. If they do, the people with 9600 bps modems will have to call the 2400 bps number and only connect at 2400 bps.

To understand whether you have connected at 2400 bps or 9600 bps or are using any data compression features, you need to watch your communications program carefully while it makes the connection. The following section illustrates a suggested procedure.

Understanding modem speed and compression

As covered in Chapter 4, the maximum possible data-throughput speed for the top-of-the-line modems has increased over the years. The early modems were only capable of transferring 300 bps, but new modems can transfer many thousands of bits in a second.

Early modems transferred one bit of data at a time, but the new modems transfer many bits at once. Additionally, modems that support a data-compression standard compress the data before sending it and uncompress it at the remote end. This compression results in the same amount of information being stored in a smaller number of bits. Consequently, the total amount of data being sent in a particular time frame is more if compression is being used.

Your modem negotiates a connection with a remote modem in two stages. It first establishes a connection speed and then negotiates any further communications protocols.

Most communications programs display the result codes being sent by your modem during the connection process. When calling another modem, you should watch the result codes carefully to see the agreed modem speed.

However, the level of detail supplied by these result codes, assuming that you can see them, may not be sufficient to supply the full connection story. For example, it may tell you that error-correction protocol is being used but not indicate which one.

If you have your modem speaker turned on, you also hear the negotiation process as the two modems exchange tones with each other. After you have connected a few times while watching the result codes, you will quickly learn to identify the difference between the sounds of the connections.

For example, it is quite easy to recognize (although impossible to describe in words) the negotiation and carrier signal for a 2400 bps connection as compared with a 9600 bps connection. You can also gain clues from the length of time it takes to negotiate the connection. (Usually, the negotiation process takes longer the faster the resulting connection.)

When the modems have agreed on a connection speed, the connection is complete, but they continue negotiation to establish any possible compression or error-correction.

Knowing what your modem is doing

The result codes sent to your modem during connection can vary on the speeds and communications standards being applied as well as the settings in various S-registers. For example, your modem may return CONNECT as a result code. Depending on your S-register settings, this may mean you have connected at 300 bps or at 19,200 bps!

Alternatively, you may see the message CONNECT 19200/ARQ, which means you have connected at 19,200 bps and are using some type of error-control technique. However, it does not tell you the precise standard, such as MNP (Microcom Network Protocol) or V.42's LAPM (Link Access Procedure for Modems).

On the other hand, if you adjust all the required S-registers so that the modem supplies full details of the connection, you may not actually achieve the connection because your communications program may not be able to handle more than one line of result code.

Exploring how to get the best connection from your modem will be pointless in some circumstances and will make tremendous differences in others. The first criterion is whether you have an alternate phone number for the online service you are calling.

When to investigate your connection if you have no alternate phone number

If you have only one phone number to call, your modem is going to connect with only one type of modem, and your connection speed and compression options will always be the same — unless you alter the options in your communications program before making the connection. In the case of only having one phone number to call, there is only one variable that can affect your transmission speed (apart from a noisy phone line). If you are transferring a lot of data across this connection, it is worth investigating the connection type.

The issue of compression type arises when you transfer files between two modems that use the MNP Level 5 compression protocol. This compression standard compresses all files sent from one modem to the other regardless of whether they have been compressed already.

In most cases, you will use a compression program, such as PKZIP, to compress the files prior to transmission. When you use MNP Level 5, the modem tries to compress the file further and actually generates a file that is larger than the compressed file. This obviously takes longer to transmit.

If you use MNP Level 5, you should compare the file-transfer speed you obtain when you transfer a file that is compressed with the same file uncompressed. The results you get will depend on the file size and in many cases only make a difference of a second or two. However, if you are transferring many files, the second or two for each file may make a big difference.

The other modem compression standards, including V.42bis, can detect whether a file is incompressable and automatically disable their own compression during the time you transfer the compressed file.

Besides investigating whether you are using MNP Level 5, if you only have one phone number to call a service, there is nothing you can do to speed the connection, except make sure that your communications program is trying to apply the maximum communications standards that your modem can achieve.

When to investigate your connection if you have alternate phone numbers

As discussed in the preceding section, if you have only one phone number for the service you are trying to connect to, you have no chance of improving your connection speed and communications standards. However, many online services, in particular BBSs, offer several different phone numbers you can call.

Data-Compression Alternatives

As you transfer a file between computers, your communications program often reports on the number of characters per second being transferred. The faster your connection speed, the more characters per second that are transferred.

If you are viewing text messages while online, you don't have the same quantitative number showing your connection speed. You can see the difference between 2400 bps and 9600 bps in the speed that messages and menus appear, but you cannot see small incremental differences so easily. However, for most people, the file-transfer speed is of more interest than the speed screens appear.

Keep in mind that the smaller the file, the faster it is transferred. If you can compress your file, it will be transferred faster because the information is stored in a smaller number of bytes. However, you need to consider whether it is better to compress the file before sending it, by using PKZIP for example, or by allowing the modem to compress it for you, by using a compression standard, such as V.42bis or MNP Level 5.

If you are using V.42bis compression, it doesn't matter where you do the compression. V.42 modems can automatically detect whether the file is compressed and will suspend their compression while the compressed file is being transferred. However, MNP Level 5 cannot make this detection and tries to compress all the data being sent from your computer. The result is that compressed files become larger with MNP Level 5 transmission.

Many online services expect you to send only compressed files. They in turn only keep compressed files in their file libraries. Most adhere to one particular standard, most commonly PKZIP. This minimizes the storage space needed to keep the files. When you call these services, you should disable MNP Level 5 compression to get the best file transmission speed. (You don't have to disable V.42 compression.)

If you use an offline reader, however, the situation may be different. Offline readers, covered in Chap-

ter 10, allow you to collect all the messages you want to read on an online service and download them as a file for later reading. This file, which contains your particular selection of messages, is generated when you call the service; it is not stored on the online service.

The sysop may choose not to compress the file, because it takes time to collect the information and it also takes more time to compress it prior to sending. When you are using a modem that has compression features, the data can be compressed during transmission, and the time the system would need to compress the file prior to sending is wasted. If you do not have compression active in your modem, the uncompressed file will take longer to transmit than if the system had compressed it prior to transmission.

I call three BBSs regularly and use their offline reader features. One does not compress the file prior to transmission, and I see a transfer speed of about 2,733 characters per second versus 1,622 when I call the other services and get a precompressed file.

At first glance, this may suggest that 2,733 characters per second is preferable to 1,622 characters per second; this is not true. Suppose that the file I wanted is 100 KB of text. It will take approximately 37 seconds to download at 2,733 characters per second. However, if the file is precompressed by using PKZIP, the 100 KB of text may be only 50 KB in size and will consequently take approximately 31 seconds to download at 1,622 characters per second. When using a modem that can compress if the file is compressable, you get the best performance possible even if the file is not compressed prior to transmission.

Advanced modem users can make the best use of their modem by considering the various options for data compression. You may want to select different configurations for when you call different online services so that you always get the data at the fastest possible speed. This does not necessarily mean you always pick every compression option available.

To find the different phone numbers, look carefully at the BBSs or online service opening screens. Make a note of the alternate numbers and also note the modem names, when available, alongside the numbers.

For example, a local BBS lists five numbers and the modem type attached to each number. The sysop uses a Smart One 2400 as the modem on node 1 (the number he advertises) and USRobotics Sportster 14400s on two of the other nodes. A Twincom 9600 and a USRobotics Dual Standard HST 16800 round out the five nodes.

The packet-switching networks, such as Tymnet and Sprintnet, often supply different local phone numbers. Some of these may be 1200 bps and some 2400 bps with MNP. It is probably worth paying slightly more for the local access call to a 2400 bps with MNP connection than to connect at 1200 bps or even 2400 bps without compression where you may have to spend twice as long on the phone.

My husband and I spent some time analyzing our local and long-distance phone rates. We determined that it was better to call long-distance to a particular online service so that we could connect at 9600 bps and get off the phone sooner than to pay the local phone company charges and connect at 2400 bps with MNP. The situation was complicated by surcharges during the day for one of the connections, different local phone call rates at different times, and different long-distance rates at different times. The results were different from when we last assessed it six months ago.

By the way, look carefully at your long-distance service. Many of them offer special promotions, such as cheap rates on weekends or reduced rates to a special person. You can probably nominate a BBS or online service for the discount. They may only apply for a few months, but you will often only want to call a BBS for a few months and then move on to new adventures. I hate to confess it, but we call a particular BBS more often than we call our family.

The following section explains a method of determining what speed and with what compression and error-detection standards you are connecting to a particular number. You should use this approach to find your best alternative and then use your normal dialing procedures for calling on future occasions.

Finding the full connection story

The general principle described in this section alters S-registers so that you see all the result codes sent from your modem. You apply this method to each of the available phone numbers for an online service and then choose the one that offers you the fastest connection.

Before calling your preferred selection, make certain that you restore your modem's profile to its normal configuration. The described method is intended only as a fact-finding approach — not the best configuration for communicating all the time.

The procedure involves three stages: altering your active configuration to get as many result codes as possible, dialing the required numbers and monitoring the result codes, and restoring your previous configuration.

Check your current configuration by using the view command and the S-register value view command described earlier. Make particular note of the settings for X, W, and S95. The values for X and W are displayed when you issue AT&V, and the value for S95 when you issue ATS95?. (They probably will be X4, W0 or W2, and S95 equal to 0 or 3.)

To alter your active configuration, perform the following steps:

1. Type **ATX4** and press Enter to enable the extended result codes. (This is usually the factory default setting.)

2. Type **ATW1** and press Enter to make the modem return the negotiation progress messages. (The factory default is typically ATW0 with these negotiation messages disabled.)

3. Type **ATS95=44** and press Enter to make the contents of S95 equal to 44. This enables the carrier, protocol, and compression messages.

To dial the number experimentally and record the result codes, perform the following steps:

1. Turn on your printer.

2. Dial the BBS's number manually by using the manual dial feature of your communications program or by issuing the command **ATD** followed by the phone number.

3. Listen to the two modems negotiate, and then as soon as the result codes are displayed, press Print Screen to print the screen's contents. (You may have to be quick to press the Print Screen key before the online service sends a new screen.)

   Alternatively, you can use the capture file feature in your communications program to capture this information. Chapter 10 explains capture files.

4. Issue the **ATH** command (or use the hang up command in your communications program) to hang up the phone and free the BBS for other callers.

5. Examine your printed results. The following example shows the results from calling one number for a local BBS:

```
CARRIER 2400
PROTOCOL: NONE
CONNECT 2400
```

Although my modem is a 9600 bps modem, it could connect only at 2400 bps. The two modems could not agree on a compression protocol, so the connection speed is the same as the carrier speed.

6. Repeat the dialing procedure for the BBS's other phone numbers if necessary.

For example, when I call the same local BBS on another number, I get the following result codes:

```
CARRIER 14400
PROTOCOL: LAP-M
COMPRESSION: V.42BIS
CONNECT 38400
```

This phone number takes advantage of all my modem's features. It uses LAP-M error-control protocol (used with V.42) and uses V.42bis. The carrier transmits data between the two modems at 14,400 bps, but because of the compression, I am actually transmitting data between the two computers at 38,400 bps. This is the phone number I want to use all the time.

7. Reset your modem's parameters. You can use the reset command to restore a saved profile. You also can exit your communications program, turn off your modem, turn it back on again, and restart your communications program. Another method is reissuing the ATX, ATW, and ATS95= commands so that the previous values are restored. Again, use the view commands to verify that your original configuration is restored.

8. Enter the most appropriate phone number for the online service in your dialing directory or activity so that you always call the best number.

Summary

This chapter showed how to make the most of your modem. This involves making adjustments to the modem's configuration to suit your needs as well as connecting to an online service at the best available connection speed.

The modem settings are adjusted by issuing AT commands. You can use *profiles* within your modem to save a series of settings. Additionally, you can issue a series of AT commands to your modem, typically known as an *initialization string*, when you start your communications program. These tools help ensure that your modem is always operating in a known configuration.

Chapter 10 introduces the extra features found in more-advanced communications programs. These help streamline your communications and remove much of the repetition and manual operation. Consequently, you will be able to reduce costs by spending less time online.

Streamlining Your Communications

This chapter discusses features that are available in more-advanced communications software programs. In particular, you will learn many methods for automating your communications, including:

- ❖ Exploiting dialing features
- ❖ Capturing your online session
- ❖ Understanding key macros
- ❖ Using script files
- ❖ Creating script files easily
- ❖ Using offline mail readers

Taking Advantage of Convenient Extras

More-sophisticated communications programs include many features beyond the minimum tools necessary to make a connection with a modem. You should explore to see what tools you can use in your particular situation. A good way to start looking is by examining the chapter headings in the documentation for your communications software. You might find that your communications software includes special features for calling a particular service, or you may be able to create separate dialing directories for each user of your computer.

Each communications program has its own advantages and limitations, and you will probably have your own particular favorite. This chapter explores three main areas of potential communications software commands. The first section gives examples of three typical features that help keep you organized. All users will benefit from these and other comparable features.

Later sections cover three other important features: macros, scripts, and offline mail readers. (You can use offline mail readers even if your communications software does not support them directly. However, some communications programs incorporate them.) In their simplest form, these features benefit all users. However, at their most advanced, they can require extensive knowledge of what you are doing.

The three examples of extras that your communications program may have are *capture files, dialing directory options,* and *redialing features.* Your communications software may include exactly the same options as explained here or may have other variations.

Capturing features

Your communications program may have several ways for you keeping a record of what has occurred during a communications session. One feature may be called a *capture file, disk capture,* or *printer capture.* Another feature may be called a *scroll back buffer* or a *peruse buffer.*

Peruse buffer

The *peruse buffer,* or *scroll back buffer,* is a temporary storage area. As you communicate, the communications program keeps the information that has "scrolled off" the top of the screen. You can use the peruse buffer to look at something you missed.

"How do I look back at material scrolled off the screen?"

Suppose that you call an online service and use the help command. You see a list of commands or an explanation of a particular command. Assume that you want to know how to edit a message you just entered and used the help edit command to get details. You then use the information to edit your message, but you forget how to tell the remote computer you're finished. You can use the peruse buffer to scroll back your screen and reread the help information.

If your communications program supports a peruse buffer, it's probably active automatically. However, you may be able to alter its size as a configuration option within your program. This size will alter how far back through your communications session you can scroll. With a PC that is not severely limited in memory, you can probably keep at least the equivalent of 10 pages of text.

The actual command for activating the read buffer varies with the communications program. If you press Alt+up-arrow key in QModemPro, you activate the read buffer and you can scroll back. You can then use cursor-direction keys, such as the arrows and Page Up and Page Down, to move around the stored information. You press Esc to return to the terminal screen.

Smartcom for Windows also includes a peruse buffer. You use the up and down scroll arrows in the scroll bar to the right of the online window to access different areas of the temporarily saved information. This is similar to scrolling through information in other Windows applications.

Although using the capture-file options is the preferred way to save a record of your communications session, your communications program probably includes a command for saving the contents of your peruse buffer to a file on disk. This command can be a lifesaver when you make a simple error.

For example, I recently logged onto an online service to send an Internet message to my brother in England. I did not turn on a capture file because I wasn't planning anything that needed saving. However, when I sent the message, it was rejected by the online service.

I wasn't very familiar with the user interface and couldn't quickly find how to read the message I tried to send. I used the peruse buffer to scroll back and find where I had written the message and found the error in my brother's address.

Then, I couldn't find the command to correct the address and decided it was quicker to delete the message and rewrite it. However, I hate retyping. I used the save peruse buffer command and logged off the online system. I used a text editor to isolate the message portion of the saved buffer and saved it as a file.

I then logged onto the online service again and created a new message (while taking a lot of care over typing the address). I then used ASCII upload to rewrite the message text and send the copy of the message. This was not rejected, so I deleted the incorrectly addressed message and logged off the system.

If I'd been better prepared, I would have written the message offline in the first place. However, my original one sentence message expanded when I was actually online, and I had to resort to the peruse buffer to bail myself out of trouble.

Capture file

If your communications program does not include capture-file features, you should consider buying a new program. The capture file feature is invaluable for beginners and advanced users — regardless of whether you are calling a new online service or the same one every time.

Unless you are using offline mail readers (which are discussed later in this chapter), capture files are the easiest and fastest way to gather the large volumes of textual information you see online. They can help you reduce your online time substantially and consequently can reduce your online costs.

Although very useful, the capture file's function is very simple. It saves to disk every action taken and displayed during an online session. This gives you a record of what occurred in the session.

"How do I keep a record of what I've done online?"

The general procedure is to turn on and provide a name for your capture file before making the connection. You then make the connection and perform all the online activities as normal. After logging off the system, you turn the capture file off.

The capture file is an ASCII text representation of your session. You can read it in a text editor, such as DOS 6's EDIT program or Windows Notepad. It shows all the menus and what you typed as well as all the information you read, such as messages and file lists.

If you do not want to save the whole session, you can turn the capture file on and off during the session if you prefer. Other options for this feature vary with the communications program, but they typically include a print capture, where every action is printed on your printer.

If you use scripts to automate your communications session, turning a capture file on and off is one of the most common items you would add to the script. Scripts are covered later in this chapter.

I keep a different capture file for each service that I call. For example, DIALOG.CAP contains a record of my activity with Dialog Information Services and GATEWAY.CAP contains a record of my activity with Gateway 2000's BBS.

Depending on your particular option selections, you can typically make your communications program append new information to the end of an existing capture file or overwrite the existing file.

Note: When you run out of space on your hard disk, examine your capture files to see whether you can delete any of them. Although they are very useful immediately after your communications session, they don't usually have long-term value.

"How do I reduce my online time?"

Capture files can speed your online communication because you don't have to take the time to read everything while you are online. Because you have a faithful record of the events, you can let information scroll by and read it at leisure when your phone bill is not mounting.

Suppose that you call a BBS each week, read the new messages, look and see what new files have been uploaded, and log off. If you are not using a capture file, you must read each message carefully and perhaps take notes on the interesting new files. If you use a capture file, you can save online time in several ways: first when reading messages; and second when looking at file lists.

An online service presents information to you one screen at a time. If you ask to read all the new messages, you see one screenful and then are prompted to press a particular key to see the next screenful. Without a capture file, you have to read these messages one screen at a time. However, with a capture file, you can select the "non-stop" option and scroll all the messages past you at once. You can't read them as they fly by, but they are saved in the capture file. You can then read them offline.

Files lists are similar. Because the list is saved to disk, you can read it offline rather than needing to take notes while online. The capture file also can be useful when more than one person is interested in the information, because the record is permanent, and all the interested people do not need to be present when the information is recorded.

When calling a new online service, particularly one that only gives you limited access until you are registered or subscribe, the capture file is helpful. It allows you to do a lot more in a limited time because you don't have to read everything in detail. You can rapidly explore the service's menus and a few sample messages or file directories and study them at leisure.

Dialing directories

Most PC-based communications programs use the concept of dialing directories. At their most basic, they keep a list of who you want to call and the applicable phone numbers.

Some communications programs, such as Smartcom for Windows, support both analogies, dialing directories and activities and connections list. You can choose the interface that suits you best.

However, your dialing directory or activity and connection documents can keep far more information. After you become familiar with communications, look again at these elements and see how much more streamlining you can do.

A dialing directory entry usually contains additional information other than the number and name. You can usually specify such items as the modem you want to use or the communications parameters, including speed and character format.

When you add new entries, consider basing your entry on an existing entry and using a copy entry command in your dialing directory.

For example, I use two main sets of parameters: one for calling BBSs and one for minicomputers. BBSs are typically PC-based and use the character format of 8N1, and most commercial online services are on minicomputers and use 7E1 as their character format. Additionally, I usually use a packet-switched network, such as Tymnet or Sprintnet, to connect with the commercial online services, and my fastest connection is often only 2400 bps with compression.

When I add a new commercial service, I copy the entry with the 7E1 and slower speed settings. When I add a BBS, I copy a BBS entry. Then, I only need to change a few settings for my new entry.

"Is there an easy way to deal with those busy signals?"

Your dialing directory may allow you to enter multiple phone numbers for the same service. The communications program tries each number in turn. This can be useful when calling a popular BBS. If one number is busy, you can try another.

Note: Many BBSs have a special telephone connection system (supplied by the phone company) that automatically routes calls to another number. You call one number and may actually be connected via another number. Sometimes, calling the alternate number doesn't buy you anything because the BBS will route you there if possible.

Your communications program may allow you to specify a group of entries to call. It then tries each entry in the list in turn. I use this feature regularly. I call about five BBSs early on Saturday morning. I make a group of these BBSs and make the communications program try each one in turn until it gets through to one.

I then collect the mail and other items of interest and log off. Because I use scripts and offline mail readers, most of the actual communications session is automated. When I log off, the communications program continues calling the remaining BBSs in the group. I don't have to supervise closely until it connects with another service.

Other useful dialing directory features include different ways of sorting your entries. For example, you may be able to make your list alphabetical. Of more interest, however, are sorting features that allow you to sort based on the number of times you have called the entry or based on the last date that you called the entry.

I regularly sort my dialing directory based on the number of times that I have called the service. This puts my favorite BBSs and online services at the top of my list.

Dialing features

Your communications program probably includes many options for dialing and redialing. You may, for example, be able to set how long the program should wait before redialing a number or how fast to dial the number.

These options adjust modem settings, some of which are discussed in Chapter 9. For example, a setting in your communications program may change your modem's result codes so that it can detect a busy signal and you can redial the number faster.

"How do I get through to an online service faster?"

Settings, such as speed of dialing and time to wait before redialing, have default values that work for most people. However, with a little trial and error, you can tailor the settings to your situation.

You can make your modem dial a number painfully slowly, and it can take say 10 seconds to dial a number. Obviously, you can make it dial faster and save a few seconds on the connection. However, you also can set your modem to dial so fast that the telephone call does not go through because the telephone exchange (supplied by local phone company) misses some or all of the digits. You need to choose a setting that is fast enough to connect every time but not too slow to waste time.

You can probably alter the time your communications program pauses before dialing the next number. Again, you can make this a very long time and waste time. If you are trying to redial a busy number, someone else might manage to dial between your calls and you will never get through.

On the other hand, if you make the pause time too slow, your phone may not have time to break the connection. You may have experienced that when you hang up the phone and pick it up again immediately; you may have been fast enough that the previous caller is still on the line.

In my situation, I need to make the delay before redialing quite long. I live in a rural area, and my local phone service seems slow to disconnect. Additionally, I use an electronic device called a *fax switch* to monitor my incoming calls and switch automatically to the stand-alone fax machine if the incoming call is from a fax machine. This switch is slow to terminate a connection.

You need to explore your communication program's documentation in detail to find many of the less commonly used features that you may find a boon. (See Appendix C for details on using Smartcom for Windows LE.) I make a point of occasionally going through the online help indexes in all my application programs, including my word processor and spreadsheet, to find words that I am not familiar with. In this way, I can learn new topics and take advantage of some less-known features. I have found many tips on solving computer games this way too!

Your communications program may include other options for dialing. For example, your communications program probably includes a feature that allows you to specify a prefix to your phone numbers. You may be able to specify several of them. This can be used, for example, to dial 1 or 9, a pause, and then 1 in front of long-distance numbers you call from your office. You may be able to keep another prefix for use when you are on the road.

"How do I disable call waiting?"

You should use the prefix feature to disable call waiting. Call waiting and modem use are incompatible. You need to disable call waiting before making a call with a modem. If you don't and a call comes through, the modem assumes that the beep or tone is data and tries to pass it to your computer. Your computer assumes it is data and will make it part of the file you are downloading or try to display it. At best, you will see some random and weird characters on-screen. At worst, your modem and computer will hang and you will have to reboot.

If you add the digits required to disable call waiting (often *70 or 1170) as the prefix sent when you dial a phone number, you don't have to add it to every entry in your dialing directory.

Note: The code for disabling call waiting may vary, depending on where you live, and you may not be able to disable it before a call. *Note:* The dialing prefix does not disable call waiting when someone calls you by modem.

Automating the Communications Process

After you make a few connections, you will begin to realize how much of what you are doing is repetitive. For example, every time you call CompuServe, you always set the same communications parameters, dial the same number, and enter the same series of information, such as user name and password, to connect with the online service.

"How do I avoid all the repetitious typing?"

Your communications program includes many features that remove the repetition in the preparation and connecting process. You also can automate the actual connection in several ways.

If you intend to call a particular person or service only once, you don't need to automate the process. However, you may want to call the same service many times and do the same things each time.

For example, you may want to call your local BBS, read all the new mail in the general section and the word processing section, see any new files that have been uploaded, and check out any new message areas. For the most part, these tasks are repetitive. There may be a different number of messages or files to see, but you will be selecting the same commands each time.

Your communications program probably includes two important features that remove the drudgery of entering the same commands and information each time: *key macros* and *scripts*.

Understanding key macros

A key macro allows you to assign a series of keystrokes to a single key. When you press that key, the communications program sends that string of characters to the modem as if you had typed them at the keyboard.

For example, you can assign your password, last name, and first name to function keys. Then, when you log onto a system and it asks for your last name, you press one key. When it prompts for your first name, you press another key. When you are prompted for your password, you press another single key.

"How do I remember my account numbers?"

You also can assign your online service account number to a key. Because this is often a number, using a key macro removes the need for you to remember it.

Although this is convenient, you need to think carefully about security before programming your password into a key macro. Read your communications software documentation to determine whether anyone else can find your password if you assign it to a key.

This security does not just apply to whether someone will "steal" your online account. If you have children and want to restrict their access, don't use key macros. Most children are completely uninhibited with computers and will press keys to see what will happen.

If you do decide to assign your password to a key, you should use the same password with all your online services. This is relatively easy for BBSs, which allow you to choose your own password. However, most commercial online services assign you with a password, and you may not be able to change it to your favorite. However, to make the best use of most commercial services, you will be using a different communications program that is tailored to that service. In this case, because you will only be calling the one service from this program, a key macro feature will not be applicable anyway.

Using script files

The other automation feature available in more-sophisticated communications programs is scripting. As its name suggests, a script file is a list of events and activities that you want followed exactly. For example, a script file may contain the information necessary to type your last name when the computer you are calling sends the prompt `Last name:`.

You create this script for an entry in your dialing directory or an activity. The script is activated when you dial the particular number. Scripts range in complexity from very simple to very complex.

The ease of creation, maintenance, and flexibility of script files are a major consideration when choosing a communications program. The particular selection depends on your programming ability. The communications program includes what is known as a *scripting language* to help you create these script files.

"I can't program. Can I use a script?"

If you have no programming experience, you should choose a communications program that has a scripting language that looks like English. Try reading the examples in the manual to get an idea of whether you will understand the commands. Do not expect to understand everything without experience, but you should at least have some idea of the general tasks being scripted.

Some communications programs include a "learn" feature that can automatically create a script file for you. In fact, you still need to edit the resulting file, but the learning feature can often take you most of way towards creating the file.

The useful qualities of scripts cannot be emphasized enough. This chapter can only scratch the surface of script file potential, but two points are important. Anyone can create scripts and use them. More-sophisticated scripts require more knowledge, but this should not prevent you from experimenting.

The examples in the remainder of this chapter assume a basic understanding of online services, including BBSs and commercial online services. You need to know that you call an online service to read and send messages and find files. The messages may be divided into topic areas known as *conferences*. The files are stored in areas called *libraries,* and the libraries may also be divided by topics. You may also call an online service to *chat* with other people.

When you call an online service, you are prompted for your name and a password. You then move around an online service to the areas of interest by selecting commands from menus. The process involved can be the same every time you call, although the details of what you read, collect, or send may vary each time. Consequently, you can use script files to remove the repetitious portion of the connection.

Calling a BBS with a script

Hayes Smartcom uses simple English to develop scripts. The following script was generated with Smartcom for Windows. It automatically connects to the Online With Hayes BBS and issues your name and password. By examining this script, you can learn how to create and modify your own scripts.

```
START CONNECTION , "9, 1 800 874 2937" ;
IF NOT CONNECTED THEN STOP "Failed to connect." ;
WAIT FOR PROMPT "First Name?" ;
TYPE LINE "Caroline" ;
```

```
TYPE LINE "Halliday" ;
WAIT FOR PROMPT "Is this correct?" ;
TYPE TEXT "y" ;
WAIT FOR PROMPT "Enter Your Password:" ;
TYPE LINE @"330<J#~6SD$ ; {Scrambled}
WAIT FOR PROMPT "-Press Any Key;" ;
TYPE KEY RETURN_Key ;
WAIT FOR PROMPT "Command:" ;
```

This Smartcom script is written in simple English to make developing scripts as easy as possible. Don't be intimidated by the appearance of this script. Ignore how it looks and concentrate on what it says, and you'll find it relatively easy to understand.

This script begins by using a START CONNECTION command to dial the Online With Hayes BBS telephone number. Then, the script waits until the BBS asks you to enter your name and password, which it enters automatically. The password is scrambled in the script for your security.

Tip: If you don't know exactly what the remote system's prompt is, enter a WAIT FOR statement that continues after 5-10 seconds. This tip is useful if you know that the service will ask you for your name or other information, but you don't know the exact prompt.

Tip: A WAIT FOR TIME OF DAY statement or similar delay statement can be used to start a script when you are away from your desk, such as at night when the rates are lower.

Using a script editor

To edit the preceding script, you use a script editor within the communications software or use a text editor. Smartcom for Windows LE (included with this book) can run but not create and edit scripts. Smartcom for Windows can run, create, and edit scripts by using SCOPE, (Simple COmmunications Programming Environment).

Most script editors enable you to use all of the major commands, such as connecting, printing, saving, typing, sending, receiving, waiting, hanging up, and quitting. These commands can be combined to automate almost any activity that you can perform manually with your communications software.

The preceding script can be extended to download all of your new mail messages, check for new files in your favorite area, or print all of your mail messages and log off. You can also modify this script to call other online services.

The following section shows a simple script file that was automatically generated by using the communications program learn feature. The section following takes this script file and enhances it.

Using learn features

A good communications program will include a scripting language feature and will have a command that automatically generates scripts for you. The learn feature is similar to a tape recorder. The program watches all the activities and learns that when you see a particular prompt from the remote system, you want to type a particular response.

"How do I create a script file?"

Because each online service you call is different, you need to generate a script file for an entry in your dialing directory. In most communications programs, one of the fields in the directory is for the script file's name. After the script file is written and associated with a dialing directory entry, the script file is executed every time you call that dialing directory entry.

The script creation procedure in QModemPro, used as the example in this chapter, is comparable with other communications programs. You start the communications program and reach the dialing directory. You select the entry of interest and activate the learn command.

In QModemPro, this is done by pressing **Q** to activate the QuickLearn command. If you have not specified a name for your script file, you are prompted to enter a filename. Type a name that relates to the entry you have chosen. For example, if you call your local BBS regularly and it is called the Nearby BBS, you may want to create a script file called NEARBY.

QModemPro displays a Q next to the entry, showing that when you dial this entry, it will generate a script file automatically. You then call the online service and go through your usual connection process.

You will create the best script file if you type carefully and only add activities that you will perform every time you call. Remember that you are recording your activities so that they can be repeated. For example, if you want to automate reading the mail, you do this activity when QuickLearn is active. However, you probably will not want to reply to a message each time, so you would not do that during this session.

The following is a sample script file generated by using QuickLearn.

```
;
;   QuickLearn Script generated at 06:53:56   02-24-94
;   May require editing before use.
;
TurnON    8_BIT
TurnOFF   LINEFEED
TurnOFF   XON/XOFF
TurnON    NOISE
TurnON    MUSIC
TurnON    SCROLL
TurnOFF   PRINT
TurnOFF   SPLIT
TurnON    STATUSLN
TurnOFF   DOORWAY
TurnOFF   CAPTURE
Capture   C:\QMPRO\CAPTURE\NEARBY.CAP
TimeOut   30     ; Set Waitfor for 30 seconds
Waitfor   "What is your first name?"
Delay     100
Send      "caroline^M"
Waitfor   "What is your last name?"
Delay     100
Send      "halliday^M"
Waitfor   "Password? [                ]^[[15D"
Delay     100
Send      "secretone^M"
Waitfor   "ue, [N]onStop, [S]top? [C]^[[D^[[D"
Delay     100
Send      "^M"
Waitfor   "ue, [N]onStop, [S]top? [C]^[[D^[[D"
Delay     100
Send      "^M"
Waitfor   "ue, [N]onStop, [S]top? [C]^[[D^[[D"
Delay     100
Send      "^M"
Waitfor   "iew the bulletin menu? [Y]^[[D^[[D"
Delay     100
Send      "n^M"
Waitfor   "Command >> ?"
Delay     100
Send      "m"
Exit
```

This script automatically types my name and password, provides appropriate responses to reach the BBS's main menu, and then selects the Mail menu.

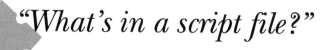

"What's in a script file?"

The problem many nonprogrammers have with understanding programs is that programs normally contain introductory information before they get to the meat of the program. The introductory information is important because it sets the rules that apply to the whole program, but it can be difficult to understand for a beginner.

Unfortunately, script files are similar, but fortunately, the introductory material is brief. Consider this script file as having a title and three parts. The title section is the lines beginning with semicolons. Part one contains the preparatory settings and consists of the lines beginning TurnON and TurnOFF. Part two is the line beginning TimeOut, and the remainder is part three of the script.

The first few lines that begin with semicolons are comments and make up the script's title. They explain that the script file was created by using the QuickLearn feature.

The next group of lines, the initial settings, beginning with TurnON and TurnOFF, are the QModemPro settings that were current when the script was created. For example, the TurnON NOISE line means that when a beep or bell is sent, you will hear it.

The TurnOFF CAPTURE line closes any open capture file. It means that if you have just called another service and have forgotten to stop recording the session, you will not record this new session with the other one.

The next line in the script turns on the capture file for your current session. In this example, it is a file named NEARBY.CAP and is saved in the subdirectory on drive C named \QMPRO\CAPTURE.

The next section in the script file contains the rules you want applied to everything in the remainder of the script. In this example, there is only one line, but this is the area where you probably will want to add lines to the script file. Before considering the TimeOut line, look at the remainder of the script.

The remainder of this script file is a series of groups of three lines. The first line in each group starts with a Waitfor instruction; the second line is a Delay; and the third line is a Send instruction.

Each set is similar; you want the script to wait until it sees a particular prompt. Then you want it to pause momentarily, and then send a particular response. However, there is a chance that the BBS or online service you call may change its menus, and your script file may never see the precise prompt. Consequently, it will then wait for a response forever.

The line beginning TimeOut specifies that if at anytime the script had waited longer than 30 seconds, you will be told so you can abort running the script.

The core of the script is the sets of three lines. Examine the first one in detail. This line instructs the script file to pause until the remote system sends the sequence of characters What is your first name?.

Note: The information in quotes must be received exactly for the script file to respond.

When you call an online system with this script, it processes the beginning of the script up to the first line beginning with WaitFor. It then stops until it sees the appropriate characters.

After these are received, you want the script to pause briefly. The Delay 100 line makes the script pause for 1/10 of a second. You need this delay because some online services get confused if you respond too quickly. They send the characters and must prepare for a response. If you respond too quickly, they may miss your response.

Another script language may not use precisely the same commands, such as WaitFor and Delay; however, it will have comparable ones with similar names. This is similar to word processors that have slightly different commands for doing the same thing.

After the delay, the Send command instructs the script to send the characters enclosed in quotes. In this example, it is the sequence caroline followed by Enter.

The actual line in the script has a caret (^) symbol followed by an M. The ^M is this script language's representation of the Enter key. Because the QuickLearn function recorded this, you would not have to know this to write the script, but you need to know to understand what the script instruction is.

The next three lines in the script are similar to the previous three. The script file sends my last name followed by Enter when it sees the prompt What is your last name?.

The next three lines are worth looking at closely to understand. The first line seems simple except for the ^[[15D on the end. This is similar to the ^M in that it is the script language's method of writing down an action that is not normally written.

To understand it (and the ^M), you need to remember that you are using a particular terminal emulation to communicate with the remote computer. In this example, the BBS is using ANSI emulation.

In your communications manual, there will be a table listing the program's representations of the special characters used in the current terminal emulation. For example, ANSI emulation has special characters for carriage return, clear screen, and delete.

The QModemPro emulation shows that the character represented by `^[[D` is cursor left. The line that shows `^[[15D` means that the cursor is moved 15 positions to the left. This is because when you are prompted for your password, the remote computer writes the prompt `Password?`, then a space, then an opening square bracket. It then leaves 14 spaces and places the closing square bracket. When it moves the cursor 15 spaces left, the cursor appears to you immediately after the opening square bracket waiting for you to type your password.

The script then delays and sends the password followed by Enter. By the way, as covered in Chapter 14, choose your password carefully. The example given is not suitable because it is easy to guess.

The remainder of the script gets you past the introductory material on the BBS and to the main menu. At the main menu, the prompt on this sample BBS is `Command >> ?`. For the example, the mail command is chosen, and the script ends with the Exit command.

At this point, you have gotten past all the repetitive material you have to do every time you log onto the system and have reached the part you are really interested in — the message area in this case.

Creating script files

You can generate scripts that are as simple as the previous example, or you can create more complex ones. For example, if you always check the new files and the new messages on a BBS, you can extend your script to look at these items automatically.

Depending on the sophistication of the script language supplied with your communications program, you can make the script do more-complex things, such as download and upload files, run other scripts from within a script, wait for a specific time, or signal you at specific points.

You can create script files from scratch. They are only ASCII text files. However, it is much easier and more efficient to base them on a QuickLearn version of the procedure. You are less likely to make mistakes.

As an example of the type of thing all users are likely to want to do to improve a script file, the following example extends the preceding example. The preceding example performs the log on process and moves you to the message menu. You might extend it to read new messages, perhaps in several conference areas, and get lists of the new files.

When you add more tasks to your script, you can quickly make very long scripts due to much repetition. Consider the preceding example.

The prompt `"ue, [N]onStop, [S]top? [C]^[[D^[[D"` appears three times. This is the last characters of the prompt `[C]ontinue, [N]onStop, [S]top?`. You are expected to press C to see the next screen of text, N to make the material scroll by nonstop, and S to stop reading. The actual syntax of this prompt varies with the online service, but all the services include a similar prompt.

If you use a capture file, you don't need to see the material one screen at a time and can let it scroll by continuously because you will be reading it at a later time. Additionally, if you are reading messages, the number of pages of text that displayed depends on how many messages there are. Using the nonstop answer in your script will work for more situations than using the continue answer.

You can write a line for your script file that looks for this prompt and supplies the same response every time it occurs. This command goes in the early section of the script file along with the time-out command. The `When` command can be used to make the script file look for alternate text strings when the `WaitFor` command is active.

To change this script, you would add the following line:

```
When "ue, [N]onStop, [S]top? [C]^[[D^[[D" "n^M"
```

This line goes immediately after the `Timeout` line and before the main portion of the script. Whenever the script is waiting for a particular prompt from the remote computer, it also looks for the prompt in the `When` line. When it sees this prompt, it will send n followed by `Enter` to make the computer display the information nonstop.

In QModemPro, you can have up to 20 `When` commands active at once. Other scripting languages will have slightly different commands and will have different limitations. You use the `When` command to amalgamate the repetitive sections in your script file only if you always want to respond in the same way.

Another modification to the script file is moving the turning on of the capture file after you enter your password. This prevents recording your last name and first name every time in the capture file. However, many online services display the time and date when you first log on and list important new information, such as new features and new phone numbers, so you shouldn't move the capture feature too far down or you will miss information.

Be sure to read your script file before using it. As the comment in the title says, you may need to edit it before using. This is particularly true if you are a poor typist. You need to correct your typing errors rather than make the same mistakes every time you call a particular online service.

Script files can be compared with DOS batch files. Everyone needs a couple of batch files, even if only AUTOEXEC.BAT. But with a little practice, you can create very sophisticated batch files that automate many tasks. Programmers have developed whole systems successfully with DOS batch files.

Similarly, script files can be elementary, such as the example here, or can be very advanced. I use a script file for almost all the online services I call. At the very least, they log me on and turn on a capture file. The more-sophisticated ones allow me to do all of my online activity without my physical intervention. I am on and off online services within 15 minutes and have literally hours worth of information to read.

Understanding offline mail readers

Offline mail readers are becoming increasingly popular, especially as we connect with more and more people online. These programs can be features in your communications program or, more typically, programs that you use in association with your communications program.

"How can I collect lots of messages fast?"

When you call an online service that supports offline readers, BBSs most commonly, you can download your mail as a file instead of reading it while you are online. This is comparable to reading your mail while standing at the mail box or being able to collect and deliver your mail but going home to read and respond to all your mail.

The general principle is that you call an online service and download a file known as a *mail packet* that contains all your messages. You then log off from the service. You then run your mail reading program and read the messages. As you read the messages, you may choose to save them, reply to them, or discard them. Any replies you create are saved in a file and are uploaded when you next collect messages.

Your communications program may include an offline mail reader, or you can obtain an offline mail reader as a separate program. Many readers are shareware and are available for downloading from online services. Although different mail reader formats are used, by far the most common is the QWK format (pronounced *quick*).

Because the online service you call must support the offline mail reader that you use, you can only use the offline mail reader format that is supported by the online service that you call.

Resource Guide to Offline Readers

Offline readers are incorporated as a part of some communications programs and are also available as stand-alone products. The following are some available products:

1stReader
Sparkware
P. O. Box 386
Hendersonville, TN 37077-0386

Blue Wave Offline Mail Reader
Cutting Edge Computing
P.O. Box 90476
Burton, MI 48509
(313) 743-9283

OFFLINE
Harvey Parisien
Box 323, Station A
Kingston, Ontario, Canada K7M 6R2

Off-Line Xpress (OLX)
Mustang Software Inc.
P.O. Box 2264
Bakersfield, CA 93303
(805) 873-2500

QModemPro
Mustang Software Inc.
P.O. Box 2264
Bakersfield, CA 93303
(805) 873-2500

Robomail
Parsons Consulting
5020 S. Lake Shore Drive, Suite 3301
Chicago, IL 60615-3249

Silver Xpress
Santronics Software
30034 S.W. 153 Court
Leisure City, FL 33033

WinQwk
Doug Crocker
PO Box 1454
Kent, WA 98035-1454

The online service can choose where to place the available commands. Consequently, you may find different commands in different places, depending on the service that you call. However, the majority of BBSs put the commands that access the mail reader with the other mail or message commands.

For example, Figure 10-1 shows the main menu from Software Creations BBS. The QMail Door option is listed at the bottom of the Mail Commands.

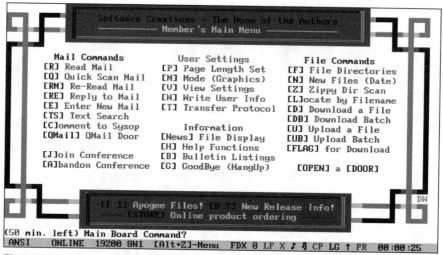

Figure 10-1: Software Creations Main Menu. The QMail Door command provides access to the mail reader features of this BBS.

Other BBSs may require you to choose mail or messages from a main menu and then list the commands for using a mail reader within the mail or message menu itself.

A *door* on a BBS is a method that allows the BBS to add extra programs and consequently extra functionality that the BBS software does not support directly. As a user, you select a door and gain access to other features. In the case of a mail reader, you access the program that creates the mail packet file that is downloaded to your computer.

When you first choose the Quick Mail Door on a BBS (or other similarly named feature), you have to perform a configuration procedure. The BBS has a series of conferences and message areas that are shown to you. You then specify the conferences of interest by choosing from the list.

When the configuration is complete, you can choose to download your selected mail. The BBS's mail reader program collects all the selected mail and makes it into a single file. You download this file to your computer and exit from the mail reading area of the BBS.

After you get offline, you start your mail reading program (from within your communications program—if it is included—or from the DOS prompt). The mail reader shows you a list of the mail packet files you have collected. You will have one for each of the services that you have accessed and used their mail reader functions.

After choosing the mail packet by name, the mail reader uncompresses the mail packet and displays a list of the conferences you have chosen to scan.

Note: As mentioned in Chapter 9, not all online services compress their mail packets.

Figure 10-2 shows a typical example collected from Mustang Software Inc., manufacturers of QModemPro communications software and WildCat BBS software.

A *mail packet* contains messages from the conferences you have expressed interest in. In Figure 10-2, you see a list of conferences. Eight of the conferences have a dot between the number and its name. This dot indicates that on this occasion (in this mail packet) you downloaded mail from those conferences. The conferences without a dot do not include mail this time (in this mail packet).

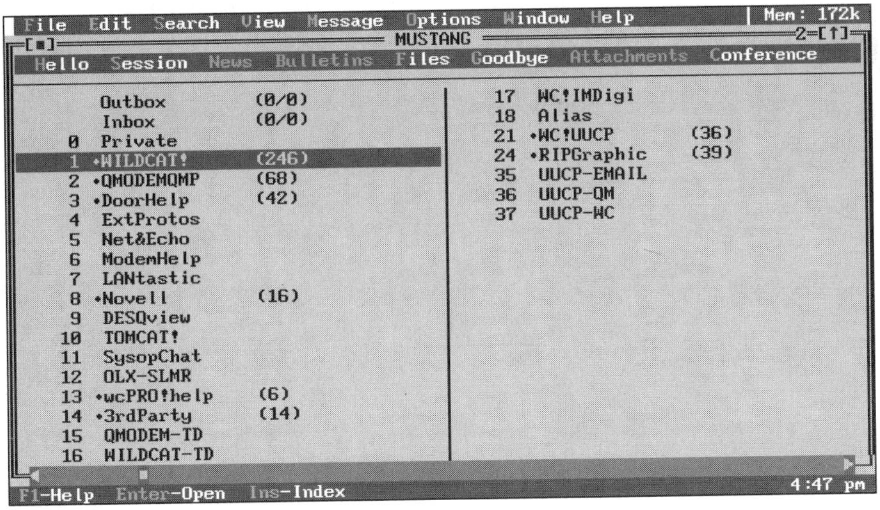

Figure 10-2: Typical mail packet conference list. The conferences and the selected messages are shown in this summary.

Figure 10-2 shows that eight conferences contain mail that was downloaded in this packet. They have a dot between the conference number and its name. For example, the RIPGraphic conference (number 24) contains 39 messages for reading.

You then read the messages in turn and can discard, save, or reply to them as you choose. The precise methods depend on the particular mail reader.

When you next access the online service and select the BBS's mail reader features, any messages that you have replied to are uploaded as a file. The selected conferences are scanned for new messages, and the resulting file is downloaded to your computer.

Taglines

One area of lighter online entertainment is message taglines. As you read messages online, you will find that many have cute footnotes. These are known as *taglines*. Most offline readers include the capability to add a tagline to your replies. You also can find many utilities for creating, managing, and adding your own taglines to your messages.

Many taglines are extremely corny, but they certainly help liven some of the messages. It is considered acceptable to "steal" someone else's tagline and use it in another message. Although not included in the following examples, some taglines make good use of ASCII characters, such as happy faces and musical notes. Others use emoticons, such as :), to show emotions. You typically read an emoticon by tilting your head to the left. For example, :) is a smiling face with the colon as the eyes and the parenthesis as the mouth.

The following are examples of taglines:

```
"640K ought to be enough for anybody." - Bill Gates 1981
"Age and treachery beat youth and talent every time."
"Creativity is the result of a BOARD mind"
"Daddy, what does FORMATTING DRIVE C mean?"
"He's dead Jim! Get his tricorder, I'll get his wallet."
"I need a home run hitter" he said ruthlessly.
"Is that computer still on the phone?"
"Misspelled? Impossible. Error-correcting modem."
"Press to test." <click> "Release to detonate."
"Put knot yore trussed in spel chequers!"
"When in doubt, use a bigger hammer."
```

Combining the script feature with a BBS's mail reader program can make your connections completely automated. My typical script file is the same as in this chapter, except that the final command accesses the Quick Mail reader rather than the mail reading command.

When the mail reader is accessed, the script selects the commands for downloading a mail packet. You can add the commands to disconnect from the system and make the whole process automatic. However, my script finishes and sounds an alarm after downloading the mail packet. This allows me to download any files from the file library that I am interested in.

Summary

This chapter introduced a variety of methods for streamlining your communications sessions. These procedures include taking advantage of the many features in your communications program. These can be organizational and involve options in your dialing directory and other connection options.

Your communications program will probably include commands that help streamline your communications while online. Most important of these features are key macros and scripts. If you are interested in messages, offline readers are important, either as a feature of your communications program or as a separate program.

Chapter 11 explains ways that you can make the most of your fax modem.

11

CHAPTER

Making the Most of Your Fax Modem

This chapter covers tools and techniques for making the most of your fax modem. Specifically, this chapter discusses the following topics:

- ❖ Reconfiguring your fax modem
- ❖ Choosing file formats
- ❖ Adding company logos and signatures
- ❖ Streamlining fax document sending and receiving
- ❖ Using special fax software features, such as mail merge and transaction logs

Essentials for Fax Software

A typical fax modem has fewer adjustable features than a typical data modem. When you send or receive a fax document, the transmission portion is automated and does not require user intervention. The user must prepare the document for sending and read the received document but does not need to interact during the transmission process itself.

A data modem, in comparison, typically requires user interaction during the communications session, but less preparatory work is necessary.

As Chapter 4 explains, your fax modem requires a serial port and comes supplied with its own fax software. Although fax modems communicate with each other by using internationally accepted standards, there is less uniformity in the way the modems are controlled by the fax software.

Consequently, you are more limited with your fax modem software selection than you are with your data modem communication software. You probably will use the fax software supplied with your fax modem and not purchase an alternative. However, you may want to supplement the fax software by using other software utility programs. You will use the fax software for the actual document transmission but are more likely to do some, if not all, of the document preparation with alternative software.

As Chapter 7 explains, your fax software can accept documents in a variety of formats and may be capable of preparing such items as a cover sheet. It can dial a telephone number and send the document to a receiving fax. The fax software also includes programs that allow you to receive a fax document and save it as a file on your disk. It probably includes a file viewer so that you can see the received document.

Although fax software is not usually as sophisticated as data modem communication software, you can look for various options when choosing a fax modem. Additionally or alternatively, you can supplement the software with other utilities.

This chapter focuses on the extras that are found in some fax software programs. In most cases, these are equivalent to the extras found in communications programs. For example, a fax program may include many options in the dialing directory configuration that allow you to sort in various ways or have several directories.

Exploiting Your Fax Software Features

This chapter divides the extra features possible in your fax software into two general topics: the features that affect your productivity by streamlining fax transmission and receipt and the features that affect the quality of the fax document and the feasibility of sending it.

Productivity features include mail merging, batch sending, and transaction logs; and feasibility features include appropriate configuration, optimum file format, and adding signatures and company logos to your fax document.

Knowing what you have

Like data modems and communication software, if you already own and use a fax modem, you should look carefully at your documentation to see whether there are any features you are not using. Check the table of contents and the index for feature names you aren't familiar with.

For example, you may find that your fax software includes a screen-capture program. This may enable you to send an image stored in a format that the fax software cannot accept directly. You can load the screen capture program, display the image, and capture it in a format acceptable to the fax software.

To make the best use of your fax modem, you also should be familiar with the other application programs you use, such as word processors and spreadsheets. The other application programs fall into two categories: the programs you use to create a document for fax transmittal and utility programs that can help prepare the document after creation.

Reconfiguring your fax modem

When you first installed your fax modem, you probably selected the default settings or only changed the minimum number of settings to make your fax modem work. You should take the time to look again at your fax modem configuration and determine whether other changes are appropriate.

"How can I make the fax modem work faster?"

Although fewer options are available than with a data modem, first look at the configuration of your fax modem to see whether you selected the correct device. Most fax modem software is written to work with several different fax modems, and you should choose the exact model name and number wherever possible. If you choose a different model, you may still be able to use your fax modem, but you may not be using all the advanced features.

The fax modem configuration, particularly if you have a data modem and fax modem combination, probably includes other options that you may not have bothered to alter when you installed the modem. Many of these settings are parallel with those found on a data modem. For example, you may be able to choose between tone and pulse dialing, alter the speed of dialing, make the fax modem detect busy signals, and alter the delays before redialing.

Chapter 10 explains some of these types of options in more detail. You can typically shave seconds off every dialing procedure and minimize wasted time by choosing appropriate configuration settings. The manufacturer chooses default settings that are going to work in almost all situations. Because these settings are conservative, you can probably get better performance.

For example, I have a less-than-optimum phone system partly due to my electronic switch that routes my phone calls. It takes several seconds for the electronic switch to hang up the phone. Consequently, I cannot reduce the delay between when the fax modem detects a busy signal and hangs up the phone and when it redials. However, when I have a dial tone, my telephone system accepts tone signals very fast, so I can increase the dialing speed and save time.

You also should check your communication parameters to verify that you are selecting the fastest speed that your fax modem can use. If the fax machine you are communicating with is not as fast as yours, the two fax modems will negotiate a lower speed automatically. Consequently, you can always configure your fax software so that it tries to operate at the fastest speed.

On a data modem, there are times when you won't want your modem to try to connect at the fastest possible speed, such as when you pay an online service for connect time. The faster speed often has a premium cost, and the slower speed may be more economical although it takes longer to get the data. Chapters 5 and 13 cover the topics of reducing online costs for data modems.

File format options

Although file formats for your fax modem are introduced in Chapter 7, this chapter revisits the topic because understanding and selecting appropriate file formats for your fax documents is the key to making the most of your fax modem.

Fax software is usually relatively unsophisticated when compared with desktop publishing programs or word processors. If you only want to send a short text message, you can use the editor in your fax software and don't need to consider many of the advanced options. However, if you send longer documents, particularly if these documents were created in a variety of application programs, you need to consider your options carefully.

Think of it as the difference between typical documents that you distribute in printed form. If you use a Post-It note or other scrap of paper, you're only scribbling a quick note and attaching it to another prepared document. If you send an internal memo, it may have a standard layout, but you don't usually need to be too concerned about its appearance or the detailed contents. However, if you prepare a document that has a wider distribution, especially when it's being sent to customers, the presentation becomes important. Not only is the content important, but the precise layout may need to conform with a corporate image.

"How do I get a document into the fax software?"

The editor in your fax software probably can handle the simple text messages where the content is brief and the format is not particularly important. You can probably create a standard fax cover sheet or use one of the supplied examples to provide a consistent image. However, you won't want to depend on this editor for long document creation, particularly when the presentation is important.

Your fax software can accept documents from your other application programs. However, it can support only a limited number of file format types, and even those it may not support completely.

Every application program has its unique way of storing the data from your documents. For example, a word processing document includes text and the special codes that indicate the word processor formatting for the text. One code indicates that the line is centered, and another shows a font change. Although you may not actually see these codes when you use the word processor, they are important when you try to send the document as a fax document with your fax software.

Note: Your fax software may accept files from WordPerfect and Microsoft Word. However, it will not support the formats from future versions of the software. Suppose that your fax software supports WordPerfect Version 5.1 but not 6.0 or later. You must understand how this affects the document you send. If WordPerfect 6.0, for example, uses different codes for centering text or creating tables than WordPerfect 5.1, your fax software cannot translate a document created in WordPerfect 6.0 correctly.

You have various alternatives for getting your document in a form suitable for sending as a fax document. You may be able to save your document in a different format from within your application program. For example, almost all word processors can save documents as ASCII text, and almost all fax software can accept ASCII text. However, ASCII text does not include different fonts or many text formatting features. Your word processor may be able to save your document in a format comparable with a previous version, as WordPerfect 6.0 can save files in WordPerfect 5.1 format.

Many word processors, spreadsheets, databases, and other application programs also can save files in alternative formats. Not only does this make it easier to transfer document files between application programs, but it gives you a better chance of being able to send a fax document that looks as much like the original as possible. A less desirable option is to use a utility program that captures the file from within your application program.

"Why doesn't my fax document look right?"

Even if your fax software claims to support a particular word processor, you need to experiment to see how complete the support is. Using an alternative file-saving format from your application program might give better output. You should do this experimentation before you have an impending deadline.

You should experiment by sending some sample documents. Examine any document viewer available in your fax software before the document is sent. Then send the document to another fax machine. (If you have two phone lines, you may want to borrow a fax machine from a friend to try this in the privacy of your own home.) Compare the received document with the original and see where the differences occur.

You won't have many problems if you send text, but you can run into problems when you send other document types. Try to include in your sample document any features you may be using in real documents. For example, if you use tables in your word processor, add graphic images on your pages, or send spreadsheets, see whether these are accepted by the fax software. If not, devise an alternative method of document preparation. This may involve using screen-capture programs, using print-capture programs, or adjusting the fonts and features you use in your documents.

Similar rules apply to graphic files. Your fax software may accept files in different graphic formats, but the level of support varies greatly. Graphics often have additional problems that you may not be aware of. Your fax modem sends documents in black and white—not color. (Color fax machines are likely to become available in the next couple of years but not yet.)

Improving Your Fax Quality

Fax modems remove one of the problems found with paper documents. You won't send a dirty document. For example, your manuscript won't have a coffee mug circle on it, dirty fingerprints, or creased pages. However, you can run into problems that affect the quality of the document you are sending.

A stand-alone fax machine is like a copy machine. The received document will look like the original document. The clarity will not be as good, but the layout, content, and completeness will be the same.

When using a fax modem, you need to consider the document's layout, content, and completeness. Experiment with your fax software so that you understand what the cover sheet and a document created in the fax software's text editor will look like. If your document is imported from another application, such as a word processor or graphic program, use the fax software's viewer to preview the fax and check the format of the document that you actually send. Many formatting details may be lost in the translation from your application program to the fax software's format.

You need to carefully consider sending color documents. Your fax modem will send documents in black and white. When you send a color document, the results are often surprising and very difficult to read. Colors that contrast well on-screen don't have the same contrast when sent in black and white.

I regularly create screen shots for publication with my articles and books. Many are reproduced in black and white. Some magazines specify the color combinations I should use to create a well-contrasting screen. I have a special color scheme for Windows, for example. It looks hideous in color, but it looks very good in black and white. I often change the background color in other application programs so that they reproduce well in black and white. If you send color pictures by fax modem, you should apply similar modifications for clarity.

Most graphic programs are in color. When you send a color graphic image, your fax software converts it to black and white before sending. This can dramatically affect the clarity of the received document, because colors that contrast well do not necessarily get converted to shades of gray that contrast well.

Graphic file formats are more standardized in some ways and more subject to different interpretation than text files in other ways. Most fax software accepts graphic images in at least PCX and a TIFF format. However, there are a couple of variations of PCX format and several different standards for TIFF files. Because you cannot read the files, finding the correct format to save the file and the correct format to import the file into the fax software is a question of experimentation.

If you cannot find a suitable format to save your files and import them into your fax software, consider a separate file-conversion program.

You also need to consider the file format for the documents that you receive. Remember that you only receive a graphic image. If you want to do more than view the document and discard it, you need a graphic program that can accept a file format that can be generated by your fax software. Again, a file-conversion program may be necessary.

"Will an OCR program save me retyping fax documents?"

To convert a received document into text, you need an OCR (optical character recognition) program. This is unlikely to be supplied with your fax software, although some manufacturers are adding it as a premium option. OCR programs vary in their capability to translate the graphics into text. Some are practically useless, and others do a reasonable job. The best can often achieve accuracy exceeding 99 percent.

Note: 99.9 percent accuracy on a single page of text still results in about two errors per page. If the document is in an unusual font or is not a particularly clean image, it may be quicker and more accurate to have the document retyped.

If you find that you regularly convert fax documents into text, consider whether you are using the correct tool for the job. You may be better off using a data modem to transfer the document as a file rather than as a fax document. PCs and modems are inexpensive enough so that purchasing an additional PC and modem may be justified when you consider the time and costs involved in conversion of graphic files to text and correction or retyping.

How OCR Works

When you receive a fax document, it is stored as a graphic image. A particular page of information is represented as a series of rows of dots. The usual description is black dots on a white page. There are typically 300 dots per inch in the horizontal direction and 150 rows per inch in the vertical direction. Text documents are also represented in this way.

The human eye is easily deceived and, rather than seeing the page as lots of dots, sees the dots in groups. You see lines of text. They might appear a bit grainy, but you usually can interpret the dots correctly.

However, your word processor, spreadsheet, database, or other text application cannot interpret the dots as text, and to load the fax image into a text application for editing, you must convert the dots into text by using an optical character recognition (OCR) program.

An OCR program is designed to look at a page of dots and "see" the dots in groups; hopefully each group is a character of text. After dividing the page into these groups, it looks at each group in turn and tries to match the pattern of dots with a character in its font library. OCR is essentially a guessing program. The program guesses each of the characters on the page.

On a clean fax document where the background is not smudged, the lines of text are straight, and the font is not too ornate, the OCR program can make very good guesses, and you probably will only need to correct a few characters. You then save the interpreted page as a text file and can put it into your text application for editing. An OCR program can only interpret the material it is given and can only match it to the character shapes it understands. You won't get good results from poor-quality fax documents.

If the page is too light, the characters will have parts missing, and the OCR program may choose the wrong character. For example, if the descender on a *y* is light, the OCR program may think the correct letter is a *v* or a *u*. On the other hand, if the fax document is too dark, the letters will be blurry, and the OCR program will have too much information for a character. For example, it will have trouble discriminating between *m* and *rn*.

Handwritten documents are not written with the same accuracy as typed or printed documents. Even if you look at one person's handwriting, the characters are not written the same each time. One time, a letter may be smaller than another or written at more of an angle. OCR programs do not do a good job of interpreting handwriting.

The OCR program will also have trouble interpreting some fonts, even ones that appear simple. Most people understand why interpreting script fonts, which emulate ornate handwriting, is difficult. However, many OCR programs have trouble even with simple italic fonts. The characters in an italic font lean, and the OCR program usually tries to divide the graphic image into a row of rectangles. When it does this with an italic font, it is more likely to get part of the previous character and possibly the next character in a rectangle it considers a character.

Adding a company logo

Your fax software may include features that allow you to add clip art or other graphic images to your fax document. You can use this feature to add a company logo or a signature.

The flexibility of this feature depends on the individual fax software. However, the general principle is to place a graphic image in a small area of your document. In the case of a company logo, you may want to place this on the cover sheet for your fax so that your fax cover sheet maintains your company image and reflects your standard letterhead.

Some fax software enables you to add several graphic images on a page and have flexible placement options. Others are more restricted in number and location for these images.

"How do I sign a fax document?"

You can treat a signature in the same way as a logo or clip art image. You place it as a graphic image in the desired location. Again, the flexibility in placement depends on the fax software. Usually, however, you can add this image only to your cover sheet or a document you have created in the fax software's text editor.

To add this image, either as a logo or a signature, you need to get the desired graphic into electronic form. The most common method is to use a scanner and scan the image into your computer. Alternatively, you may be able to use a graphic program and re-create the image electronically.

You can purchase scanners that range from very inexpensive hand-held devices, to large, fast, page scanners that can scan engineering drawings. In general, you get what you pay for. However, many scanners include an OCR program as part of the supplied software.

Note: You should think carefully before putting your signature on your computer in electronic form. You must understand the security implications and your vulnerability. Anyone who has access to the files on your computer will have access to your signature. On the other hand, having your signature stored electronically compensates for one of the fax modem's shortcomings: its inability to send handwritten material.

Streamlining Your Fax Sending and Receiving

Because you don't interact with your fax modem while it sends or receives a fax document, the methods you employ to streamline your fax use relate more to the preparation and organization of your document and phone books than to techniques applicable during the actual transmission.

Document organization

Your fax software may include various options that can help you organize your fax documents. You usually can select directories where your received fax documents are placed. You may have other organizational options, such as a default directory for a copy of sent documents, or other storage aids.

"Where are my received fax documents?"

If you will send or receive many fax documents, you should decide on a procedure so that you know where you stand. You should employ a file-naming method that you can understand so that you can separate the read files from the unread files.

Think about your file-naming and organization system carefully. DOS has a serious limitation by allowing only eight characters in the main part of a filename. You need to choose a naming system that you will understand several months or years from now.

You also need to separate fax documents into different locations. At its simplest, you need an area for documents ready to send, another for sent documents, another for received documents, and another for received and read documents. Bear in mind that the received document is a graphic file, and graphic files tend to be extremely large. You can rapidly fill a hard disk if you get a lot of fax documents.

I use a system where my data files are divided by project. When I contact a potential customer, the information is stored in a directory named JOBS. When the job becomes a reality, it gets its own directory based on the customer's name. When the job is completed, I back up all the files and remove the directory.

I divide customer directories into project directories when applicable. It takes a couple of minutes to make sure that any generated document, such as a received fax, is immediately transferred to the correct directory, but it makes it very easy to find later. (It also has the added benefit of appearing efficient to my customers.)

My file-naming system is not very imaginative and varies with my mood. However, I always separate the files by projects and take care to name the files by type, such as .FAX for fax documents and .WP for word processing files. This means I am only looking through a few files when I search for information.

Transaction logs

Many stand-alone fax machines offer a feature known as *transaction logging*. The machine keeps lists of all the fax documents that have been sent or received. It also typically notes whether the document was sent or received successfully. Your fax software may offer a similar feature so that you can track your fax documents. Desirable extras for this feature include a record of the filename of the document.

"Can I keep a record of the fax documents I've sent?"

Although you won't suffer from document paper jams when you send a document by fax modem, your document may not be sent completely for other reasons. These include the receiving fax machine running out of paper or disk space or some sort of error with the document you are sending where the fax software is unable to convert the supplied file into a form suitable for transmission.

Mailing lists

Your fax software probably can store the names and fax phone numbers for the people you call. This capability is equivalent to the dialing directory for data communications software.

Some fax software includes extra features in the dialing directory area. If you need to send the same document to multiple locations, you may be able to establish mailing lists. These lists are equivalent to a circulation list on a memo.

"How do I send the same fax to many people?"

If you need the fax software to send a copy of the document to each person on the mailing list, this task can be implemented in a variety of ways. You may need to choose several people from your dialing directory and then issue the command to send a fax document. Alternatively, when you fill out the cover sheet, the fax software may be able to pick up the addressees automatically.

The flexibility of specifying what you want and then letting your computer software handle the distribution list is a feature that separates fax modems. Look carefully at this area when you choose a fax modem.

Mail merging

In some cases, you need to send the same message to a variety of people, but you don't want the other people to know. This process is equivalent to doing a mass mailing.

In the mass mailing situation, your needs are different than when you want to send a document to a circulation list. A good mass mailing uses personalized features that tailor each document to the receiving person.

Consider the customized junk mail you receive that says "Dear Mr. Smith. We are currently offering discounts on aluminum siding for people located in the Boston area." At first glance, the letter looks individually written but is in fact a mass mailing where the "Mr. Smith" and "Boston" are inserted automatically.

Like the group mailing feature, mass mailing features separate various fax modems. Some fax software does not support this type of feature; other fax software has particularly flexible mail merging options.

For example, some fax software allows you to use a special coding system when preparing your cover sheet or document. You write something like **%%FAXNAME%%** in your document where you normally write the name of the recipient and **%%FAXTEL%%** where you normally place the recipient's fax telephone number. You generate a separate text file that contains a list relating all the names you want to place in the %%FAXNAME%% and %%FAXTEL%% locations. The fax modem software takes the sample document file and the name file and generates a fax document for each person listed in the text file and then sends it to the specified number.

Choosing whether to use the fax software's mail merging capabilities can be a trade-off. Most good word processors include mail merging capabilities that far exceed any of the mail merging features found in a fax software program. However, if you use the word processor, you need a way to tell the fax software that you have a list of files to be sent as fax documents. You also need to tell the fax software which telephone number to dial for each document. The balance between how much to do in your word processor and how much to do in the fax software varies with the particular fax software.

Scheduling fax delivery

When you use a fax modem as a major source of document distribution, you can see the cost of telephone calls mount. Although sending a single page fax document can be less expensive than regular mail, when you start sending multipage documents, the costs mount rapidly and quickly exceed the costs of overnight courier services.

"How do I cut my phone costs?"

One way to reduce costs is to use the scheduling feature of your fax software. You can write and schedule your faxes for delivery but delay the actual sending until a later time. For example, you can delay the actual sending until the telephone rates go down in the evening or on the weekend.

Although I am only a small business and have very tight control of my expenses, I can reduce my phone bill by about a third by calling internationally during reduced times and delaying sending faxes within the U.S. until the evening.

Scheduling the fax transmittal until a later time has two additional advantages. If you wait until evening or night time to send the fax to a business, you are more likely to get straight through without a busy signal.

Additionally, delaying the fax sending also gives you a performance advantage. Most fax software can send your fax and allow you to continue using your computer while the fax document is being sent. Because the computer is dividing its resources so that it can do more than one thing simultaneously, it is less responsive to you while it sends the fax document. Delaying the actual sending until you are no longer using the computer allows you to continue working without a performance degradation.

Summary

This chapter showed how to make the best use of your fax modem. Most optimization features involve streamlining your document preparation and file handling. You need to determine the best combination of file formats to give you the best results.

Other keys to making the most of your fax modem involve using the extra features supplied with your fax software. The software may include flexible mail merging, logging, and scheduling features that can reduce your online costs.

Chapter 12 introduces special-purpose communications, such as using your modem on the road, using remote control software, and connecting internationally.

12
CHAPTER

Special-Purpose Communications

This chapters covers special-purpose communications, including the following topics:

- ✤ Understanding remote control software
- ✤ Using your modem on the road
- ✤ Using your modem internationally
- ✤ Creating a mini-BBS by using host mode
- ✤ Communicating with computer types other than PCs

Understanding and Using Host Mode

Bulletin board systems are introduced in Chapter 13 and are explained in detail in Chapter 14. They are probably the most common application for modems. You use your modem and communications software to call a remote computer. The remote computer runs special communications software, known as bulletin board software. This allows you to control both ends of the connection.

When you are connected, the BBS software displays a menu of selections, and you choose from that menu. You can read stored messages or select a file for transfer. The BBS software is designed to allow you access to the remote computer.

"Can I turn my computer into a BBS?"

Although BBSs use special communications software, there are many instances when you can benefit from having your own "mini-BBS." You can set up a computer as a BBS and call it from a remote location, for example. Suppose that you are on the road but need to pick up some files from your computer. If you leave your computer configured as a BBS, you can call in and collect the files without coordinating with someone else.

Alternatively, if you want to exchange files with a friend, it is much easier to set up one of the computers as a BBS and have the other person call this computer remotely. Then, when you connect, rather than typing messages to each other like **I am going to download the file now**, you can select from menus.

Apart from being an additional program you need to purchase, BBS software is very sophisticated and can do far more than the relatively simple task of downloading or uploading a couple of files. However, many communications software programs include a feature, known as *host mode*, that acts like a mini-BBS.

"Why would I use host mode?"

When you activate host mode, you make your communications program wait for an incoming phone call. It answers the phone, establishes the connection, and presents a menu of selections for your caller. You use host mode only on the remote computer;

the person calling the remote computer uses the typical communications program mode to dial a phone number and connect with the other computer.

Although limited in features, host mode usually has several essential security features that you can activate. First, most programs only allow the caller to access a particular subdirectory on your hard disk. If the file the user wants is not in that subdirectory, the user cannot access the file. This feature allows you to copy the files you want the caller to access to that subdirectory yet protect the other files on your disk.

Another common feature is password-protection. The caller must give a name and password that are acceptable to your system before seeing the host mode menus. The need for this feature depends on your circumstances. If you leave your computer in host mode for hours or days at a time, an unauthorized person could call the number with his/her modem and have access to your system. (Some people call numbers randomly with a modem in an attempt to find computer systems that they can access.)

I don't bother using the password feature. I set host mode on my computer only when I know a friend is going to call in the next few minutes. The extra configuration necessary to set up the password checking and tell the friend the password does not seem worth it for my potential exposure. However, I do take advantage of the other host mode features that allow access only to a particular directory. This way, the friends calling can easily remind themselves of the names of the files they want to download without wading through hundreds of other files on my computer.

Note: Although host mode allows you to control the activities you want to perform on a remote computer, it does not give you access to the programs on the remote computer. The typical activities involve downloading and uploading files and reading or leaving messages. You cannot, for example, run a spreadsheet on the remote computer. This requires remote control software.

Understanding Remote Control Software

Remote control software allows you to connect with another computer from a remote location by using modems and operate the remote computer as if you were sitting at the remote computer itself. For example, you can use remote control software to call your office computer from home and use the word processor or spreadsheet located on the office computer. It's like giving a computer an extremely long keyboard and display cables.

Consider a typical communication session when you use your normal communication software. You call another modem by using your modem, and the two modems connect. You run communication software on your computer, and the remote computer also runs communication software. The remote computer may run communication software similar to yours, or it may run specific software, such as bulletin board software. As explained earlier in the chapter, some communication software includes host mode, which is equivalent to running BBS software. When the remote computer uses communication software, you need someone to operate the remote computer. In the case of BBS software, you can control the remote computer by using the remote computer's communication software. However, you are only controlling the communications software on the remote computer—not any of the other programs on that computer.

When two people are involved in using communication software, your communication session involves transferring files from one computer to another or typing messages to each other. When you call a computer running BBS software, the processes are similar, but you control both ends of the connection. You transfer files from one computer to another or you send and read messages.

"How can I run my computer's programs remotely?"

Remote control software is different because it seems like you are sitting in front of the remote computer. For example, you can see a DOS prompt, use DOS commands, or type the command to start your word processor. You can run your word processor and save files to disk. The disk the files are saved on is the one on the remote computer.

This type of software is useful in two specific situations. First, you can use it to operate the computer from a remote location—to use the office computer when at home, for example. Second, it can be used as a technical support tool.

Suppose that you supply technical support to a remote location and are responsible for training users in their word processors. If someone has a problem, you can connect with his computer by modem and run remote control software. You can then watch him operate the word processor and see the mistakes he's making. Additionally, you can operate the application program by remote and show the user how to perform a task. The keys the user presses on his keyboard cause the application program to respond, and the keys you press on your keyboard also cause the application program to respond.

This can be an invaluable tool compared to a typical telephone technical support call. When you make a telephone call, communicating can be difficult because you don't have visual feedback from the other person. Remote control software helps you "see" what the other person is doing with the computer.

To run remote control software, you install the software on two computers, the one you will call from and the one you will operate remotely. Depending on the particular product chosen, this may require you to purchase a copy of the program for each end of the connection. When comparing prices, look carefully to determine how many copies of the software you need. Because you will run the communications software on two computers, you probably will need two copies of the software. This may be supplied in a single box, or it may require two complete copies.

Resource Guide to Remote Control Software

Close-Up
Norton Lambert Corp
P.O. Box 4085
Santa Barbara, CA 93140
(805) 964-6767

Central Point Commute
Central Point Software, Inc.
15220 NW Greenbrier Parkway, Suite 200
Beaverton, OR 97006
(800) 445-2110

Carbon Copy for DOS
Microcom Inc.
500 River Ridge Dr.
Norwood, MA 02062
(617) 551-1000

Crosstalk Remote2
DCA Inc.
1000 Alderman Dr.
Alpharetta, GA 30201
(404) 998-3998

Norton pcANYWHERE
Symantec Corp
10201 Torre Ave.
Cupertino, CA 95014-2132
(408) 253-9600

PC MacTERM
Symantec Corp
10201 Torre Ave.
Cupertino, CA 95014-2132
(408) 253-9600

To simplify the remaining explanations, consider the following remote control connection. Suppose that the computer containing the application software, such as a word processor, is the remote computer in your office, and the computer linking to the remote computer is in your home.

You run remote control software by loading a TSR (terminate and stay resident) program on your office computer. This makes the office computer answer the phone and give you control of this computer when you call it from your home.

You run the companion portion of your remote control software from your home. In most cases, this is the same product as installed on your office computer, but some remote control products allow you to call from ordinary communications programs by running a special script file. (Script files are covered in Chapter 10.)

After you have established the connection between your home computer and office computer, you can run your application programs. The communications software can display the same thing on your home computer's screen as on the remote computer's screen. The software can deal with such items as different video screen resolutions and keyboards to make your home computer appear as close as possible to your office computer.

"Why can't I use remote control software to receive faxes?"

For remote control software to work, the TSR must be loaded in the office computer. Consider a fax modem, where you can't receive fax documents unless you have the relevant TSR loaded into memory. You can't have multiple TSRs loaded into memory when they try to do the same job. A fax modem TSR uses the modem to answer the phone when it rings, as will a remote control TSR. You have to choose which one you load in memory. For similar reasons, you can't use remote control software to run communication software on your office computer. You are already using the modem to make the connection.

Remote control software has various other limitations. Most are due to the computer hardware rather than the remote control program limitations. The problems relate to available DOS memory and the differences between your screen at home and in the office.

In reference to the memory limitations, when you call your office computer, the TSR activates itself to make the connection. This program is always running while you are connected to the office computer. Consequently, it always uses some of the memory on your office computer. This leaves less memory available for your application program. You may not be able to load your application program because you don't have enough memory available after the remote control software's TSR is in memory.

This limitation can apply even if you have 16 MB of RAM in your office computer. The critical memory is the amount of base memory available to DOS. You can determine this by using the DOS MEM command. Most application programs, such as word processors and spreadsheets, specify that they need a certain amount of free memory to load, such as 480 KB. This amount must be available after you load the remote control software's TSR.

There are many techniques for maximizing the amount of free base memory in your computer, especially in 386-based computers (or better). These techniques can involve using memory-manager programs, altering your CONFIG.SYS and AUTOEXEC.BAT files, or using different command line switches when you start your application program.

In addition to memory limitations, you may encounter device limitations with the remote control software. These problems depend on the particular combination of software and hardware that you run. For example, you may not be able to access a CD-ROM drive using remote control software, or you may not be able to see the correct screens on your home computer. In most cases, there are workarounds that can solve your problems, but you may need to spend some time with the remote control software technical support technicians to make your particular configuration work.

You should consider the impact of your computer crashing while running remote control software. Regardless of the configuration, you probably will need to reboot the remote computer at some time. Look carefully at the remote control software to determine what happens if someone breaks the connection while in an application program. This may happen intentionally or accidentally. Remember that you are depending on a telephone connection to maintain the link between the two computers. You may get a noisy connection or may be unexpectedly disconnected.

It is very inconvenient to need to reboot the office computer by being physically present. After all, the whole point of remote control software is being able to use your computer when you are not sitting at it. Being able to reboot remotely is a good feature but can expose you if the wrong people can reboot the computer.

Consider the situation where you set up a remote computer with a database library on it. You can supply many people with the remote control software to access this computer remotely. Because only one person can be connected to the computer at one time, you aren't violating any copyright rules on the database software, yet many different people have access to this computer. In the case of some very expensive databases, such as medical or legal libraries, the remote control software costs are minimal compared with supplying multiple copies of the database.

However, if the users accessing the database hang up without exiting the database, the database will not be available to any user until you reboot the remote computer unless your remote control software can handle the rebooting automatically. If you are offering access to the database as a service, having the database unavailable due to the system needing rebooting is probably unacceptable.

Other issues you should examine relate to security. If you leave your office computer in a mode where you can connect to it remotely, you leave it in a mode where others also can connect to it. When using host mode in your communication program, you only expose one or two directories on your hard disk to the caller. In the case of remote control software, you expose your application programs to the caller.

Be sure to look at the security features in the remote control software. These include password security access. They also may include callback features where the remote computer calls the caller back at a previously specified number. This enables you to make the office computer pay for the phone call but limits where the caller can be located.

Remote control software provides features not usually found in other communication programs. You may be able to run the desktop publishing program in your office from your laptop or finish other projects from your home. You may be able to reduce the number of on-site technical support calls you need by using remote control software and linking to a consultant's or trainer's office.

In the past, remote control software was not particularly popular because of the programs' responsiveness. The modems had to pass a lot of information between the two computers, resulting in sluggish application program response. The new generation of high-speed modems are fast enough that you will be able to run most applications without unacceptable speed reductions because the two modems will be able to transmit and receive the necessary data fast.

However, remote control software is more difficult to set up and manage than typical communication software. If you only want to exchange a few messages or transfer files, stick with ordinary communications programs. As its name suggests, remote control software is suitable when you want to actually operate a computer remotely.

Communicating with a Macintosh

In a way, this section is unnecessary in this book, but a frequently asked question is "How do I connect with a Macintosh or other computer?" The earlier chapters emphasize that when you make a telecommunication connection, you control a modem with your computer. The modem connects with another modem, which in turn is connected to another computer or device.

The two computers at each end of the connection don't have to be the same. You can link PCs, Macintoshes, minicomputers, or mainframes, and any combination of computers. Each computer must be able to communicate with a modem, and the two modems do the actual linking. Because modems adhere to international communication standards (not computer standards), the computer types do not matter.

Now that I've said that you can link any two computers, there are limitations as to the value of linking the two computers. Most computers support the sending and receiving of ASCII text, so you can type information on your keyboard and have it appear on the remote computer, and the remote computer can send ASCII text to your computer and it will appear on your screen.

However, the ASCII character set on one computer may not be the same as the ASCII character set on another computer. The ASCII character set consists of 128 defined characters. However, on computers that can store information in 8-bit characters (chunks of data) rather than the 7-bit characters found on mainframe computers, the ASCII character set is extended another 128 characters. (There are 128 unique combinations of bits with 7 bits of binary data and 256 unique combinations with 8 bits of binary data.) Because these are not part of the internationally accepted standard, many different variations occur. If you only exchange data with PCs within the U.S., you'll probably always use the same character set. However, there are different standards for different countries as well as different standards for special purposes. The differences may allow you to use accented characters, different punctuation symbols, or different line drawing characters.

Apart from character transfer, most communications programs support file transfer, regardless of the computer they run on. If the two computers support the same file-transfer protocol, you can transfer files between the two computers. The important issue is what can be done with the files after they are transferred. Suppose that you transfer a spreadsheet file from a PC to a Macintosh. You can only use that PC file on the Macintosh if you have a Macintosh application program that can read the PC spreadsheet file. This applies to any file. The file may be transferred correctly, but it can only be used if the receiving computer's application program can read it.

Note: This disregard for *computer type* is why commercial online services can work. You transfer your file to the online service, even though the computer may be a mainframe computer. The online service never actually uses the file; it only stores it. Another user downloads the file from the online service to his PC and then uses it.

As more people connect different computer types together, more DOS-based and Apple-DOS application programs support a common file format so you can use a file on either computer, which makes transfer between computer types more valuable and more streamlined. This occurs frequently when you use application programs that are available on different platforms, such as WordPerfect and Microsoft Excel, which are available for the PC and the Macintosh. You are more likely to be able to use files created by the other computer type than if you try to import a file created by a less common application program.

Remote control software also allows you to link your PC to a Macintosh. For example, with the right software, you can call a PC from your Macintosh and run PC applications on your remote PC.

Using Your Modem on the Road

As covered in Chapters 7 and 11, your fax modem can accept and send fax documents as if it were a stand-alone fax machine. If your fax modem is installed in or attached to your laptop, you can send and receive fax documents wherever you are located—if you know the receiving fax machine's telephone number.

Data modems also can be installed in most laptop computers or can be attached to a laptop's serial port. Although you can use a full-sized external modem with a laptop, you can also purchase small-sized modems (and some that are combination fax and data modems) for use with your laptop. Chapter 4 explains modem selection and the relevant considerations and trade-offs when selecting a modem and communications software for your laptop.

If you have access to the RJ-11 jack for a telephone, you can attach your modem to the telephone system and send data via modems. However, using your modem while traveling can be more difficult than when in a home or office. The problems are not usually due to the modem but relate to how you connect to the telephone system.

"How do I use my modem in a hotel room?"

Hotels and conference centers are becoming more aware of the traveler with a laptop computer, and they make RJ-11 sockets increasingly available for their visitors. They often advertise their modem support in their hotel guides. In some cases, there is an extra socket on the telephone, and you just plug your modem into it. In other cases, the hotels have only a few phones with the modem socket on it, and you have to ask for the correct phone to be installed in your room. In other instances, you may have to use the hotel or conference center's business office. Although frustrating, this latter alternative is preferable to not being able to connect at all.

Tip: If you are in a hotel and do not have a printer, sending a fax to the hotel's fax number is an alternative for printing a document.

I make a point to ask a hotel about connecting my modem to the phone when I confirm my reservation. (I also ask about any fees for receiving fax documents.) I am unlikely to stay at a hotel without convenient modem hookups more than once.

If you have doubts about whether the plug in the back of a hotel phone really is an RJ-11 and is not a similar-looking connector, ask the hotel staff. If you make the wrong judgment, you can damage your modem permanently. Some, if not most, hotels use a special telephone system, similar to a company using its own telephone exchange system (PBX). Depending on the type of PBX and the equipment installed, you may not have suitable access to the telephone service by simply plugging in your modem.

"How do I use my modem from a public pay phone?"

If you do not have a phone jack connector suitable for your modem, you still have several other options. You can purchase a device called an *acoustic coupler* to make the connection. You may have seen pictures of these in movies that now seem antiquated. The telephone receiver is placed in a box that has two cradles for the earpiece and mouthpiece. Other acoustic couplers are two round cups that you strap onto the telephone receiver, usually with Velcro straps. The cups or box are attached to a cable with an RJ-11 connector on the end, and you can plug your modem into this connector.

Note: Acoustic couplers, as the name implies, use the microphone and speaker in the telephone receiver. They "listen" to the data being sent and "talk" into the telephone mouthpiece. This connection is less ideal than sending and receiving the data directly from the phone cable. However, this provides a method of connecting a modem to a public pay phone as well as an obscure hotel telephone.

Even with the modem physically connected, making a connection is typically more complicated when staying in a hotel or sending data from an airport than when dialing from your home or office. It is often a balancing act of dialing the correct sequence of numbers with the appropriate delays. In some cases, you can create a dialing string in your communications program. In others, you will have to dial the number by hand and then transfer control from the telephone handset to your communication program.

When you first learn to make a telecommunication connection, you must consider the steps involved in the process. These involve connecting the modem to the telephone line, configuring the modem correctly, dialing the required numbers, letting the modems negotiate a connection, and then performing the character and file transfer desired. When considering telecommunication on the road, you need to reconsider these steps. The first hurdle is the physical connection, and the second is dialing the correct number.

Earlier chapters, including Chapter 9, show techniques for using dialing string prefixes and dealing with extra-long dialing strings. You may need to employ these techniques when using an unusual telephone.

For example, you may need to use a long-distance calling card. You will probably need to dial an access number as well as account number information before dialing the telephone number of the computer you are calling. If you are calling from a hotel room, there may be additional numbers required to actually get a normal telephone company dial tone.

One of the problems with using the modem to do all the dialing is that you have to add delays into your dialing string. This gives the hotel's telephone system time to give you an outside line. Then, after you connect with your long-distance telephone service, it gives time for the long-distance service's computer to accept your account information.

Additionally, the typical default S-register setting (S7) for the length of time between when you start to dial and when the modem expects to negotiate a connection is only 30 seconds. It can take longer than that to dial all the relevant digits. You may need to alter S7's contents to allow for the longer time required. Chapter 10 covers altering the S-register contents. As you move from location to location, the necessary dialing sequence may vary. For example, one hotel may need a 9 and another an 8 to get an outside phone line.

It may be easier to manually dial the necessary phone numbers and only use the modem after the phone number is dialed. To do this, you need the phone and the modem connected at the same time. You can purchase adapter cables, known as RJ-11 splitters, that consist of a single RJ-11 connector at one end of the cable and two RJ-11 connectors at the other. You connect one end into the phone jack in the wall and the other ends into the phone and modem. Alternatively, you can use the acoustic coupler system and strap the handset onto the acoustic coupler after you dial the number.

This procedure involves telling the modem when you want it to start controlling the connection. You can configure some communication programs, such as Smartcom for Windows, so you can switch from voice to data with a keystroke. In other cases, you need to issue the **ATO** command from the terminal screen. You make adjustments by choosing the Settings menu on the main menu bar and then choosing Modem. From the Select Modem & Settings box, you choose Settings. You then uncheck the Monitor call for dial tone and Monitor call for busy signal checkboxes. Then, when you select the phone icon, you do not enter a phone number but press OK and connect.

Because you want to switch from voice to data quickly, you must set up your communication program and modem so that you can switch with a single keystroke. Turn on your modem, load your communications program, and get to the terminal screen.

As explained in earlier chapters, when you type at the terminal screen, the keystrokes are passed to the modem. However, the modem does not accept a command until you press Enter at the end of the command string. When you turn on your modem, it comes up in command mode, ready to receive instructions.

Type **ATO** at the terminal screen in preparation for completing the command. (The ATO command makes the modem take the phone off the hook.) Then, manually dial the required number with the handset.

When you hear the remote modem signal that it has answered the phone, transfer control to the modem. (If you use an acoustic coupler, quickly strap it onto the phone.) Press Enter to send the ATO command to the modem, and the modem negotiates the connection. You can hang up the handset.

You may need to perform a comparable procedure when sending a fax document with your fax modem. You prepare the fax communication software so that a single keystroke will take the phone off hook, and then you dial the phone manually. When the other fax machine answers, you transfer control to the fax modem. This also can be achieved by strapping on an acoustic coupler and pressing the correct key to complete the command or pressing the correct key to complete the command if the fax modem and the phone are attached to the phone line.

International Communication

The telephone system in the U.S. is taken for granted by most of the population. Stories of waiting six months to be assigned a phone number and phone charges that are a substantial portion of a paycheck seem incredible to Americans. However, these facts not only apply to Third World countries but also apply in many other countries throughout the world.

In many countries, the telephone company is government controlled, and in many cases, funds are not assigned for delivering phone lines to all residences. The concept of a phone being a necessity rather than a luxury is really only prevalent in the U.S.

International telephone communication may also be limited in other countries. Remember that when you make a telephone call, you actually are making a link between the location you are calling from and the location you are calling to. Although the signal may be transmitted between two points, the route must be available for the connection to be made. Although there are many international phone lines connecting the U.S. with other countries, another country may only have a few international connections. In some countries, you even need to schedule international phone calls.

"Can I call internationally with my modem?"

The easiest way to connect reliably with other countries is to use a commercial online service, such as CompuServe. You then make a local phone call and post your message or file. The recipient makes a phone call, local or long distance, to connect with the same service and pick up the sent information.

Part IV covers the various online services available. Many are available overseas. Alternatively, many offer connection to the Internet, an international network system. You send a message to the Internet through a commercial online service, and your recipient connects to a different online service available in his country to pick up the message. (Chapter 17 discusses the Internet exclusively.)

Some Internet connections offered by commercial online services only include messaging services and not file transfer. However, the Chapter 17 sidebar, "Transferring Binary Files with 7-Bit Systems," shows another method that allows you to transfer files over an Internet connection, even if file-transfer facilities are not available.

"Can I use my modem in Europe?"

Using your modem overseas is more complicated and may be illegal. Just as the modem you use in this country must be approved for use on the phone system in this country, most other countries also insist that telephones, modems, and other devices must be approved for use in that particular country. In many cases, this means you must use a modem supplied by the telephone company in that country.

Each country has its own standards, and these are probably not the same as the ones used by the U.S. Although many modem manufacturers sell their modems in different countries, the exact settings or modem models may be different to conform with local regulations. (Hayes modems are available in more than 65 countries worldwide.) This variation applies in Europe from country to country as well as in Asia, Africa, and the Middle East.

Note: Different countries also have different AC power circuits. The U.S. standard of 115V 60Hz AC is not typical. Different countries use different power cables as well as different voltages and frequencies. Your computer and modem must be able to connect to these services unless you are only running from a battery or are able to use appropriate adapters and transformers.

If you want to travel to other countries and use a modem, the best advice is to set it up beforehand and make arrangements to buy or borrow equipment in the relevant country. If you want to call another country from the U.S., the procedure is the same as if you are calling within the U.S., except that the telephone number is typically longer. You may need to adjust the S7 S-register to allow time for a connection to be made. However, if you use a modem that supports a V.21 or better standard, and the other modem also supports that standard, you will be able to make a connection.

Some early U.S. modems only support the Bell 103 or Bell 212A standards. These are U.S. standards and were not adopted internationally.

Note: The quality of phone line connections in the U.S. is substantially better than in many other countries and is improving. You may not be able to connect internationally at high speed without getting some data errors. Be sure to use error-detection wherever possible.

Summary

This chapter introduced some of the more unusual connections you may make with your modem. These include using the host mode in your communication software to set up a mini-BBS or using remote control software to run application programs from a remote location.

Other topics covered include communicating with other types of computers, such as a Macintosh, and communicating internationally.

Part IV, "The Online World Tour," introduces the wide variety of online services available to you. Chapter 13 provides an overview of the various services, and later chapters focus on more-specific applications.

IV

PART

The Online World Tour

Part IV introduces the limitless world of online data. Thanks to the remarkable proliferation of computers and telephone systems throughout the world, we can access more information from more sources, faster and more economically than previously possible.

Chapter 13 introduces all the online database services in a general way and differentiates between the most popular services based on their most common uses. Chapter 13 also introduces packet-switched networks, which allow you to access the online services potentially at a more economical telephone service rate, and the variety of ways that online services interconnect to provide you with more opportunities for reaching a wider user base. The subsequent chapters, Chapters 14 through 18, focus on each of these major purposes for online services in turn.

Beginners should read Chapter 13 carefully to determine what type of service is useful and then focus on the following corresponding chapter for more detail. Experienced modem users should skim the introduction to online databases in Chapter 13 to understand the divisions made before exploring the more detailed chapters. You may find a different service fits more of your particular needs than the one you were considering.

13
CHAPTER

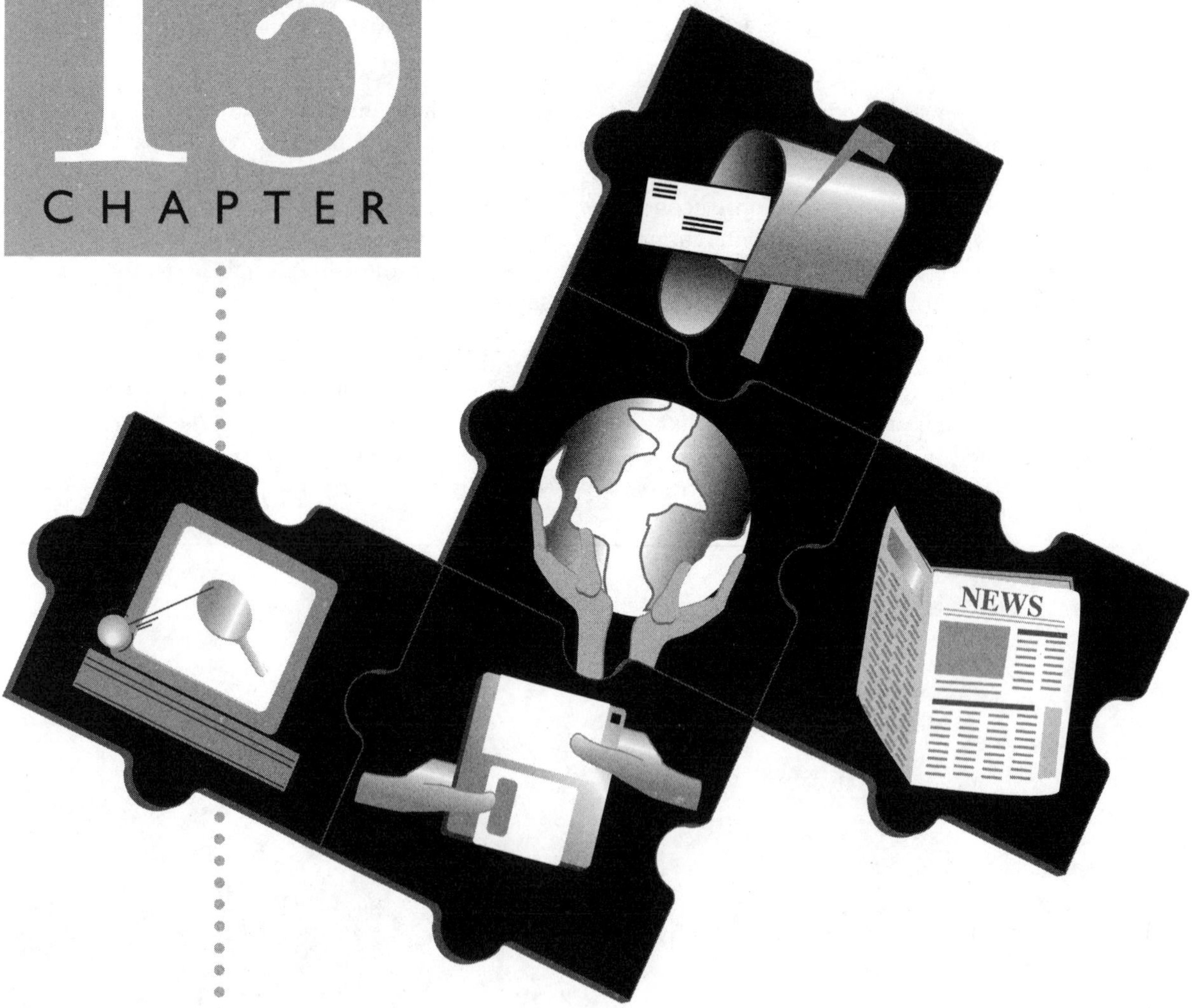

Choosing
the Data Source

This chapter covers the following main topics:

- ❖ Understanding online databases
- ❖ Introducing bulletin board systems
- ❖ Introducing messaging services
- ❖ Introducing information-exchange services
- ❖ Introducing information-searching services
- ❖ Appreciating packet-switched networks
- ❖ Getting online with the whole world

Introduction to Online Databases

Armed with a computer, modem, and telephone line, the world is literally at your fingertips. If you can think of the question, it can be answered by telecommunicating. You can perform obvious tasks like calling your office, collecting or sending files, or sending messages to your colleagues. However, there literally are thousands of specialized online services that you can call. Chapter 2 introduces the three main purposes for telecommunicating and online services: chatting, messaging, and exchanging files.

Chatting is connecting to another computer via modems and interacting with the other computer operators. You type on your keyboard, and the words appear on the other computer screens. The other computer operators in turn type responses on their keyboards. This interaction is often called *conferencing* because it is very like holding a conference call. (**Note:** The term conference is also used with messaging as a method of dividing the messages into related topics known as *conferences.*)

"Why would I want to chat online?"

If you've never chatted online, it may seem strange that people want to interact this way — especially if you aren't a rapid typist. However, consider the anonymity factor. You can't be seen or known by the other participants. Everyone is truly equal. Consequently, you can express views that you ordinarily wouldn't and not be judged by your sex, age, race, profession, or religion, unless you choose to disclose such information. Even poor spelling may be disguised as bad typing.

Although online services usually require you to register your correct name, for chatting, you can usually choose a name that is shown to the other users on the system. This pseudonym is often referred to as a *handle.* Handles can preserve your anonymity or reveal a lot. Consider the images portrayed by: Fred the Brain, Conan the Great, and Jill the Joker — compared with Jo or Al.

Online services are more frequently used for *messaging.* You send a message to someone specific or to all the users on a system. You can read messages sent to other people if they are marked for public viewing, and if you desire, you can join in with the exchange by replying to the messages. The primary advantage of messaging over chatting is that you are not present when the message is posted, and you can read the exchanges when you choose to get online. Another advantage is that you have the chance to get replies from more than the people currently online.

"*Can anyone read a message I send?*"

Depending on the service, messaging can be public or private. In a public message, the idea is to exchange information with other users — perhaps giving you a forum for your opinions or a searching tool to find help with specific questions or problems. In a private message, the idea is an alternative to the mail system. You can send messages and perhaps files that are intended for specific individuals. These individuals can call the online service from anywhere and collect their messages.

Although chatting and messaging aspects are important in specific instances or for particular personalities, the file exchange aspects of telecommunicating are cited as the most important reason individuals purchase modems and get online. People want more software for their computers.

Online services can provide you with far more software, both programs and data, than you can possibly ever use. In most cases, you can obtain a particular file from a variety of different sources. If file collection is your primary motivation for telecommunicating, regularly reconsider the most economical method to find and download the file.

"*Which is the best online service?*"

Some online services offer chatting, messaging, and file exchange, and others only offer one or two of these main functions. As you investigate online services, keep in mind the type of information you want to find and the typical user of that service.

For example, if you want to play interactive computer games, do not expect to find many kids playing on an expensive business-oriented system. If you want to talk to a Russian rocket scientist, you are unlikely to find a suitable candidate on a small local BBS that is not connected to other BBSs.

Generally, you can divide the available services into two categories: BBSs and commercial online services. That doesn't mean that all BBSs are free and none are run as commercial ventures; it is more a statement about how you learn where the systems are. In fact, any generalization you make about the available online services is inaccurate or incomplete. Because they are all essentially a community of computer users, trying to categorize is like trying to pigeonhole people. Bear this in mind as this chapter tries to divide the online world into meaningful categories.

Understanding Viruses

It is a fallacy that you are bound to get a computer virus by using a modem. However, the more files you exchange with other computers, the more likely you are to expose your computer to a computer virus. As you use a modem, you are more likely to increase the number of files you exchange and consequently increase your risk.

You can minimize the risks by understanding the following concepts:

❧ Viruses are small programs that can self-replicate and can damage system areas and files on your computer. They are hidden in files or on computer disks.

❧ You can get a virus only by transferring an infected file onto your computer or by accessing an infected disk.

❧ Although there are thousands of different viruses, very few have caused any widespread damage. The majority of reported incidences are either isolated cases, instigated by personal revenge motives, or are operator or system errors.

As a modem user, use the following procedures to minimize your exposure:

❧ Check that all your computers are currently virus-free. Several virus-checking programs, shareware and retail, are available.

❧ Establish a virus-checking procedure and follow it religiously. This is even more important than following a backup procedure for your hard disks.

❧ Immediately after hanging up the phone, verify that each file you transfer onto your computer does not contain a virus. (You need to uncompress the file and run the virus-checker.) Do not try the programs first.

❧ If you think you have a virus, stop. Don't do anything with your computer. Note any displayed messages and call the virus-checker manufacturer's technical support for assistance.

Although viruses are widely publicized, they are extremely rare. However, they can cause such devastation that precautions are worthwhile. Remember that your exposure is not limited to the files you obtain from online services; the disk you receive from a friend and even retail software is a potential risk.

A *BBS* (bulletin board system) is typically run from a PC or a series of networked PCs. Many are run by hobbyists from their basements and have only one telephone line. However, some have more than one hundred phone lines and are frequently used by thousands of users.

Commercial online services are typically run from minicomputers or mainframes and are linked via local telephone access number throughout the country. As some BBSs increase in popularity and offer local telephone access, the distinction can become blurred.

Some important commercial online services are focused for a business audience. They offer private messaging services or information searching in specialized categories, such as medicine, investment, or law. Others focus on information exchange via messages, chatting, and file exchange.

The following sections introduce the four categories for online services: BBSs, messaging systems, information exchange, and information searching. Appendix B is a resource guide to online services and gives phone numbers for reaching them.

Understanding BBSs

BBSs are almost always run from PCs, advertised by other BBS operators or users, and with more than 200,000 BBSs estimated in the U.S., they make up the bulk of online services.

BBSs are relatively easy to set up. You need a phone line, modem, special communication software, and your PC. In fact, some communication software includes commands that let you set up a mini-bulletin board. (Chapter 12 covers host mode.) As a result, many hobbyists set up BBSs as an extension of their PC hobby.

Besides the BBSs run from a hobbyist's basement, you probably have many other BBSs in your geographical area. Your local library probably has a card catalog system online where you can find books, reserve them, and even find out if there is a copy on the shelf. The Internal Revenue Service has a BBS you can call to get tax information, and the Social Security Administration has a BBS you can call to get information on your Social Security benefits. NASA also has a BBS that provides information on the space program.

In the last couple of years, with the dramatic cost reductions in the PC market, many PC software and hardware companies are looking to BBSs to reduce their technical support costs by supplying a BBS that their users can call. Other companies, professional associations, and volunteer groups are also finding BBSs a convenient and inexpensive way to disseminate and collect information.

Many local computer clubs have BBSs that tell you about upcoming meetings, exchange information, and want ads. Many associations use BBSs as means of communication, including membership lists, want ads, and general information exchange.

"What's the cheapest online service?"

BBSs are the best online services to try as a beginner to communications. This is particularly true if you are comfortable with your computer but not with the telephone charges. They are typically run by volunteers for fun, so you can often get help and make friends at the same time.

However, if new software intimidates you, consider a graphical online service, such as Prodigy or America Online, as a starting point. These are considered information exchange services and are detailed later in this chapter and in Chapter 16.

BBSs also are the best resource if you are very price conscious. Many BBSs are free or charge a nominal annual fee, and you only pay for the phone call.

I find BBSs the best online service for regional information. If I want to know what people think of a new restaurant, where to buy new carpeting, or find information on the latest local tax hike, I go to a local BBS. When I lived in Chicago, there were more than 300 BBSs within my local calling area. Even in the rural area where I now live, there are several within a few miles.

There are less than a dozen popular BBS software companies that sell the computer programs necessary to make a BBS. Consequently, you will find many common elements between different BBSs. For example, a main menu on one board will have similar choices to another board.

"Are all BBSs alike?"

When you try a couple of BBSs, you will be able to call almost any BBS and transfer your knowledge to the new BBS. The BBS software can be, and often is, customized, depending on the system operator's (known as a *sysop*) choices, but you are unlikely to have difficulty with operating a different BBS. BBSs do have character, however, and these are typically a reflection of the system operator's characters and the regular users. If you do not like a BBS, try a different one.

Chapter 14 covers BBSs in more detail and gives you a sample guided tour. Appendix B gives a sampling of a variety of boards arranged by area code so you can find ones in your region.

Understanding message-based services

Electronic mail, frequently abbreviated to *e-mail,* has been an integral part of some companies' communication system for many years. One person types a message on a computer or computer terminal and sends it to another person. The recipient reads the mail from the computer or computer terminal.

In some cases, all the users are operators of terminals attached to a central computer; in others, they are linked by a local area network (LAN). Some companies extend this connection further in a variety of ways and allow users to call via modem and collect their messages.

Some commercial online services offer a comparable service independent of your company. You purchase an account and can call the service, send a message to another subscriber to the service, and have the message delivered automatically and instantaneously. Some services allow you to attach a file to a message.

These services are equivalent to a mailing service. You direct your message to another user, and only the recipient can receive and read the message or the accompanying file.

"How do I send private messages instantly?"

The three major advantages of a message-based service are the inexpensive cost, more or less instantaneous delivery, and the service's accessibility from any location. The user is identified by name and password. You don't send the message to the recipient's physical location.

The typical home user isn't interested in this type of service, but this is the only electronic online service described that sends messages privately. In all other services, someone else, even if it is only an employee of the online service, has accessibility to the messages and in some cases the power to censor them. The cost per message is equivalent to typical mailing charges, but it is less expensive than courier services. Message-based services are alternatives to fax machines and fax modems, particularly if you need to keep the message private.

Apart from the basic concept of sending a message to someone else subscribing to the same service, the messaging services offer more-sophisticated and alternative options. In many cases, they provide links to other online services, so if you subscribe to one service, you can often send messages to or receive messages from subscribers to another service. Chapter 15 explains the potential problems with this approach in reference to security.

Additionally, the messaging services may include other mailing services. For example, you may be able to send a message to a recipient who is not a subscriber and who is on the other coast. The message is transmitted to the closest physical office to the recipient, printed, and then mailed automatically. You then save the time necessary to transport the mail coast to coast and reduce your costs by not using an overnight courier service. (Chapter 15 explains additional options for messaging services. However, most are of particular interest to sales personnel for links to the central office and pursuing sales leads.)

Understanding information-exchange services

Apart from BBSs, information-exchange services are the most widely known online services available. These commercial services can be thought of as very large BBSs. They are run from minicomputers or mainframes — in most cases, multiple minicomputers or multiple mainframe computers. They offer messaging and file exchange and, to a lesser extent, chatting.

These services should appeal to all users because they have so many different services and features. They do, however, cost money to access. Depending on the service, it may be a flat monthly fee, but in most cases, there is an additional charge, called a *connect charge*, where you pay for the time that you are actually connected to the service.

"What types of commercial online services are available?"

From a user interface standpoint, there are two types of services: *graphical interface* and the more traditional *text interface*. The graphical online services are particularly appealing to those intimidated by learning new software or who do not want to learn any commands. However, in comparison to the information-exchange services with a text interface, graphical services are incredibly slow.

In many cases, people initially subscribe to a graphical online service, and after gaining experience, consider the alternative services. This migration depends on your goals. The other online services tend to attract more computer literate users who are interested in computer topics, and the graphical services offer more readily accessible general material to a less technical audience.

For the home user, any of these services is desirable, and the most applicable depends on your particular interest. Chapter 16 gives examples of topics on some services and a guided tour to a graphical and textual information exchange service.

You will find advocates of each service. I find the graphical services frustrating because I am not interested in reading the news or seeing a weather forecast from my computer. However, these are precisely the reasons cited by a very technical friend of mine. She does not have time to read a newspaper, and the graphical service gives the information to her quickly in a format she likes.

The textual online services include vast amounts of information, and if you know where to look, you can find almost anything. However, because you are being charged a connect time charge, you need to be as efficient as possible. The major services offer software, in most cases for free, that help you navigate the areas of interest very rapidly. Chapter 10 details the advantages of this type of product. (There are equivalent products for BBSs.)

The messaging facilities available on these commercial information-exchange services are equivalent to BBSs in that you can read messages related to a particular topic and respond if you desire. However, because of the larger number of subscribers to the services, you will see opinions from a larger pool of people. As with the messaging services, you can send messages to other subscribers to the service and, in many cases, can send messages to subscribers to other services.

Understanding information-searching services

Another type of specialized online service is the *information-searching service*. These services are huge databases of information that are regularly updated. You call the database and search for information of interest.

These services are expensive when compared with the other online services and are not intended for the casual home computer user. It is not unusual to spend hundreds if not thousands of dollars a month to use them. However, for the right purpose, they are invaluable and cannot be underestimated. Additionally, many service companies, sometimes owned by the online services themselves, will inexpensively and automatically do the searching for you. In some cases, you can establish search criteria and have the online service automatically supply any data as it becomes available.

"How can online research help me?"

Chapter 18 covers these information-searching services in detail and gives a guided tour of one of them. Because they are designed for very specific purposes, a general description is too superficial to be illuminating, but consider the following applications.

You may need a newspaper clipping service. The online service may carry the full text of hundreds if not thousands of different newspapers from around the world. You can search for any references to your company, your industry, or your competitors. You can typically read an abstract of a reference and obtain full text of desired articles. Electronic document searching is much more accurate than any visual system.

The online service may catalog patent applications, current government legislation, and stock information. You can do a patent search and see what patents your competitor has filed or bought. You can keep current on new regulations that may affect your business or investment information. The information is not always so directly related to business. One particular service specializes in chemical compound information; another specializes in current law. Other equivalent services specialize in other areas.

If you are not currently doing business involving database searching, this type of service may seem fanciful and impractical. Although it has been made a cliché by the media, the world *is* getting smaller, and you must think globally to stay competitive. If you don't know what the competition is doing, understand market trends, or have the latest in technology, you may not survive.

Different Connections

The following sections cover alternative ways you can connect with your favorite online service and introduce some of the ways the online services connect with each other to your benefit.

Understanding packet-switching network access

As covered extensively in early chapters in this book, you make a connection between two modems by dialing a telephone number. The two modems negotiate a connection, and your computer is linked to the serial device that is connected to the other modem. In the case of online services, the other modem is attached to a computer. This other computer may be a PC, minicomputer, or a mainframe. It runs computer software that you control from your PC.

"Should I call the local phone number or the long-distance one?"

In most cases, if you call a BBS, you dial the BBS directly. When you dial the number, the modem attached to the BBS detects the phone ringing and answers the phone. The actual routing of the telephone call from the outlet in your wall to the receiving computer's outlet is under the control of your local or long-distance telephone company. The receiving computer does not care whether you are calling from around the corner or around the world.

Commercial online services and a few very large BBSs offer an alternative method of connecting. Rather than dialing the computer directly, you call a local telephone number. This is the number for a telephone service called a *packet-switched network*. Two popular examples are Sprintnet and Tymnet.

A packet-switched network is a computer-controlled telephone system with digital telephone lines that can route your telephone call more efficiently and with higher fidelity than the regular analog telephone system. It is so-named because it divides the data being transmitted into small chunks called packets. (In some cases, your ordinary long-distance telephone call may be routed through a packet-switched network for part of its route.)

When you call the packet-switched network, you connect with the packet-switching network's computer. You identify the online service you wish to connect to by following the instructions supplied when you register with your chosen online service, and the packet-switching network links you to your online service's computer.

The online service has established an account with the packet-switched network company and pays the packet-switched network for the time that you are connected. The online service typically passes these charges on to you. For example, the online service may quote one price per hour of connect time if you call a particular number and a different price if you call a different number.

As covered in the sidebar "Calculating Connect Charges" it may be more economical to call a service directly, or you may save money by using a packet-switched network connection. Be sure to review your selection regularly, because this is one of the charges that varies over time as the online services offer different deals.

Linking with the world

Although interconnection between online services has been around for many years, it is probably the fastest growing area of interest in PC telecommunications. As more people accept modems as a commodity rather than a specialized device that you only own if you have a particular task to do, the communicating itself is becoming more commonplace. A few years ago in most circles, it was an adventure to link with a few hundred other users and find their opinions and exchange files with them. Now it is possible to link with literally millions of users worldwide.

In the BBS world, several fairly informal systems were established for allowing BBSs to exchange messages. This procedure usually is called *echoing mail*. The most common are Fidonet and RIME. You call your local BBS and read the messages relating to a particular topic, and you can respond to some of the messages. The sysop (system operator) of the BBS calls another BBS and, through the specialized software, passes on the messages you responded to and receives the new messages. When you next call the BBS, the new messages are available. Each BBS passes the information to the next link in the chain. Each sysop pays only a small portion of the cost because he or she is usually calling a nearby BBS.

Calculating Connect Charges

The relative costs of different online services can be dramatic. One may be free — another may cost tens of dollars an hour. The charges may vary depending on your modem speed and which phone number you use to access the service.

The costs fall into two categories: the access charges for the service and the telephone costs. Many services offer discount schemes, and you need to compare the costs to choose the best for you. Unfortunately, it is like a school mathematics exercise.

For example, a service may have a fixed monthly charge of $15 with five hours connect time free and $6 an hour after that. Compare this with $4 an hour all the time. You need to judge whether you will use the service less than three hours a month or more than eight hours.

Remember to regularly reassess the amount you use an online service because your needs change with time. For example, one year I spent hundreds of dollars with a particular service submitting my magazine articles. The following year, a different magazine was my major customer, and I stopped using the service but didn't cancel my subscription. However, it was only when I got the annual renewal bill for the service that I realized I was wasting my money. The service was just as good, but my needs had changed.

When comparing the services, don't overlook the other costs: telephone charges. The online services do not factor in these charges because they vary, depending on your location. Consider all the different ways in which you can access the service when considering relative costs. You may be able to call a local phone number, an intrastate state number, a long-distance number, or an 800 number.

Commercial online services often offer a regional phone number for access and not just a single national number. If you call the national number, you are paying the long-distance telephone charges. If you call the local access number, you pay the local telephone call charge, and the online service pays for the long-distance charge. This charge is often passed on to you by a higher cost in accessing the service through this local number.

Depending on where you live, the local access method may prove more expensive than using a direct long-distance number, and the cost difference may surprise you. Take the time to calculate the relative costs by making an estimate of your online time. For example, calculate the per hour costs for being online.

Do not overlook the special discounts offered by long-distance telephone companies. Many relate to calling the same number or set of numbers regularly. Because I live in a rural area, for example, the local access numbers for online services are intrastate calls. (Even the local pizza store is long-distance, although they do deliver.) I have joined every special program offered by my long-distance phone company and added the online service phone numbers to my "calling list." In most cases, it is cheaper for me to call the national number and pay the long-distance carrier than to pay the local telephone company.

As the cliché goes, "your mileage may vary," but I estimate that I have saved hundreds of dollars by regularly reconsidering how I access online services and how much I am actually using them. (Although calling online services is a passion for me, my combined online service charges are less than my electricity bill.)

You may wonder why a sysop would be interested and willing to bear the cost. Depending on the geographical location, a local BBS has a limited population of callers. To attract these people, the messages need to be of interest and current. To help make running the BBS interesting, the sysop also wants to reach other people who are not local. Picking up the messages from one of these mail-echoing exchanges gives the appearance of a BBS having more users and helps provide interesting interchanges.

"What is the Internet?"

Another much older network has only relatively recently become accessible to PC users. All the descriptions are rather vague because it is such a mixture of computers, located in a mixture of establishments, in many different countries. Chapter 17 covers the Internet in more detail.

The Internet is a network of networks that can all communicate with each other. They use a protocol (equivalent of language) called TCP/IP (Transmission Control Protocol/Internet Protocol) as the basis for that communication, and each attached computer is allocated a name. The connected computers are in universities, research establishments, government sites, and commercial companies.

In a way comparable to Fidonet and RIME, where each participating BBS bears a small portion of the cost, the sites connected to the Internet freely exchange electronic mail and files with each other. If you can find a way to connect with a computer on the Internet, you can literally exchange messages with the world for free.

Although The Internet Society allocates ID numbers to various Internet sites, the Internet itself is not a fixed entity and has seen explosive growth recently as many PC users have found ways to access the system. As a PC owner, you can access the Internet in one of several ways. Keep in mind that you can do two things with the Internet: send and receive messages and send and receive files. A supplier may only offer messaging services and not file-exchange services.

Note: People make a big deal about whether you are *on* the Internet. In general, almost all PC owners are not on the Internet. However, you can send and receive messages or files to a computer that is on the Internet.

At the most sophisticated end, beyond the scope of this book, you can set up an Internet node, get an ID from The Internet Society, and you are connected. In this case, you are considered *on* the Internet. However, this connection is not particularly straightforward because The Internet Society has procedures and rules that must be followed.

At a simpler level, more appropriate for almost all PC owners, you can access the Internet via most online services including from BBSs. Commercial online services are rapidly responding to customer pressure and are supplying Internet electronic mail services. A few have added file-exchange services as well.

As the popularity increases, the current limitations imposed by commercial services will probably disappear. For example, an online service may limit the amount of electronic mail or files that you can receive or send via the Internet in a month. Commercial online services typically charge you to send messages via Internet. In some cases, this is per message; in others, it is a nominal monthly charge with volume limitations.

This topic is probably the most speculative of all the topics covered in this book because it is changing daily. However, even with the online service charges, connecting is inexpensive. For example, I currently pay $3 a month and can send up to 50 messages. (I send some to my brother in England who works for a research establishment on the Internet. Now if I could just persuade him to reply. . . .)

Access to the Internet has also become popular with BBSs. The new versions of BBS software have, or will soon have, the necessary facilities so that BBSs can be on The Internet. One concept is that the BBS software manufacturer becomes an Internet node, and each BBS that uses that manufacturer's software becomes a user on the BBS software manufacturer's Internet node. You, the caller to the BBS, are considered a user of the BBS and can in turn access the Internet.

Summary

This chapter introduced online services. You can use your modem for three main functions while online: chatting, messaging, and file exchange. Each online service supplies one or more of these features. However, most online services emphasize a particular aspect.

BBSs are the most common online service. They vary in size from being operated from a single telephone line to hundreds of telephone lines. They are typically smaller in scope than the commercial online services. They are often regional or specialized on a particular topic. Increasingly, BBSs are being used by PC companies to provide technical support, and many national groups have one. Most BBSs offer file exchange and contain libraries of software you can download. Most BBSs also offer messaging where all the callers can read the messages and contribute responses. Less commonly, BBSs offer chatting, where you can interact with other users on the system.

Some online services emphasize messaging. They are like electronic mail services that extend beyond the bounds of your company. The message you send is not read by the online service and is only accessible to the recipient. In some cases, you can attach a file to a message. Messaging services do not have public forums, file libraries, or offer chatting. They are like a form of postal service.

Other online services emphasize information exchange. They also usually support messaging, but the messages are not completely private. They are intended as forums for exchanging information with an unknown group of individuals. Like BBSs, the information exchange services typically have large file libraries of software that you can download. Depending on the service, they may also offer chatting.

Another online service category is information-searching services. These are typically more expensive and are aimed at business or professional users. They have enormous, continually updated databases that you can search. They are the equivalent of electronic libraries. They do not offer messaging, chatting, or file exchange, except that you can usually obtain the full text of a reference you have found. A typical application is using the service as a newspaper clipping service.

This chapter also introduced packet-switched networks, which are used by many online services as means for connecting to their computers.

The global nature of communication is becoming a reality for PC users as an increasing number of methods emerge for exchanging messages and files economically with people around the world. The long-established Internet is now becoming available to PC users and is likely to become a favorite.

Chapter 14 explores BBSs in more detail. Chapter 15 focuses on messaging services, and Chapter 16 covers information-exchange services. Chapter 17 introduces the Internet. Chapter 18 explores information-searching services.

14
CHAPTER

BBSs for Everyone

This chapter introduces the immense world of BBSs. In particular, the following topics are covered:

- ❖ Types of BBSs
- ❖ A sample tour of two BBSs
- ❖ What to look for on a BBS
- ❖ How to find BBSs

Understanding BBSs

BBSs are the most common type of online service available. As covered in Chapter 13, BBSs offer messaging, chatting, and file exchange. Some offer each function and are general purpose, and others specialize by focusing on a particular topic, geographical region, or function.

Regardless of your taste, there are many BBSs around that are suitable for you. Everyone who calls BBSs is exercising the human desire to communicate. Some people only call to collect software — others only to espouse their favorite political agenda. However, they are all communicating.

Any BBS you call, and for that matter any online service you call, is made up of two components: the computer with its software and the other BBS users. The other BBS users make up a community, and the BBS software supplies the neighborhood.

A BBS really is a living, breathing community of people. Just as in real life, you'll meet people you love, hate, or share some similar opinions with. Some BBS users, often known as *lurkers*, are invisible to the community because they look around but do not contribute. Other BBS users are loudmouths who have an opinion on everything and can't let a single topic go by without extensive comment. Another element, often known as *flamers*, extends their opinions to personal affronts and can make discussions escalate into nuclear war very rapidly.

Unless you call for the file-exchange services only, you will run into the other members of the community, and you will be considered part of that community. The success or failure of a BBS depends on that community. If you do not like the atmosphere on a BBS, either work to correct it or go somewhere else. In telecommunicating, you don't have to move your home to meet new neighbors.

"Where do I get help on a BBS?"

Because all BBS users are trying to communicate, you will find that almost without exception they are very willing to help. Don't be afraid to ask where to find information. When approached appropriately, almost all users like to help because it gives great satisfaction to be needed or considered authoritative.

On-Line Etiquette

When you communicate with an online service, you connect to someone else's computer, and they are entitled to set the rules you must conform to. For example, a BBS typically limits how long you can be online each day so that many users get the opportunity to call. Other rules may apply to how many files you can download without uploading files.

Most of the operational rules are easy to live with. However, when you start reading messages or chatting, you can quickly meet people who intentionally or unintentionally abuse the system.

As a neophyte leaving messages, the first rule is to keep it simple and do not type your whole message in uppercase letters. Typing with Caps Lock on is considered shouting, and someone will reprimand you. If you read a series of messages and come across one that is written in uppercase letters, it seems to leap off the screen. If you cannot touch type well, do not use any uppercase letters at all.

Poor spelling and bad grammar are fine online, but bad taste is not. It is always exaggerated online and often quickly escalates into war. An offhand comment that your friends may think is funny, because they know your character, religion, and national origin, can be especially offensive. For example, ethnic jokes are not funny even if you are from an ethnic minority. You are not in that minority when online.

Before writing or sending a message, take a second to be certain that you did not miss a critical "not." Before responding to an apparently inflammatory message, reread it to be sure you did not misread. A sysop described his golden rule of etiquette to me as "Take aim at the topic and not the author".

You can get a lot of help online with solving your PC problems. Remember that not all the advice supplied will be accurate, but you should, more importantly, supply feedback when a solution is found. It is not only a matter of courtesy to thank someone for free consulting services, but it supplies the confirmation many other readers of the messages may be looking for.

In some cases, particularly on the larger and more complex boards, you may be guided to another area of the BBS to pose your question. In other cases, you can find the name and number of another BBS that can fill your need.

For example, if you want to find a BBS that has users interested in genealogy (a surprisingly popular topic), ask. Many BBS users frequent multiple boards, and unless you ask, they are unlikely to mention it. Many sysops encourage you to explore other boards. It either shows how much better their own is, or it allows them to focus on the topics of interest to them instead of needing to be all things to all callers.

The following sections introduce a few of the myriad types of BBSs. The purpose is to show you what is available — the list is not exhaustive. As mentioned in Chapter 13, each online service is unique, and you can find what you are looking for in a variety of different places. The key to the best use of online services is finding the most appropriate mix of services for the most economical use of your time and money.

Understanding local BBSs

One of the first BBSs you are likely to try calling is your local BBS. At its most expensive, it will cost you the price of a few local phone calls while you get the hang of it. Many local BBSs are run by PC enthusiasts as extensions of their hobby. They often have only one telephone line and are located in someone's basement. For the most part, especially when they are first established, they are general purpose and offer messaging and file exchange.

They do not usually offer chatting services. It is obvious why chatting is not supported. Chat boards require a minimum of two phone lines so that you can chat to the other person online, and until there is a core of users on the board, you will be the only one calling at one time even if there are two phone lines. If a board is being run by volunteers, the cost of one or two phone lines may be an acceptable burden to a sysop, but having many more phone lines installed makes it much more of a serious business proposition.

Many local BBSs are free and have no annual maintenance charges. Some do not charge but have certain usage rules. For example, you may have to upload one new file for every five that you download, or you have only a very limited time online unless you contribute financially or materially with new files for the file library. Other BBSs charge a nominal annual fee, which is intended to defray expenses. For example, several of my local BBSs charge $25 per year. This is probably enough for the sysop to pay the phone bill and buy a couple of CD ROM disks for the file library each year.

Local BBSs vary in quality and diversity. If you live near a major metropolitan area, you can easily have tens if not hundreds to choose from. Appendix B lists a selection of BBSs arranged by area code. Some magazines publish lists from time to time, and most BBSs contain a file that lists hundreds of BBSs. The section on invaluable files later in this chapter explains more about this list.

Obviously, the larger BBSs must be located locally to some people, so you may be fortunate to have one that is only a local phone call for you. The character of a BBS is reflected in its callers. Many local BBSs have less than 100 regular callers, and you can really get to know the individuals more easily than with services who get hundreds of callers a day.

Many local BBSs are extensions of the local computer club and are particularly beneficial for meeting people who know about PCs (or think they do). You must remember that the advice you see on a BBS is only as good as its source. I have seen many beginners who did not know what question to ask or where to start sorting out a problem get guidance from BBS users.

"What will I find on a local BBS?"

You will typically find file exchange and messaging on your local BBS. Depending on the number of users, you may find only one communal message area, or you may find a main area and a couple of specialized topic areas called *conferences*, on such topics as politics, parenting, or word processing. Messages are often referred to as *mail.*

There is an increasing interest in parents letting children use BBSs to exchange information. The local BBS is a great place to let your child communicate with friends and make new friends. It is a safe environment and can provide excellent education. You should to take an active interest in your child's online activities. Apart from the potential increase in telephone bills, insidious elements in our society are just as present here as everywhere else.

BBSs are great places to frequent when there are national or local crises occurring. If you listen to the radio, watch TV, or read a newspaper, you are presented with a diluted compilation of information. If you get on a BBS and read the messages, you get much more of a raw opinion and typically get another perspective on the topic. For local news, local BBSs provide a different gauge of interest.

Do not assume however, that a local BBS will not have up-to-date files available. You may be able to get the new printer driver for Windows from your local BBS within a couple of days of release and not have to subscribe to a national service to get it.

For example, I subscribe to a national BBS because some of my interests are not served by my local BBSs. I am very interested in the latest in PC communications information and several very specific PC topics but have not found other fanatics near me.

I am also addicted to computer games, particularly those that are not "shoot-em up" ones. I get the games from the national board and immediately upload them to my local BBS. You can get the new public domain or shareware games from my local BBS within a couple of days of their release. I call my local BBS for local information because the BBS picks up some messages on PC communication from a national source.

Listening for New Technology

Browsing around BBSs is an excellent way to keep in touch with new technology and new issues. For example, when the former U.S.S.R. collapsed, thousands of computer users around the world followed the action by communicating via BBSs with Russians. The Russians were sending messages to the West, and these messages were echoed throughout the world.

On a less world-shaking level, you can often pick up information on new technology or different interests from BBSs. You can certainly hear about the obvious, such as a new computer from IBM or new prices for online services. But more interestingly, you can hear how people like these new things and what they use them for. For example, the popularity of the Internet for PC users mushroomed in the space of only a few months because of BBSs. The Internet was not news; it had been in place for over two decades; but PC operators had only recently discovered it.

The timetable for acceptance of V.34 modems will depend on the reaction of BBS operators. Many people will not purchase new technology until they read about success stories on the BBSs. Offline readers are gaining in popularity rapidly because of

the "good press" they are receiving online. RIP (Remote Image Protocol), a graphical interface for BBSs, is gaining in popularity because of the interest by users of BBSs.

You can also learn about other interests. Because these may never have a big following but are of particular interest to a small group of people, the international nature of BBSs gives these interests a forum. For example, a class of programs known as *demos* are popular in Europe and are gaining an interested following in the U.S. via BBSs. A demo is a program written typically as a collaborative effort by programmers. There is a competition each year for the best. A demo is intended to show the skills of the programmers.

Demos are typically self-running and show lots of objects moving around on your screen. You have probably seen pictures of bouncing balls on chessboards on the television. These demos are similar but are written for the PC. A casual PC user probably would look at a couple of demos and say, "Pretty pictures — so what?" However, to someone with programming knowledge, even very elementary knowledge, the programming skills required are apparent.

I consider it mutual cooperation. I get the PC communication information from my local BBS because the sysop collects and posts it, and he gets the latest games because I collect them and pass them on. By the way, supporting your local BBS is one of the best ways to get involved in BBSs, especially if you are considering running your own BBS. Many sysops welcome volunteers, and many waive subscription fees if you prove an asset to the BBS.

For example, you may volunteer to moderate some of the chat or message areas or help with the routine maintenance. Running a BBS is rather like running a restaurant, however. The image portrayed to the public ignores the mundane essential tasks, such as dishwashing and trash collection. Additionally, the sysop and his helpers supply a service — not the loudest voice.

Understanding national BBSs

Some BBSs have become so popular that they have become known nationally and have avid followers. They are no different than the local BBS except that they manage to pull users from all over the country. If a board is popular, it has lots of callers, and its user community gets larger and more diverse. However, if you call the board and only get busy signals, you will try another board. Some local BBSs are so popular, they do not have the phone line capacity.

The incremental cost for sysops to add more than a second phone line begins to mount because they need special computer hardware to allow multiple users on the BBS and have sufficient serial ports to attach to the phone lines. This is in addition to the costs involved with having many phone lines installed.

Consequently, there is a division between a local BBS and a BBS with many phone lines. The BBSs with more phone lines tend to be run more as commercial enterprises. Although only a few are big money-makers and allow the sysop to be a full-time BBS operator, many make small supplemental incomes for the sysops.

"What do I find on a national BBS?"

These boards tend to have more of everything. The national BBSs tend to have faster computer equipment, so they are more responsive, and have faster modems, so you can connect with a fast modem. Additionally, they often have more storage space, so they can hold more files. The larger user base encourages more messages, so they tend to have more general messages and many more topical conferences.

Additionally, the national BBSs tend to be more involved with interconnection. They often pick up echo mail, from such networks as Fidonet or RIME, or have links into the Internet. If you want to know what it is like to live in Israel, Estonia, or Australia, you only have to send a message to find out.

Chat boards

BBSs that offer chatting are far fewer in number than those that only offer messaging and file exchange. However, as a BBS becomes sufficiently popular to justify more than one telephone line, chatting is often listed as a feature even if it is not used all the time.

Next time you are on your favorite BBS, look carefully at the menus because you may see an option that says something like "who's on." This tells you the name of any other caller who is currently online. Depending on how the sysop has set up the system, you may be able to invite someone to chat with you. If he or she agrees, you type your message, and he or she types an answer.

A few BBSs have expanded their chat features so that they are a major or the only focus of the BBS. These typically charge a few cents an hour for you to chat with other callers. As with most BBSs, you can typically look around for a limited time for free. You may, for example, be able to chat for ten minutes a day for a month before subscribing.

"What will I find on a chat board?"

As covered in Chapter 13, chatting permits individuals to exploit their alter egos. Because of the relative anonymity, you can express opinions that you would not ordinarily do. If you are someone who carefully weighs everything you say before speaking, stay off the chat boards and stick with messaging systems or elementary chatting to find out who else is on the same BBS as you. If you are easily offended, by perhaps a comment on the President's new health plan, or whether women should stay at home and have babies, keep away. If you enjoy a good argument, try a chat board.

Some of these BBSs are adult only — others are not. However, even the adult boards have various sections. For example, an area may support very heated political or religious discussions, and another support more sexually oriented topics.

Another form of chatting is interactive game playing. You call a BBS and play a game with other users who are online. For example, you may choose to play a game where you are driving a tank and you fight other tanks that are controlled by other users.

A more common interactive game involves role playing and is similar in concept to the popular Dungeons and Dragons game. It is actually a form of chatting that follows rules while you express an alter ego. Interactive games are usually found as part of national BBSs. Some commercial online services also offer this and chat forums as does the Internet.

Messaging boards

Messaging boards are commonly found on local and national BBSs. Again, the character of the board is dictated by the users who call it. The more diverse the user base, the more diverse the topics under discussion.

As shown in the guided tour later in this chapter, boards that focus on messaging segregate the messages into topics. These topic areas are often called *conferences*. They permit you to call the board and read only the messages that may be of interest to you. Many boards get hundreds of messages a day, and you are unlikely to be interested in every topic. When you call the board, you look only at the message conferences that interest you. For example, you may look at the general conference, the education conference, and the movie review conference.

Many of the national messaging boards emphasize a particular topic and often name their boards appropriately to attract interested people. For example, there is at least one BBS focused on gay rights, another on education, and another on bird watching. The messaging boards typically include file libraries in addition to messaging. Many also pick up echo mail, such as Fidonet, RIME, or the Internet, to expand their message base.

Messaging boards can be a lot of fun, but the volume of messages can be overwhelming. Offline mail readers quickly become valuable, and you need to call a BBS regularly if you want to follow the messages on an ongoing basis. Calling occasionally often makes the messages seem very disjointed.

File library boards

Many message boards that are not focused on a particular topic also carry many file libraries. Many other BBSs tend to have minimal messaging areas but have gigabytes of files for downloading. Collection of new software is the most frequent reason given by users for using BBSs and online services.

Like message boards, the large file libraries are typically divided into topic areas to help you find things. For example, you may choose between word processing, games, utilities, and general. You can typically search for files in a variety of ways, including by filename, key topics, or date. You also can search for new files — perhaps files that have been added since you were last on the BBS.

Your best approach with a new board is to get an idea of the topics for the files and download the file or files that contain the lists of all the BBS files. Most BBS software can be set up automatically to create this file, so it will probably be updated regularly by the sysop. A later section explains what typical file names to look for.

"What files can I get from a BBS?"

You should understand clearly the type of files that are available online and the type of files that are suitable for uploading to BBSs. Software falls into one of three general categories: commercial, shareware, and public domain. WordPerfect is an example of commercial software; PKZIP is an example of shareware; and LZH (another file compression program) is an example of public domain software.

Public domain software, as the name implies, is available to everyone, and you can use it freely and copy it for your friends. Shareware programs are commercial programs distributed in a unique way. You may freely copy shareware programs. You may use shareware programs for a limited period, typically 30 days, free of charge. However, if you continue to use a shareware product, you must register it with the vendor. The registration form is included with the product files. If you do not use the shareware product, you are obliged to delete it from your computer. Shareware works as an honor system; if you use it, you are required to register it.

Some of the very best software available is shareware, and it is hard to use BBSs without encountering shareware. PKZIP, an essential program for BBS users, is a shareware product, and if you download files, you should be using a registered version of PKZIP. Some communication software does not support the ZMODEM file-transfer protocol, and you may decide to use the shareware add-on program. Again, this product should be registered. The most popular antivirus programs, SCAN and CLEAN, also are shareware programs.

Commercial software should not be found on BBSs, and you should not upload it. For example, it is illegal to upload WordPerfect, Windows, or DOS onto a BBS. Although most sysops go to great lengths to check that none of the files on their BBS are commercial, some programs slip by them. If you find that you have downloaded one, delete it, and leave a message for the sysop next time you call the BBS.

By the way, some people alter commercial software and upload it with the copyright screen removed or some other such modification. I am highly suspicious of programs obtained from a BBS that appear to be commercial even if I do not see any real evidence of tampering. I feel that someone who is corrupt enough to modify a commercial program and pass it off as public domain software may have the mentality necessary to place a virus within the modification.

There are several variations on the general definitions of shareware and public domain software. Some people distribute limited versions of their products for free and provide the full working version when you register the software. (These are not considered true shareware as approved by the Association of Shareware Professionals.)

Note: Software can be copyrighted even if it is public domain. This usually means you are not allowed to modify the software and pass it off as your own.

You may find files that are supplied by a commercial vendor on BBSs. For example, you may find a new mouse driver, video driver, or a bug fix for a program. Although these are parts of commercial products, they are typically legal on the BBS. On their own, these little files are useless, but if you own the relevant product, these files can upgrade your setup. These files are found most often on technical support BBSs.

For example, Qualitas had an interim update for their product 386MAX on their BBS. Users downloaded the file and ran the program. The program looked for 386MAX on your hard disk, and if it found it, updated it. If you did not have 386MAX installed on your hard disk, the downloaded file was of no use to you.

Another type of file that is fairly popular on BBSs is graphic files showing high-resolution pictures. Unfortunately, this area is very controversial because it is difficult to control for two reasons. As mentioned before, many BBSs expect you to maintain a particular upload-to-download ratio. For example, you may need to upload one file for every five that you download. Where do you get the files from? Some people use a scanner and scan pictures from magazines and books and upload them to a BBS. This is illegal. The photographer or publisher of the magazine or book owns the copyright on the printed photograph, and you may not copy it. You can scan only your own photographs and upload them.

The other problem associated with these graphic files is adult material and pornography. There are well-defined laws defining pornography and who can have access to it, but these are not yet well defined in the electronic media and specifically on BBSs. Ignoring the legal implications, there is no doubt that you can obtain plenty of pornographic pictures from some BBSs. As with the chat boards, if you find this material offensive, avoid the adult file areas, and if you let your children have free rein on BBSs, be aware that they may find access to this type of material.

Technical support boards

As the price of computer software and hardware continues to tumble, many companies are reassessing how to provide quality technical support at a more economical price. One solution is running a technical support bulletin board.

BBSs have the advantage that the user can call any time and the messages can be processed at a different time. Technical support technicians are regularly asked the same questions, and a BBS enables a company to post the most frequently asked questions so that they can be read without requiring a technician's intervention.

Technical support boards also offer the opportunity to provide software bug fixes or new printer or display drivers inexpensively. The user calls the BBS and downloads the driver of interest. The user also can leave messages for a technician to answer. In general, the messages on these BBSs are not read by all the users but are earmarked for the receiving technicians. (Companies offering technical support boards include Hayes, WordPerfect, and Gateway 2000.)

The problem with technical support BBSs is that some are very good and some are very bad. In many cases, the user calling needs to be fairly sophisticated to know what information to supply with a question and how to handle a modem and communications software. The lack of direct interface between the technician and the user can be frustrating because the user may omit information when asking the question, or the technician may omit information when answering the question. Consequently, getting the answer to a relatively simple question may take a couple of iterations.

I find the technical support BBSs very useful, but I am also very willing to call technical support directly when I have problems. I use the BBS to find out whether there is a new driver or any known incompatibilities. I call technical support by telephone when I have a question that cannot be asked in a couple of sentences.

Some technical support BBSs boast an interactive database where you can search for keywords and find any questions and answers that have been asked on a similar topic. I have been unsuccessful with these because I do not use quite the right search word. For example, I may ask for *printer, page jamming* when I should have asked for *printer problems, output.*

Some BBSs also offer a fax-back service. (Some telephone systems also offer this.) You call the BBS, request information, and it is faxed to the number you request within a few minutes. This is particularly useful for application notes that are so detailed it is hard to communicate them verbally. For example, an *application note* (a written piece of paper that shows how to do something specific) may show the switch settings for a sound board or the pin connections for an audio cable.

Association and government agency boards

In the current electronic world, you can find a BBS relevant to whatever topic you can conceive. Many associations, societies, and clubs use BBSs as a communication medium. In some cases, the organization may have an area on a commercial online service and require membership to subscribe to the service.

Additionally, many government agencies run BBSs that can be accessed by the general public. These include the IRS, Social Security Administration, Department of Defense, Department of Energy, Environmental Protection Agency, and Small Business Administration. Some of these even have 800 numbers.

Files containing lists of these BBSs are found on most BBSs. The one for the government agencies is commonly called GOVT.ZIP. A later section in this chapter lists the typical file names to look for and how to go about extending your search.

Overview of Your First Encounter with a BBS

The first time you call a BBS is different from the rest. In almost all cases, you are expected to register with the BBS. This allows the sysop to have a record of who you are and how to contact you. Although you may consider this information prying and unnecessary, bear in mind that you are actually using someone else's modem and computer. The sysop is entitled to know some basic information.

The typical information that you will be asked for is your name, address, phone number, and the password you want to use to access the system. In some cases, you are also given the opportunity to choose how your name will appear in messages. This is known as your *handle*. You may be named Frederick, for example, but want to be known on the board as Fred or even Skip. Another common option allows you to pick a default file-download protocol. If your communications program supports ZMODEM, and it is offered as an option, you will want to choose ZMODEM.

If you consider asking for this information prying, you probably will not find any online service satisfactory, because they all want it. In some cases, the BBS uses a callback system, where the BBS automatically calls you back at the given phone number to verify that you are a legitimate user. Beware of this if you call a BBS from work but give your home phone number, for example.

You need the name and password each time you call a BBS. Be very careful about what you use as a password. Most people choose a child's, pet's, or spouse's name, or their telephone number. Avoid this, especially if you are paying for the service, because it is very easy to guess a password and someone else can access the system by using your name. Consider basing it on a phone number that you remember, perhaps the local dry cleaner's or your doctor's.

Some BBSs ask for additional information, such as the type of computer you are using, the modem type, and other computer information. From the sysop's viewpoint, it is interesting to know something about the demographics of the callers. Filling out this information is typically a condition of becoming registered with the BBS. I think of it as a rite of passage. You are unlikely to be asked for the information again. It may prove useful to you. If you have a fast modem, for example, you may encourage the sysop to add a fast modem to the BBS by filling out this form.

"Why do I have to register with a BBS?"

However, some BBSs also ask for information that you may not be willing to give, such as age and gender. Before refusing to give your age, consider the board you are calling. If it contains adult material, the sysop must provide some method of filtering minors. Although it is less offensive to some people to be asked whether you are over 21, some people get upset however the question is phrased. Some BBSs require proof of age in writing before you are accepted to the BBS. This is often a copy of your driver's license.

You also may be asked for a credit card number. Again, consider the BBS carefully before giving this number. You should have an opportunity to explore the board in a limited way without subscribing, and you should be able to send a check instead of using a credit card if you prefer. However, the sysop is entitled to make sure the check clears before altering your access status to the board.

In addition to filling out some type of questionnaire, you will be shown the rules of the BBS. This will include the subscription charges, time limitations, and other details. For example, a BBS may have a rule of no profanity or that messages must be less than 25 lines. Remember that you are a guest on someone else's computer. If you do not like the rules, find another BBS.

After completing the questionnaire, you will have the opportunity to explore the BBS a little or will be instructed to call back the next day. The sysop takes the supplied information and upgrades your status on the BBS so that you have access as a registered user.

Note: Every time you call the BBS, you will be asked for your name and your password. These are the keys to your access. You must use exactly the same name each time you call. For example, Jon Smith is a different person than J Smith, or Jonathon Smith.

If you do forget your password, reregister by using a slightly different name; use your initial instead of your full name. Then leave a message for the sysop explaining why you are reregistering and specifying what you actually want your name and password to be. The sysop will compare the other information you gave, such as your address and phone number, and will clear up your error for you.

Five-Minute Tour of a BBS

Assuming that you are registered with a BBS, you will be able to access it by supplying your name and password when the BBS answers your phone call. The process of accessing the BBS is known as *logging on*. Similarly, the process of leaving the BBS is known as *logging off*.

BBSs are typically running one of about a dozen popular BBS software programs. However, each board has an individual character. Some are rather clinical and austere; others are so user-friendly that you have to plow through lots of menus to get anywhere.

To get around a BBS, remember the following hints:

- ❖ Read the menus and prompts carefully.
- ❖ If all else fails, log off and recall the system.
- ❖ Use the capture feature of your communication software and look at it offline.

For a brief introduction to a BBS, I called Software Creations, the largest BBS in the U.S. Figure 14-1 shows the opening screen.

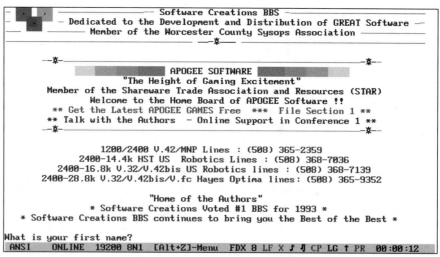

Figure 14-1: Software Creations opening screen. A BBS's opening screen should show the phone numbers for access as well as give a brief overview of where you have called.

The first prompt on most BBSs is for your first or last name. This is the first step in the logon process. The Software Creations opening screen is fairly typical although more colorful than many BBSs.

Notice the useful list of phone numbers in the center. If you have a faster modem, you can call a different number and log on at a faster speed. Software Creations is a national BBS that offers subscribers alternative phone numbers that are less likely to be busy. As it is an extremely popular BBS, the subscription is well worth the money.

After typing your first name, you are prompted for your last name. The BBS then repeats your name and your location and requests your password. You type your password, and when the BBS verifies it, you are logged onto the BBS. You continue to follow any prompts, such as Do you want to read your mail before proceeding? and then you reach the main menu.

The Main Menu shown in Figure 14-2 is an example of a particularly well-equipped BBS. However, it is very similar to many BBSs. The available items are arranged in groups, such as mail commands, user settings, and file commands. Within each group is a list of available commands, such as read mail or enter new mail. The letter or letters enclosed in square brackets before the command name are the letters you must press at the prompt to access the command. The overall menu is surrounded by a border that helps give the BBS character.

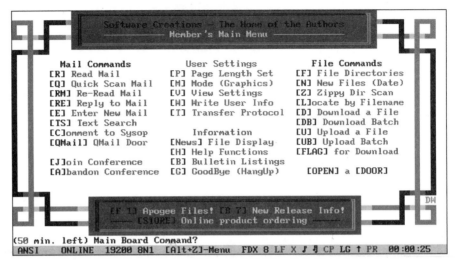

Figure 14-2: Main Menu. The actual items on this menu can vary with the BBS as well as with your status on that BBS.

Notice in particular the information displayed at the command prompt. On the sample screen, the very bottom line is displayed by the communications software and gives status information, such as the terminal emulation, the character format, and the amount of time since the connection was made. The line above is the terminal screen and shows the BBS's command prompt. In this case, the prompt is (50 min. left) Main Board Command?.

The prompt will show you where you are in the BBS. For example, it will say the Main Board, File Menu, or Mail Read menu. It usually also shows how much longer you have for today. Many boards restrict the length of time for which you can access the board in a single day so that other users get a chance to use it too.

You type the command of interest at the command prompt. In this example, I press R to read mail and get to the read mail command prompt. At this prompt, I could press H to get help on the available read commands or type a read command immediately. Pressing R S, for example, is the quick way to read all messages since you last read messages.

For this example, I press J to join a mail conference. This opens the mail conference menu, as shown in Figure 14-3.

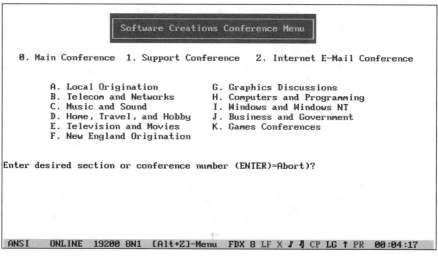

Figure 14-3: Software Creations mail conferences. The mail is divided into topics known as conferences.

This BBS has many different conferences available. Figure 14-3 shows the summary screen. The conferences are divided into categories based on subject, such as Music and Sound or Business and Government. There are further conferences for e-mail of a general nature, such as Internet e-mail or for users of this particular BBS. You press the number or letter for the conference of interest. For example, if you want to read the messages on the main board, you press 0, or if you want to read about games, you press K. Figure 14-4 shows the first screenful of gaming conference selections. The selections are color-coded to show their origin. This particular screen, the first of two, shows conferences from the Internet as well as from echo mail and a local conference. Again, you select the number of the conference of interest. For example, you type 52 to read about Nintendo gaming or 89 to read about Sega gaming.

When you are in a conference, you will be reading mail relating to that particular conference topic. You can read as many or as few messages as you like and can choose different conferences. However, if you are going to do much exploring of the messages, you will probably want to read the messages offline. As explained in Chapter 10, an offline reader can automatically create a file containing the messages from your chosen conferences and download it to your computer. You then log off from the BBS and read the messages at your leisure without incurring the telephone charges while you read.

When you finish reading the messages of interest, you can return to the main menu for other commands (or to log off). To illustrate a file library system, Figure 14-5 shows the screen displayed if you press F at the main menu.

```
Enter desired section or conference number (ENTER)=Abort)? k

Yellow = local    Cyan = Internet    Green = Echo

Gaming Conferences

1    Software Support                Talk to the authors here
9    INFINITY Machine                Support and codes from REM Software
14   comp.sys.ibm.pc.games          General Games Discussions
33   rec.games.design               Game Design
52   rec.games.video.nintendo       Nintendo Gaming
86   rec.puzzles                    Puzzles and Crosswords
89   rec.games.video.sega           Sega Gaming
90   alt.netgames.bolo              Bolo Network Gaming
111  rec.games.hack                 Nethack, Rogue, et al
130  rec.games.board                Board Games
131  rec.games.pinball              Pinball Games
132  rec.games.trivia               Trivia Style Games
134  rec.games.video                Video Games - Atari, 3DO, etc.
142  comp.sys.ibm.pc.games.action    Action Games Discussion
143  comp.sys.ibm.pc.games.adventure Adventure Games Discussion
144  comp.sys.ibm.pc.games.announce  Announcements of Game Releases
145  comp.sys.ibm.pc.games.flight-sim Flight Simulators
(55 min left), (H)elp, More?
 ANSI    ONLINE  19200 8N1  [Alt+Z]-Menu  FDX 8 LF X ♪ ♪ CP LG ↑ PR  00:06:10
```

Figure 14-4: Software Creations Gaming Conferences. The mail that you can select from is obtained from a variety of sources.

```
═══════════════ Software Creations * Home of the Authors ═══════════════
   ◆─── Apogee Software ───◆      ◆─── Software Creations ───◆
   Apogee Releases.......... 1    SWC Releases ............... 3
   Apogee Dist. Network...... 2    SWC Vendors/Sysops ........ 38

  ──── You Can Also Order These File Areas By Mail — Open Door #5 ────
  Arcanum Computing... 4   Id Software ...... 47   Boxer Software...... 6
  Alive Software .... 63   Boardwatch Contest. 62  ImagiSOFT ......... 61
  Gamer's Edge ...... 5    Favorite Authors....65  GameByte Magazine.. 66

Educational ........ 7    Utils, Files ....... 16   Windows, Games ..... 67
Games A-L .......... 8    Utils, Printers .... 17   Windows, General ... 20
Games M-Z .......... 9    Utils, Video ....... 18   Windows, Fonts ..... 69
Game Accesories ... 10    Utils, Menus ...... 102   Windows, Wallpaper . 70
MS-DOS ............ 15    Utils, Memory ..... 103   Windows, Drivers ... 71
OS/2 .............. 98    Utils, Keyboard ... 104   Windows, Printers .. 72
Unix .............. 99    Utils, Disk/Tape ... 14   Windows, Video ..... 73
Multi-tasking .... 100    Music/Sound Programs 11   Windows, Icons ..... 74
Device drivers ... 101    Music/Sound Files .. 12   Windows, Programing  75
4DOS Related ...... 79    Windows: Utils ..... 68   Windows, Sound ..... 76

(52 min left), (H)elp, More?
 ANSI    ONLINE  19200 8N1  [Alt+Z]-Menu  FDX 8 LF X ♪ ♪ CP LG ↑ PR  00:08:34
```

Figure 14-5: The Software Creations File menu. This BBS divides its huge file collection into directories by topic.

Again, Software Creations has an extensive list of available topics. You choose your topic by its number and can see a list of available files. If you choose topic number 39, Astronomy, for example, you see a screen similar to Figure 14-6.

```
(H)elp, (1-200), File List Command? 39
Filename        Size      Date      Description of File Contents
===============================================================================

ACE1.ZIP        163028   12-13-93   General Purpose Astronomy Software Package
                                    Files: 12  Oldest: 9/26/86  Newest: 1/24/87
                                    Uploaded by: Steve Meade
ALW32S.ZIP      1322267  07-14-93   ASTRONOMY LAB version 1.2
                                    for Windows 3.1 and Windows NT
                                    includes win32s for W31
                                    brought to you by HZZ
                                    Files: 3  Oldest: 5/28/93  Newest: 7/14/93
AMKP0111.ZIP    13202    09-02-92   AMSAT-formatted satellite elements as of
                                    01/01/92.
AMST0111.ZIP    14320    09-02-92   AMSAT-formatted orbital elements as of
                                    01/11/92.
ASTINFO.ZIP     101984   08-12-93   Astrological Information Viewer
                                    Shows BioRythm etc..
                                    Files: 4  Oldest: 1/17/93  Newest: 1/17/93
ASTLAB.ZIP      661111   11-22-93   Astronomy Lab for Windows
                                    Files: 20  Oldest: 6/10/92  Newest: 10/2/93
                                    Uploaded by: Bob Oxberger
(52 min left), (H)elp, (V)iew, (F)lag, More?
 ANSI    ONLINE  19200 8N1  [Alt+Z]-Menu  FDX 8 LF X ♪ ♫ CP LG ↑ PR  00:09:19
```

Figure 14-6: File library list. The directory listing shows the available files.

On this BBS, you can continue to get a list of filenames with short descriptions of the files, or you can flag a particular file for downloading. If you choose flag, you are prompted for the filename, and it is marked as being a file you want to download. You then continue looking at lists of files and can download all your chosen files at once.

On many BBSs, there are literally hundreds of files on a particular topic, and you shouldn't search through them all. As shown later in the chapter, most BBSs have a file or series of files that you can download. These files contain a list of all the available files on the BBS. If you download one of these, you can then just look at any new files when you log onto the board.

In the same way that the mail menu has read commands that allow you to read only the messages you have not read since a particular date, the file menu has equivalent commands so that you can see which files have been added since you were last on the board or since a particular date.

If you need help at any time, you can press H or type **help** at the command prompt for a list of the currently available commands. As a newcomer to a BBS, you should choose one command at a time. However, as you gain experience, you can learn how to get through the menus more rapidly or activate a series of commands with a single command line.

To leave a BBS, you must log off from the system. In most cases, the command is G, **goodbye**, or **bye**. Remember that you can use this to exit the BBS when you get lost in the menu structure. Whenever you re-call the BBS, you start at the main menu again.

Logging off from a system rather than just issuing the hang up command to your communication software is a useful habit to cultivate. If you are paying for your online time, the BBS will not know immediately that you have hung up and will assume you are about to type on your keyboard. It will hang up eventually, but the few seconds to few minutes before it considers you to have hung up because there is no activity will cost you. Even if you are not paying for the time but have a restricted amount of time online, the BBS will continue to count your time down until it resets itself.

One-Minute Look at a Graphical BBS

A new generation of BBSs is gaining popularity. These use a graphical user interface called RIP (Remote Image Protocol) as the terminal emulation. If your software can support RIP — and increasingly communications software is supporting this standard — you can use your mouse online and have screen buttons to press instead of commands to type.

Note: All BBSs that support RIP also support another terminal emulation standard such as ANSI. To take advantage of RIP, you need to choose RIP emulation before dialing the BBS.

As an example of how RIP can completely change a BBS's user interface, see Figures 14-7 and 14-8. Figure 14-7 is the main menu from a BBS I called by using ANSI terminal emulation, and Figure 14-8 is the same BBS I called by using RIP terminal emulation.

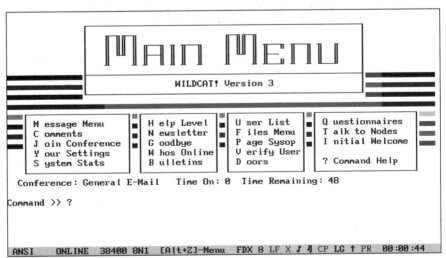

Figure 14-7: BBS main menu with ANSI terminal emulation. ANSI terminal emulation gives colors but is totally textual in appearance.

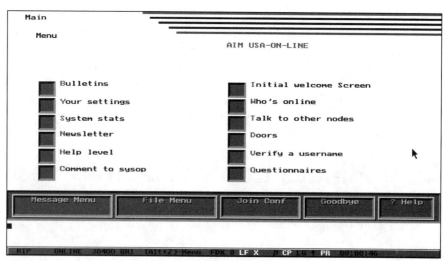

Figure 14-8: BBS main menu with RIP terminal emulation. RIP provides a graphical interface and mouse support for a BBS.

If you look carefully, you can see the same menu options on both screens despite the totally different appearance.

What to Look for on a BBS

If you look hard enough, you can find BBSs to fit your tastes — no matter how eclectic they may be. However, the following sections give a brief overview of items to look for when choosing a BBS, particularly a messaging and file-exchange BBS. They include the board's organization, files to look for, and the file-exchange services offered.

Organization

A BBS presents itself to you one screen at a time. A good BBS is one that is easy to navigate. It is amazing how many BBSs are very difficult to use. Consider the following items when assessing a BBS:

✤ Does it contain the information *you* want?

✤ Is it easy to *find* the information you want?

- Is the grouping, such as conferences and file libraries, *logical* to you?
- Can you *search* for the files you want?
- Is there a *regular flow* of traffic?
- Are the menus *consistent?*

Most of these topics have been covered elsewhere, but it is worth doing a critical assessment of the online services you use from time to time so that you continue to get the most from them.

A BBS should contain information of interest to you, where you can find it, and arranged in a fashion that is obvious to you. The organization may seem very logical to the sysop but not to you. For example, one sysop may keep all the word processing utility files in the word processing library, but another puts them into various categories, such as printers, video, and mouse sections. Both are reasonable places, but one will seem more logical to you.

When you first log on to a BBS, the amount of accumulated information can seem exciting and endless. However, the information may not change, perhaps because not many callers contribute to the messages or supply new files. These BBSs can quickly become boring because you are not seeing new material. Similarly, when you first log on to a BBS, you may be overwhelmed by the amount of information and may be intimidated. Find a BBS with more-limited information and get used to that before considering another one.

Beware of some BBSs that use the same letter command for different purposes depending on which is your current menu. For example, a BBS may use S in the message menu to send a message and S in the file menu to search for a file. These BBSs can be very irritating to use, especially when you reach the point where you stop reading the menus carefully. These include compression and uncompression utilities, lists of conferences, lists of files, and possibly lists of other BBSs to call.

Invaluable files

Almost all BBSs have a few files that are worth collecting. These include compression and uncompression utilities, lists of conferences, lists of files, and possibly lists of other BBSs to call.

First, you need a file compression and uncompression utility program. Most files are stored on the BBS in compressed form to save disk space and to reduce the time needed to download them. The compression program also allows multiple files to be stored in a single compressed file. Consequently, you download a single file that may be comprised of many individual files needed to run the program you have selected.

"What are the most important files to get from a BBS?"

The market leader is PKZIP from PKWARE and is typically named PKZ204G.EXE. The 204G portion of the filename refers to the version number — in this case, Version 2.04G. Consequently, when a new version becomes available, this filename will change. Files that are zipped with PKZIP have a file extension of .ZIP.

The file PKZ204G.EXE is a special type of compressed file, known as a self-extracting file. You download this file to your computer, type its name at the DOS prompt, and then press Enter. The file automatically uncompresses all its component files, and you end up with, among other important files, the compression and uncompression programs. Be sure to read the supplied documentation to understand how to use PKZIP.

Some BBSs and online services use other file compression utilities. The most common are ARC and LZH (typically found as ARJ202.EXE and LHA212.EXE respectively.)

Most BBSs include a file that lists all the files found on that BBS. They may also keep a list of available conferences in a file. It is found under a variety of names, so you may have to leave a message if you cannot find it. However, common names are FILES.ALL, DIR.ALL, or variations on the name that include the date the file was compiled, such as FILE0294.ALL, meaning February 1994's list. This file is sometimes listed as a menu item on its own. For example, Software Creations lists ALLFILES as a directory item of its own and has a separate directory of "free needed files" that includes such things as PKZIP.

Another commonly found file is a file containing a list of BBSs that you can call. It is sometimes called BBSLIST.ZIP. The file GOVT.ZIP, is a list of BBSs run by government agencies. However, if looking for these files does not reveal a BBS that you are particularly interested in finding, consider the following search strategies. Call the BBS manufacturer's BBS. Each of the companies that sells BBS software runs a BBS.

For example, Mustang Software, who makes QModem, runs a BBS. Mustang allows its registered BBS software owners to advertise their BBSs. Last time I looked, they had more than ten pages of BBS ads in their file listing. Several were for overseas BBSs, such as in England or Trinidad.

If you have a more specialized interest, call the national association, the local club, or look in a relevant magazine. For example, Antiquenet, a BBS for antique dealers, advertises in one of the antique dealer magazines.

File exchange with a BBS

If you intend to do much downloading of software, you should carefully examine your options after you have mastered the basics. The following sections give an overview of the most important items to look for, including supported file protocols, libraries, and quotas.

Supported protocols

In most cases, you want to select a BBS that supports the ZMODEM file-transfer protocol. You will want to choose a version of XMODEM as a backup. Practice down-loading files with both protocols, and make a note of the preferred choices for that particular BBS. (Chapter 6 explains the potential discrepancies between XMODEM file-transfer protocols.)

You should weigh the advantages of using ZMODEM in batch mode, where you can specify a series of files for downloading at one time, with the speed differences. For example, a BBS that supports 2400 bps and ZMODEM batch mode may be preferable to a BBS that supports 9600 bps, but you must specify each file in turn.

I would look for a BBS that has it all: fastest speed with compression, ZMODEM batch mode, and the capability to hang up automatically after downloading files. However, I have a high-speed modem, a husband who considers high phone bills a trivial detail, and a second phone line in my home.

Libraries

When considering a BBS's file libraries, you should look for logical organization and a reasonable searching mechanism. You also want to see that new material is being added regularly and that the older material is being removed or moved out of the way so that accessing the newer material remains efficient.

Suppose that you want to look for a genealogy program. A directory labeled something like genealogy or family history, would be ideal; but on smaller BBSs, you may need to choose a more general library topic that suggests genealogy, such as history or personal. Now suppose that you find the topic, download a few files, and try out a few programs.

A few months go by and you decide to get interested in genealogy again but want to see whether there's anything better. When you call the BBS, you don't want to wade through all the same material you saw before to find the one new file of interest. Therefore, you need to evaluate whether the BBS lists files by date or another element that indicates clearly how new they are.

The BBS needs to supply easy ways to find what you are looking for, even if you do not know exactly what you are looking for! Although this may seem a tall task, it is surprising how some BBSs seem to do this effortlessly and others do not.

Quotas

Some BBSs use file quotas or ratios to encourage new files on the BBS. You may have to upload one file for every five you download, for example. If you call several boards regularly, it is quite easy to maintain this quota.

Other boards offer alternative pricing that you will want to select based on your use of the BBS. Some may offer a quota system for free, a more liberal quota system for a small subscription, or unrestricted downloading for a more generous subscription. Other approaches include more liberal time online per day for subscribers, or alternate and less busy phone numbers for subscribers.

This is one area where BBSs are likely to be much more economical than commercial online services. Many online services charge for connect time and charge a premium if you connect at a higher speed. Most BBSs charge an annual or monthly subscription if they charge at all.

Desirable extras for messages

Other items to consider when choosing a BBS relate to messaging rather than file exchange. If you are going to do much message reading, offline mail reader support becomes a vital rather than desirable extra. Additionally, support for echo and relay mail systems, such as RIME, Fidonet, and the Internet, may be important to you if you want to reach or hear from a wider audience.

Summary

This chapter introduced general categories for BBSs based on size and function. Local BBSs tend to be small and may focus on regional topics. National BBSs with huge followings have a wide user base, extensive libraries, and messaging services. Chat boards, the best of which draw users from a national audience, allow you to express your alter ego. BBSs are run as hobbies, by associations, by clubs, and by companies as technical support tools.

A BBS is a community of its BBS software and its users. As with all communities, you will find a wide diversity of opinions and views. Don't be afraid to contribute to the community. If you find it really does not suit you, there are hundreds of thousands more BBSs you can call.

This chapter scratched the surface of my favorite type of online service: BBSs. There is a BBS out there for everyone — you only have to find it.

15

CHAPTER

Message-Based Services

This chapter introduces commercial electronic mail service companies. These companies offer private messaging and file-exchange services. In particular, this chapter covers the following concepts:

- Privacy with e-mail
- Available commercial services
- A tour of MCI Mail
- Sending files, faxes, and telexes via e-mail
- The potential for e-mail

Understanding E-Mail

As its name implies, electronic mail, commonly abbreviated *e-mail*, consists of messages that you send electronically. Apart from file exchange, the most common use for online services is sending messages or e-mail. However, there is a distinction between sending messages and sending e-mail. (Both terms are used synonymously.) The issue is privacy, and it can be very significant.

If you call a BBS or a typical commercial online service, such as CompuServe or Prodigy, you can send messages to other people who call the BBS or commercial online service. You usually can mark the message as *private* so that all users of the system cannot read it. However, the message is not completely private, and the sysops, or their designated staff, can read those messages even if they have been marked private.

"How do I send a private message?"

Some commercial companies offer an electronic mail service that keeps your message private so that it can be read only by the intended recipient. This is the service to use if you want to send confidential information. For example, a private message on a BBS or typical commercial online service is fine for inviting a friend to dinner or talking about the great computer deal you made. However, these are not the services to use to send private messages showing your company sales reports, employee performance reviews, or other private negotiations, such as contract bids, potential products, or patents.

Note: The weakest point for privacy in your electronic mail may be your own computer. Although a sysop can read all the messages, the volume is so high that messages are not typically read in detail. However, someone with direct access to your computer is more likely to have a vested interest in the contents of your messages.

Internal e-mail

Many companies use e-mail extensively as an internal communication method. Most LANs (local area networks) include an e-mail system where you can send electronic messages to anyone on the network. The e-mail program installed on your network is an application program, equivalent to using a word processor or spreadsheet. Although you pay for the e-mail application program, you do not pay for each message sent because the message is internal to your company.

Depending on the e-mail program, you can establish users on the LAN who are not physically located within your company. These people, such as sales staff, call into the LAN via modem and pick up their messages from their assigned electronic mailboxes. In this case, the salesperson calling in for the message incurs the cost of a phone call to collect the messages.

As with internal messages, you don't pay for each message but only pay for the telephone charges, because you supply the electronic mail services. Every person trying to receive or send e-mail must be a user on the LAN. If you have a preferred supplier or customer, for example, you can give her an assigned mailbox on your network. However, the intent of a LAN is to provide full network access to each user and enable all users to share the application programs, such as word processors and spreadsheet programs. Although there are situations where you may wish to establish a nonemployee as a remote user of your LAN, you probably won't want to do this in all cases.

E-mail via online services

A better alternative when you want to communicate with more than your fellow employees is to use commercial online services for e-mail. You establish an account with an online service and can send messages to anyone else with an account on that service. (In many cases, the service can exchange messages with other commercial services, which extends the potential recipient base substantially.)

When you start considering commercial online services as a method of contacting people, you need to consider the issue of privacy. In this book, the term *commercial online service* applies to online services whose primary goal is information and file exchange. The intent is to share information. They are covered in more detail in Chapter 16.

Although you can send a message addressed to a particular subscriber of a commercial online service, you cannot usually send a file for receipt by that individual. Additionally, you cannot be certain that the message will not be read by another person. This person would be authorized by the service to monitor and maintain the messages and would not be a casual user.

The costs incurred in sending a message depend on the service but include telephone charges and any connect time charges. A few services charge an additional fee per message over a monthly minimum. For example, the first 30 messages may be free, and then each costs 10 cents.

E-mail via commercial mail service

This chapter addresses a different message delivering category, *commercial mail services*. These services offer message and file-transportation services, and their intent is to deliver information and not share it. A message or file cannot be read by anyone except the recipient.

A subscriber pays for an electronic mailbox with the mail service. Although there may be a nominal annual fee, you usually pay only for each message that you send, and there is no connect time fee. Because of the narrow focus of these services, they are relatively easy to use. However, they offer unique services that can be powerful marketing tools and cost savers.

The three major players in commercial mail services are MCI Mail, AT&T Mail, and SprintMail. Of these, MCI Mail is the most appropriate for an individual user. AT&T Mail and SprintMail are intended for medium to large corporations.

A Brief Tour of MCI Mail

In principle, using MCI Mail is similar to calling a BBS or commercial online service. You open an account with MCI Mail and access it by calling a phone number from your communication program with your modem. You type your account name and a password to gain access to your account. After you access your account, you can use the messaging facilities.

MCI Mail uses the concept of an office Desk for your mailbox. You have an Inbox, an Outbox, a Desk, and a Pending area. The Inbox contains all the messages that have been sent to you that you haven't read. The Outbox contains all the messages you have sent. The Desk contains the messages you have read. The Pending area contains the messages you are currently creating.

These areas of your Desk are completely separate, and you need to be aware of which area you want to work in. You issue the Scan command, as in Scan Outbox, to view a summary of the contents of the desired area. The Scan command numbers the items in that area for reference. For example, if you have four unread messages, issuing the command Scan Inbox assigns the numbers 1 through 4 to the waiting messages. You can then issue commands, such as read 1 or read next, to read messages.

"What costs do I incur with MCI Mail?"

Using MCI Mail for simple message creating, sending, and receiving is particularly easy. You only need to learn a few commands, and even if you forget them, help is easy to find. Additionally, because you call an 800 number to reach MCI Mail — and are charged for the messages you send, not how long it takes you to create a message — MCI Mail is an economical service.

However, MCI Mail also includes more-advanced features that make the service more than a simple e-mail exchange service. You can, for example, attach files to your message, send a message and have it received as a fax document, or even send documents to nonsubscribers. The following sections illustrate sending a message, reading a message, and getting help. Later sections show how to take advantage of MCI Mail's more advanced features.

To access MCI Mail, you must first open an account with MCI and choose such items as your customer name and user name. MCI Mail then mails you the enrollment kit that contains your password. When you have your password, you can start to use the system. From your computer, you run your communication program and make it dial the central access number for MCI Mail. At the prompt `Please enter your user name:`, you type the user name you have selected and press Enter. This is a single word, typically a contraction of your name or your company name.

At the `Password:` prompt, you type your assigned password and press Enter. MCI Mail displays a summary of today's headlines, a notice about whether there are any messages waiting to be read, and the command prompt. Your screen will be comparable to Figure 15-1.

Sending a message

You control MCI Mail by typing commands at the command prompt `Command:`. To send a message, for example, you type **create** and press Enter.

```
Welcome to MCI Mail!

Need information from the White
House on the North American
Free Trade Agreement?

Type VIEW WHITE HOUSE FOREIGN
for details.

Today's Headlines at 12 pm EDT:

--Arkansas Judge Rules Wal-Mart
    Guilty Of 'Predatory Pricing'
--GE's 3rd-Quarter Net Rose 8.6%
      * Corporate Earnings Report * .

Type //BUSINESS on Dow Jones for details.


MCI Mail Version V11.3.H

    There are no messages waiting in your INBOX.

Command :
 ANSI    ONLINE  38400 8N1  [Alt+Z]-Menu  FDX 8 LF X ♪ ♩ CP LG ↑ PR  00:00:08
```

Figure 15-1: MCI Mail opening screen. MCI gives a brief news headline summary, status of your Inbox, and the command prompt when you first log on.

Creating a message is similar to creating a memo. You first generate the address portion followed by the text content. For example, you specify who will receive the message, who will get a "carbon copy," and then generate the subject of the message. When you need to edit a message, MCI Mail considers everything except the text itself as the envelope.

After typing **create**, MCI Mail prompts with TO:. You type the name of the recipient, in our example, **Sandy Reed**. MCI Mail displays the name and customer number for the recipient or provides further information. For example, if you only type the name **Reed**, MCI Mail needs you to choose the correct customer amongst its many Reeds. On the other hand, if no subscriber is found, MCI Mail reports that you must try a different name. MCI Mail continues to prompt you for additional addressees until you press Enter without typing a name. In this way, you can send the same message to several different people.

After choosing the recipient, you are prompted by CC:. At this prompt, you type the name of someone who should receive a copy of the message but is not the addressee. It is equivalent to cc: on a letter. You may, for example, send a message to a manufacturer complaining about a product and send a copy to the store manager where you bought the defective product.

Again, MCI Mail continues to prompt you for more names until you press Enter without typing a name. At the `Subject:` prompt, you type the subject of your message, which is **Meeting Confirmation** in this example. (As shown in the following section, the message recipient sees the `Subject:` in the message summary section.)

After the subject, you are prompted for the main text of your message. Figure 15-2 shows a typical message creation screen.

```
Command: read inbox
Your INBOX is empty.

Command: create

TO:      Sandy Reed
           382-6179 Sandy Reed                    -              Saratoga, CA
TO:

CC:

Subject: Meeting Confirmation

Text: (Enter text or transmit file. Type / on a line by itself to end.)

Hello!
Thanks for taking the time to talk to me this morning. This message
is to confirm our meeting on Friday at 12 noon. I will be standing
under the clock in Paddington Station wearing a red carnation and
carrying a portable computer.
I will be on the lookout for a tall dark stranger with the Times
newspaper under one arm and a modem (with phone cable and power
cord) under the other.
 ANSI    ONLINE  38400 8N1  [Alt+Z]-Menu  FDX 8 LF X ♪ ♫ CP LG ↑ PR  00:05:37
```

Figure 15-2: Message creation with MCI Mail. Messages in MCI Mail have a similar structure to memos with the addressees and subject followed by the main text.

If you are used to word processors, or even BBSs and some commercial online services, you will find that the message creation editor in MCI Mail is not very sophisticated. In a word processor, when you run out of space on a line of text, the word processor automatically wraps your word onto the next line. Many BBSs also support this feature in their message editor. MCI Mail does not and expects you to press Enter at the end of each line.

Although you can type longer lines in MCI Mail, you can get into very confusing situations. MCI Mail warns you if the line is too long, and you can reformat by using the editing commands. However, the result is not always what you would expect and can result in a mixture of long and short lines. You must remember to press Enter at the end of each line or type the message offline and use the more advanced upload text command introduced later in this chapter.

MCI Mail's message editor also requires that you end the message in a particular way. When you finish typing all your text, you need to type / on its own on a new line to signal the end of the message. If you press Enter without any text on the line, MCI Mail assumes you want to leave a blank line in your message and does not assume that you have finished typing. Fortunately, the slash (/) requirement is displayed as a reminder at the top of the message during creation.

"How can I separate my e-mail charges by project?"

After typing /, MCI Mail prompts you for the message-handling requirements. If you have no special requirements, you press Enter to ignore this option. Several handling options are available, including charging the message to a particular project, or giving a message priority-delivery status so that the recipient realizes it is urgent, or requesting a notification that the message was read by the recipient.

I think the handling options are particularly valuable even to infrequent users. I use the charge option to split my MCI Mail bill into projects. I can then submit expenses to my customers without having another customer's expenses appear on the same billing page. The receipt option is particularly useful if you have trouble contacting someone and want to know whether he is ignoring you or simply not checking his mail.

You are then prompted to send the message. If you choose yes, your message is sent and a copy is placed in your Outbox. If you choose no, the partially written message is kept in the Pending section. You can edit the message by using the edit commands or can delete the message without sending it.

Reading a message

Finding your messages can be tricky with MCI Mail, unless you remember the areas of your mailbox. As mentioned previously, your Inbox contains unread messages; your Desk, messages you have read; Pending, messages you have started to create but have not sent; and your Outbox, messages you have sent.

When you log on to MCI Mail, the message line above the command prompt tells you whether your Inbox contains any messages. To read these messages, you must first scan your Inbox by typing **scan**. MCI Mail then assigns numbers to each message and presents a summary list. You read the first message by typing **read 1** (or a different message with a different number). MCI Mail then displays the message along with its contents.

After you read a message from your Inbox, it automatically moves to the Desk area. Figure 15-3 shows the contents of a typical mailbox, where all the messages have been read and one message is in the Pending area. In this example, to read the message from Dan Sommer, you type **read 9,** and MCI Mail displays its contents. To read the draft message in Pending, you type **read 10**.

```
Command: scan inbox
Your INBOX is empty.

Command: scan desk

  4 messages in DESK

No.  Posted        From              Subject                    Size
  6  Sep 20 10:24  John P. Davis     RE: New email product      119
  7  Sep 27 12:55  Kimberly M. Crew                             993
  8  Sep 27 12:56  Kimberly M. Crew  Welcome Aboard!            953
  9  Oct 01 14:03  Dan Sommer        reaching IW via MCI        744

Command: scan pending

  1 message in PENDING

No.  Posted        From              Subject                    Size
 10  Oct 12 Draft  To: Sandy Reed    Meeting Confirmation        398

Command: scan outbox
Your OUTBOX is empty.

Command:
ANSI     ONLINE  38400 8N1  [Alt+Z]-Menu  FDX 8 LF X ♪ ♫ CP LG ↑ PR  00:08:18
```

Figure 15-3: MCI Mail mailbox. As soon as a message is read, it moves from the Inbox to the Desk area.

Getting help

MCI Mail makes getting help particularly easy, so even if you are an infrequent user, you can find out how to perform tasks from the command prompt. (The supplied quick reference guide is also clear.) To get help while online, you type **help** followed by a command name. For example, to get help on editing a message, you type **help edit,** or you type **help mailbox** to get a list of your mailbox areas and the typical commands you may need to use.

Ancillary services

At its simplest, MCI Mail allows you to send and receive text messages. However, it actually offers many more features. It is not a general-purpose online service but includes many different features relating to sending messages. The following sections summarize some of the features you may want to explore.

Compare the U.S. Postal Service. At its simplest, you can send a letter for delivery. However, you can actually do much more. You can send parcels as well as letters or send material express, priority, certified, or bulk mail.

Sending to a nonsubscriber

MCI Mail allows you to send messages to people who are not subscribers to an online service. You prepare and send a message to a person and specify that it can be sent on paper. The message is printed at the physical MCI Mail location that is closest to the recipient and is then mailed to the recipient. You can specify that you want an overnight delivery, and the message will be delivered by courier.

This method has several advantages. In the U.S., for example, you can send a message up to 11 p.m. EST and have it delivered the next day. Depending on your location, the overnight courier services may have final pickup time much earlier.

"Why should I use MCI Mail to send a message overseas to a nonsubscriber?"

Additionally, this method may be advantageous in cost and time for overseas delivery. MCI Mail may have locations or agreements with other companies that have locations close to your recipient. You can save the time that would be necessary to physically fly your letter to the required country. In some cases, this can reduce the delivery time by days.

Apart from the time-reduction aspects, paper delivery allows you to add a signature to your letter. You can arrange for your letterhead and a signature (or multiple versions) to be registered with MCI Mail and your account. Then, when you specify paper, the message is printed with your letterhead and signature.

Sending a fax or telex

Using a method comparable to sending a message to another online service, you can use MCI Mail to send fax or telex documents. You specify fax or telex during the addressing process and supply the necessary fax phone number or telex number.

"How can I send a telex?"

In many areas of the world, the telex remains the only electronic contact method besides the telephone. In the U.S., telexes are becoming scarce. MCI Mail enables you to send and receive telexes without extensive special consideration. However, telexes have a maximum of 69 characters on each line of text.

With the typical cost of a fax modem, you probably won't use this approach as an alternative to using your own fax modem, but don't dismiss the MCI Mail fax feature. It can provide a convenient method of sending a message, even if it is not the most economical. Additionally, you can use MCI Mail to send a fax document when you do not have access to a fax machine or fax modem.

Sending to other online services

MCI Mail is connected to other online services, including CompuServe and AT&T Mail, and you can send messages to subscribers of those services. To do this, you use a special address.

You begin creating a message in the usual way, but when prompted by the TO: prompt, you type the name followed by (**EMS**). You then include additional information at the electronic mail service (EMS) prompts to enable MCI Mail to route the message. The precise details of what to add to the address depend on the service you are trying to reach.

To send a message to someone on CompuServe, for example, you need to know the person's name and CompuServe ID number. After typing the name and (EMS), MCI Mail prompts you for the name of the electronic mail service by displaying EMS:. You type **CompuServe** and press Enter.

MCI Mail then prompts you for the mailbox information. At the first MBX: prompt, you type **P=CSMail** and press Enter. At the second MBX: prompt, you type **DDA=ID=99999,999** where 99999,999 is the recipient's CompuServe user ID number.

MCI Mail can connect to any electronic mail system that employs the X.400 connection standard. Some large corporations use this standard, as do other mail systems, such as AT&T Mail. People who have mailboxes on these systems can supply the precise mailbox address information you need to supply.

Consider your mail's privacy when sending information to another system. MCI Mail offers a completely private service, and messages cannot be read except by the recipient. However, this privacy may not apply to messages sent on another system.

Interesting extras

MCI Mail has several other features you can use. The most important is the capability to attach binary files to your messages. You might use this to send a copy of a budget spreadsheet to outside sales staff along with a message requesting that they fill out their particular section and return it. To attach a file to your message, you issue the upload command when you are prompted for the text for your message. To read a message with an attached file, you issue the download command to collect the file.

Although powerful features, the upload and download commands are not particularly easy to understand in MCI Mail. If you plan to attach files to your messages, you should use a special program, such as MCI Express (formerly Lotus Express), or an offline mail reader, such as OLX (part of QModemPro). These automate the uploading and downloading process so that you are less likely to make a mistake.

MCI Mail also provides access to the Dow Jones News Retrieval Service, which also is accessible from other online services. It is an online service that contains current and historical information relevant to business and finance from around the world. For example, it contains the full text of *The Wall Street Journal, The Wall Street Journal Europe,* and *The Asian Wall Street Journal.* You need to subscribe to this in addition to MCI Mail.

"Can I have a "toll-free" mailbox?"

Other MCI Mail features enhance your mailing facilities. For example, you can set up a *toll-free mailbox* so that the recipient rather than the sender pays for the message. You can have your mail automatically forwarded to other recipients, use electronic forms, or share your mailing lists with other subscribers.

An additional feature of MCI Mail allows you to establish a bulletin board that can be accessed by the people you specify. A corporation, for example, may want to establish a bulletin board that can be read by sales staff and provide a medium for discussion via electronic mail.

One disadvantage to electronic services is the need to supply precise information to find a subscriber. Sometimes, it can be difficult to find someone because you are misspelling the name slightly. To help, MCI Mail allows you to search its subscriber list. Consequently, you can turn this disadvantage into an advantage. (The same is true for commercial online services.) You may be able to find a subscriber from a particular company where you are interested in making contacts. Use the FIND command or other similar commands, and see who is a subscriber.

Tip: I find MCI Mail particularly useful when I try to get industry quotes for an article. I send a message to people who are extremely busy and don't have time to talk to me on the telephone. Because they actually get my message when they, or their assistants, are prepared to read messages, they will often rattle off a quick reply that I can use. If I call, I always manage to interrupt a meeting and catch them off guard. By using electronic mail, my response rate is maximized, and the amount of time I invest in getting the quote is minimized.

Simplifying Your Message Distribution

With the various online services available, you may find that the people you regularly contact do not all subscribe to the same service. Keeping in touch and feeling confident that you have actually contacted all the relevant people can become an administrative nightmare.

If used appropriately, MCI Mail provides you with a single account from which to send your messages to a wide variety of destinations. You may be able to get a similar service from another online service, such as CompuServe, but depending on your emphasis, the mailing facilities may be more important and economical than the file exchange and forums offered on CompuServe.

Suppose that you have ten different people to contact. Two subscribe to MCI Mail, one to AT&T Mail, two to CompuServe, three have fax machines, one has a telex, and the other has no electronic mail facilities at all. Coordinating sending messages to this group and making sure that the information was received can be difficult. However, the MCI Mail facilities enable you to create a single message and address it to each recipient in different ways. As far as your records are concerned, you send a single message to ten different people, but MCI Mail routs the messages in several different ways.

Note: MCI Mail also allows you to store lists of people that you want to send messages to. These ten people with their different addresses need to be entered only once, and you can choose them from a list when you need to send more messages to them.

Automating your account

Like all electronic mail, the service is useful to you only if you regularly check your mailbox. You should establish a procedure, such as checking the mailbox once a day, to be the most effective. You can purchase products that automate your MCI Mail use. Products include MCI Express (formerly named Lotus Express), Norton Express, and in a more limited way, the offline reader in QModemPro.

"How do I automate my MCI Mail usage?"

MCI Express is a communication program and a message-handling program. You can only use it to call MCI Mail and not as a general-purpose communication program. MCI Express is extremely valuable, especially if you need to send many messages and keep records over a long period of time. MCI Mail only keeps a record of the messages you have sent for a couple of weeks. After that time, they disappear from your Outbox. MCI Express requires you to explicitly delete the message from your Outbox.

Other advantages of MCI Express include the capability to easily attach binary files and easily read binary files attached to messages. The text editor for typing your message is also slightly better than the one on MCI Mail itself. You can set up MCI Express to call your MCI Mail account automatically. You load it as a TSR and specify how often it should call. For example, you can make it call once an hour or once a day.

Note: You don't want MCI Express loaded as a TSR if you are going to use your modem to call other services. Norton Express offers comparable features for MCI Mail.

QModemPro, a general-purpose communication program, includes an offline reader that is particularly useful for collecting messages from BBSs that support the quick mail (QWK) mail packet format. However, you can also use another supplied offline reader program (QGate) for reading your MCI Mail and responding to messages. (It also offers comparable features for CompuServe.)

You don't get the same level of automation and organization that is possible from MCI Express and similar products with QGate. You can't, for example, make the program call every hour. However, you can automate your message sending and retrieving.

Summary

This chapter introduced online mail services, in particular MCI Mail. These services provide a method of sending private mail and files to another subscriber. You can also use the service to send faxes, telexes, and messages to subscribers of other online services.

In its simplest form, MCI Mail is very easy to use. However, it includes flexible features that can streamline your messaging. With a single message, you can send e-mail, fax, telex, and paper output, depending on the recipient.

You can purchase programs that automate the process further and supply a more complete record of your online activities.

With a little exploration, you can use MCI Mail to find new contacts and link with other services that you may not find on other services. MCI Mail also supplies a gateway into the Dow Jones News Retrieval Service, a business and financial online service.

16

CHAPTER

Information-Exchange Services

This chapter introduces information-exchange services. These commercial online services offer the widest variety of features of any online service. In particular, this chapter covers the following topics:

- ✦ Understanding information-exchange services
- ✦ Understanding graphical services
- ✦ A brief tour of a graphical service
- ✦ Understanding text-based services
- ✦ A brief tour of a text-based service
- ✦ Typical features of online services

Understanding Information-Exchange Services

After BBSs, commercial online services are the most commonly found online service. Some people prefer commercial online services to BBSs, and others prefer BBSs to commercial online services. In general, BBSs are preferable because you don't pay for connect time. Although you pay for the phone call, you aren't usually running up a bill with a BBS for the time you are online.

In general, commercial online services are preferable because they have more users and you consequently have a more diverse user base. Because you do pay a connect charge, you are not limited in the amount of time you can spend online. BBSs typically restrict you to about an hour a day maximum.

"Why should I subscribe to an information-exchange service?"

Information-exchange services are usually general purpose and offer messaging, file exchange, and chatting online. They offer more features than most BBSs and are not as limited in the number of phone lines. You are unlikely to find a busy signal when you call a commercial online service. A popular BBS may have busy signals and be unaccessible at peak usage periods.

Like BBSs, commercial online services emphasize information exchange. Although they do offer messaging services, which are used extensively, much of the messaging is not private and is for public discussion. These large systems are divided into sections so that you can focus on a particular area of interest. These commercial online services each have hundreds of thousands of users. If you have an interest in a particular topic, you should be able to find someone else with a similar interest if you look hard enough.

This chapter avoids prices for these services because they change so frequently. However, most services offer a special promotion, and you should watch out for opportunities to try new items inexpensively as you use a service. For example, a special recently offered by a couple of the services was five hours connect time for $5.

Balancing Online Costs

The "Calculating Connect Charges" sidebar in Chapter 13 explains the various costs involved in using online services, including telephone charges as well as any connect time charges. The connect time charges can vary with the connection speed as well as the time of day. Depending on what you actually do online and when you do it, online charges can mount very quickly. A common fear for newcomers is large unexpected bills. Some services have complicated pricing structures; others have deceptively simple ones.

Most services offer a basic service where you pay a fixed price, typically between $10 and $20 per month. This may entitle you to unlimited time on the service or give you the first *x* hours free. However, most services also include extra cost items. For example, a stock quote may cost a few cents, or sending mail via the Internet may have a monthly minimum fee. The services do clearly state what costs more and usually warn you when you move to an area where extra fees apply.

Until you are familiar with the service, you should avoid the extra cost items. But don't overlook their value. It may cost a dollar or two, but if it gets you an answer you would have to spend days finding or would have to drive to the library to look up, it can be worth it.

There are many ways to economize. The telephone networks, such as Sprintnet and Tymnet, are much less expensive during nonworking hours. If you can find one or two services that fill all your needs, even if another service is quicker to use, you may save money. Don't overlook the opportunities of BBSs. Although they don't usually have current, constantly changing information, such as news, weather, or stock information, they do have the latest computer games and lots of messages from users interested in specific topics.

Getting online has become part of my daily and weekly routine. I check my mail daily, which takes a couple of minutes, and then I call a few BBSs and a couple of online services on a weekly basis for about an hour. My expenses, both phone bills and online service charges, vary little from month to month unless I am working on a special project.

However, you had to use the time within the calendar month or you lost it. Another service offered one hour of free access to a games area one month and one hour free access to the business news area the next.

The problem with describing any of these services is that they are diverse, and you can find more or less anything on any of them. However, each has an individual character that you may or may not like.

In general, commercial online services can be divided into two types: graphical and text-based. The two most popular graphical services are Prodigy and America Online. The most popular (with the most subscribers) text-based services are CompuServe and Genie. However, other text-based services have a loyal following too because they are less general purpose in nature.

Introduction to Graphical Services

Graphical information exchange services offer ease of use as their main strength. When you subscribe to a graphical service, you are supplied with a program that you install on your computer. This is a communication program written especially to interface with the service.

"What is a graphical online service?"

You can, and will probably prefer to, use a mouse with these services. Wherever possible, the communication program removes the details of the connection, and you make selections from the screen as if you were running an ordinary application program. You may not even realize that you are communicating with another computer via telephone. Generally, graphical services are very simple to use. However, they have a tendency to run slowly and can be frustrating to wait for unless you have a powerful computer.

Understanding a Slow Graphical Online Service

In general, the speed of your computer does not make much of a difference to your communication speed. The speed of an online service is much more dependent on your modem speed and the speed of the computer you are connected to.

However, graphical online services can be an exception to this generalization. These services use a program running on your computer as part of the communication process. In part, they depend on the processing power of your computer to display and redraw screens.

Consequently, on a slow computer, the service can appear to be slow. On a 386-based computer or better, any delay due to the computer's speed is insignificant; however, on a PC or AT-compatible computer, the performance can be frustrating.

This slow speed is not apparent on text-based systems. The text can be displayed on your computer more or less as fast as it can be sent from the remote computer. The information is not processed by your computer's microprocessor before display, so the speed is independent of your computer's speed.

You don't have to remember commands to use these graphical services, because the menus are displayed or are accessible from the screen. However, after you are familiar with one aspect of the service, it is worth learning any shortcut keys to help speed your progress from one area to another.

Many people, especially non-technical people, find the graphical online services wonderful. Others, particularly those who are not intimidated by complicated computer commands, find the graphical online services frustrating. I believe these services can be used by anyone who can read. However, I also know a lot of people who used these services as an introduction to online services and then moved on to a text-based service, where the depth of information, particularly technical information, is greater.

The most suitable service for you is the one that contains the information that you need and presents it in a manner you can understand. You don't need to know much about modems to access and use an online service, particularly a graphical online service. The two most popular graphical online services are Prodigy and America Online. The following lists indicate the features offered for each type of service.

Prodigy

Service topics offered by Prodigy include:

* Business and finance

  Automatic bill-paying services, real estate, tax, investment, and travel information

* For your kids

  Encyclopedia, teenager message area, Sesame Street area, and games, such as Where in the World Is Carmen Sandiego?

* Fun, games, and adventure

  Chess, brain teasers, golf, armchair baseball, and a games message area

* Bulletin boards and messaging

  Singles, seniors, computers, careers, pets, medical, genealogy, and hobbies

* Travel

  EEASY SABRE, a travel reservation service; weather; and city, vacation, and restaurant guides

❦ Arts and entertainment

TV reviews, news, and schedules, plot summaries of soap operas, book reviews, movie reviews, and music reviews and charts

❦ News and information

Headline news, national, political, and international news, lottery results, and columnists on politics and Washington

❦ Sports

Sports message area, sports results and headlines, auto racing, horse racing, golf, football, boxing, and bowling information

❦ Computers

Software guide, Macintosh column, consumer reports, multimedia, computer club, and best-selling software charts

❦ Homelife and shopping

Cookbooks, wine reviews, health, home business, do-it-yourself, gardening, and online shopping for cameras, books, clothes, sporting goods, toys, and entertainment products

America Online

The following lists features offered by America Online:

❦ Learning and reference

Library of Congress Online, CNN Online, *National Geographic*, and Teacher's Information Network

❦ People connection

Public and private chat areas, message boards, and event schedules, as well as special conference events

❦ Travel and Shopping

EAASY SABRE travel service, flower shop, Comp-U-Store, classifieds, and office products

❦ News and finance

U.S. and world news, sports, editorial, weather, stock quotes, business, and finance

* Life-styles and interests

  Chatting and message areas for variety of topics, including disabilities, seniors, pets, aviation, and food and drink

* Computing and shareware

  PC file library, news, reference, and messaging areas

* Games and entertainment

  Multiplayer online games, casino games, and entertainment news

A brief tour of America Online

As an introduction to a graphical online service, the next sections present a brief online session with America Online. When you enroll with America Online, you are given the choice of two PC communications programs — one for DOS and one for Windows. The features are the same with both programs, although the screens look slightly different. (The following example shows the Windows version of the program.)

After starting Windows, you double-click the America Online icon to start the program. You are prompted for your user name and password. Prodigy and America Online allow you to establish several different users for the same account. For example, you may be one user and your son another. You are charged as though one person uses the account.

After selecting the user name and typing your password (each user has a different password), you choose Sign On to proceed, and the program automatically connects you with the service. The icons on-screen show the call's progress. They show the phone number being dialed, the modems link being established, and the password being checked. Your screen then looks like Figure 16-1.

The opening screen shows your name as it is known on the system. The window offers four topics of interest, such as the top news story and new record releases. Because the screen was captured near Halloween, another suggested topic is Halloween Art. You are also given an icon that indicates whether you have any mail. In this example, I chose the button Browse the Service. Your screen will look like Figure 16-2. The eight departments show America Online's main topic areas as mentioned in the features list.

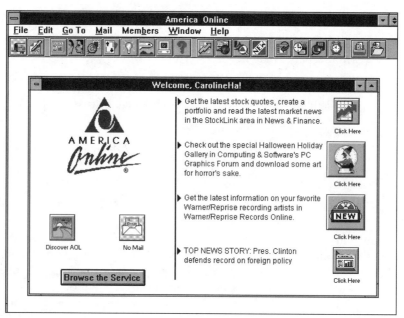

Figure 16-1: America Online's opening screen. All commands can be selected from the screen icons.

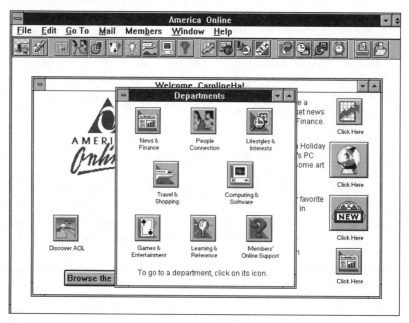

Figure 16-2: America Online's Departments. America Online divides its activities into eight topic areas.

I decided to visit the People Connection section and chat with other people online. The first area I visited, the Lobby, did not have any interesting conversation, although 22 people were in that area. I chose to look at the *room*, labeled Sports. After watching for a minute, my screen looked like Figure 16-3.

The five people in the sports chat area were discussing football. To join in, I could type my comment at the bottom of the screen and press the Send button to have it added to the list. However, because I was hoping they would be talking about the World Series and not football, I decided to leave.

From the department window, I selected the Games and Entertainment department and checked my horoscope, as shown in Figure 16-4. After reading that my financial outlook for today was poor, I decided to look at more entertainment.

I picked the message board area and looked at the messages on the topic of oxymorons. Figure 16-5 shows part of the list of messages. After reading some of the messages and adding a message containing my own favorite oxymoron (initial deadline), I returned to the Departments window.

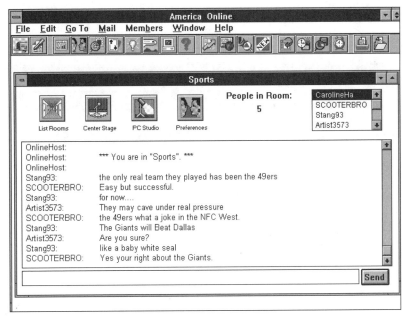

Figure 16-3: Sports chat room. Each participant in a chat session types his or her comments and reads other people's comments.

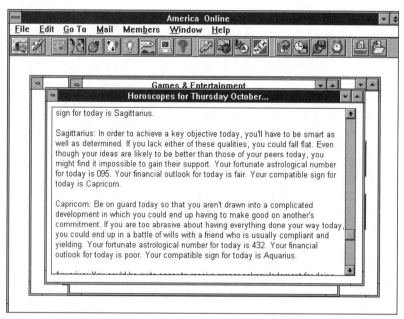

Figure 16-4: Horoscope. Each topic is displayed in a window. Where applicable, scroll bars and icons are available.

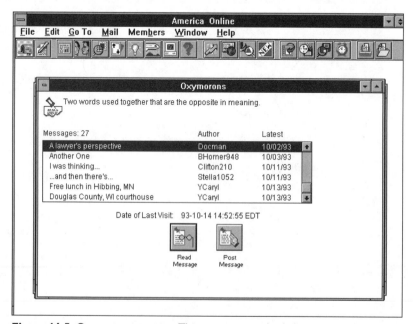

Figure 16-5: Oxymoron messages. The messages are divided into topics. You can choose to read all messages, or only some, as well as respond.

From the Departments window, I chose Learning & Reference. Figure 16-6 shows some of the available topics. Comptons Encyclopedia is online as well as many specialized topics. I was particularly interested in Smithsonian Online and explored that area before choosing Sign Off from the Go To menu at the top of the screen to end my session.

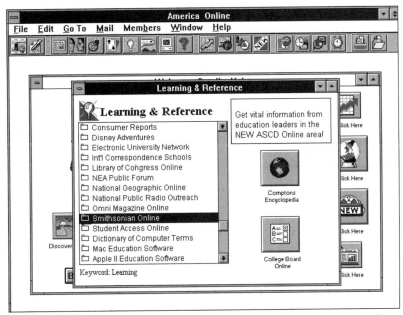

Figure 16-6: Learning & Reference Department. Many different topics can be chosen, including College Board Online and Omni Magazine Online.

Introduction to Text-Based Data Exchange Services

Like the graphical-based systems, the text-based data exchange services also attract hundreds of thousands of users. The most popular services, in terms of the number of subscribers, are CompuServe and Genie. However, BIX, Delphi, The Well, and others also have large followings.

"What does a text-based online service offer?"

In general, these services offer messaging, file exchange, forums, and games. Each has a leaning towards one or more of these features. CompuServe, for example, has a large number of forums, many supported by computer software and hardware manufacturers. The typical user tends to be fairly computer literate and technical.

As another example, The Well emphasizes messaging and has hundreds of different topic areas. It has had a long history and has a very loyal following. It does not have live chatting or online games.

Imagination is specifically targeted towards games and entertainment. It has live chatting and many games. You can find terminals in bars, restaurants, and hotel lounges around the country.

The following lists give a brief summary of features offered by the most popular services: CompuServe, BIX, Genie, and Delphi.

CompuServe

- Electronic mail
- Online reference material
- Travel services
- Weather feature
- Shopping
- Investor services
- Leisure-time games
- Forums
- Software exchange
- Chatting

BIX

- Electronic mail
- Conferences
- MicroBytes industry news briefs
- Software exchange

Genie

- Multiplayer games
- Chatting
- Electronic mail
- File exchange
- Investment and financial services
- Electronic text of publications, company profiles, and patent information

Delphi

- Electronic mail
- Messaging areas
- Chatting
- File exchange

A brief tour of CompuServe

Most online services offer a multitude of services and options. Although you can call the services and find your own way around, most services offer a software program, variously referred to as an *information manager* or *a front end.*

These programs are essential for economical and efficient use of the service. You can make your selections for the areas of interest and proceed directly to them instead of learning a lot of commands. Although these programs may have a text-based user interface, they allow you to choose commands and areas of interest from lists of commands.

The following example is a brief tour of CompuServe. The CompuServe Information Manager (CIM) was used to make the selections. CompuServe supplies this program with its enrollment fee. Like the graphical-user interfaces, the Information Manager hides the details of the modem use from view. You start the program and select the topic you want to browse. CompuServe Information Manager then makes the connection automatically. (The following example shows the DOS version of the program.)

Unlike Prodigy, where you are prompted to choose your user name and type the password, CIM stores your user name and password. You can only have one user for each CompuServe account.

CIM displays a series of cascading windows that show where you are in the service. In Figure 16-7, for example, there are four windows on-screen. One, in the lower-right corner, indicates that mail is waiting, and the one in the upper-right corner shows highlights of the service this week. The other two windows show the selections made prior to connection.

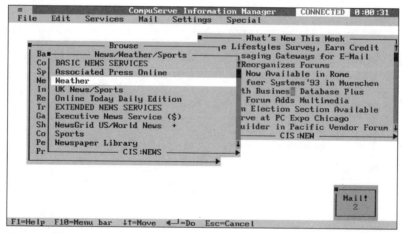

Figure 16-7: CompuServe connection. CIM presents a series of cascading windows to navigate the system.

After starting CIM, I decided to view a weather map. I chose News/Weather/Sports from the Browse window, and CIM automatically connected with CompuServe. The current connection status is shown at the top of the screen. In Figure 16-7, it shows CONNECTED, but at other times it may show WORKING or DISCONNECTING. The length of time that you have been connected is also shown at the top of the screen.

The News/Weather/Sports window opens on top of the Browse window and summarizes the available topics. After choosing Weather from this list, your screen will look like Figure 16-8.

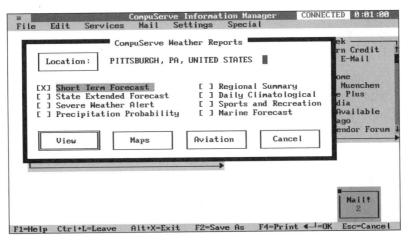

Figure 16-8: Available weather reports. You can choose from a variety of weather forecasts and maps for any location.

The available weather forecasts cover most requirements. For example, you can see a short-term forecast, extended forecast, or a regional summary. In addition to reading a forecast, you can see a map of the chosen forecast. Although CompuServe assumes that you want a forecast for your location, you also can choose the location. For this example, I chose to view a map of the current weather. The screen looked like Figure 16-9.

Figure 16-9: Weather maps. The map shows a graphical view from the current weather radar.

After viewing the weather map, I decided to explore one of CompuServe's most popular areas, the computing support areas. These forums are supplied by computer software and hardware manufacturers. You usually can get technical support; news information; and, in some cases, updated device drivers or other utilities. Some of these forums are very formal; others provide interesting insight. These forums are often a way to communicate with the company executives.

I chose Computer Support from the Browse menu and then Hardware Forums from the Computer Support menu. I then chose Hayes from the extensive list of hardware manufacturers and groups.

Each forum is different and is structured by the particular company that supports that forum. However, they are all similar in presenting a list of options for you to choose from, and you gradually focus on the item of interest. For example, after choosing Hayes from the Computer Support menu, I chose Special Support programs and discovered that Hayes offers three special support programs: one for registered dealers, one for developers, and one for sysops. I could choose one of these for more details about the current programs.

After viewing the special support for sysops, I moved to the forum area itself to read messages about Hayes products. As shown in Figure 16-10, the messages are divided into topics, and you choose a topic of interest to see the relevant messages.

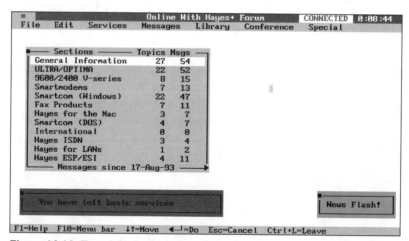

Figure 16-10: Typical CompuServe forum. The messages are divided into topics to make finding them easier.

After looking in the forums, I took a look in the shopping area. I picked Shopping from the original Browse menu. I then searched The Electronic Mall by product to find some cookies. As shown in Figure 16-11, the index starts with general topics and then focuses on the more specific items.

I chose the Index, Gourmet Foods, and then Candies/Cookies/Cakes and was presented with a list of companies that will accept my order online. These include a cookie company, a steak company, fruit shippers, and a coffee company. I spent my allowance and then chose Disconnect from the File menu. CIM then automatically disconnected me from the service.

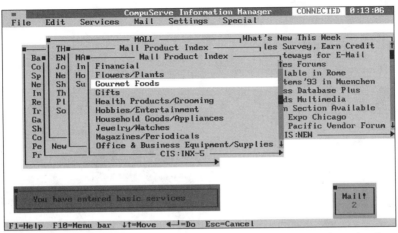

Figure 16-11: Shopping mall. You can purchase many different items from the electronic mall.

Summary

This chapter introduced the commercial information exchange services. These offer similar features to BBSs but on a larger scale and for a higher cost. Depending on the particular service, you can connect with services offering general interest or very focused interests.

The commercial information-exchange services typically include material, such as news and weather, that is regularly updated. Most include an encyclopedia.

The graphical services, such as Prodigy and America Online, offer menus and icons for your selections. They are easy to use but tend to be slower than the text-based services.

Most of the text-based services offer a front-end program that makes navigating the vast array of options easier. These front-end programs allow you to pick from a list of choices. However, you can also access these systems directly from your own communication programs. As an advanced user, this may save you time.

Chapter 18 introduces Information-Searching services that specialize in supplying database information for business applications.

17

CHAPTER

The Internet

This chapter introduces the Internet. This network of networks includes all the features of the other online services, but because it is not owned or run by a single organization, it doesn't fit a neat explanation in the same way as the others. In particular, this chapter covers the following topics:

❖ Understanding the Internet

❖ Getting access to the Internet

❖ Typical features found on the Internet

❖ Typical utilities to navigate the Internet

Understanding the Internet

Understanding the Internet is like appreciating astronomy. I know that the Earth is a planet spinning on its own axis and moving around the Sun. I also know that the moon spins on its own axis and moves around the Earth. My mind can grasp the concept of light years and billions of galaxies. However, somewhere between this elementary level and discussions on event horizons, pulsars, quasars, and arithmetic involving numbers approaching infinity, my mind locks up.

At a simple level, the Internet also seems logical. As an interconnected computer system, it seems understandable. However, when you try to pin an item down or grasp an overall understanding, the terms become esoteric, the experts become more vague or more technical, and comprehensible explanations are elusive.

At first glance, understanding the Internet is easy. It is a network of interconnected computers. You, a computer user, access one of the interconnected computers and, as a consequence, communicate with others (people and computers) on the Internet. You have access to information that is stored on the computers in the network. Keep this simple description in mind as you expand your understanding.

The computers linked together in the Internet all use a communications protocol called TCP/IP (Transmission Control Protocol/Internet Protocol) for their communication. This protocol specifies the form of data and how the data is passed between computers. It is a *packet-switching protocol*, which means the data is divided into chunks (known as *packets*) for transmission. Each computer and each user on that computer on the Internet has an address, and the packets of data include the addresses of the sender and receiver. The addresses help the computers route the information packets. The packet is passed from the sending computer to the next computer in the net until it reaches its destination.

So far, the description doesn't sound much different from a typical online service, such as a BBS or CompuServe, except that more computers are involved. However, the Internet is different because there is no central computer that you are calling. The available resources are scattered around all the different computers. No single group owns all the computers, and it is a continually changing network as computers are added or are taken out of service (temporarily for service or permanently). Estimates of thousands of new computers being added every month are not exaggerated.

The computers are located in universities, research establishments, government sites, and commercial companies literally around the world. Some computers are linked by very high speed connections, others by slower links. (These are still much faster than a typical asynchronous modem connection.) The costs involved are borne by the various computers that are connected together. For example, computer A, linked to computer B and C, may pay communications charges for the data being passed from A to B and C. Or, computer B pays for the data it passes to computers A, D, and E.

The link between the computers is not an asynchronous link, as has been discussed in the rest of this book. The computers are linked via leased lines, and the connection is permanently open (except when closed for maintenance or breakage). As a result, to the organizations owning the computers, the connection charges are constant and continual. You, or other Internet users, adding your data to the flow does not alter the costs. (It may alter the performance in some cases, because there is a limit to the amount of data that can be sent at once.)

The packets are passed from one computer to another based on the address in the packet. Any particular computer in the Internet knows the addresses of the computers it is attached to, and it passes a packet to a computer that it considers "closer" to the destination address.

The actual route taken by a packet depends on many factors, including the source and destination of the packet. Some interconnections between computers are intended for specialized use, such as research or education. These connections allow packets that are sent to or from research or educational addresses only. Commercial use of the Internet, although becoming commonplace, was not the original intent. However, there are enough computers on the Internet, so that, although a commercial message may take a different route, it still arrives at its destination.

"Should I be on the Internet?"

The Internet has existed and flourished for many years. Most computer users who have dabbled with Unix-based computers at college have visited the Internet. PC users, who typically use DOS or Windows as an operating system, have found the Internet in only the last few years.

Whether you need an Internet address depends greatly on your communication needs. You may even have an Internet address and not know it. (Most online services are indirectly or directly connected to the Internet.) Without doubt, more information is stored on the Internet than is available from online services, and more people are connected to the Internet than to online services. However, you must weigh whether you care about this access.

The following section gives an overview of some of the information available on the Internet. Subsequent sections explain how to get access to the Internet and how to find items on the Internet.

Typical Features on the Internet

Plumbing the depths of the Internet does not simply involve choosing items from a menu. The information and people are there, but you have to find them. If you are adventurous, you can have a lot of fun or find invaluable information, but you can compare it with the way you use a library. If you like to randomly pick books from the shelves, you will have fun on the Internet. If your research material is not available elsewhere in an easy to find form, the Internet may be your only source. However, do not expect to find an index or directory that describes the Internet's contents. You will find hundreds, if not thousands, of lists describing where to find items.

You can chat, send and receive messages, and transfer files on the Internet. As on BBSs and commercial online services, this means you can send and receive e-mail, send and collect files, and potentially chat with other Internet users by typing at your keyboard. However, the ease with which you can do these things varies greatly, depending on the type of connection that you have. The following section describes the differences between types of connections.

"What information is on the Internet?"

Because the Internet is many computers that are organized in different ways, the information available is not arranged in a coherent manner. (This is where understanding the Internet moves from tangible numbers to numbers approaching infinity.) Imagine a network with five computers for a moment. If each computer has a different directory structure and different application programs, accessing each computer may require you to learn five approaches to finding information. Suppose that each computer offers different levels of access, and the information you can reach varies. Now expand the network to tens of thousands of computers, and you get some idea of how the Internet is a whole universe to explore.

As a small chapter in a communications book, generalizations on the Internet are necessary in this book. The following descriptions only scratch the surface of the available information.

You can send e-mail on the Internet. Your connection includes (or you obtain) a mailing program that can send messages. You supply the Internet address for a message's recipient, write the message content, and send the message. The message is passed via the Internet to the computer where your recipient is connected and where it can be read.

Note: There is no privacy on the Internet. The message can be read on its way to its destination. This is not important when announcing your child's birth but may be important when handling delicate business negotiations. If you use an online service that offers complete privacy for your messages and you also send messages via the Internet, remember that this privacy is lost once the message gets to the Internet.

By using e-mail, you usually send a message to a single recipient, but you can widen your audience to include *newsgroups* and *mailing lists.* These are similar to conferences on BBSs and other online services. (In some cases, as shown in Chapter 14, the conferences found on BBSs or online services are Internet newsgroups.) You read the mailing by using a mail program, and you read the newsgroup by using a news-reading program. (Your connection may not include both programs.)

The newsgroups focus on particular topics, and you can choose groups that you want to "subscribe" to. For example, you may choose to read the conferences on IBM PCs and organic gardening. The messages posted to these conferences are sent to your e-mail address. You can add your own contributions or remain passive. In some cases, this may result in two or three messages a week; in others, it may mean two or three messages a minute.

Using newsgroups is a very interesting way to exchange ideas with other interested people, but as you can guess, you need to check your mailbox regularly and remove or add newsgroups as your interests change. You may be able to filter the information you read from a newsgroup, depending on the particular software you are using to pick up the information.

Another variation on the e-mail topic is subscribing to mailing lists. You can sign up to receive mailings from various places on the Internet. As the name suggests, you then receive any mailings from that location. For example, you can sign up to get all the White House press releases or weather reports twice a day. Other services, such as newswires, are also available on the Internet, but you may have to pay to subscribe.

Note: Most newsgroups and mailing lists have a special message known as an *FAQ list.* This itemizes the frequently asked questions about the group. As a newcomer, you should read this information before posting a question of your own.

As part of your exploration of the Internet, you will quickly learn that there are many lists of lists. For example, you can find lists of available newsgroups and lists of available mailing lists. Most Internet books, including *the Internet For Dummies,* give you a sampling and show how to find the lists listing more.

In addition to various e-mail features, many computers on the Internet have files that you can download. After all, the computers are connected so that information can be passed from one computer to another. Many of these computers require you to have an account with them to access the files. However, thousands support nonsubscribers and give you access to a small area of the available information. You log on to the computer as a person named "anonymous" and gain access to the public area.

In some cases, the computers provide a convenient storage area, and the files are of a general nature. For example, you can find most shareware and public domain software that you would find on a BBS or commercial online service on the Internet. In other cases, the information is supplied as a service. The Library of Congress and the Smithsonian Institution have files containing digitized pictures of exhibits.

In principle, you download these files in a comparable way as downloading a file from a typical online service. You run a program at both ends of the connection to transfer the file from one computer to the other. Two popular programs are FTP (file transfer protocol) and RCP (remote copy protocol).

In practice, your particular Internet connection may not support file transfer. Although this limitation is changing with time, most commercial online services can provide you with an Internet e-mail address but cannot supply file transfer facilities for the Internet. (Delphi is a notable exception and currently offers the easiest and most economical connection for the typical PC user.) The sidebar "Transferring Binary Files as ASCII Text" explains how you can transfer a file to someone via e-mail if you don't have file transfer facilities. However, this will not allow you to transfer files from another computer.

You can find the computers on the Internet that have files you can download by exploring. You find a list of places to call, which in turn leads you to further places. To explore with any degree of efficiency, you need to learn new jargon and be prepared to read pages of information for one nugget of information.

You also can chat over the Internet. This is how you can talk to people in Russia, Australia, and Africa, for free, all at the same time. Again, you need a program; IRC (Internet Relay Chat) is a popular choice. You type your comments, and the other people online at the same time respond. CB radio is a good analogy. You talk to whomever is listening. If this interests you, there is a newsgroup (named alt.irc) that gives more information. Many connections do not offer this feature, because it arguably uses computer resources for little value.

Transferring Binary Files
without Internet File-Transfer Capabilities

Chapter 5 introduces the ASCII character set and the extended ASCII character set. Each character in the ASCII character set can be represented by using 7 bits of data. (The extended character set uses 8 bits of data.) Most electronic mail systems, especially those on types of computers other than PCs, handle only 7-bit ASCII text files. If you are connected to the Internet and can only send e-mail, this method applies.

As a PC owner, these electronic mail systems allow you to send messages to other computer owners without problems. However, if you want to transfer a binary file, you use a special file-transfer protocol, such as XMODEM, that can handle the 8-bit data. A *binary file* is a program or data file containing a series of 8-bit characters.

If the computer you are calling is unable to support file transfer, or the intended recipient cannot download the file from his system, consider using the ASCII text message features to send the binary file instead. This involves converting your program file from a binary file to an ASCII representation of the program file. You then send the ASCII file as if it were a message to the recipient. The recipient converts the received message back into a binary file for use.

The method is used most frequently when communicating via the Internet where file-transfer protocols are not always supported. The most commonly used conversion utility files are found on Unix-based systems because until recently most computers linked to the Internet were Unix-based. These files are known as UUENCODE and UUDECODE. UUENCODE converts the binary file to ASCII text, and UUDECODE converts the ASCII text into a binary file.

For a PC running DOS, shareware or free conversion utilities are available, including encode and decode utilities from Sabasoft Inc. and Richard Marks. They are often named or referred to as UUENCODE or UUDECODE because of their Unix origins. I use Wincode from Snappy Inc., which is written by G. H. Silva. It is a Windows-based encoder and decoder that is available free of charge and has several particularly nice features. (Like PKZIP, it's available from online services, BBSs, and The Internet.)

You can compare the encoding and decoding procedure with using a file-compression program, such as PKZIP. When the file is compressed (or converted into ASCII text), it is unusable. The encode and decode utilities are tools that allow you to do something you could not do with the file in another form.

If you use a commercial online service as your Internet connection, you need to look carefully at the service's charges and limitations. Limits on the size and number of messages that you can send affect how you choose to convert your binary file. Some encoders can split your binary file into multiple ASCII text files of an appropriate size. The decoder can reassemble these files upon receipt.

Chatting over the Internet seems to me like stopping people in a grocery store and talking to them. I can understand people wanting to chat on BBSs or online services where the topics, such as politics or sports, are defined, but just chatting for the sake of doing it does not appeal to me.

You also can play games on the Internet. These may be familiar board games, such as chess or go, or may involve many players at once. These Multi-User Dungeons (MUDs), which are also known by many similar names such as MUSEs (multi-user shared environments), are variations on the chatting approach. They are roughly equivalent to the role-playing fantasy game Dungeons & Dragons. If this interests you, a newsgroup supplies a weekly list of available MUDs.

Getting Access to the Internet

All the computers on the Internet communicate by using TCP/IP protocols. Consequently, for you to be *on* the Internet, you need to use or connect to a computer that supports TCP/IP. If you are a home user with a stand-alone PC and a modem, you are not connected to the Internet. But if you use a PC in a business, particularly where you are on a LAN, you may already be on the Internet or can arrange to access the Internet. If you have a system administrator, *ask*. If you have access to a college computer — and in some areas, local schools — you may have access to the Internet. Several of my friends "talk" daily to their college-age children via the Internet.

If you subscribe to a BBS or commercial online service, you may already have access to the Internet. For example, you can send and receive messages to and from the Internet with your MCI Mail account, your CompuServe account, or your Delphi account. (In most cases, you will pay the service to send and receive messages. This may be a fixed monthly fee or may be a per message fee.) In most cases, this access is limited to sending and receiving messages.

Some BBSs connect to the Internet to pick up newsgroup mail. As explained in Chapter 14, they show up as conferences of messages that you can read. You may be able to suggest further newsgroups for your BBS to collect.

"How do I connect to the Internet?"

Another resource is an Internet Service Provider. These companies will provide you with access to the Internet for a monthly fee. They assign you a mailbox on their computer so you have an Internet address. When you have an account, you call the service provider from your PC and use the computer as your access to the Internet.

These service providers typically offer two types of connection: *terminal* and *network host*. They also offer different schemes (for different charges) that are typically volume related. For example, you may be charged $20 a month for a mailbox that you can access for an hour a day or $400 a month for unlimited access, multiple mailbox addresses, and other features.

The two types of connection are important to understand. By using a terminal connection, you call the service provider with your modem and communications software, such as Smartcom for Windows or QModemPro, and use the Internet access tools that they provide. For example, they may offer FTP as a file-transfer program, finger as a program to find who else is connected to the Internet, and IRC as a chat program. You cannot use your own selection of programs for this type of connection. When choosing a service provider, look carefully at the utilities offered and their user interface. (This is the type of connection currently offered by Delphi.)

As a network host, you make your computer actually attach itself to the network. This allows you to choose the software programs you run. This is particularly interesting for PC users who may find the commonly used utilities archaic and frustrating. It also allows you to take advantage of a relatively new trend. Many new software programs are becoming available, particularly for Windows, that provide a more familiar user interface for PC users with network host abilities.

For the typical single PC user, running a small business for example, the Internet service provider may allow you an economical way to connect with the Internet for a minimal cost. Using a special type of connection, SLIP (serial line IP) or PPP (point-to-point protocol), you can call the service provider via an ordinary telephone line with your modem and become a network host for the duration of the call. Although you may need support from your local supplier to install the required software to start with, this need not be an expensive alternative. (It's as complex as installing a very small LAN.)

Note: You are not paying an Internet organization; you are paying the provider who supplies you with your connection to the Internet. As a consequence, your charges and facilities may be very different from other Internet users. It is well worth shopping around.

Typical Utilities for Navigating the Internet

To communicate with other computers on the Internet, you will need to run software programs. You will, for example, need a mail-reading program to read mail and a file transferring program to download files. As explained in the preceding section, whether you can choose your own programs or must use the ones supplied by the Internet service provider depends on the type of connection you have.

However, because the Internet has been around for many years, there are several programs, some newer than others, that people tend to talk about. (This is where the astronomy analogy comes in again. Other Internet users may sound like they are talking in technical detail about event horizons or black holes.)

PC users have their own jargon they use without being aware of it. Internet users do the same. For example, we talk about zipping a file and using PKZIP. This is actually a product name. We mean compressing, but we don't say that. The good Internet providers will supply information on the utilities they provide. Increasingly, providers are adding menu-driven user interfaces to make your job easier. You will probably have to read the instructions and probably the FAQ (frequently asked questions) information to get started.

"What do I use to search the Internet?"

To understand this process, you need to learn two more terms: *server* and *client*. The term server on the Internet (and other computer systems) means the computer that supplies (stores and can run) the application program. You need to run an appropriate client (a piece of software) to access the server application. This client is a utility program that may be located on your local computer, the server you are accessing, or even another server on the Internet. The utilities your Internet provider supplies are examples of client software. This explains how different Internet servers can be accessed by dissimilar computer systems (Unix, PC, Mac, etc.) by means of an appropriate client for each system. The server behaves the same, no matter which system the client software is running to access the server.

In some cases, you may need to run one client software program on your local computer to connect with another server and use another client software program on that server to access the application program of interest. For example, a Gopher server is the computer that contains the Gopher program and the computer that is actually running the Gopher program for you. You use the expression *connect with a Gopher server* to indicate that you are running the Gopher program. You can use Gopher client software located at your local computer, in which case the Gopher client software makes the connection and runs the Gopher program. Alternatively, you can use a different program, such as Telnet, to make the connection with a Gopher server and run the Gopher client software as well as Telnet. To compare this with typical asynchronous communication, you run a communications program with terminal emulation to make the connection with another computer, but you may use a second program from within the communications program that supports file-transfer protocols to transfer the file. As a user, you probably don't realize that you are running two different programs; you only care that you have made the connection and accessed the desired function.

Telnet

This most basic utility allows you to log into a remote computer as a *terminal*. As explained in Chapter 5, when you link your PC to another computer as a terminal, you control the remote computer from your PC.

Finger and Whois

These are two commands available on many systems that allow you to find other people on the Internet. The finger command tells you about who is currently logged into the Internet at the address you specify. The whois command tells you about the addresses of people on the Internet. The whois directory does not contain all Internet user names but contains many people who are involved in the working of the Internet and doing network research.

FTP and RCP

These programs allow you to download and upload files to the Internet.

Archie

This program searches the Internet for files that meet your description. You access an Archie server (a computer that has Archie available for use) and run Archie from there. You may have Archie available at your connection (if your Internet provider offers it). Or you can use Telnet to access the Archie server. You are then logged in as a terminal to the computer that can run Archie for you. Alternatively, you can send e-mail to an Archie server and receive the response as a (potentially huge) e-mail message.

Gopher

Gopher is a menu-driven program that helps you look for documents and files on the Internet. It is an attempt to make navigating the Internet easier. You run Gopher from your connection or Telnet to a Gopher server. When you find something of interest, you can access this data from Gopher.

The Gopher program is an example of why the Internet is so powerful yet hard to understand. Anyone who wants to can set up a Gopher server and provide menus that show the features of their particular computer. This Gopher server can also provide links to features of other computers. As a result, you may find the menus inconsistent, because so many different people may have been involved in setting up the menus. (Keep in mind that the Internet is a network of networked computers without a centralized system.)

Veronica

Veronica (Very Easy Rodent-Oriented Net-wide Index to Computerized Archives) is a database that shows all the locations of available Gopher servers. (There are so many Gopher servers that the index is very useful.) It is typically available from all other Gopher servers. You pick the menu selection, such as Veronica or Other Gophers. It is roughly equivalent to Archie, where Archie is an index to FTP files on the Internet. Veronica can find Gopher servers that meet your search criteria.

Wide Area Information Servers (WAIS)

Wide Area Information Servers (WAIS, pronounced *ways*) is another form of index on the Internet. It looks inside the documents and files rather than at only the titles (like Archie and Veronica) for the words that meet your search criteria. However, not all documents and files on the Internet have the necessary indexes for WAIS to be able to find them.

WAIS has a reputation of having a very difficult user interface, but you can often access WAIS through Gopher menus, which makes life much easier (but more limited).

World Wide Web (WWW)

The World Wide Web (WWW or the Web) is another document index that explores the information on the Internet by using hypertext links. You access a hypertext browsing program and see a summary or part of the document. Certain words are highlighted or numbered, and you can select one of these linking words or phrases to jump to another area of interest. In fact, the link may not be a word or phrase, but may be a pointer to a picture.

You probably have encountered hypertext in Windows help files. You display an index of information and click a hypertext phrase to jump to information on that phrase. When in the new area, you can jump to another highlighted phrase to get other related information.

Most of the documents that WWW can search are also WAIS documents and files. Consequently, you can consider WWW as being a preferable user interface to access WAIS information.

Summary

This chapter introduced the Internet. It is a rapidly growing collection of interconnected computers. Each computer in the chain passes data to the next computer in the chain to make a world-wide network. There is no "central computer."

You can connect to the Internet in a variety of different ways. If you subscribe to an online service or BBS, you may already be part of the Internet community. This may limit your connection to sending and receiving mail.

An Internet service provider can provide two other forms of connection that give you even greater access. As a *terminal*, you can call the provider and use the utilities supplied by the provider to read mail, search for information, and do file transfer. As a *network server*, you can use your selection of utilities rather than depending on the service provider's choices. The connection as a network server may be continual or may be via a SLIP or PPP connection where you are actually only connected to the Internet for the duration of the phone call.

Chapter 18 covers information-searching services, which provide vast sophisticated databases useful for specialized applications, such as patent searching, following news wire services, and other electronic database searching.

18

CHAPTER

Information-Searching Services

This chapter covers information-searching services. In particular, you will learn about the following topics:

- ❖ When to use an information-searching service
- ❖ The types of information-searching services
- ❖ Tours of two different searching services
- ❖ Using a third-party to search efficiently

Understanding Information-Searching Services

Unlike the other online services covered in Part IV, this chapter covers services intended almost exclusively for professional use. These services are vast databases that are valuable to business, academic, and research staff. Although connect time charges can be more than $10 per minute, when used for the right purpose, these services can easily save a company more than that amount.

Information-searching services are similar to your accounting system. When you are a small company, you can handle the accounts and payroll with one individual and PC. As you grow, you reach a point where it is more economical to pay an outside service to do some of the work, keep up with the government and tax regulations, and ensure that the job is done on time. However, you may reach a point where is it better to have the relevant skills in-house, and some of the responsibility returns to your company.

"Who needs an information-searching service?"

Information-searching services are not really suitable for individuals, but when chosen judiciously, small businesses may get a large competitive edge from them. If you need to follow an industry, particularly one that has government regulations, these services can keep you informed.

The information falls into two categories: current and historic. The current information includes such items as today's newspapers from around the world, regional and even local newspapers, and current stock market quotes and newswire information.

As you might expect, the historical information includes back issues of the newspapers, periodicals, and financial data. However, it also includes much more. You can find such diverse topics as worldwide patent and trademark information, books in print, government publications, labor statistics, zoological information, and toxicology and other medical data. The information is particularly relevant if you do research. There are many chemical and legal databases. Most, if not all, the information is available from other sources. However, the advantage of having a single source in which the information is stored electronically cannot be ignored.

Consider a simple example of research done the manual way. About a year ago, I needed to find the source for a quote made by John Walker, the founder of Autodesk, Inc. and creator of AutoCAD. I read the quote in a magazine article and wanted to read the context in which it was said. Most of my research work was done because I knew the title of the book where the quote was taken from. However, because I didn't have access to an information-searching service, finding a copy of the book and then finding the quote in the book took several hours, with several days' delay.

This type of research problem occurs in most businesses. A new company calls, and you need to know something about it, the people, and the financial information. You are considering names for your product but need to check trademarks of other companies. You need to find out as much as possible about new businesses your competitors are exploring. You want the best newspaper clipping service possible. You meet with an executive to get him to support a philanthropic endeavor, and you want to do some research about what causes he's interested in.

Using an information-searching service is similar to using another online service. You call the service with your modem and communication software. You then connect to a remote computer that contains all the database information. You search for the desired information by specifying such items as where you want to look for the information and what information to look for.

"What can I find on an information-searching service?"

The commercial online services covered in Chapter 16 are aimed at a general audience and include relatively intuitive user interfaces and common features, such as messaging, file exchange, and chatting. The information-searching services tend to be more targeted and are not particularly easy to use. However, they are no more difficult to use than a specialized application program.

Like other online services, you can get the same information from a variety of sources. For example, the Dow Jones News Retrieval service, a business and financial news information service, can be accessed directly or via other online services, such as MCI Mail (see Chapter 15), or DataTimes. Certain newspapers and magazines are available online from other services. For example, America Online has *USA Today*, and Prodigy contains *Consumer Reports*.

The following sections summarize the available features of three popular information searching services: Dow Jones News Retrieval, DataTimes, and Dialog Information Services Inc.

Dow Jones News Retrieval

The Dow Jones News Retrieval service emphasizes business and financial data. It includes worldwide news information as well as data on companies, stocks, and mutual funds. However, it also includes more general services, such as college selection services, sports, movie reviews, weather, and shopping. Electronic mail services are supported via MCI Mail. You can use MCI Mail from Dow Jones News Retrieval in the same way that you can use Dow Jones News Retrieval from MCI Mail. However, you do need to subscribe to the two services separately.

The services offered include the following:

- Business and world newswires

  Business and Finance Report, Japan Economic Daily, Dow Jones Business Newswires, and Dow Jones News Service

- Dow Jones Text Library

  Current business articles, *The Wall Street Journal,* and other national, regional and industry publications

- Company and industry information

- Dun and Bradstreet market identifiers and financial records, Zacks corporate earnings estimator, Standard and Poors profiles and earnings estimates, corporate ownership watch, worldwide corporate reports, and corporate Canada online

- Quotes, statistics, and commentary

  Historical Dow Jones averages, Dow Jones quotes, future and index quotes, mutual fund performance reports, and "Wall $treet Week" transcripts.

- General services

  Book reviews, career management advice, encyclopedia, travel, college selection, and weather reports (electronic mail services via MCI Mail)

DataTimes

DataTimes boasts more than 2,000 local, regional, national, and international newspaper, newswire, trade, and industry sources. Its emphasis is on printed material.

❧ National news sources

   Newswire services include Associated Press and US Newswire. Magazines and newspapers include *The New York Times, USA Today, The Wall Street Journal, The Washington Post, Money Inc., Barron's,* and *American Banker.*

❧ Broadcast transcripts

   Including CNN's news, specials, "Crossfire"; "Inside Business"; National Public Radio's "All Things Considered," "Morning Edition," and "Weekend Edition"; "Frontline"; "Nova"; and "Washington Week in Review"

❧ Local and regional newspapers

   Divided by state and individual papers. For example, North Dakota sources are *Grand Forks Herald* and *Fargo's Forum,* while 21 New York newspapers are available.

❧ International newspaper and business sources

   General international sources include *NTIS Foreign Technology Newsletter, Electronic World News,* and *International Country Risk Guide.* More specific sources are from Africa, Asia, Australia, Canada, Europe, Latin America, the Middle East, as well as Russia and the Commonwealth of Independent States. Examples include *Southern African Freedom Bulletin, South China Morning Post, Ottawa Citizen, Euromarketing, Tehran Times,* and *Soviet Aerospace and Technology.*

❧ Company and industry databases

   Same-day regional business news from such newspapers as *The Kansas City Star* and the *Houston Chronicle.* Additionally, many Dow Jones News Retrieval services, such as newswire, business and financial news, SEC Online, Dun's Financial Records, and quotes and statistics.

Dialog

Dialog is an immense online database with a mixture of reference material and current news. It claims more than 450 separate databases containing more than 330 million articles, abstracts, and citations. It emphasizes news, business, science, and technology.

❀ Business

General business and industry, such as *Moody's Corporate News, Harvard Business Review,* and *Standard and Poor's Daily News.* Business statistics, U.S. and international directories and company financials, product information

❀ Dialog reference files

Includes product name finder, journal name finder, company name finder, electronic mail, and newsletters

❀ Law and government

Includes Congressional Information Service, American Statistics Index, Federal Register abstracts, Laborlaw, and British Official Publications

❀ General

REMARC (Library of Congress books), books in print, British books in print, academic index, OAG electronic edition, encyclopedia of associations, public opinion online

❀ News

Indexes for over 100,000 articles and full text to over 60 newspapers, wire services including Reuters, and PR Newswire; and international news services, including Kompass International and Global News

❀ Patents, trademarks, and copyrights

U.S. copyrights; several U.S. Patent related databases; U.S., UK, and Canada trademarks and world patents.

❀ Science

General topics include agriculture and nutrition, chemistry, computer technology, energy and environment, medicine and biosciences, pharmaceutical, science, technology, and engineering. Specific databases include aerospace database, consumer drug information, zoological record, *New England Journal of Medicine,* oceanic abstracts, Datapro software directory, polymer online, and food science and technology abstracts.

❀ Social sciences and humanities

The available databases include education index, religion index, philosopher's index, mental health abstracts, and music literature international.

A brief tour of the Dow Jones News Retrieval

As the name suggests, the Dow Jones News Retrieval service focuses mainly on news, financial, and business-related material. To illustrate a couple of its features, the example in the brief tour shows how to find recent news stories for particular companies as well as the stock symbol for companies. The subsequent example shows more of the available financial information.

When you have been issued with a password to Dow Jones News Retrieval, you log on by calling the relevant phone number, typically your local Tymnet or Sprintnet number, and issuing the commands to connect your computer with the service's computer.

Dow Jones News Retrieval divides its services into topics, such as stock quotes, news wire services, and Official Airline Guide (OAG). In this example, I looked for the recent articles and newswire information on IBM.

You access the newswire service by typing //**WIRES** at the command prompt. Your screen will look like Figure 18-1.

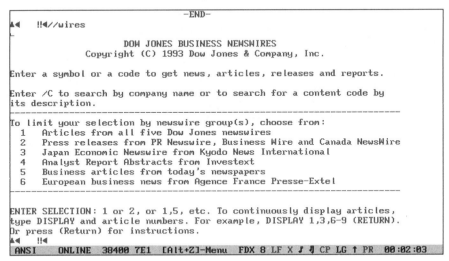

Figure 18-1: Dow Jones Business Newswires. You can search for news on a particular company or based on the news supplier.

You can limit your search by choosing the newswire or news service. For example, you can choose to search only the European business news or the business articles from today's papers. For this example, I searched all the services but looked only for articles referring to IBM. To do this you type /**C,** press Enter, type **IBM**, and then press Enter. Your screen will look like Figure 18-2.

```
  5    Business articles from today's newspapers
  6    European business news from Agence France Presse-Extel
──────────────────────────────────────────────────────────────────────────

ENTER SELECTION: 1 or 2, or 1,5, etc. To continuously display articles,
type DISPLAY and article numbers. For example, DISPLAY 1,3,6-9 (RETURN).
Or press (Return) for instructions.
▲◄   !!◄/c

ENTER AS MUCH OF THE COMPANY NAME AS YOU KNOW AND PRESS RETURN.
▲◄   !!◄ibm

YOU ENTERED: IBM

FIND STORIES ON:
  1   IBM         IBM
  2   G.IBM       IBM DEUTSCHLAND GMBH
  3   F.IBM       IBM FRANCE
  4   I.IBM       IBM ITALIA S.P.A.
  5   J.IBM       IBM JAPAN LTD.
                             —END—

ENTER A SELECTION, /T FOR TOP, OR HELP.
▲   ◄   !!◄
 ANSI    ONLINE  38400 7E1 [Alt+Z]-Menu  FDX 8 LF X ♪ ♫ CP LG ↑ PR  00:01:25
```

Figure 18-2: Searching by company name. Dow Jones News Retrieval prompts you for the company of interest to avoid ambiguity.

Dow Jones News Retrieval notes that five companies match the requested IBM. They include IBM France and IBM Japan. To focus in on IBM France rather than IBM, you choose 3 from this menu. However, if you choose 1, Dow Jones News Retrieval displays the latest articles available on IBM. Your screen will look like Figure 18-3.

This shows a list of the 18 most recent news items on IBM. (Further lists are displayed by pressing Enter.) The first six articles show a time rather than a date because they are taken directly from the newswire services and today's papers. For example, article number 1 is from the PR Newswire service. The older articles (yesterday's in this example) show the headlines and date for the article. Notice that articles 13 through 15 are all on the same topic; remarketing Evans & Sutherland Accelerators.

Article number 18 is a notification of IBM's second quarter financial statements that are filed with the Securities and Exchange Commission. To view this, you type **18** and press Enter. The financial statements or article is displayed one screen at a time. Obviously, if you call the service on a different day, the newest articles would be different. You can perform a similar search for articles on another company or in a particular industry, such as railroads or tobacco. Other searching options are also offered.

```
┌─────────────────────────────────────────────────────────────────────┐
│ BUSINESS NEWSWIRES - IBM                          HEADLINE PAGE  1     │
│                                                                        │
│   1 PR    09:34 HOW DO YOU MOVE 2,367,096,000,000 BYTES OF INFORMATION FROM... │
│   2 BW    08:22 Adobe's Display PostScript Level 2 Supports New IBM PowerPC... │
│   3 WJ    06:16 Digital A Surprise Contender In Video Servers Market   │
│   4 AX    05:01 ALITALIA REPORTEDLY TO CONTRACT BOOKING SYSTEM TO IBM, SIP... │
│   5 SFC   03:13 Many Layoffs Are Planned For the Future               │
│   6 HOU   02:18 Expo to guide firms through computer-buying maze       │
│   7 IN    10/19 IBM/Interactive -3: No Consensus On Best Hardware System │
│   8 IN    10/19 IBM/Interactive-2: Bell Atlantic Says IBM Strong Contender │
│   9 IN    10/19 (WSJ): IBM In The Running For Bell Atlantic Video Project │
│  10 DJ    10/19 IBM Eliminates Use Of Ozone Depleting CFCs In Mfg Process │
│  11 BW    10/19 IBM 0662 Model S12 1.05GB Drive is PC Magazine's Editors'... │
│  12 BW    10/19 IBM eliminates worldwide CFC emissions from manufacturing... │
│  13 DJ    10/19 IBM - Evans & Sutherland -2-: Accelerators Available Next Yr │
│  14 DJ    10/19 *IBM To Remarket Evans & Sutherland Accelerators >ESCC │
│  15 BW    10/19 IBM to remarket high-end graphics accelerators from Evans &... │
│  16 WJ    10/19 IBM Picks Welsh For New Post                          │
│  17 WJ    10/19 Bull To Get A Cash Injection One Last Time From Government │
│  18 FF    10/19 INTERNATIONAL BUSINESS 2Q Fin'l Statements            │
│ ─────────────────────────────────────────────────────────────────────│
│ SELECT STORY, ENTER PRINT COMMAND OR PRESS (RETURN) FOR MORE HEADLINES.│
│ ▲◄   ‼◄                                                                │
│ ANSI    ONLINE  38400 7E1  [Alt+Z]-Menu  FDX 8 LF X ♪ ♫ CP LG ↑ PR  00:02:35 │
└─────────────────────────────────────────────────────────────────────┘
```

Figure 18-3: Newswire listing for IBM. The latest headlines for newswire reports and articles for IBM are shown.

For many of the topics available on Dow Jones News Retrieval, you need to know the company name and its stock symbol that you are interested in. These can be found online by using the symbols database. If you type //**SYMBOLS,** your screen will look like Figure 18-4.

```
┌─────────────────────────────────────────────────────────────────────┐
│                      DIRECTORY OF SYMBOLS                             │
│                      COPYRIGHT (C) 1993                               │
│                   DOW JONES & COMPANY, INC.                           │
│                                                                        │
│ To find a stock symbol, enter at least 3 characters of a company name │
│ and press (Return). Or you can enter one of the following selections: │
│                                                                        │
│  1     Stock Symbol When Company Name or Cusip Number is Known        │
│  2     Company Name When Stock Symbol is Known                        │
│  3     Summary of Codes and Symbols for a Company                     │
│  4     Mutual Funds                                                   │
│  5     U.S. Corporate Bonds                                           │
│  6     U.S. Treasury Issues                                           │
│  7     Foreign Bonds                                                  │
│  8     Companies in Dow Jones Industry Group Indexes                  │
│  9     Information on codes used in //WIRES, //CLIP, //DJNEWS and //TEXT │
│           available exclusively in //GUIDE Code Directory (selection 8)│
│ 10     Recent Symbol Updates                                         │
│ 11     Option Symbol and Code Information                             │
│ Note: Media General Industry Code Information is now in //MG          │
│ ─────────────────────────────────────────────────────────────────────│
│ Press (Return) for general instructions and help.                    │
│ ▲◄   ‼◄                                                                │
│ ANSI    ONLINE  38400 7E1  [Alt+Z]-Menu  FDX 8 LF X ♪ ♫ CP LG ↑ PR  00:01:12 │
└─────────────────────────────────────────────────────────────────────┘
```

Figure 18-4: Symbol Directory. Many searches require a company stock symbol and not the company name.

This directory allows you to find the stock symbol or abbreviation for the chosen item. Typing **IBM** and pressing Enter at the command prompt, for example, opens the screen in Figure 18-5.

```
4       Mutual Funds
5       U.S. Corporate Bonds
6       U.S. Treasury Issues
7       Foreign Bonds
8       Companies in Dow Jones Industry Group Indexes
9       Information on codes used in //WIRES, //CLIP, //DJNEWS and //TEXT
            available exclusively in //GUIDE Code Directory (selection 8)
10      Recent Symbol Updates
11      Option Symbol and Code Information
Note: Media General Industry Code Information is now in //MG
─────────────────────────────────────────────────────────────────────
Press (Return) for general instructions and help.
▲◄    !!◄ibm
└SYMBOL
                            STOCKS

D.IAD     IBM CREDIT CORP. - NA
G.IBM    *IBM DEUTSCHLAND GMBH - GE
F.IBM    *IBM FRANCE - FR
I.IBM    *IBM ITALIA S.P.A. - IT
J.IBM    *IBM JAPAN LTD. - JA
IBM      *INTERNATIONAL BUSINESS MACHINES CORP. - NY
                            -END-
▲◄    !!◄
 ANSI    ONLINE  38400 7E1  [Alt+Z]-Menu  FDX 8 LF X ♪ ♫ CP LG ↑ PR  00:01:44
```

Figure 18-5: Symbol searching. Dow Jones News Retrieval reports on the companies with names similar to that specified.

Like the newswire service, several companies fit the name description of IBM. These include IBM Germany and IBM Credit Corp. When searching for stock information on these companies, you must use the correct symbol. For example, to search for International Business Machines Corp., you use IBM. To search for IBM Credit Corp. you use D.IAD. If you look for Microsoft, you find that the symbol is MSFT, and no other companies use Microsoft as part of their name and Microsoft does not have other separate companies.

Dow Jones News Retrieval is particularly useful for finding financial and business information. Much of this is updated on a continual, daily, or weekly basis. For example, you can access the MMS Weekly Market Analysis. These are the weekly survey results generated by MMS International. They gather the data from more than 200 economists, traders, and money dealers nationally and internationally. They assess the economy, foreign exchange, and equity markets.

To reach this analysis, you type //**MMS** at the command prompt to open the screen in Figure 18-6. You can view economic summaries, equity, currency, and debt commentaries. You can also view a calendar that shows the upcoming economic events such as housing starts.

```
FINAL PAGE OF TEXT IN THIS SECTION.

PRESS FOR
 T   TOP MENU
 M   PREVIOUS MENU
▲◀   !!◀t


                    MMS Weekly Market Analysis
                         Oct. 17, 1993
                       Copyright (c) 1993
                      MMS International Inc.


        1       MMS Weekly Economic Survey:
                   Summary & Analysis and Survey Medians & Ranges
        2       Weekly Equity Market Commentary
        3       Weekly Currency Market Commentary
        4       Weekly Debt Market Commentary
        5       Calendars of Economic Events
        6       MMS Forecasts of Monthly and Quarterly Indicators
        7       MMS Biweekly Economic Briefing

    Enter selection.
▲◀   !!◀
─────────────────────────────────────────────────────────────────────
 ANSI    ONLINE  38400 7E1  [Alt+Z]-Menu  FDX 8 LF X ♪ ♫ CP LG ↑ PR  00:03:34
```

Figure 18-6: MMS Weekly Market Analysis. You can view analysis on various economic markets.

If you press **7**, you will see a multipage summary of the current and forecasted economic state. You can read this compiled text information. If you press **6**, you can get tables of monthly or weekly economic indicators. Figure 18-7 shows one page from the summary of monthly economic indicators. For example, it shows that imported car sales are expected to grow in the next few months, and domestic car sales will also grow.

```
MMS                                             P103 ENDS AT 105

        MMS Forecasts: Monthly Economic Indicators
                 Last Reviewed OCT/15
```

REAL SECTOR	JUL	AUG	SEP	OCT	NOV	DEC
CIV.UNEMPLOYMENT	6.8%A	6.7%A	6.7%A	6.6%	6.6%	6.5%
NONFARM PAYROLL	237KA	−41KA	156KA	165K	165K	180K
DOMESTIC AUTO SALES	6.7MA	6.7MA	6.6MA	6.9M	7.0M	7.1M
IMPORTED AUTO SALES	2.0MA	2.0MA	1.9MA	2.0M	2.1M	2.1M
PPI	−.2%A	−.6%A	.2%A	.2%	.1%	.2%
RETAIL SALES	.5%A	.5%A	.1%A	.6%	.4%	.3%
IND.PRODUCTION	.2%A	.1%A	.2%A	.5%	.3%	.3%
CAPACITY UTILIZATION	81.6%A	81.6%A	81.6%A	82.2%	82.3%	82.4%
WHOLESALE SALES	.9%A	1.1%A	.2%	.4%	.4%	.4%
HOUSING STARTS	1.23MA	1.32MA	1.30M	1.35M	1.35M	1.35M
PERSONAL INCOME	−.3%A	1.3%A	.2%	.5%	.5%	.5%
PERS. CONS. EXPEND.	.4%A	.4%A	.3%	.5%	.5%	.4%
CPI	.1%A	.3%A	.0%A	.4%	.3%	.3%
DUR GDS ORDERS	−2.8%A	2.3%A	1.0%	2.0%	1.0%	.5%
DUR GDS SHIPMENTS	−4.3%A	3.6%A	1.0%	1.0%	.5%	.5%

```
▲◀   !!◀
─────────────────────────────────────────────────────────────────────
 ANSI    ONLINE  38400 7E1  [Alt+Z]-Menu  FDX 8 LF X ♪ ♫ CP LG ↑ PR  00:01:33
```

Figure 18-7: Monthly Economic Indicators. The economic indicator data is summarized in tabular form.

You disconnect from Dow Jones News Retrieval by typing //**DISC**.

A brief tour of Dialog

Dialog Information Services Inc. has an extensive series of databases that you can search through. Generalizing a typical search is very difficult because the range of supported topics is so diverse. All information-searching services require a knowledge of what you are searching for and some idea of where you will be able to find it. In many cases, you will look in the more general databases and then move to the more specialized databases.

Suppose that you have invented a new chicken-flavored crunchy snack food. You are considering product names, and your short list includes Crickles and Chickles. You can use Dialog to search for other companies that may have trademarked your proposed product name.

You log on to Dialog in a way comparable to other online databases. However, you typically connect via a packet-switched network such as Tymnet or Sprintnet. You call the local number, specify the service you want to connect to — in this case Dialog — and enter your user number and password.

You can select different user interfaces when you set up your account. This chapter uses an account that provides more menus and help with the user interface. This is easier to use than the more curt user interface, but it takes longer to move around the system.

After logging in, you can begin your search. From the catalog, I determined that the U.S. Federal Trademarks are stored in database number 226. (Dialog also includes U.S. State, Canadian, and UK trademark information in separate databases.)

You gain access to the database of choice by using the Begin command. At the command prompt, you type **begin 226**. You then choose key words that you want to search for. In this example, the key words are Chickles and Crickles.

You type **select crickles** to make a selection set of all the records in the database that contain the word crickles. Dialog searches the database and reports back. As shown in Figure 18-8, the results for set number one (S1) found one item with the word crickles.

```
    Enter an option number or a Begin command and press ENTER:
    /H =Help              /L =Logoff         /NOMENU =Command Mode
?◄begin 226

        19oct93 15:45:51 User073296 Session D64.1
           $0.09    0.006 Hrs FileHomeBase
    $0.09  Estimated cost FileHomeBase
    $0.05  TYMNET
    $0.14  Estimated cost this search
    $0.14  Estimated total session cost    0.006 Hrs.

File 226:TRADEMARKSCAN  OG:10/05/93 AP:08/11/93
    (Copr. 1993 Thomson & Thomson)
***   PRELIMINARY RECORDS THROUGH 09/16   ***


    Set   Items   Description
    ---   -----   -----------
?◄select crickles
    S1       1   CRICKLES
?◄select chickles
    S2       1   CHICKLES
?◄
 ANSI    ONLINE  38400 7E1  [Alt+Z]-Menu  FDX 8 LF X ♪ ♫ CP LG ↑ PR  00:01:57
```

Figure 18-8: Dialog selection set. Dialog searches the chosen database for the chosen items.

Similarly, you type **select crickles** to make a second selection set. Dialog creates a second set (S2) and reports that it found one item with the word chickles in it.

You can view the specific references to crickles and chickles. You can have them displayed one screen at a time, continuously, or printed out and mailed to you. In this example, if you type **d s1/2/1**, your screen will be similar to Figure 18-9. This command instructs Dialog to display set number 1, with a format style of number 2 (a summary), and the record you want displayed is the first one.

As shown in Figure 18-9, the word Crickles was first used in 1968 and was trademarked in 1970 by John E. Cain Co. It is used for a brand of pickles.

Using the same display command, but this time requesting information for the second set, you can see the information for Chickles as shown in Figure 18-10. In this case, Chickles is a registered trademark for a soft toy with a light-actuated noisemaker. It was first registered by Animal Fair, Inc., and has been assigned to Manhattan Toy/Carousel, L.P.

It looks like your snack will have to have another name to avoid using another company's trademark.

```
?◄d s1/2/1
        Display 1/2/1

          02372210 DIALOG File 226: TRADEMARKSCAN(r)-Federal
CRICKLES      Stylized Letters
          INTL CLASS:  29 (Meats & Processed Foods)
          U.S. CLASS:  46 (Foods & Ingredients of Foods)
          STATUS: Renewed
          GOODS/SERVICES: PICKLES
          SERIAL NO.: 72-372,210
          REG. NO.: 924,777
          REGISTERED: November 30, 1971
          FIRST USE: September 1968 (U.S. Class 46)
          FIRST COMMERCE: September 1968 (U.S. Class 46)
          FILED: October 1, 1970
          PUBLISHED: September 14, 1971
          RENEWAL FILED: June 20, 1991
          RENEWED IN OG: October 1, 1991
          AFFIDAVIT SEC.: 8-15
          ORIGINAL REGISTRANT: JOHN E. CAIN CO. (Massachusetts Corporation)
            , 678 MASSACHUSETTS AVE., CAMBRIDGE, MA (Massachusetts), 02139,

                              -more-
?◄
  ANSI    ONLINE  38400 7E1  [Alt+Z]-Menu  FDX 8 LF X ♪ ♫ CP LG ↑ PR  00:02:35
```

Figure 18-9: Dialog record display. Dialog can show the selected database records in a variety of formats.

```
?◄d s2/2/1
        Display 2/2/1

          03632067 DIALOG File 226: TRADEMARKSCAN(r)-Federal
CHICKLES
          INTL CLASS:  28 (Toys & Sporting Goods)
          U.S. CLASS:  22 (Games, Toys, & Sporting Goods)
          STATUS: Registered
          GOODS/SERVICES: SOFT TOY WITH LIGHT-ACTUATED NOISEMAKER
          SERIAL NO.: 73-632,067
          REG. NO.: 1,444,296
          REGISTERED: June 23, 1987
          FIRST USE: June 12, 1986 (Intl Class 28)
          FIRST COMMERCE: June 12, 1986 (Intl Class 28)
          FILED: November 24, 1986
          PUBLISHED: March 31, 1987
          ORIGINAL REGISTRANT: ANIMAL FAIR, INC. (Minnesota Corporation),
            MINNEAPOLIS, MN (Minnesota), USA (United States of America)
          ASSIGNEE(S): FIRST BANK NATIONAL ASSOCIATION (Incorporated
            association)
            Assignor(s): MANHATTAN TOY/CAROUSEL, L.P. (Delaware

                              -more-
?◄
  ANSI    ONLINE  38400 7E1  [Alt+Z]-Menu  FDX 8 LF X ♪ ♫ CP LG ↑ PR  00:02:58
```

Figure 18-10: Patent summary. Each patent is a separate record within the database.

This example shows the most simple search possible on Dialog. Typically, you will search with far more complex criteria. Suppose that you want to look up patents for magnetic stripes and, more specifically, you want to know who has an international patent on the magnetic heads that are used to read magnetic stripes on credit cards.

The general procedure would be to search in a patent database. For example, database number 351 contains the world patent index. You may issue the following select command: **select magnetic and stripe**. This searches the patents for instances where the words magnetic and stripe occur in the record. As shown in Figure 18-11, Dialog may report back that there are 155,392 records with the word magnetic, 4,478 with the word stripe, and 360 with both words.

```
      1981+;DW=9335,UA=9331,UM=9309
**FILE351: Attention Derwent subscribers: Markush DARC on DIALOG is
   available.  Begin WPILM to access.

   Set  Items  Description
   ---  -----  -----------
?◄select magnetic and stripe
        155392  MAGNETIC
          4478  STRIPE
   S1     360  MAGNETIC AND STRIPE
?◄select s1 and card and head
          360  S1
        19626  CARD
       149168  HEAD
   S2      46  S1 AND CARD AND HEAD
?◄select s2 not reader
           46  S2
        13620  READER
   S3      27  S2 NOT READER
?◄select s3 not manufacture
           27  S3
       202001  MANUFACTURE
   S4      27  S3 NOT MANUFACTURE
?◄
 ANSI    ONLINE  38400 7E1  [Alt+Z]-Menu   FDX 8 LF X ♪ ♫ CP LG ↑ PR  00:10:48
```

Figure 18-11: Dialog search criteria. Dialog accepts typical Boolean expressions in its search criteria.

If 360 records are too many to look at, you can choose to refine your selection by searching the selected records for those that contain the words card and head. The command is **select s1 and card and head**. This searches set number one for those records with the words card and head. Dialog reports that there were 360 records in set one; 19,626 records contain the word card, and 149,168 contain the word head. The combination, called set number two (S2), contains 46 records.

Your search continues by widening and narrowing the search criteria. Dialog supports Boolean expressions, such as AND, OR, NOR, and NOT. These are familiar to many technical PC users, especially engineers and programmers. And they are relatively easy to understand because they act exactly as their names suggest.

The AND command gives you a record selection only when both the word before and the word after the and are in the record.

The NOT gives you the records that are selected that do not contain a keyword. For example, continuing the credit card example, if you try and eliminate patents relating to card readers, you can type **select s2 not reader**. This reduces the number of selected records to 27.

To remove records related to the manufacture of these magnetic stripe heads, you type the command **select s3 not manufacture**. Unfortunately, the resulting set number four also has 27 records. Although Dialog found 202,001 records with the word manufacture, none were in the selected set.

You can string a series of selection options together, similar to a mathematical equation, on a single command line to speed the process. Dialog offers technical support and training programs to help you search more effectively.

Dialog also includes other commands that help you find appropriate references. For example, a better way of searching for records that relate to magnetic stripes is to use the near command. This specifies that the words must be near each other in the record. If you type **select magnetic(5N)stripe**, you would find records where the words magnetic and stripe appear within five words of each other.

These types of commands are particularly valuable on full-text databases. For example, if you are looking in a database related to education, you may find many records with the words head and start in them. However, using the Near command helps narrow your focus to records more likely to be covering the specific education program called Head Start.

Choosing a Service

Because of the emphasis on news and financial information, the most common use for Dow Jones News Retrieval is for information that ages very quickly. For example, you can use the service to get current stock quotes (delayed by 15 minutes). It also includes performance information. For example, you can find the best-performing mutual funds, information on the Dow Jones Industrial Average, and financial statements for publicly held companies.

Although Dow Jones does not use typical PC commands for navigation, the user interface is relatively easy and consistent. The help information is also considered a database and is accessed by using the //**HELP** command.

Data-Searching Services

Like most PC applications, almost all users can operate information-searching services, but only a proportion of users make efficient use of them, and only a smaller proportion can exploit their potential.

Information-searching services are more expensive than any other online service, and inefficient use can be very costly. Although inefficient use of CompuServe may cost tens of dollars a month, inefficient use of an information-searching service may cost hundreds of dollars a month.

This is the fault of the user, not the information service. Some services offer training seminars that can be invaluable. Most services, and many independent contractors, also offer consulting services and some type of tailored service. These are well worth considering for two reasons. Not only can you make the most efficient use of the service, but you can get the ongoing material essentially automatically.

Consider a newspaper clipping service. Manual methods depend on the readers being able to spot every incidence of your company name, competitor's names, industry name, and whatever other words you request. An electronic method will not miss any of these references. Additionally, it is only incrementally more expensive to widen the search to more newspapers and publications.

You can also access current-awareness services, which can give you information on national health care and the Americans with Disabilities Act (ADA), for example.

A consulting service can help you establish search criteria and collect the material regularly. Some services even offer an automatic searching system. For example, you might establish that all articles relating to your industry are printed and sent regular mail, while all articles mentioning your company name are faxed to your company immediately.

Dialog's user interface is harder to use than the Dow Jones News Retrieval service, but it is much more powerful. Other services, such as DataTimes, have yet another user interface. The costs for using each service can be dramatically different, and it is important to understand which service is most applicable for your situation.

My minimal needs, where I may need a few news-breaking stories and a couple of historical searches in a month, may cost less than $100 but save me hours searching in libraries and phone calls. On the other hand, I interviewed a professional librarian employed to do research for a multimillion dollar company who said a $10,000 monthly bill for online services was not unheard of.

Summary

Online information searching services offer unique opportunities for gaining a competitive advantage in business. Because you pay according to the type of information retrieved, these services can be expensive but can be invaluable.

Each service offers a different collection of information and is suitable for different purposes. Some are tailored to news information, others to data of long-term interest, or specialized disciplines.

Most services offer consulting services where the ongoing searching can be done for you. Additionally, independent companies that specialize in searching can provide beneficial help.

V

Appendixes

Part V provides several appendixes that provide valuable reference material.

Appendix A includes a thorough list of AT commands that are applicable to most modems.

Appendix B provides listing of online services that are organized according to function and area code to save you money.

Appendix C provides concise documentation for using the Smartcom for Windows LE software that is included with this book.

Appendix D lists all the frequently asked questions that appear throughout the book and the page where you can find the answers.

AT Command Set

Your modem should support the Hayes Standard AT Command Set common to all modems. Additional commands your modem supports vary with supported standards and the manufacturer. This appendix contains a list of commonly used AT commands, S-registers, and result codes.

AT Command Descriptions

The following tables list and describe each of the AT commands. Default settings for Hayes modems are listed in **bold**.

Note: Type **AT** before each of the following commands.

Command	Description
A	Enter answer mode, go off hook, attempt to answer incoming call, and go online with another modem.
A/	Re-execute previous command line (this command is not preceded by **AT** nor followed by pressing the Enter key).
B0	Initiate calls by using ITU-T V.22 at 1200 bps.
B1	Initiate calls by using 212A at 1200 bps.
B15	Initiate calls by using ITU-T V.21 at 300 bps.

(continued)

Command	Description
B16	Initiate calls by using 103 at 300 bps.
B30	Initiate call by using V.22 bis at 2400 bps.
B41	Initiate call by using ITU-T V.32 at 4800 bps.
B52	Initiate call by using V.32 bis at 7200 bps.
B60	Initiate call by using ITU-T V.32 at 9600 bps.
B64	Initiate call by using V.FC at 9600 bps.
B75	Initiate call by using V.32 bis when handshake begins at 14400 bps.
B76	Initiate call by using V.FC when handshake begins at 14400 bps.
B81	Initiate call by using V.FC when handshake begins at 16800-28800 bps.
D	Enter originate mode, go off-hook, and attempt to go online with another modem. The dial modifiers (see following table) tell the modem what, when, and how to dial.

Dial Modifiers	Description
0-9 * # A B C D	Specifies letters, numbers, and symbols the modem uses when dialing.
T	Dials by using tone method.
P	Dials by using pulse method.
,	Pauses before continuing the dial string.
W	Waits for second dial tone.
$	Waits for "bong" tone (for calling card number entry).
@	Waits for quiet answer.
!	Issues hookflash.
R	Places call in reverse mode (to call an originate-only modem).
;	Returns to command state after dialing and maintains the connection.
S=n	Dials telephone number n (0-3) stored with the **&Zn=x** command.

Note: The **comma** (,) and the **W** dial modifiers should be used only within a dial string and following the **D** command.

Command	Description
E0	Do not echo characters from the keyboard to the screen in command state.
E1	Echo characters from the keyboard to the screen in command state.
H0	Hang up and place modem in command state.
H1	Go off hook and operate auxiliary relay.
I0	Display numeric product code.
I2	Verify ROM checksum (OK or ERROR).
I7	Display the product version number. **Note:** I7 is supported only by OPTIMA 288 V.FC + FAX.
L0, L1	Set low speaker volume.
L2	Set medium speaker volume.
L3	Set high speaker volume.
M0	Turn speaker off.
M1	Turn speaker on until carrier detected.
M2	Turn speaker on.
M3	Turn speaker on until carrier detected, except while dialing.
N0	When originating or answering, handshake only at speed specified by S37.
N1, N2	When originating, begin negotiations at the highest DCE line speed specified in S37 and fall back to a lower speed if necessary. When answering, handshake at the highest speed allowed by S37 and fallback if necessary.
N3, N4	When originating, handshake only at the speed specified by S37. When answering, handshake at the highest speed allowed by S37 and fallback if necessary.
N5	When originating, begin negotiations at the highest DCE line speed specified in S37 and fall back to a lower speed if necessary. When answering, handshake only at the speed specified by S37. **Note:** The maximum handshaking speed is determined by the specific features of your modem.

(continued)

Command	Description
O0	Go to online state.
O1	Go to online state and initiate equalizer retrain sequence.
O3	Go to online state and initiate ITU-T V.32 *bis* rate renegotiation sequence.
	Note: O3 is not supported in OPTIMA 24 + FAX96, OPTIMA 24B + FAX96, OPTIMA 96 + FAX96, or OPTIMA 96B + FAX96.
P	Select pulse dialing method.
Q0	Return result codes.
Q1	Do not return result codes.
Q2	Return result codes in originate mode, do not return result codes in answer mode.
Sn?	Read and respond with current value of register n (n is the register number; ? requests the value assigned to that register).
Sn=value	Set the value of register n to value.
T	Select tone dialing method.
V0	Display result codes as numbers.
V1	Display result codes as words.
W0	Do not return negotiation progress messages.
W1	Return negotiation progress messages.
W2	Do not return negotiation progress messages and return CONNECT messages using modem-to-modem (DCE) speeds instead of modem-to-DTE speeds.
X0	Provide basic call progress result codes: CONNECT, NO CARRIER, and RING.
X1	Provide basic call progress result codes and appropriate connection speed (e.g., CONNECT 1200, CONNECT 2400).
X2	Provide basic call progress result codes, connection speed, and DIALTONE detection.
X3	Provide basic call progress result codes, connection speed, and BUSY signal detection.

Command	Description
X4	Provide basic call progress result codes, connection speed, BUSY signal detection, and DIALTONE detection.
Y0	Do not respond to long space disconnect.
YI	Respond to long space disconnect.
Z0	Reset and recall stored user profile 0.
ZI	Reset and recall stored user profile I.
&A0	Connect as answering modem when auto-answering.
&AI	Connect as originating modem when auto-answering.
&B0	Disable V.32 Auto-Retrain.
&BI	Enable V.32 Auto-Retrain. **Note:** This feature is not supported in OPTIMA 24 + FAX96 or OPTIMA 24B + FAX96.
&C0	Assume presence of carrier detect signal.
&CI	Track presence of carrier detect signal.
&C2	Assume presence of carrier detect signal until online, then track presence of signal.
&D0	Ignore status of DTR signal.
&DI	Monitor DTR signal. When an on-to-off transition of DTR signal occurs, enter the command state. Return to the online state when the O0 command is issued (if the connection has not been broken).
&D2	Monitor DTR signal. When an on-to-off transition of DTR signal occurs, hang up and enter the command state.
&D3	Monitor DTR signal. When an on-to-off transition of DTR signal occurs, hang up and reset.
&F	Recall factory configuration as active configuration.
&G0	Disable guard tones.
&G2	Use 1800 Hz guard tones.
&K0	Disable local flow control.
&KI	Enable RTS/CTS local flow control.

(continued)

Command	Description
&K2	Enable XON/XOFF local flow control.
&K3	Enable RTS/CTS local flow control.
&K4	Enable XON/XOFF local flow control.
&K5	Enable transparent XON/XOFF local flow control.
	Note: Local flow control is unidirectional in &Q6 mode and bidirectional in &Q5 mode.
&Q0	Communicate in asynchronous mode.
&Q1	Communicate in synchronous mode 1. Async-to-Sync.
&Q2	Communicate in synchronous mode 2. Stored Number Dial.
&Q3	Communicate in synchronous mode 3. Voice/Data Switch.
&Q4	Communicate in synchronous mode 4. Hayes AutoSync.
&Q5	Communicate in error-control mode.
&Q6	Communicate in asynchronous mode with automatic speed buffering (ASB) — for interfaces requiring constant speed between the DTE (computer/terminal) and the DCE (modem).
&Q8	Communicate in MNP error-control with 2:1 data compression. If an MNP error-control protocol is not established, the modem will fallback according to the current user setting in S36.
&Q9	Communicate in V.42 bis/MNP2-4 error-control. Attempts to negotiate a V.42 bis error-control link upon connection. If V.42 bis (or V.42) is not achieved, MNP2-4 will be attempted. If neither error-control protocol is established, the modem will fallback according to the current user setting in S36.
	Note: &Q1, &Q2, and &Q3 are not supported in board-level modems.
&R0	CTS tracks RTS while the modem is online.
&R1	CTS is on while the modem is online; RTS is ignored.
&S0	Assert DSR signal always.
&S1	Assert DSR signal before handshake only.
&S2	Assert DSR signal after handshake negotiation, but before CONNECT XXXXX result code is sent to the DTE.

Command	Description
&T0	Terminate any test in progress.
&T1	Initiate local analog loopback.
&T3	Initiate local digital loopback.
&T4	Grant request from remote modem for remote digital loopback.
&T5	Deny request from remote modem for remote digital loopback.
&T6	Initiate remote digital loopback.
&T7	Initiate remote digital loopback with self-test.
&T8	Initiate local analog loopback with self-test.
&T19	Determine whether RTS and CTS circuits are supported in the DTE cable.
	Note: The **&T** commands must be entered when the modem is configured for &Q0 (unbuffered asynchronous mode). Also, your terminal software must support the function of &T19 to work with &T19.
&U0	Enable trellis coding (ITU-T V.32 9600 bps only).
&U1	Disable trellis coding.
	Note: OPTIMA 24 + FAX96 and OPTIMA 24B + FAX96 do not support &U0 and &U1.
&V	View active configuration, user profiles, and stored telephone numbers.
&W0	Write storable parameters of current configuration in memory as profile 0.
&W1	Write storable parameters of current configuration in memory as profile 1.
&X0	Modem generates transmit clock.
&X1	DTE generates transmit clock.
&X2	Modem derives transmit clock from receive carrier signal.
&Y0	Specify stored user profile 0 as power-up configuration.
&Y1	Specify stored user profile 1 as power-up configuration.
&Zn=x	Store phone number *x* in location n (n=0-3).

Result Code Descriptions

Hayes modems are factory-set to monitor calls and report the following result codes (**X4**).

Number	Word	Description
0	OK	Command executed.
1	CONNECT	A connection has been established.
2	RING	Ring signal indicated.
3	NO CARRIER	Carrier signal not detected, or lost, or inactivity for period of time set in the automatic timeout register (set with **S30**) caused the modem to hang up.
4	ERROR	Invalid command, checksum, error in command line or command line exceeds 255 characters.
5	CONNECT 1200	Connection at 1200 bps (disabled by **X0**).
6	NO DIALTONE	No dial tone detected. Enabled by **X2** or **X4**, or **W** dial modifier.
7	BUSY	Engaged (busy) signal or number unobtainable signal detected. Enabled by **X3** or **X4**.
8	NO ANSWER	No silence detected when dialing a system not providing a dial tone. Enabled by **@** dial modifier.
10	CONNECT 2400	Connection at 2400 bps (disabled by **X0**).
11	CONNECT 4800	Connection at 4800 bps (disabled by **X0**).
12	CONNECT 9600	Connection at 9600 bps (disabled by **X0**).
13	CONNECT 14400	Connection at 14400 bps (disabled by **X0**).
14	CONNECT 19200	Connection at 19200 bps (disabled by **X0**).
15	CONNECT 28800	Connection at 28800 bps (disabled by **X0**).
18	CONNECT 57600	Connection at 57600 bps (disabled by **X0**).
24	CONNECT 7200	Connection at 7200 bps (disabled by **X0**).
28	CONNECT 38400	Connection at 38400 bps (disabled by **X0**).
31	CONNECT 115200	Connection at 115200 bps (disabled by **X0**).
33	FAX	FAX connection.
35	DATA	DATA connection.
65	CONNECT 230400	Connection at 230400 bps (disabled by **X0**).

Negotiation Progress Result Codes

A special set of result codes can be enabled to monitor error-control negotiation. Hayes modems are factory-set to disable the display of negotiation progress messages (**W0**). If your communications software supports this level of result code monitoring, you may wish to enable the display of negotiation progress result codes by selecting the **W1** command.

Note: Whether or not some of the result codes are fully enabled (used and viewed) may depend on the compatible settings of an **X**n command and the **S95** register.

Number	Word	Description
40	CARRIER 300	Carrier detected at 300 bps
46	CARRIER 1200	Carrier detected at 1200 bps
47	CARRIER 2400	Carrier detected at 2400 bps
48	CARRIER 4800	Carrier detected at 4800 bps
49	CARRIER 7200	Carrier detected at 7200 bsp.
50	CARRIER 9600	Carrier detected at 9600 bps.
51	CARRIER 12000	Carrier detected at 12000 bps.
52	CARRIER 14400	Carrier detected at 14400 bps.
54	CARRIER 19200	Carrier detected at 19200 bps.
53	CARRIER 16800	Carrier detected at 16800 bps.
38	CARRIER 21600	Carrier detected at 21600 bps.
37	CARRIER 24000	Carrier detected at 24000 bps.
36	CARRIER 26400	Carrier detected at 26400 bps.
55	CARRIER 28800	Carrier detected at 28800 bps.
66	COMPRESSION: CLASS 5	MNP5 compression negotiated.
67	COMPRESSION: V.42 bis	V.42 bis compression negotiated.
69	COMPRESSION: NONE	No compression negotiated.
70	PROTOCOL: NONE	Asynchronous mode.
77	PROTOCOL: LAPM	V.42 LAPM
80	PROTOCOL: ALT	Alternative protocol (MNP compatible).

S-Register Descriptions

S-registers are special memory locations in the modem for storing specific configuration and operating parameters. S-registers typically hold some type of counting, timing, ASCII character, or feature negotiation value.

S-registers can be adjusted to configure the modem from the range of values indicated in the Range/Units column in the following chart. Values assigned to these registers (except **S1**, **S3**, **S4**, and **S5**) can be stored in user-defined profiles with the **&W** command.

Sn=value is the command to change an S-register (for example **ATSn=value** Enter key, where n is the S-register to be changed, and n is the value to be assigned to the S-register). **Sn?** is the command to read the value currently stored in an S-register (for example **ATSn?** Enter key, where n is the S-register to be read).

Register Setting	Description	Range/Units	Default
S0	Select ring to answer on.	0-255 rings	0
S1	Ring count (incremented with each ring).	0-255 rings	0
S2	Escape sequence character.	0-127 ASCII	43
S3	Carriage return character.	0-127 ASCII	13
S4	Line feed character.	0-127 ASCII	10
S5	Back space character.	0-32,127 ASCII	8
S6	Wait before blind dialing.	2-255 sec	2
S7	Wait time for carrier/silence.	1-255 sec	50
S8	Duration of delay for comma.	0-255 sec	2
S9	Carrier detect response time.	1-255 1/10 sec	5
S10	Delay carrier loss to hang up.	1-255 1/10 sec	14
S11	Duration/spacing of DTMF tones.	50-255 msec	95
S12	Escape sequence guard time.	0-255 1/50 sec	50
S16	Test in progress.	0-6	—
S18	Select test timer.	0-255 sec	0
S25	DTR change detect time.	0-255 1/100 sec	5
S30	Automatic timeout (S30 monitors the activity on the line; the factory-set default is 0, which disables the timer).	0-255 10 sec	0

Register Setting	Description	Range/Units	Default
S31	XON character select.	0-255	17 (DC1)
S32	XOFF character select.	0-255	19 (DC3)
S36	Negotiation fallback.	0,1,3,4,5,7	7
S37	Maximum DCE line speed.	0-12, 15, 26, 29, 33, 34	0
S38	Delay before forced hang up.	0-255 seconds	20
S43	Current DCE speed.	0-12, 15, 26, 29, 33, 34	—
S46	Error-control protocol selection.	2, 136, 138	2
S48	Feature negotiation action.	0, 3, 7,128	7
S49	Buffer lower limit.	1-249 bytes	64
S50	Buffer upper limit.	2-250 bytes	192
S69	Link layer window size.	1-15 frames	15
S70	Maximum number of retransmissions.	0-255 retries	10
S71	Link layer timeout.	1-255 1/10 sec	2
S72	Loss of flag idle timeout.	1-255 seconds	30
S73	No activity timeout.	1-255 seconds	5
S82	Break signaling technique.	3, 7, 128 values	128
S86	Connection failure cause code.	0-19	—
S91	PSTN transmit level adjustment.	0 to -15 dBm	10
S95	Negotiation message options.	1,2,4,8,32	0
S97	V.32 automode V.22/V.22 bis probe timing.	15 to 70 (1.5 to 7.0 seconds)	30
S108	Signal quality selector.	0-3 values	1
S109	Carrier speed selector.	0-4094 decimal values	4094
S105	V.42 frame size.	4-9 octets	7
S110	V.32/ V.32 bis selector.	0-2 values	2
S113	Calling tone transmission.	0-1	0 (off)

APPENDIX

Resource Guide to Popular Online Services

The following is a sampling of available online services. The services are divided in the same way as the chapters in the book. The topics are BBSs, Messaging Services, Information Exchange Services, and Information Searching Services.

The service is listed under the heading that is most appropriate. That does not mean that a particular service does not offer services that belong in another category. For example, a service listed under information exchange services may include messaging services as well.

The phone numbers given for the BBSs are the online numbers that you can call with your modem. The phone numbers given for the other services are the voice information numbers where you can get further information and open an account.

BBSs

The following list of 100 BBSs represents a good mix of the typical types of BBSs you can find. They include messaging, file exchange, and chat boards. Some BBSs have only a couple of phone lines; a few have hundreds of lines. Most sysops are volunteers. The BBSs are listed by area code so that you can save money by choosing from your region.

BBS Phone No.	BBS Name	Sysop Name	Description
201-935-1485	Starship II BBS	Phil Buonomo	General interest, 10Gig, Chat, 100+ message areas
203-371-8769	Psycho Ward BBS	Dennis Ryan	Free system, 13Gig, IBM, Amiga, MAC
203-738-0342	H H Infonet	Lee Winsor	Professional, technical, & business oriented, Windows files
205-660-1763	The Unearthed Arcana BBS	Slayer/Lady Morgan	Adult, occult, automotive CD-ROM online, files, messages, online games†
206-692-2388	TCSNet	Al Charpentier	Newsgroups, Rime, MetroLink, online services
206-956-1206	Capital City Online	Joe Goeller	Internet, Usenet, 12Gig, 100+ online games, chat
209-357-8424	Aces Place	Bill Paez	Message areas, new files, helpful staff
212-274-8905	Invention Factory	Michael Sussell	250,000+ files, newsgroups, large adult section, USR V32bis modems†
212-888-6565	Computers & Dreams	William P. Stewart	Internet, Usenet, Rime, 40 doors, 10,000+ new files
213-933-4050	Westside	Dave Harrison	SprintNet access, very large file base, many great features
213-962-2902	BCS BBS	Bill Weinman	Home of Cal-Link, ilink, e-mail, general interest†
214-497-9100	Texas Talk	Sunnie Blair	Adult chat, matchmaking, games, parties, CD-ROMs
214-690-9295	Chrysalis	Garry Grosse	Internet, Connex, 30Gig, chat, encyclopedia
215-439-1509	Father and Son BBS	Dale Lloyd	Fidonet echoes, 10Gig, large adult area, chat, OS/2 files
215-443-9434	Datamax/Satelite	Ron Brandt	Live ftp & telenet, 10Gigs, large adult area
216-691-3025	PC-OHIO	Norm Henke	Internet, 3,000 message areas, 400 file areas, 250 doors†
216-726-3619	Rusty and Edies BBS	Rusty Hardenburgh	All shareware, 9Gig, huge adult section, USR 168 modems†

BBS Phone No.	BBS Name	Sysop Name	Description
219-256-2255	Radio Daze BBS	Michael Shannon	Worldwide echoes, 63 Gig, 65,000+ files, USR HS modems
219-696-3415	Toolkit	Ken Prevo	Resource for programmers and power users
303-933-0701	Eagle's Nest BBS	Ron Olsen	Free access to all, 13Gig, very nice single-line system
303-534-4646	File Bank	Brian Bartee	Astronomy, ham radio, programming, adult files
305-346-8524	Looking Glass	Kenneth Wiren	Files, conferences, doors
310-371-3737	Source BBS	Chip North	General interest, Fidonet e-mail, new files daily
312-907-1831	Zoo BBS	Chuck Goes	Adult social network, chats, gay, bi, straights welcome
313-238-1178	Totem Pole BBS	Alan Myers	4Gig, 97 file areas, 419 message areas, 24 doors
313-776-1975	Legend of Roseville BBS	Richard Leneway	45Gig, message areas, files
314-446-0475	Batboard	Mark Chambers	For BATMAN fans, RIP, NAPLPS, custom GIF & FLI files
317-357-1222	Some Place	Mike Shepard	Fee-based system. Best place to find the hardest-to-find files[†]
401-732-5290	Eagles Nest Communications	Mike Labbe	Internet, Usenet, RIME, Ilink, Paranet, 50,000+ files
403-299-9900	Logical Solutions	Hans Hoogstraat	The Information Exchange, technical advice, PD software, FidoNet message bases plus Netmail, Internet workgroups plus Email, online games, etc.[†]
404-992-5345	Hotlanta BBS	Mike Deen	Social chat system for open minded & adventurous adults
405-325-6128	OU BBS	Ronnie Parker	Internet, telenet, 3Gig files, online games, PIMP, chat

(continued)

BBS Phone No.	BBS Name	Sysop Name	Description
407-635-8833	Techtalk	Jerry Russel	Six CD-ROMs, USR 168 modems, PIMP, Internet, techtalkcom
408-655-5555	Monterey Gaming System	David Janakes	Chat, messages, e-mail, online games, fun entertainment
408-737-7040	Higher Powered BBS	Bob Jacobson	Ilink, SmartNet, SciFact, FredNet, 1 Gig files
413-536-4365	Springfield Public Access	Matthew De Jongh	Internet e-mail, focus on Genealogy, Ham Radio, Windows
414-789-4500	EXEC-PC	Bob Mahoney	World's largest BBS, 35Gig, most anything you need†
415-323-4193	Space BBS	Owen Hawkins	Internet e-mail, 3,000 newsgroups, Rime, Ilink, a most active BBS
415-495-2929	Studs	Hans Braun	Adult conversation, AIDS/ HIV news and information
416-213-6002	CRS	Neil Fleming	Canada's largest online system, very large file area
501-753-8575	USA BBS	Jeff Johnson	Internet, all major filebone areas, online games, 10Gig
503-639-4135	PCs Made Easy BBS	Ken Rea	This BBS is aimed at the programmer and the home brewers (beer) in Oregon†
504-756-9658	Cajun Clickers BBS	Michael Vierra	Online games, 44Gig, no fees, 11,000+ files
505-294-5675	Garbage Dump BBS	Dean Kerl	Adult chat, dating registry, games, national access
505-299-5974	Albuquerque ROS	Steven Fox	Home of ROS BBS, 60,000+ files, active social issues
508-368-7139	Software Creations	Dan Linton	Home BBS for Apogee, and many other shareware producers
509-943-0211	One Stop PCBoard BBS	Gary Hedberg	USR 168 modems, 8Gig, 70 doors, 900 messages areas
510-736-8343	Windows On Line	Frank Mahaney	Premier Windows file service, 10,000+ 3x files

BBS Phone No.	BBS Name	Sysop Name	Description
510-849-2684	Planet BMUG	Dong-Gyom Kim	100 forums, gateways to OneNet & BMUG Boston
512-320-1650	After Hours	Conrad Ruckelman	Best little BBS in Texas
512-345-5099	Nightbreed	Randy Faulk	Games, messages, files, users
514-597-2409	S-Tek	Eric Blair	Montreal's premiere Gay & Lesbian BBS, G&L BBS List
515-386-6227	Heat In The Night	Rob Murdock	Free Adult BBS, chats, dates, and fun
516-471-8625	America's Suggestion Box	Joe Jerszynski	Focused on collecting & distributing consumer feedback
516-689-5390	Lifestyle	Marc Kraft	Adult lifestyles, personal ads, e-mail, personal contacts
517-695-9952	Wolverine	Rick Rosinksi	Official SkyGlobe support, Searchlight sales & support
518-581-1797	NightOwl BBS	Greg Lake	Files, online games, message board†
602-294-9447	Arizona Online	Shawn Striplin	Massive adult area, 20,000+ files, 3Gig online
604-536-5885	Deep Cove BBS	Wayne Duval	Internet, 7Gig file area, CD-ROMs, ZyXEL modem sales
609-764-0812	Radio Wave BBS	Tyler Myers	ASP BBS, RIME, 4Gig files, 4,000+ newsgroups
612-633-1366	City Lights	Brian Elfert	Adult files & echoes, 600 message areas, 57Gig, 35,000+ files
614-224-1635	Wizard's Gate BBS	Joseph Balshone	FREE, no fee, ASP BBS, full access on first call 12Gig
615-227-6155	3rd Eye BBS	Michael Vetter	Adult system serving the responsible swinging life-style
615-383-0727	Nashville Exchange	Ben Cunningham	Internet, Usenet, Fidonet, 10Gig files, online games
617-354-8873	Channel 1	Brian Miller	3,500 message ares, 120 online games, Internet, 30Gig

(continued)

BBS Phone No.	BBS Name	Sysop Name	Description
617-721-5840	BMUG Boston	Roz Ault	East coast BMUG, gateways to OneNet & Planet BMUG
618-453-8511	Infoquest	Charles Strusz	RIP, Fidonet, Internet, VNet, 100,000 files, many online games
619-737-3097	Cloud 9	Devin Singleton	Chat, Internet e-mail, trivia, 50000+ files, online CPA
701-281-3390	Plains Bulletin service	Rob Kirkey	Great Plains Software support for GPS Partners
702-334-3308	Advanced System BBS	Alan McNamee	Internet, Fidonet, 16Gig, TBBS enhancements
703-385-4325	0S/2 Shareware	Pete Norloff	5,000+ 0S/2 files, 25 areas, 50 message area
703-578-4542	GLIB	Jon Larimore	Information serving the gay, lesbian, and bisexual community
704-254-4714	Yes Net	Burton Smith	Networking local environmental groups, schools, and businesses†
708-564-1069	Windy City Freedom Fort	Robert Copella	Adults only, over 4,000 original scanned graphics
708-827-3619	AlphaOne	Toby Schneiter	Online shopping, 30+ games, 200+ echoes, 30,000+ files
713-596-7101	Fantasy Party Line	Charles Henderson	Social gatherings, live chats, great users
714-636-2667	Kandy Shack	Mike Bernstein	Ilink, U'NI-net, ASP member, 24Gig online, USR 168 modems
714-996-7777	Liberty BBS	Stephen Grande	Nationwide chat, e-mail, news, games, Internet
716-461-1924	Frog Pond	Nick Francesco	Supporting MS-DOS & cp/M with great files and zany users
718-837-3236	The Consultant BBS	Jay Caplan	Specializing in ASP shareware programs†
719-578-6088	CoSNUG BBS	Joe Adams	Mainly for Seniors, open to the public
800-874-2937	Online With Hayes	Ricky Lacy	New products, technical support, order small parts, and download SCOPE scripts†

BBS Phone No.	BBS Name	Sysop Name	Description
804-490-5878	Pleasure Dome	Tom McElvy	Sexually explicit, adults only, ladies free
804-790-1675	Blue Ridge Express	Webb Blackman	Message areas, 84+ files areas, 21,000+ files
805-964-4766	Seaside	Les Jones	ASP BBS, 100+ online games, 450 message areas
812-428-3870	YA WEBECAD	Dan Habegger	PSL library, ASP BBS, 72,000+ files, 118Gig, adult file area
812-479-1310	Digicom BBS	Gary Barr	Product Support BBS list, adult area with games, 27Gig
813-289-3314	Godfather	Jim Sharrer	Fidonet, Usenet, adult areas, graphics, GIFs, new files
813-321-0734	Mercury Opus	Emery Mandel	Internet, 80,000+ files, MS-DOS, Windows, OS/2
816-587-3311	File Shop BBS	Walt Lane	RIP, 2,200 file areas, 28Gig, 310,000+ files, 85 online games
817-662-2361	File Quest	Jim Ray	General purpose, 2.5GB files, FidoNet, Echonet[†]
818-358-6968	Odyssey	Michael Allen	Where adults come to play and meet, active chats
818-982-7271	Prime Time BBS	Bill Martian	Live multi-user games, chat, Interlink, files
904-874-1988	Baker Street Irregular	James Young	Variety of general interest conferences and shareware downloads[†]
908-494-8666	Microfone Infoservice	John Kelly	Fidonet, 14 CD-ROMs, online games, since 1982
914-667-4567	Executive Network	Andy Keeves	10Meg new files daily, 4,000 message areas, Internet
916-448-2483	24th Street Exchange	Don Kuhworth	General IBM MS-DOS files and support, ASP BBS, Fidonet, chat[†]
918-665-0061	Wayne's World	Wayne Greer	Large filebase, online games, latest new files

(continued)

| 919-481-9399 | deltaComm BBS | Zack Jones | Support board for Telix Communications software |
| 919-779-6674 | Micro Message Service | Mike Stroud | Internet, excellent ham radio area, 7Gig, family BBS |

† Indicates a BBS that uses a Hayes V.FC Modem

Messaging Services

MCI Mail
1111 Nineteenth St N.W.
Washington DC 20036
800-444-6245

SprintMail
US Sprint
12490 Sunrise Valley Drive
Reston, VA 22096
800-736-1130

Information Exchange Services

America Online
America Online, Inc.
8619 Westwood Center Drive
Vienna, VA 22182
800-827-6364

BIX
General Videotext
1030 Massachusetts Ave.
Cambridge, MA 02138
800-695-4775

Compuserve
CompuServe, Inc.
P.O. Box 20212
Columbus, OH 43220
800-848-8199

Delphi
Delphi Internet Services Corp.
1030 Massachusetts Ave.
Cambridge, MA 02138
800-695-4005

Genie
P.O. Box 6403
Rockville, MD 20850-1785
800-638-9636

Prodigy
445 Hamilton Ave.
White Plains, NY 10601
800-822-6922

The Well
27 Gate Five Road
Sausalito, CA 94965
415-332-4335

Information Searching Services

Dialog
Dialog Information Services
3460 Hillview Ave.
Palo Alto, CA 94304
800-334-2564

Dow Jones News/Retrieval
P.O. Box 300
Princeton, NJ 08543-0300
800-522-3567

NEXIS / LEXIS
Mead Data Central
P.O. Box 933
Dayton, OH 45401
800-227-4908

BRS/After Dark
Maxwell Online Inc
8000 Westpark Drive
McLean, VA 22102
800-289-4277

DataTimes
14000 Quail Springs Parkway,
Suite 450
Oklahoma City, OK 73134
800-642-2525

Guide to Smartcom for Windows LE

APPENDIX C

Smartcom for Windows LE is an asynchronous communications software package for Windows Version 3.1. Based on Hayes Smartcom for Windows, this fully-functional *limited edition* program gives you a chance to experience the power of Hayes Smartcom communications software. If you find that there are additional features you would like, chances are they are in Smartcom for Windows. Call Hayes Customer Service at (404) 441-1617 to order your copy. Use the coupon from Hayes at the back of the book for a discount on your upgrade.

Some additional features of Smartcom for Windows include:

- ❖ The Smartcom Communications Editor combines text with color and ANSI character graphics to create high-impact, exciting messages.

- ❖ English, French, German, Spanish, and Italian program files let you standardize on one program for international data communications.

- ❖ You can download and view .GIF images.

- ❖ Additional file-transfer protocols and terminal emulations give you more error-free options and increase your communications capabilities.

- ❖ The SCOPE script compiler lets you create scripts to simplify communications by automating repetitive tasks.

- ❖ You can communicate with popular communications servers and networks plus TCP/IP Telenet communications and NetBIOS connections support.

Installing Smartcom for Windows LE

To properly install, configure, and operate Smartcom LE, you need the following:

❧ An IBM AT, PS/2, or 100%-compatible computer with a 286 processor or greater.

❧ 2 MB or more of available RAM.

❧ A hard drive.

❧ Microsoft Windows version 3.1.

❧ A monitor and video adapter capable of EGA resolution (640 x 350) or better.

❧ AT-compatible modem. Although it supports all popular modems for personal computers, Smartcom LE automatically assures Hayes modem users the full benefit of its special features while maximizing the throughput performance and capability of Hayes modems.

❧ Mouse. Although all Smartcom LE functions can be accessed via keyboard, you should use a mouse connected to your computer for maximum speed and flexibility.

Use the following steps to install Smartcom for Windows LE:

1. Make backup copies of the Smartcom LE master disk. Install Smartcom LE by using the copies. If something happens to one of the copies, you can make another copy from the master disk. Store your master disk in a safe place.

2 Verify that Windows is running on your computer and that the Windows Program Manager or the File Manager is open.

3. Insert the Smartcom LE disk in the floppy drive you want to use to install the program.

4. Choose Run from the File menu. The Run dialog box opens. In the Command Line text box, type:

    A:\SETUP

    (If you are installing from a different drive, type that drive letter instead of A:. Or, if you are in the File Manager, you can simply go to drive A and double-click SETUP.EXE.)

    Then click OK.

5. The Smartcom for Windows dialog box opens. If your computer system is using virus protection software, disable it now and then click OK.

   If your computer system is not using virus protection software, click OK.

6. A dialog box then displays information about the README file that comes with Smartcom for Windows LE. This file contains the latest information about Smartcom LE. Take a few minutes to read it.

   Click Continue when you are ready to move on.

7. After you finish reading the information text, Smartcom LE automatically checks your system hardware and software.

   If Smartcom LE cannot install for any reason (if you aren't using Windows 3.1, for example), a dialog box appears and explains the reason. After you resolve the problem, begin the Setup program again.

8. If no problems are found with your system, the Names dialog box opens. Enter your name and your company's name, and click Continue.

9. The Select Directory dialog box opens. Select the drive and directory where you want to install Smartcom and click OK.

   The default path is C:\SCWINLE. If you want to select a different path, backspace over the defaults and type your new path. The Setup program creates the directory if it does not exist and then installs Smartcom LE files in the following subdirectories:

Files	Where Installed
Program files	Smartcom LE program files are copied into C:\SCWINLE (or the subdirectory you indicated).
Communications documents	When you create communications documents—which contain modem settings, telephone number, terminal emulator, and so on—they are stored in C:\SCWINLE\COM, unless you specify another directory location when you save them.
Receive files	When you download files from BBSs, information services, and other remote systems, they are stored in C:\SCWINLE\RCV, unless you specify another directory location at the time of downloading. Files that are automatically downloaded to your system also will be placed in this subdirectory.
Temporary files	Any temporary files that Smartcom LE creates are stored in C:\SCWINLE\TEMP.

10. The Select Modem & Settings dialog box appears. If you are using a Hayes modem, accept the default Hayes by clicking OK.

If you are not using a Hayes modem, select your modem vendor, and the supported models display. Choose your modem from the list and click OK.

If your modem vendor is not listed, select Other 2400, Other 9600, or Other 14400, depending on your modem's maximum baud rate.

Note: Smartcom LE assumes the modem is installed on COM1. If you need to change this communications port configuration, see the section "Selecting the communications port."

Note: If you need to reconfigure Smartcom LE for a another modem after the installation procedure, you can pull down the Settings menu and choose Modem.

After confirming that your hard drive has enough memory space for Smartcom LE, the Setup program copies the program files from the floppy disk to your hard drive and indicates the status of the installation process on your screen.

If your computer has insufficient disk space to install Smartcom LE, a warning message appears. Click Cancel to exit the Setup program. Delete enough files from your hard drive to make room for Smartcom LE, and begin the Setup program again.

11. When the installation is complete, the Successful Installation dialog box appears. Click OK to exit the Setup program.

After clicking OK, the Smartcom for Windows LE group icon displays in the Windows Program Manager.

Registering Smartcom LE

Registering your Hayes products makes you eligible for free Customer Support.

To Register Smartcom LE, double-click the Smartcom for Windows LE group icon in the Windows Program Manager. Double-click the Product Registration icon. A Smartcom Script asks you questions and prompts you for answers. Follow the prompts, and the script makes a toll-free connection with a Hayes BBS (bulletin board service) and registers your Hayes product. Smartcom tells you when your registration is complete.

Note: This registration procedure uses your modem, so the modem must be connected to your computer before registering your Hayes products.

Starting Smartcom LE

Double-click the Smartcom for Windows LE program-group icon from the Windows Program Manager. Double-click the Smartcom for Windows LE telephone icon. When Smartcom LE first starts, you will briefly see the sign-on screen.

If you want to quickly dismiss this sign-on screen, press the spacebar. If another Smartcom LE communications document is already open, the sign-on screen will not appear.

After a few moments, the application displays with a default communications document called Untitled-1 open. This is where you change settings, place calls, and perform communications activities with Smartcom LE.

Note: There are certain operations (like creating custom buttons) that are not allowed when you are working with the default document. To enable these operations, save the default document as a specific communications document.

Accessing Online Help

Smartcom LE has an online, context-sensitive Help menu. You can access help at any time by selecting Help and then choosing a topic. If you select Context-Sensitive Help from the Help menu, Smartcom LE provides online assistance on the last action performed. Also, Hayes Microcomputer Products, Inc. offers free technical support.

Calling the Online With Hayes BBS

Online With Hayes is a BBS dedicated to Hayes products. After you access Online With Hayes, you can read information about new products, obtain technical support, order small parts and download SCOPE scripts and other files. Follow the instructions in this section to log onto the Online With Hayes BBS.

Smartcom LE comes with a communications document called Online With Hayes. This communications document is configured with an auto-logon script and the settings needed to log you onto the Online With Hayes BBS (U.S.). This document demonstrates some of the customization options available to you, including the button set interface.

If you want to connect to the Online With Hayes BBS quickly, the easiest way is to use the Online With Hayes communications document. Also, because of common default settings and Smartcom LE special modem control, you can simply click the phone icon, enter a phone number and go online.

Note: Most BBSs limit how long you can stay connected during a 24-hour period. You may call Online With Hayes up to three times per day, but your total connection time cannot exceed 30 minutes per day. This is to prevent individuals from monopolizing the phone lines and to give everyone a chance to call.

Creating a Communications Document

Smartcom LE uses *communications documents* to control communications with remote systems. A communications document contains the settings necessary to connect and interact with a remote system, including a remote system's telephone number, connection speed, character format, and terminal emulation. SCOPE scripts, macros, and custom keyboard layouts are also stored in communications documents.

You'll probably create custom documents for the various systems you call. After you create the communications documents you want, you can automatically start Smartcom LE with the document of your choice by double-clicking that document in the Program Manager, by using the File Manager's drag-and-drop function, or by using the File menu or Phone Book button to select the document you want, after starting Smartcom LE.

Selecting the communications port

Before you can telecommunicate successfully, you need to select a COM port for serial connections. Serial connections are used when you are using either a modem or a direct connection through a serial port on the PC and you are not using a network. Smartcom LE recognizes both external and internal modems.

To select a COM Port, follow these steps:

1. Select Choose Port in the Connection pull-down menu. The Choose Port dialog box appears.

2. Click Program Default if you want to specify a default for all communications documents that have this option selected. If you want to specify a default for the current communications document only, then click Document Only.

3. Click the serial port (COM1, COM2, etc.) that you have configured for your modem. Click OK.

The COM port you select for your modem depends on how your computer is configured. Depending on your PC and its configuration, in addition to selecting a COM port in Smartcom LE, you may also have to select the same COM port in your computer's setup and/or, if you are using an internal modem, on your modem.

Quick Settings

Quick allows you to set those most commonly used settings. Or you can use Speed & Format, Modem, Terminal, and File Transfer Protocol from the Settings menu if you need to further redefine your configuration.

When you select Quick from the Settings menu, the Quick Settings dialog box appears.

Note: You can also access this screen by clicking the Phone Book button and then selecting Settings.

Selecting the type of terminal emulation

Many BBSs (including Online With Hayes) use ANSI BBS emulation to produce multicolor graphics. To use ANSI BBS emulation, select Terminal from the Settings menu. The Terminal Settings dialog box appears.

Note: You can also select a terminal emulator by choosing Quick from the Settings menu.

Select the Emulator drop-down list box to see the choice of emulators. Choose ANSI BBS, for use with Online With Hayes. TTY and VT102 would also work, but you would not see the Online With Hayes color graphics.

Selecting the type of file-transfer protocol

Smartcom LE supports the file transfer protocols XMODEM and ZMODEM. Your computer and the remote system must use the same file-transfer method.

Note: If it is supported by the remote system, ZMODEM often has a clear advantage in speed, features, and ease of use. Other ZMODEM features include the selective transfer of groups of files based on size and date changes and interrupted file transfer recovery.

If you want to select the XMODEM protocol, go to the Settings menu and select File Transfer. The following dialog box appears. Click the file transfer list box and select XMODEM.

Note: You can also select a File Transfer Protocol by choosing Quick from the Settings menu.

Entering the remote system's phone number

The final parameter you need to add is the phone number of the remote system. Select Phone Number from the Connection menu.

Enter the phone number of the remote system you wish to call, and click OK. Later, when you save this communications document, the phone number will be stored with any other changes that you have made.

If you are calling the Online With Hayes BBS, type 1-800-USHAYES in the U.S.; 011 44 81 569-1774 in Great Britain; or 011 852 887-7590 in Hong Kong.

Note: If you enclose alphabetic characters in quotation marks, Smartcom LE converts them to numbers.

The following table describes the dial modifiers that can be used to tell Smartcom LE how to dial:

Dial Modifiers	Description
0-9 * # A B C D	Numbers, letters, and symbols that Smartcom LE recognizes when dialing
T	Specifies dialing using tone (DTMF/touch-tone) dial method
P	Specifies dialing using pulse (rotary) dial method
, (comma)	Pauses before continuing the dial string
W	Waits for dial tone before continuing the dial string
@	Waits for quiet answer
!	Issues hookflash

Pull down the Connection menu again, and make sure that the **Connect Through Phone** and **Originate** options are both checked. You are now ready to save the communications document.

Saving Your Communications Document

Choose Save As from the File menu. Complete the File Name and Description boxes, and click OK.

Note: Remember to follow DOS file-naming conventions—.SCW is the common extension for Smartcom LE communications documents.

There is usually no need to change the default drive, directory, or file type. Smartcom LE saves the communications document under the name you selected as the standard directory for communications documents.

Placing the Call

You are now ready to place a call to the remote system by using your newly created communications document. To place the call and go online, double-click the Phone button. Smartcom LE displays a Call Progress box with sequentially highlighted graphics to indicate the program's progress as it attempts to make a connection.

If the connection is established, you see whatever screen information the remote system sends to you when you are connected; you may have to press the Enter key to make this happen. The first time you log onto a BBS, for example, you usually have to answer some questions identifying yourself and your computer system. If you are not calling Online With Hayes, follow the prompts that the remote system gives you.

Using the Phone Book

The Phone Book allows you to view all your Smartcom LE communication files, their phone numbers and descriptions. You can select a particular communication document and copy, delete, or cancel it. You also can change the settings and initiate a connection.

To use the Phone Book, follow these steps:

1. Click the Phone Book button.

    Note: You can also pull down the Connection menu and select Phone Book.

2. Select a communications document by file name, phone number, or description. Click Browse to peruse the communications document.

3. After you select a communications document, you can do one or all of the following actions:

    ♣ Initiate a connection by clicking Connect.

    ♣ Change the settings of a communications document by clicking Settings. Smartcom LE prompts you with the Quick Settings dialog box.

    ♣ Create a new communications document by clicking New. Smartcom LE prompts you with the File Save dialog box and then the Quick Settings dialog box.

    ♣ Copy an existing communications document by clicking Copy. Smartcom LE prompts you with the File Save As dialog box, which contains a name and description field.

    ♣ Remove an existing communications document from the Phone book by clicking Delete.

4. To save your changes, click Done.

Logging Off Your Remote System Connection

After finishing your BBS connection, you need to log off. Clicking the Phone button severs the connection; however, you should exit a system via its menu commands. If you are communicating with an information service, this ensures that your session is terminated and that you are not being charged while the host is waiting for a time-out condition to occur. This also ensures that you receive all information that the BBS has to send you. (Some BBSs display one last screen after you log off.)

Exiting Smartcom LE

To exit Smartcom LE, follow these steps:

1. Select Exit from the File menu.

    If you have made changes to the current communications document and have not saved them, Smartcom LE displays a dialog box.

2. Click Yes to save and exit, No to exit without saving, or Cancel to return to the program without saving or exiting.

    Smartcom displays a dialog box that asks whether you want to save the information in the peruse buffer.

3. Click Yes to save and exit, No to exit without saving, or Cancel to return to the program without saving or exiting.

Running SCOPE Scripts

SCOPE (Simple COmmunications Programming Environment) is the programming language developed especially for automating data communications by using Smartcom products. SCOPE scripts can perform the following functions:

*   Automate repetitive tasks
*   Create menu-driven interaction with remote systems

♣ Trigger events according to a specific time, keyboard input, or remote system response

♣ Process and transfer files

With Smartcom LE, you can run existing Smartcom scripts. You can download scripts from Online With Hayes or use SCOPE scripts from other Hayes Smartcom products (Smartcom III, Smartcom Exec, or Smartcom for Windows).

Smartcom LE allows you to run existing scripts, but if you want to create your own scripts, upgrade to Smartcom for Windows and take advantage of a significant savings from Hayes.

With Smartcom LE you can run existing scripts created in other Smartcom products the following four ways:

♣ From the SCOPE menu.

♣ By using a Smart Button.

♣ From the Windows Program Manager.

♣ If you have a script called AUTOEXEC, it automatically runs when you open the communications document.

100 Most Frequently Asked Questions

APPENDIX

Chapter 10: Streamlining Your Communications

Chapter 11: Making the Most of Your Fax Modem

Chapter 12: Special-Purpose Communications

Notes

Notes

INDEX

D

example, 252
explained, 170–171, 249–254
faxes and, 252
limitations, 252–253
    device, 253
    memory, 253
passwords and, 254
PC/Macintosh links, 256
problems with, 50–51
resource guide, 251
running, 251
security and, 254
setup/management of, 254
speed reductions, 254
TSR, 252
uses, 50, 249, 250
See also communications software; host
    mode
remote modems, 115–116
research, 27
resource guides
    BBS, 396–401
    offline readers, 224
    remote control software, 251
result codes, 112
    descriptions, 390
    enabling, 185
    examples, 116
    function of, 196
    getting, 114
    negotiation progress, 391
    recording, 200–201
    short form of, 185
RIME, 278, 291
RIP (Remote Image Protocol), 108, 305
    BBSs supporting, 305
RJ-11 phone jacks, 40, 62, 90
    external modems and, 91
    in hotels, 257
    internal modems and, 93
    on the road, 256
    tip and ring, 62–63
    wires, 62–63
    See also telephone lines

RJ-11 splitters, 259
RJ-12 phone jacks, 63
    See also telephone lines
RS-232 standard, 65
    PCs and, 66
    revision D, 65
    short cables and, 81

scan lines, 48
scanners, 240
SCOPE scripts, 405
    functions, 415–416
    running, 415–416
screen-capture program, 146
script files, 165–166, 215
    capture files and, 222
    contents of, 219
    creating, 221–223
        learning process for, 217–218
    ease of use, 216
    example, 222
    introductory material, 219
    learn features, 217–221
    online services and, 220
    QuickLearn sample, 218
    using, 215–223
        reading before, 223
scripts, 165–166
    language for, 220
    online services and, 216
    SCOPE, 405
        functions, 415–416
        running, 415–416
    See also script files
scroll back buffer, 206–208
    defined, 206
    function of, 206
security
    host mode, 249
    remote control software and, 254
    See also passwords

GEnie®
The most fun you can have with your computer on.

No other online service has more cool stuff to do, or more cool people to do it with than GEnie. Join dozens of awesome special interest RoundTables on everything from scuba diving to Microsoft to food and wine, download over 200,000 files, access daily stock quotes, talk to all those smart guys on the internet, play the most incredible multi-player games, and so much more you won't believe your eyeballs.

And GEnie has it all at a standard connect rate of just $3.00 an hour.[1] That's one of the lowest rates of all the major online services! Plus -- because you're a reader of *The Official Hayes Communication Companion* you get an even cooler deal.[2] When you sign up we'll waive your first monthly subscription fee (an $8.95 value) and include ten additional hours of standard connect time (another $30.00 in savings). That's fourteen free hours during your first month - *a $38.95 value!*

You can take advantage of this incredible offer immediately -- just follow these simple steps:

1. Set your communications software for half-duplex (local echo) at 300, 1200, or 2400 baud. Recommended communications parameters 8 data bits, no parity and 1 stop bit.
2. Dial toll-free in the U.S. at 1-800-638-8369 (or in Canada at 1-800-387-8330). Upon connection, type **HHH** (Please note: every time you use GEnie, you need to enter the HHH upon connection)
3. At the U#= prompt, type **JOINGENIE** and press <Return>
4. At the offer code prompt enter GAD225 to get this special offer.
5. Have a major credit card ready. In the U.S., you may also use your checking account number. (There is a $2.00 monthly fee for all checking accounts.) In Canada, VISA and MasterCard only.

Or, if you need more information, contact GEnie Client Services at 1-800-638-9636 from 9am to midnight, Monday through Friday, and from noon to 8pm Saturday and Sunday (all times are Eastern).

1 U.S. prices. Standard connect time is non-prime time: 6pm to 8am local time, Mon. - Fri., all day Sat. and Sun. and selected holidays.
2 Offer available in the United States and Canada only.
3 The offer for ten additional hours applies to standard hourly connect charges only and must be used by the end of the billing period for your first month. Please call 1-800-638-9636 for more information on pricing and billing policies.

Effective date as of 7/1/93. Prices subject to change without notice. Offer limited to new subscribers only and one per customer.
©1994 by General Electric Company   Printed in the U.S.A.

Put the power
of CompuServe
at your fingertips.

Join the world's largest international network of people with personal computers. Whether it's computer support, communication, entertainment, or continually updated information, you'll find services that meet your every need.

Your introductory membership will include one free month of our basic services, plus a $15 usage credit for extended and premium CompuServe services.

To get connected, complete and mail the card below. Or call 1-800-524-3388 and ask for Representative 607.

Yes! I want to get the most out of my PC. Send me my FREE CompuServe Introductory Membership, including a $15 usage credit and one free month of CompuServe basic services.

Name: _____

Address: _____

City: _____ State: _____ Zip: _____

Phone: _____

Clip and mail this form to: CompuServe
P.O. Box 20212
Dept. 607
Columbus, OH 43220

CompuServe.
The difference between your PC collecting dust and burning rubber.

No matter what kind of PC you have, CompuServe will help you get the most out of it. As the world's most comprehensive network of people with personal computers, we're the place experts and novices alike go to find what's hot in hardware, discuss upcoming advances with other members, and download the latest software. Plus, for a low flat-rate, you'll have access to our basic services as often as you like: news, sports, weather, shopping, a complete encyclopedia, and up to 60 e-mail messages a month. And it's easy to begin. All you need is your home computer, your regular phone line, a modem, and a CompuServe membership.

To get your free introductory membership, just complete and mail the form on the back of this page. Or call 1-800-524-3388 and ask for Representative 607. Plus, if you act now, you'll receive one month free unlimited access to basic services and a $15 usage credit for our extended and premium services.

So put the power of CompuServe in your PC — and leave everyone else in the dust.

CompuServe®

The information service you won't outgrow.™

Hayes®

Upgrade your Smartcom™ for Windows™ LE to Smartcom for Windows

The fast, powerful Windows communications software for everyone.

You Get Everything - The FULL Retail Package, Plus More Terminal Emulations and File Transfer Protocols, Text Editor, .GIF Viewer, Network Support, and More

- Use any modem- Smartcom automatically selects the fastest, most advanced features
- Graphic call progress and file transfer displays keep you informed
- SCOPE scripts make it easy to perform complex or lengthy communications activities
- Just click on the phone to connect and Smartcom takes care of the rest
- Capture information to printer and disk at the same time

- Use customized Smart Buttons to automate any task
- Fast download and display of .GIF files
- Access network modems, LAN async comm servers, and TCP/IP Telnet communications

Hayes™
Increasing The Speed Of Business.™

Special Discount Coupon

Qty.	Product	Your Price	
_____	Smartcom for Windows Special Upgrade Price	$49	_____
	SubTotal		_____
	Tax only for Residents of GA 5%, CA 8.25%		_____
	Shipping and Handling	$10.00	
	Total		_____

Shipping Address

Name

Title

Company

Address

City _____ State _____ Zip _____

Phone _____ FAX _____

Payment Method

☐ Check   ☐ Money Order   ☐ VISA   ☐ MasterCard

Card Number _____ Exp. Date _____

Signature _____

For Canadian pricing and information call 519 746-5000.
For European pricing and information call + 44 252 7755 44.
For Asian pricing and information call + 852 887 1037.
For Australian pricing and information call + 612 959 2340.

Order by Phone

Call today
404 441-1617
Ask for the Official Companion offer

Order by Mail

Return this form with payment to:
Hayes Microcomputer Products, Inc.
Customer Service
P.O. Box 105203, Atlanta, GA 30348

Order by FAX

FAX this form
to 404 449-0087

Hayes®

Your Fast, Reliable Communications Link to the Electronic World.

From the creator of the legendary Hayes® Smartmodem™

ACCURA™ 288 V.FC + FAX
ACCURA™ 144 + FAX144

The easy way to call other PCs, online services, or Bulletin Boards and send or receive FAXes.

Practically operates without you - error-control and data compression. 28,800 bit/s or 14,400 bit/s external data and FAX modem with free Smartcom™ for Windows™ data and FAX software and cable.

Hayes® ESP® Communications Accelerator

Hit the Accelerator!

Ultra-fast serial port that helps prevent data loss and overruns in a Windows communications environment.

Hayes®
Increasing The Speed Of Business.™

Learn to Surf the Internet with The Internet For Dummies™!

over 6 million IN PRINT!

Get up and running on the Internet the fun and easy way with *The Internet For Dummies*. This down-to-earth reference cuts through the jargon and helps you get to the best resources the Internet has to offer. From swapping e-mail, to conversing on bulletin boards, and downloading software and data, this is the only book you need! Covers DOS, Mac, & UNIX platforms.

$19.95 USA/$26.95 Canada/£17.99 UK and Eire

PC WORLD

PC WORLD MICROSOFT ACCESS BIBLE
by Cary N. Prague & Michael R. Irwin

Easy-to-understand reference that covers the ins and outs of Access features and provides hundreds of tips, secrets and shortcuts for fast database development. Complete with disk of Access templates. Covers versions 1.0 & 1.1

ISBN: 1-878058-81-9
$39.95 USA/$52.95 Canada
£35.99 incl. VAT UK & Eire

PC WORLD WORD FOR WINDOWS 6 HANDBOOK
by Brent Heslop & David Angell

Details all the features of Word for Windows 6, from formatting to desktop publishing and graphics. A 3-in-1 value (tutorial, reference, and software) for users of all levels.

ISBN: 1-56884-054-3
$34.95 USA/$44.95 Canada
£29.99 incl. VAT UK & Eire

PC WORLD DOS 6 COMMAND REFERENCE AND PROBLEM SOLVER
by John Socha & Devra Hall

The only book that combines a DOS 6 Command Reference with a comprehensive Problem Solving Guide. Shows when, why and how to use the key features of DOS 6/6.2

ISBN: 1-56884-055-1
$24.95 USA/$32.95 Canada
£22.99 UK & Eire

QUARKXPRESS FOR WINDOWS DESIGNER HANDBOOK
by Barbara Assadi & Galen Gruman

ISBN: 1-878058-45-2
$29.95 USA/$39.95 Canada/£26.99 UK & Eire

PC WORLD WORDPERFECT 6 HANDBOOK
by Greg Harvey, author of IDG's bestselling 1-2-3 For Dummies

Here's the ultimate WordPerfect 6 tutorial and reference. Complete with handy templates, macros, and tools.

ISBN: 1-878058-80-0
$34.95 USA/$44.95 Canada
£29.99 incl. VAT UK & Eire

PC WORLD EXCEL 5 FOR WINDOWS HANDBOOK, 2nd EDITION
by John Walkenbach & Dave Maguiness

Covers all the latest Excel features, plus contains disk with examples of the spreadsheets referenced in the book, custom ToolBars, hot macros, and demos.

ISBN: 1-56884-056-X
$34.95 USA/$44.95 Canada /£29.99 incl. VAT UK & Eire

PC WORLD DOS 6 HANDBOOK, 2nd EDITION
by John Socha, Clint Hicks & Devra Hall

Includes the exciting new features of DOS 6, a 300+ page DOS command reference, plus a bonus disk of the Norton Commander Special Edition, and over a dozen DOS utilities.

ISBN: 1-878058-79-7
$34.95 USA/$44.95 Canada/£29.99 incl. VAT UK & Eire

OFFICIAL XTREE COMPANION, 3RD EDITION
by Beth Slick

ISBN: 1-878058-57-6
$19.95 USA/$26.95 Canada/£17.99 UK & Eire

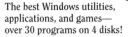

Order Form

Order Center: (800) 762-2974 (8 a.m.-5 p.m., PST, weekdays) or (415) 312-0650

For Fastest Service: Photocopy This Order Form and FAX it to: (415) 358-1260

Quantity	ISBN	Title	Price	Total

Shipping & Handling Charges

Subtotal	U.S.	Canada & International	International Air Mail
Up to $20.00	Add $3.00	Add $4.00	Add $10.00
$20.01-40.00	$4.00	$5.00	$20.00
$40.01-60.00	$5.00	$6.00	$25.00
$60.01-80.00	$6.00	$8.00	$35.00
Over $80.00	$7.00	$10.00	$50.00

In U.S. and Canada, shipping is UPS ground or equivalent.
For Rush shipping call (800) 762-2974.

Subtotal _____

CA residents add
applicable sales tax _____

IN and MA residents add
5% sales tax _____

IL residents add
6.25% sales tax _____

RI residents add
7% sales tax _____

Shipping _____

Total _____

Ship to:

Name _____

Company _____

Address _____

City/State/Zip _____

Daytime Phone _____

Payment: ❑ Check to IDG Books (US Funds Only)   ❑ Visa   ❑ Mastercard   ❑ American Express

Card# _____ Exp._____ Signature_____

Please send this order form to: IDG Books, 155 Bovet Road, Suite 310, San Mateo, CA 94402.

Allow up to 3 weeks for delivery. Thank you!

Hayes Microcomputer Products, Inc. Limited Warranty — English/U.S.A.

(This Limited Warranty applies to Products sold within the borders of the United States of America.)

Who is Covered by This Warranty? This limited warranty ("Warranty") is extended by Hayes Microcomputer Products, Inc. ("Hayes") only to the original end user purchaser of the accompanying HAYES HARDWARE PRODUCT ("Hardware") and/or HAYES SOFTWARE PRODUCT ("Program") (separately and together, "Product").

What Does This Warranty Cover? This Warranty covers defects in materials and workmanship, under normal use and service, in the Hardware and Program magnetic diskettes ("Defects"). This Warranty also covers any failure of the Product to perform substantially in accordance with the description in the documentation accompanying the Product ("Performance"), unless the packaging or documentation of the product indicates that the product is intended for use only in a specified country or countries. If the product is designated for use only in a specified country or countries, then this Warranty covers any failure of the product to perform substantially in accordance with the description in the documentation accompanying the Product only when used within the borders of the country or countries designated on the Product package ("Country Performance"). This Warranty is in lieu of all other express warranties which might otherwise arise with respect to the Product. No one is authorized to change or add to this Warranty.

What Does This Warranty NOT Cover? Hayes does not warrant or guarantee you uninterrupted service, the correction of any error or elimination of any "bug". You are solely responsible for any failure of the Product which results from accident, abuse, misapplication, alteration of the Product, or use of the Product outside of the borders of the country or countries shown on the Product package. Hayes assumes no liability for any events arising out of the use of any technical information accompanying the Product. THIS WARRANTY APPLIES TO THE PRODUCT ONLY AND DOES NOT COVER ANY OTHER SOFTWARE OR HARDWARE WHICH MAY BE INCLUDED WITH YOUR PURCHASE OF THE PRODUCT. WITHOUT LIMITING THE GENERALITY OF THE FOREGOING, ANY SOFTWARE OTHER THAN THE PROGRAM IS PROVIDED "AS IS" AND WITHOUT WARRANTY OF ANY KIND. INCIDENTAL AND CONSEQUENTIAL DAMAGES CAUSED BY MALFUNCTION, DEFAULT, OR OTHERWISE WITH RESPECT TO BREACH OF THIS WARRANTY OR ANY OTHER EXPRESS OR IMPLIED WARRANTY ARE NOT THE RESPONSIBILITY OF HAYES AND ARE HEREBY EXCLUDED BOTH FOR PROPERTY AND, TO THE EXTENT NOT UNCONSCIONABLE, FOR PERSONAL INJURY DAMAGE. Some states do not allow the exclusion or limitation of incidental or consequential damages, so the above exclusion or limitation may not apply to you. This Warranty gives you specific legal rights and you may also have other legal rights which vary from state to state.

What is the Period of Coverage? The period of coverage for the enclosed Hardware and/or Program is set forth in the Warranty Period section of this Guide. If this section indicates that Hayes offers an Extended Protection Plan ("Plan") for the enclosed Hardware and/or Program and you select the Plan, the period of coverage for the Hardware and/or Program would be the total of the original Warranty Period and the Plan period. ANY AND ALL IMPLIED WARRANTIES OF MERCHANTABIL- ITY AND FITNESS FOR A PARTICULAR PURPOSE SHALL TERMINATE AUTO- MATICALLY UPON THE EXPIRATION OF THE PERIOD OF COVERAGE. Some states do not allow limitations on how long the implied warranty lasts, so the above limitation may not apply to you.

What Will Hayes Do to Correct Problems? In the event of a malfunction attributable directly to Defects or Performance, Hayes will, at its option, repair the Product, to whatever extent Hayes deems necessary to restore the Product to proper working condition, or replace the Product with a new or functionally equivalent product of equal value, or refund an amount equal to the lesser of (1) the purchase price paid for the Product or (2) the then effective Hayes Estimated Retail Price for the Product. THE REMEDY DESCRIBED ABOVE IS THE EXCLUSIVE REMEDY EXTENDED TO YOU BY HAYES FOR ANY DEFAULT, MALFUNCTION, OR FAILURE OF THE PRODUCT TO CONFORM WITH THIS WARRANTY OR OTHERWISE FOR BREACH OF THIS WARRANTY OR ANY OTHER WARRANTY, WHETHER EXPRESSED OR IMPLIED.

How Do You Obtain Warranty Service? To obtain warranty service, you must either call the appropriate Customer Service number or write to Customer Service at the appropriate address listed at the end of this section. You must return the Product, along with the return authorization number given to you by Customer Service and proof of date of purchase, or after expiration of the Warranty period, Hayes will, at its option, repair the Product and charge you for parts and labor or replace the Product and charge you the then effective Estimated Retail Price for the Product, unless Hayes has discontinued the manufacture or distribution of such products because of techni- cal obsolescence.

Warranty Period

Your modem includes a two-year limited warranty, and an optional two-year extended protection plan is also available. Hayes software includes a 90-day limited warranty.

Statement of Copyright Restrictions

(This Statement applies to Hayes Software Products sold outside the borders of the United States of America)

The Hayes Microcomputer Products, Inc. ("Hayes") program that you have purchased is copyrighted by Hayes and your rights of ownership and use are subject to the limitations and restrictions imposed by the copyright laws and international treaty provisions outlined below.

It is against the law to copy, reproduce or transmit (including without limitation, electronic transmission over any network) any part of the program except as provided by the Universal Copyright Convention of Geneva and the copyright laws of your country (the "Laws"). However, you are permitted by Hayes to write the contents of the program into the machine memory of your computer so that the program may be executed by a single user. You are also permitted by Hayes to make a back-up copy of the program subject to the following restrictions:

1. Each back-up copy must be treated in the same way as the original copy purchased from Hayes;

2. If you ever sell or give away the original copy of the program, all back-up copies must also be sold or given to the same person, or destroyed; and

3. No copy (original or back-up) may be used while any other copy (original or back-up) is in use.

If you make a back-up copy of the program you should place the copyright notice that is on the original copy of the program on every back-up copy of the program.

The above is not an inclusive statement of the restrictions imposed on you under the Laws. If you are in any doubt as to whether your proposed use of the program is prohibited, you should seek appropriate professional advice.

Certain programs sold by Hayes are copy-protected (in addition to copyright protected) - that is, the diskette on which the program is recorded is physically designed so that the program cannot be copied or reproduced. If the program you have purchased is copy protected and a back-up copy of the program has been provided to you by Hayes, your rights in the back-up copy are also subject to the restrictions under the Laws referred to above.

To the extent that any of the terms and conditions of the English version of this Statement of Copyright Restrictions conflict with any of the terms and conditions of any translation thereof, the terms and conditions of the English version will prevail.

Service Address

Americas   Hayes Microcomputer Products, Inc.
Region   Attention: Customer Service
                  P.O. Box 105203
                  Atlanta, Georgia 30348-9904
                  Telephone: (404) 441-1617 Telefax: (404) 449-0087
                  Telex: 703500 HAYES USA

                  Online with Hayes BBS: (404) HI MODEM or (800) US HAYES
                  and Hayes forums on CompuServe (GO HAYES) and GEnie
                  information services.

                  For unit repairs:
                  5953 Peachtree Industrial Blvd.
                  Norcross, Georgia, 30092

Canada Office   Hayes Microcomputer Products (Canada) Limited
                  295 Phillip Street, Waterloo
                  Ontario, Canada N2L 3W8
                  Telephone: (529) 746-5000

Europe   Hayes Microcomputer Products, Inc.
Region   Millennium House, Fleetwood Park
                  Barley Way, Fleet
                  Hampshire GU13 8UT
                  United Kingdom
                  Telephone: + 44 252 775544 Telefax: + 44 252 775511
                  Online with Hayes BBS + 44 252 775599

Asia Pacific   Hayes Microcomputer Products, Inc.
Region   39/F, Unit B, Manulife Tower
                  169 Electric Road, North Point, Hong Kong
                  Telephone + 852 887-1037, Telefax + 852 887-7548
                  Telex: 69381 HAYES HX
                  Online with Hayes BBS: + 852 887-7590

IDG Books Worldwide License Agreement

Read this agreement carefully before you buy this book and use the programs contained on the enclosed disk.

By opening the accompanying disk package, you indicate that you have read and agree with the terms of this licensing agreement. If you disagree and do not want to be bound by the terms of this licensing agreement, return the book for refund to the source from which you purchased it.

The entire contents of this disk and the compilation of the software contained therein are copyrighted and protected by both U.S. copyright law and international copyright treaty provisions. The individual programs on this disk are copyrighted by the authors of each program respectively. Each program has its own use permissions and limitations. You may copy any or all of these programs to your computer system. Do not use a program if you do not want to follow its licensing agreement. Absolutely none of the material on this disk or listed in this book may ever be distributed, in original or modified form, for commercial purposes.

Disclaimer and Copyright Notice

Warranty Notice: IDG Books Worldwide, Inc., warrants that the disk that accompanies this book is free from defects in materials and workmanship for a period of 60 days from the date of purchase of this book. If IDG Books Worldwide receives notification within the warranty period of defects in material or workmanship, IDG Books Worldwide will replace the defective disk. The remedy for the breach of this warranty will be limited to replacement and will not encompass any other damages, including but not limited to loss of profit, and special, incidental, consequential, or other claims.

5¼", 1.2MB Disk Format Available. The enclosed disk is in 3½" 1.44MB, high-density format. If you have a different size drive, and you cannot arrange to transfer the data to the disk size you need, you can obtain the programs on a 5¼" 1.2MB high-density disk by writing: IDG Books Worldwide, Attn: *Official Hayes Modem Communications Companion*, IDG Books Worldwide, 155 Bovet Rd., Suite 310, San Mateo, CA 94402, or call 800-762-2974. Please specify the size of disk you need, and please allow 3 to 4 weeks for delivery.

Copyright Notice

IDG Books Worldwide and the authors specifically disclaim all other warranties, express or implied, including but not limited to implied warranties of merchantability and fitness for a particular purpose with respect to defects in the disks, the programs, and source code contained therein, and/or the techniques described in the book, and in no event shall IDG Books Worldwide and/or the authors be liable for any loss of profit or any other commercial damage, including but not limited to special, incidental, consequential, or other damages.

Installation Instructions for Smartcom for Windows LE

Before you install the contents of Smartcom for Windows LE, please read the notices on the preceding pages. Smartcom for Windows LE is described fully in Appendix C, "Guide to Smartcom for Windows LE."

Installing Smartcom for Windows LE

Perform the following steps to install Smartcom for Windows LE:

1. Make backup copies of the Smartcom LE master disk. Install Smartcom LE by using the copies. If something happens to one of the copies, you can make another copy from the master disk. Store your master disk in a safe place.

2. Verify that Windows is running on your computer and that the Windows Program Manager or the File Manager is open.

3. Insert the Smartcom LE disk in the floppy drive you want to use to install the program.

4. Choose Run from the File menu. The Run dialog box opens. In the Command Line text box, type:

    `A:\SETUP`

    (If you are installing from a different drive, type that drive letter instead of A:. Or, if you are in the File Manager, you can simply go to drive A and double-click SETUP.EXE.)

    Then click OK.

5. Follow the on-screen prompts to complete the installation and setup program.

See Appendix C, "Guide to Smartcom for Windows LE" for more details on the installation process.

IDG BOOKS WORLDWIDE REGISTRATION CARD

RETURN THIS REGISTRATION CARD FOR FREE CATALOG

Title of this book: Official Hayes Modem Communications Companion

My overall rating of this book: ❏ Very good [1] ❏ Good [2] ❏ Satisfactory [3] ❏ Fair [4] ❏ Poor [5]

How I first heard about this book:

❏ Found in bookstore; name: [6] _____

❏ Advertisement: [8]

❏ Word of mouth; heard about book from friend, co-worker, etc.: [10]

❏ Book review: [7]

❏ Catalog: [9]

❏ Other: [11]

What I liked most about this book:

_____

_____

What I would change, add, delete, etc., in future editions of this book:

_____

_____

Other comments:

_____

Number of computer books I purchase in a year: ❏ 1 [12] ❏ 2-5 [13] ❏ 6-10 [14] ❏ More than 10 [15]

I would characterize my computer skills as: ❏ Beginner [16] ❏ Intermediate [17] ❏ Advanced [18] ❏ Professional [19]

I use ❏ DOS [20] ❏ Windows [21] ❏ OS/2 [22] ❏ Unix [23] ❏ Macintosh [24] ❏ Other: [25] _____
(please specify)

I would be interested in new books on the following subjects:
(please check all that apply, and use the spaces provided to identify specific software)

❏ Word processing: [26]

❏ Data bases: [28]

❏ File Utilities: [30]

❏ Networking: [32]

❏ Other: [34]

❏ Spreadsheets: [27]

❏ Desktop publishing: [29]

❏ Money management: [31]

❏ Programming languages: [33]

I use a PC at (please check all that apply): ❏ home [35] ❏ work [36] ❏ school [37] ❏ other: [38] _____

The disks I prefer to use are ❏ 5.25 [39] ❏ 3.5 [40] ❏ other: [41] _____

I have a CD ROM: ❏ yes [42] ❏ no [43]

I plan to buy or upgrade computer hardware this year: ❏ yes [44] ❏ no [45]

I plan to buy or upgrade computer software this year: ❏ yes [46] ❏ no [47]

Name: _____ Business title: [48] _____ Type of Business: [49] _____

Address (❏ home [50] ❏ work [51] /Company name: _____)

Street/Suite# _____

City [52] /State [53] /Zipcode [54]: _____ Country [55] _____

❏ **I liked this book!** You may quote me by name in future IDG Books Worldwide promotional materials.

My daytime phone number is _____

IDG BOOKS

THE WORLD OF COMPUTER KNOWLEDGE

❏ YES!

Please keep me informed about IDG's World of Computer Knowledge. Send me the latest IDG Books catalog.